NEW SCREEN MEDIA
CINEMA/ART/NARRATIVE
EDITED BY MARTIN RIESER/ANDREA ZAPP

bfi Publishing

Center for Art
and Media
Karlsruhe

First published in 2002 by the
British Film Institute
21 Stephen Street, London W1T 1LN

The British Film Institute is the UK national agency with responsibility for encouraging the arts of film
and television and conserving them in the national interest.

Cover design: Cube/Paul Wright
Cover installation: *Landscape One*, Luc Courchesne, 1997 – photography: Richard-Max Tremblay

Text design: ketchup
Set by Fakenham Photosetting, Norfolk
Printed by Cromwell Press, Trowbridge, Wiltshire

British Library Cataloguing-in-Publication Data
A catalogue record for this book is available from the British Library

ISBN 0–85170–864–1 (pbk)
ISBN 0–85170–865–X (hbk)

Contents

PART ONE: ORIENTATIONS: HISTORY AND THEORY

Definitions

Origins

Beyond the Screen

The Personalised Interface

Notes on Contributors

Zoe Beloff
Grew up in Edinburgh, Scotland, and moved to New York in 1980. She has exhibited internationally, including the Museum of Modern Art, New York, the *New York Film Festival*, the *Rotterdam Film Festival*, *Pacific Film Archives*, the Centre Pompidou in Paris and the *Whitney Museum Biennial*. Zoe works with moving images, film, stereoscopic projection performance and interactive media. She sees her work as the production of philosophical toys, objects to think with and through, more or less tangible. All her work centres around a desire to get beneath the skin of everyday life by 'dreaming' her way back into the past. More and more she finds herself fascinated by phantoms, by images that 'are not there'. She would like to think of herself as an heir to the nineteenth century mediums whose materialisation séances conjured up unconscious desires, in the most theatrical fashion. Though lacking psychic abilities she confesses to relying on cinematic illusionism or what one could call the cinematic 'medium'. She teaches film and digital media at New York City College.

Annika Blunck
Born in 1967 in Kiel, lives in Karlsruhe. She works as a research associate at the ZKM (Zentrum für Kunst und Medientechnologie) Institute for Visual Media. She has developed a number of different projects for international exhibitions centring on media art. At the ZKM she contributes and supports the collaborations between commissioned media artists and hard- and software developers. Her publications and research deal with the evaluation of interactive installation in relation to information technology.

Michael Buckley
Born in Dublin in 1955. Michael Buckley has had an intrepid life and chequered career in many fields, including newspaper boy, golf caddy, wool store worker, Hudson Bay Fur Trading Company employee, grape picker, dishwasher, billiard table remover, teacher, Lecturer at the University of Swinburne, documentary/experimental film-maker, animator and more recently a multimedia artist. His multimedia works include: *The Swear Club* (1994, interactive CD-ROM), *The Good Cook* (1996, interactive CD-ROM), *High Art* (1996, interactive CD-ROM).

Alex Butterworth
Alex Butterworth is a writer and dramatist with a specialist interest in interactive stories. Having written stage and screen plays, he is currently developing an emergent narrative system for a series of

console-based projects and working with an academic research consortium on the use of augmented reality in site-specific opera and drama. In his spare time he is writing quite a linear novel. He has studied at the National Film and Television School, is a graduate of Oxford University and the Royal College of Art., and is currently Researcher, University of Nottingham/Illuminations, London.

Luc Courchesne

Born in 1952 in St-Léonard d'Aston, Québec. He studied at the Nova Scotia College of Art and Design, Halifax (Bachelor of Design in Communication, 1974), and at the Massachusetts Institute of Technology, Cambridge (Master of Science in Visual Studies, 1984). He has since produced more than a dozen installations including *Encyclopaedia Chiaroscuro* (1987), *Portrait One* (1990), *Family Portrait* (1993), *Hall of Shadows* (1996), *Landscape One* (1997), *Passages* (1998), *Rendez-vous* (1999) and *The Visitor* (2001). His work has been shown extensively in galleries and museums worldwide: Sydney's Art Gallery of New South Wales, New York's Museum of Modern Art, Tokyo's InterCommunicationCenter (ICC), Paris's La Villette, Karlsruhe's ZKM/Medienmuseum, Montreal's Musée d'Art Contemporain among others. His installations are part of the collections of the National Gallery of Canada (Ottawa), the ZKM/Medienmuseum (Karlsruhe), the NTT InterCommunication Center (Tokyo) and the Museum of Communication (Bern). Luc Courchesne was awarded the Grand Prix of the *ICC Biennale '97* in Tokyo and an Award of Distinction for Interactive Art at *Prix Ars Electronica* 1999 in Linz, Austria. Based in Montreal, Luc Courchesne is Professor of Information Design at the Université de Montreal and president of the Société des Arts Technologiques. Marc Lavallée and Étienne Desautels have been his two main collaborators since 1996.

Sean Cubitt

Professor of Screen and Media Studies at the University of Waikato, New Zealand. His most recent books are *Digital Aesthetics* (Sage 1998) and *Simulation and Social Theory* (Sage 2001). He has published widely on contemporary arts, media and culture and is currently researching a book on special effects cinema.

Söke Dinkla

Born in Wilhelmshaven in 1962, studied Art History, Literature, Ethnology and Biology at the Universities of Kiel, Hamburg and Bielefeld. She worked as a curator in Munich, Hamburg, Essen and Duisburg, Germany. In 1993 she was a scholarship holder of the Institute for Cultural Studies, Essen, Germany; and in 1994 from the DAAD (German Academic Exchange) in the United States; in 1996 she received a PhD from the University of Hamburg with a dissertation on the history and aesthetics of interactive media art and culture. She lectured at international congresses such as *XXVIII International Congress of the History of Art*, Berlin, Germany; *5th International Symposium on Electronic Art (ISEA)*, Helsinki, Finland, 1994; Center for Art and Media (ZKM), Karlsruhe, Germany; *Ars Electronica*, Linz, Austria, 1997; *Interfacing Publics*, V2 Organisation, Rotterdam, Netherlands, 1999; *Media Art Perspectives*, Cultural Department of the City of Munich, Germany, 2000. In 1997 she curated the exhibition *InterAct!* at the Wilhelm Lehmbruck Museum in Duisburg, Germany and published the standard reference book *Pioneers of Interactive Art*. In 1999 she curated *Connected Cities – Processes of Art in the Urban Network*, an art event in the urban space of the Ruhr, Germany. In 2000 she was Artistic Director of the series *Dance and New Technologies* at the Choreographic Center North-Rhine Westphalia, Essen, Germany. Since 2000 she has been Director of the Festival Department, City of Duisburg, Germany.

Toni Dove

An artist who works primarily with electronic media, including virtual reality and interactive video laser disk installations that engage viewers in responsive and immersive narrative environments. She also creates linear narrative fictions. Her work has been presented in the United States, Europe and Canada as well as in print and on radio and television. *Mesmer, Secrets of the Human Frame* has been shown as an installation, aired as a radio show and was published by Granary Books as a limited edition book; The *Blessed Abyss – A Tale of Unmanageable Ecstasies* has been exhibited as a performance/installation and aired as a radio piece; *Archeology of a Mother Tongue*, a narrative virtual reality installation, was created with Michael Mackenzie at the Banff Centre for the Arts, and the video installation *Casual Workers, Hallucinations and Appropriate Ghosts* was commissioned by Creative Time. It has also been shown at festivals and on cable as a video. *Artificial Changelings*, 1993–8, is an interactive narrative installation that debuted at the *Rotterdam Film Festival* in 1998 and was part of the Exhibition *Body Mécanique* at the Wexner Center for the Arts. It was exhibited at the Computing Commons Gallery at Arizona State University during the *Performance Studies International Conference* in March, 2000 and was part of the exhibition *Wired* at the Arts Center for the Capitol Region, 2000. Her current project under development is *Spectropia*, a supernatural thriller about the infinite deferrals of desire. It will be an interactive feature film performed for and by an audience.

Jon Dovey

A writer, producer and lecturer, Jon Dovey currently lives in Bristol and lectures at the School of Cultural Studies of the University of the West of England. As a film and TV programme maker, his most recent broadcast credit is as Associate Producer on the series *Reel Truths*. Previous credits include writing the BFI film *Zygosis*, researching and writing for the series *Spitting Image*, and several multimedia pieces. He has developed and exhibited his own multimedia productions, including *The Desktop Theatre of Amnesia* on *The Toybox* CD-ROM and has collaborated as part of *Ship of Fools* in *Media Myth and Mania* (1993) and *Dreamhouses* (1997). He has written and published widely on the subject of new media. He is the editor of *Fractal Dreams* (Lawrence & Wishart 1996) and most recently *Freakshow – First Person Media and Factual TV* (Pluto Press 2000).

Timothy Druckrey

An independent curator and writer concerned with the history and theory of media and the transformation of representation, communication and art in an increasingly electronic culture. He co-edited *Culture on the Brink: Ideologies of Technology* and edited *Iterations: The New Digital Image* and *Electronic Culture: Technology and Visual Representation*, and *Ars Electronica: Facing the Future* (all MIT Press). He lectures internationally about the social impact of digital media, the transformation of representation, and communication in interactive and networked environments. Currently he is editing a series of books for MIT Press – *Electronic Culture: History, Theory, Practice*.

Ken Feingold

Born in the United States in 1952, he has been recognised during the past decade as an innovator in the field of interactive art after 15 prior years of making films, video art, objects and installations. His work includes *The Surprising Spiral* (1991), *JCJ Junkman* (1992), *Childhood/Hot & Cold Wars* (1993), and *where i can see my house from here so we are* (1993–5), among many others. In recent years, his work *Interior* (1997) was commissioned for the first *ICC Biennale '97*, Tokyo, *Seance Box No. 1* (1998–9) was produced for the ZKM Karlsruhe, and *Head* (1999–2000) was commissioned by the Kiasma Museum of Contemporary Art, Helsinki. He is presently developing an interactive permanent public artwork commissioned by the Cardiff Bay Arts Trust, which will have both physical and online components, and will evolve during its existence. After first studying at Antioch College (Yellow Springs, Ohio) he received his BFA and MFA degrees in 'Post-Studio Art' from California Institute of the Arts, Valencia, California. He has taught at Princeton University and Cooper Union for the Advancement of Art and Science, among others. His works are in the permanent collections of the Museum of Modern Art, New York; Centre Pompidou, Paris; Kiasma, Helsinki; ZKM Center for Art and Media, Karlsruhe, and others. He lives in New York City.

Chris Hales

Studied PhD research on Interactive Film Art at the RCA Film and TV Department, and taught as Senior Lecturer at the Faculty of Art of the University of the West of England (Bristol) until 2001. His publications include *LAB002: Twelve* published on the Laboratory label by Research Publishing, 1997; *The Morph Meadow*, interactive piece published on *Toybox*, a CD-ROM by Video +/Moviola, 1995; *Jinxed!* demo on Creative Review cover disk, 1998; *Bliss* CD-ROM (various artists), published in limited edition by ARTEC, 2000. *Six of the Best* and *Grandad* (Mac CD-ROMs of various movies) are produced by the artist.

His interactive films and CD-ROMs have been shown to date at film/new media festivals in Sheffield, Perth, Melbourne, FCMM Montreal, Brisbane, Oberhausen, Hong Kong, Helsinki, Rotterdam, *Videonnale* Bonn, Palermo, *Transmediale* Berlin, Tallinn, *dART* Sydney (+ tour), *EMAF* Osnabrück, *WRO* Wroclaw, Split (Croatia), *Athens Festival of New Media on Art*, *Videolisboa* Lisbon, Sheffield Documentary, Bergen, Wroclaw (British Art CD-ROM show).

His *Interactive Cinema* installation showing selections of interactive movies has been shown at: *ARTEC 95* Nagoya, Japan, *EMAF* Osnabrück, Germany 1995, *IMPAKT* Utrecht, Holland 1996, *Language of Interactivity*, Sydney, Australia 1996, Oberhausen *Kurzfilmtage*, Germany 1997, *FCMM* Montreal, Canada 1997, *CILECT* Conference 97, European Film School, Denmark, Living Arts

Museum, Reykjavik, Iceland, *FUSE 98*, San Francisco, *Creative Futures*, London 1998, *Visual Extension of the Photographic Image*, Seoul, South Korea 1998–9, *LAB7/Centre* for Contemporary Art, Ujazdowski Castle, Warsaw, 1999, *Electrohyp/Kajplats 305*, Malmo, 2000.

Graham Harwood

Harwood started out as an artist during the 1980s. He was involved with publishing initiatives such as *The Working Press*, *Underground Newspaper* and books such as *Unnatural – Techno Theory for a Contaminated Culture*. In 1995 he produced a piece for Video Positive in Liverpool. He worked at Ashworth maximum security hospital and created the installation *Rehearsal of Memory*. As an educationalist he worked on various new media courses and advised many other academic media initiatives. Disappointed with the state of academic education, Harwood was invited to work with Artec (London Arts Technology Centre), where he provided innovative training for the long-term unemployed. With Artec and ex-trainees he produced and published the CD-ROM version of *Rehearsal of Memory*. Harwood has spoken and exhibited at numerous events, in England, France, Austria, Australia, Germany, Canada, Portugal, Finland, Holland and Norway. In 1997 he formed Mongrel, with Matsuko Yokokoji and Richard Pierre-Davis. Their collaborative, socially-engaged cultural products include *National Heritage* and the *National Selection Search Engine*. In 1999 Harwood/Mongrel received the *Clarks Digital Bursary* and the *Imaginaria* award, from which emerged the software *Linker*, shown at ICA, London, and Watershed, Bristol. Currently Harwood is concentrating on research on software as culture and the history of medicine, and is Artist in Residence, Tate Modern, London.

George Legrady

George Legrady Studio is a research and development office specialising in interactive digital media art installations and publications. Emphasis is on the intersection of fine arts practice, interactive media and multidisciplinary theory through an in-depth exploration of new forms of cultural narratives.

George Legrady is Professor of Digital Media at the University of California, Santa Barbara and has also taught at the Merz Akademie, Stuttgart, Germany, San Francisco State University, UCLA, University of Southern California, California Institute of the Arts and the University of Western Ontario. His interactive installations have recently been exhibited at the Museum of Contemporary Art, Los Angeles, the Kunsthalle in Bonn, Haus der Kunst, Munich, Projects Studios One, New York, the National Gallery of Canada, the Palais des Beaux-Arts, Brussels, and the Centre Pompidou in Paris. Awards include a National Endowment of the Arts Visual Fellowship, Canada Council Computer Integrated Media Awards in 1994 and 1997, the *New Voices, New Visions* prize from Voyager and Honorable Mentions at *Ars Electronica*, Austria in 1989 and 1994. Digital interactive publications include the National Gallery of Canada, *Catalogue George Legrady: From Analogue to Digital* (1998); *Slippery Traces*, in *artintact 3*, ZKM, Karlsruhe, Germany (1996); and *An Anecdoted Archive from the Cold War*, HyperReal Media Production (1994).

Malcolm Le Grice

He began making films in 1965, and made his first computer performance work and film in 1969. He published a history of experimental cinema, *Abstract Film and Beyond*, in 1974 and his film and later video work is regularly shown internationally. Since 1983 he has had three feature-length and other shorter works screened on television. In the past ten years he has concentrated on video and computer art, and on publishing theoretical articles on the implications of digital concepts particularly as they relate to the forms and language of cinema. He is Professor at Central Saint Martins College of Art and Design, London.

Lev Manovich

Artist, theorist and critic of new media. He is the author of *The Language of New Media* (MIT Press 2001), *Tekstura: Russian Essays on Visual Culture* (Chicago University Press 1993) as well as over fifty articles which have been translated into many languages and published in over twenty countries. Currently he is working on a new book provisionally titled *Info Aesthetics*. His art projects include *Little Movies*, the first digital film project designed for the web (1994–) and *Freud-Lissitzky Navigator* (1999–), a conceptual software for navigating twentieth-century history.

Merel Mirage

A Dutch media artist based in Amsterdam and Cologne, Germany. She is Lecturer at the Media, Institute, Cologne. She has lived in Nicaragua, Japan, Tibet, and the internet, and her work often explores the conjunction and conflict of diverse realities. Her videos, films, installations and internet projects have been awarded prizes and exhibited internationally in such places as the Stedelijk Museum (Amsterdam), the Reina Sofia Museum (Madrid), the ICA (London), the *International Rotterdam Film Festival*, and the *Venice Biennale*.

Martin Rieser

Born in 1951 in London, and educated in English Literature and Fine Art. He has exhibited internationally using a variety of media, including graphic arts and photography. He works as a lecturer, writer and media artist. He curated *The Electronic Print* (Arnolfini 1989), and directed *Media Myth & Mania* for the *Silver to Silicon* CD-ROM (1993), exhibited at Watershed (Bristol), Focal Point (Southend), Photographer's Gallery, London, ICA (London) and Milia (Cannes). Interactive exhibitions include *Screening the Virus* website (ArtAids 1996), *Understanding Echo* interactive installation (Cheltenham Festival of Literature 2000), *Labyrinth*, CD-ROM and installation 1998 (F-Stop, Bath), and *Electronic Forest* interactive installation 1990–1 (Prema/Bristol). He has presented papers and work at international conferences including the Oberhausen *Kurzfilmtage*, Germany 1997, *ISEA 95* Montreal, *ISEA 96* Rotterdam, *ISEA 97* Chicago, and *Creativity and Cognition* Loughborough University 1999. He has been involved with digital media as an electronic artist since 1981 and has worked intensively with interactive multimedia for the past ten years. Currently he is Senior

Lecturer in Digital Media at Bath Spa University, formerly he lectured at Napier University, Edinburgh, and the University of the West of England, Bristol.

Jill Scott

Jill Scott was born in 1952, in Melbourne, Australia. She has exhibited many video artworks, conceptual performances and interactive environments in the United States, Australia, Europe and Japan. In 1973, she completed a degree in Film, Art and Design from Prahran Institute of Technology, Melbourne. From 1975–82 she lived in San Francisco, where she finished a Masters in Communications from San Francisco State University, and became the Director of *Site, Cite, Sight*, an alternative Gallery for Sculptural Installation. In 1982 she returned to Australia to lecture in Media at the University of New South Wales, College of Fine Arts, Sydney, and since then has worked with computers leading to 3D animation and interactive art. In 1992 she was invited to be a Guest Professor for Computer Animation in the Hochschule für Kunst, Saarbrücken, Germany, and in 1993 she won a second prize for Interactive Art at the *Prix Ars Electronica*. From 1994–7 she was an Artist in Residence and project co-ordinator for the Medienmuseum at ZKM in Karlsruhe, as well as a Research Fellow at the Centre for Advanced Inquiry into the Interactive Arts, University of Wales, Newport, where she was awarded a doctorate in Media Philosophy. Currently she is Professor for Installation Design in the Media Faculty at the Bauhaus University in Weimar.

Bill Seaman

Received a PhD from CAiiA, the Centre for Advanced Inquiry into the Interactive Arts, University of Wales, Newport, 1999. He holds a Master of Science in Visual Studies degree from the Massachusetts Institute of Technology, 1985. His work explores text, image and sound relationships through technological installation, virtual reality, linear video, computer-controlled laserdisc and other computer-based media, photography, and studio-based audio compositions. He is self-taught as a composer and musician. His works have been in numerous international festivals where he has been awarded prizes such as the *Prix Ars Electronica* in Interactive Art, 1992 and 1995, Linz, Austria; *International Video Art Prize*, ZKM, Karlsruhe, Germany; Bonn *Videonnale* Prize; First Prize, *Berlin Film/Video Festival, for Multimedia* in 1995; and the *Awards in the Visual Arts Prize*. Selected exhibitions include *Mediascape*, Guggenheim, New York 1996; the premiere exhibition of the ZKM in Karlsruhe, Germany 1997, Barbican Centre London 1997, C3 – Center for Culture and Communication, Budapest, Hungary 1997; *Portable Sacred Grounds*, NTT-ICC, Tokyo 1998; *Body Mécanique*, the Wexner Center, Columbus, Ohio 1999. He recently collaborated with the dancer Regina Van Berkel on the installation entitled *Exchange Fields*, which was commissioned by the *Vision Ruhr* exhibition, Dortmund, Germany. He was also commissioned by the National Gallery of Canada for the interactive work *Red Dice/Dés Chiffrés*, which is touring. He is currently Professor in the Department of Design/Media Arts, UCLA, where he is exploring issues related to the continuum between physical and virtual/media space. He is also working on a grant from Intel to create a computer-based Hybrid Invention Generator.

Jeffrey Shaw

Born in 1944, in Melbourne, Australia. Lives and works in Karlsruhe, Germany. Since the late 1960s Jeffrey Shaw has pioneered the use of interactivity and virtuality in his many art installations. His works have been exhibited worldwide at major museums and festivals. For many years he lived in Amsterdam where he co-founded the Evenstructure Research Group (1969–80). At present Shaw is director of the Institute for Visual Media at ZKM, Karlsruhe. He heads a unique research and production facility where artists and scientists are working together and developing profound artistic applications of the new media technologies.

Eku Wand

Born in October 1963 in Düsseldorf, Germany. From 1984–9, he studied at the Hochschule der Künste Berlin, finishing with a diploma degree. From 1984–7 he worked on various experimental theatre projects and he was front man and guitarist of the music band 'Diva Bleux'. From 1989–90 he did research work for SK4, a digital TV project in Berlin and from 1990–1 he was Art Director for Computer Animation and Video Productions at Cinepool GmbH, Berlin. From 1991–3 he worked as co-founder, manager and creative director of Pixelpark Multimedia Produktionsgesellschaft GmbH, Berlin. In 1993 he founded ScreenDesign, an office for interactive multimedia projects in Berlin, including Project 11ï23, a video beamer and slide installation for an event with Neville Brody in Berlin, in 1993. From 1994–6 he was teaching in Berlin and Zürich, Switzerland. From 1993–8 he created and published *Berlin Connection* – an interactive documentary thriller on CD-ROM. In 1998 he renamed his company eku interactive e. K., Berlin. From 1996–2000 he was Visiting Professor at the KHM Cologne, the Bauhaus University Weimar and since 2001 he has been Professor at the HBK Braunschweig. From 1999–2001 he was producer, director and designer of *Darksome Secrets – An Interactive Documentary Thriller* on CD-ROM. In 1991 he received various prizes and distinctions at *Imagina* and *Siggraph* among others, and in 1993 at the *Prix Ars Electronica*.

Peter Weibel

Born 1944 in Odessa. He lives in Karlsruhe, Germany, and Vienna, Austria. He studied Literature, Medicine, Logics, Philosophy and Film in Paris and Vienna. He works as polyartist, art- and media theoretician and exhibition curator. From 1976–81 he was Lecturer for Theory of Form and from 1981–4 Visiting Professor for Design and Art Education at the Hochschule für Angewandte Kunst in Vienna. In 1981 he was Visiting Professor at the College of Art and Design, Halifax, Canada, in 1979–80 Visiting Professor for Media Art and in 1981 Lecturer for Perception Theory. From 1982–5 he was Professor for Photography at the Gesamthochschule Kassel and from 1984–9 Associate Professor for Video and Digital Arts at the Center for Media Study, State University of New York at Buffalo. From 1989–94 he was Director of the Institut für Neue Medien at the Städelschule in Frankfurt am Main. From 1984–98 he was Professor for Visual Media Art at the Hochschule für Angewandte Kunst in Vienna. From 1986–95 he worked as artistic advisor and since 1992, as Artistic Director of the *Ars Electronica* in Linz, Austria. From 1993 to the present day he has been curator of the Neue Galerie am Landesmuseum Joanneum in Graz, Austria. From 1993–9 he was the Austrian commissioner of the *Venice Biennale* and since 1999 he has been Chairman and CEO of ZKM in Karlsruhe, Germany.

Grahame Weinbren

Has worked in film and video since the early 1970s and was one of the first artists to apply interactivity to the moving image. His interactive cinema installations have been exhibited internationally since 1984 and his most recent documentary (the feature-length *George* made in collaboration with Henry Corra) was broadcast in 2000 on HBO, the American national cable channel. He is an editor of *Millennium Film Journal*, and his writings on cinema, new technology and media art have been widely published. As a video artist, interactive video designer and consultant, and film-maker, he has exhibited widely at Centre Pompidou, Paris; Caixa de Pensions, Barcelona; Whitney Museum of American Art; The Kitchen; Museum of Contemporary Art, Los Angeles; Jewish Museum; Hallwalls, Buffalo; Walker Art Center, Minneapolis; and the Oberhausen Film Festival, Germany.

Paul Willemen

Received a PhD in Art and Design History (Middlesex). He was formerly Professor of Critical Studies at Napier University, Edinburgh. Currently he is Professor of Media and Cultural Studies at the University of Ulster, Coleraine. He previously worked as programmer for the Cinemathèque Royale de Belgique in the late 1960s, then at the Netherlands Filmmuseum and, since 1976, in various capacities at the British Film Institute. He has served on the editorial boards of *Screen*, *Skrien* and edited *Framework*. He is the author of books on Tashlin, Jacques Tourneur, Corman, Amos Gitai, Pasolini and of *Looks and Frictions* (BFI 1994), *Encyclopaedia of Indian Cinema* (with A. Rajadhyaksa, Oxford University Press 1994) and *Questions of Third Cinema* (with Jim Pines, BFI 1989).

John Wyver

A writer and producer, and chairman of the Illuminations Group, a close association of three independent production companies creating innovative and distinctive television, films, multimedia and convergent media. The co-founder of Illuminations Television in 1982, John Wyver has produced numerous programmes with the company, mainly about the arts and digital media. In 2000 he was awarded the Royal Television Society's Silver Medal in recognition of Distinguished Services to Television. He has been Series Editor of the BBC2 magazine *strand* about digital culture, *The Net* (1994–8), and also Series Editor of the contemporary cultural documentaries *Tx.* (BBC2, 1995–9). His work has won a number of major awards, including a 1995 *BAFTA for Best Arts Programme* awarded to his production for *Tx.* of David Hinton's film *Children of the Revolution*. In 1996 John Wyver's production *The Waste Land*, directed by Deborah Warner and featuring Fiona Shaw, was an Official Selection for the *Cannes Film Festival*. Subsequently, he produced a two-hour television version of Deborah Warner's staging of Shakespeare's *Richard II*, with Fiona Shaw as the King. In

1999 he co-produced with Shaun Deeney a film drawn from Phyllida Lloyd's stage production for Opera North of Benjamin Britten's *Gloriana*. This production won the *Performing Arts International Emmy* in 2000.

Andrea Zapp

Born in Germany, she lives in Manchester and works as a lecturer and media artist. Her projects focus on digital networks as a model for digital drama and user participation, the most recent one currently supported with a stipend from the Leverhulme Trust London. She received an MA in Film and Media Theory, Russian Language and Literature from the Philipps-University in Marburg in 1990. She has taught at the Academy of Film and Television in Potsdam-Babelsberg and at the Universities of Marburg and Leipzig, Germany. She was Visiting Lecturer at Arteleku San Sebastian, Spain, and at the State University of Santiago de Chile. In 1997 she was an Artist-in-Residence at the Future Lab of the Ars Electronica Centre in Linz, Austria, and in 2000 Visiting Artist at the Goethe Institutes in Latin America. She was nominated for the *International Media Art Award* 2000 and 2001 in Karlsruhe and received an Honorary Mention for Interactive Art at the *Prix Ars Electronica 2000* and at the *Art on the Net 2000* Competition, Machida City Museum of Graphic Arts, Tokyo. Her works have been shown widely on the net and in international exhibitions throughout Europe, the United States and Japan.

List of Artworks on the DVD-ROM

(accessible via artist's name in **DVD Quicklinks** or main menu unless stated otherwise in brackets)

Beloff, Zoe
- *Where Where There There Where* (interactive and QTVR images)
- *Beyond* (interactive and QTVR images)

Bielicky, Michael, Bernd Lintermann & Torsten Belschner
- *Room with a View* (movie [see Peter Weibel])

Blast Theory
- *Desert Rain* (movie [see Peter Weibel])

Blum, Heiner
- *Augentauschen* (movie [see Peter Weibel])

Buckley, Michael
- *The Good Cook* (interactive)

Butterworth, Alex & John Wyver
- *Avatar Farm* (movie and images)
- *Out of This World* (images)

Courchesne, Luc
- *Landscape One* (movies and images)
- *Panoscope* (movies)
- *Encyclopaedia Chiaroscuro* (image)

Dodge, Chris
- *The Winds that Wash the Seas* (movie [see Peter Weibel])

Dove, Toni
- *Artificial Changelings* (movie and image)
- *Spectropia* (images)

Feingold, Ken
- *The Surprising Spiral* (movie and image)
- *Interior* (movie and image)

Feingold, Ken (cont.)
- *where i can see my house from here so we are* (movie and image)
- *Self-Portrait as the Center of the Universe* (movie)
- *Head* (image)
- *Séance Box No 1* (image)
- *Jimmy Charlie Jimmy* (image)

Fietzek, Frank
- *Tafel* (movie [see Peter Weibel])

Fujihata, Masaki
- *Impalpability* (movie [see Peter Weibel])
- *Nuzzle Afar* (movie [see Peter Weibel])

Grzinic, Marina & Aina Smid
- *Troubles with Sex, Theory and History* (movie [see Peter Weibel])

Hales, Chris
- *Grandad* (interactive)
- *Tallinn People's Orchestra* (image)
- *Messed Up* (image)

Harwood, Graham & Mongrel
- *National Heritage* (movie)
- *Colour Separation* (images)
- *Heritage Gold* (image)

Hoberman, Perry
- *The Sub-Division of the Electric Light* (movie [see Peter Weibel])

Legrady, George
- *A Sense of Place* (interactive)
- *Slippery Traces* (movie [see Peter Weibel])

Le Grice, Malcolm

- *Digital Still Life* (movie)

Lintermann, Bernd & Torsten Belschner

- *Sonomorphis* (movie [see Peter Weibel])

Mirage, Merel

- *Subject: emotions encoded* (movie and images)

Rieser, Martin

- *Understanding Echo* (movie)
- *Screening the Virus* (interactive)

Rieser, Martin & Ship of Fools

- *Labyrinth* (interactive)
- *Media Myth and Mania* (images)

Scott, Jill

- *Beyond Hierarchy?* (movie)
- *A Figurative History* (movie)
- *Frontiers of Utopia* (movie)

Seaman, Bill

- *The World Generator* (movie and images)
- *Passage Sets* (movie [see Peter Weibel])

Shaw, Jeffrey

- *Place Ruhr* (movie)
- *conFiguring the Cave* (movie and images)
- *Movie Movie* (movie)

Spiegel, Stacey & Rodney Hoinkes

- *Crossings* (movie [see Peter Weibel])

Wand, Eku

- *Berlin Connection* (interactive and image)

Weibel, Peter

- *On Justifying the Hypothetical Nature of Art and the Non-Identicality within the Object World* (movie)

Weinbren, Grahame

- *Frames* (movie)

Zapp, Andrea

- *Little Sister* (website)

Zapp, Andrea & Paul Sermon

- *A Body of Water* (movie)

List of Book Illustrations

Acknowledgements

The authors would like to thank the following for their support and interest in the realisation of this project:

First of all, we are very grateful to all the contributing authors for their patience, dedication and responsiveness during the making of this book and for their inspirational and essential participation. The Center for Art and Media (ZKM) in Karlsruhe and The British Film Institute (BFI) in London for entering an unusual trans-national agreement in co-producing the DVD as an innovative supplement to the book. The ZKM Institute for Visual Media, headed by Jeffrey Shaw, for the initiative, support and encouragement in realising the DVD. Andrew Lockett and Tom Cabot from the BFI for their careful editing and advice. We thank the *Leonardo* Journal for their kind permission to reproduce texts by Merel Mirage and Grahame Weinbren. All those who have given permission to use and quote from their work throughout the essays. Judith and Paul for unfailing support and encouragement.

Martin Rieser and Andrea Zapp 2001

Preface

Timothy Druckrey

Traditional assessments of the effects of cinema have focused on the reciprocity between ideology and reception. These crucial arenas have provided a foundation for deconstructing the cinematic experience as a rich source for the emergence of cultural metaphor and the 'political unconscious', against the backdrop of the cinematic production as itself a subject of discourse. Indeed, the trajectory of critical writing on cinema (from Kracauer to Jameson, Bazin to Bellour, and including a newer generation of feminist and psychoanalytic theorists: Kaja Silverman, Margaret Morse, Constance Penley, Slavoj Žižek, etc.), from theories of the 'cultural industries' and mass psychology, to those of the psychology of the 'gaze' and of the incipient dominance of strategies of narrated power, have concentrated on the increasingly detailed micro-reading of semiotics and the ideologies of spectacle.

While the persuasiveness of these approaches is clear, the history of cinema, with its roots firmly embedded in technology, also challenges notions of causality, outside those of sheer literary readings of formal narrative technique. Almost from its beginnings (in the films of Méliès, for example), the cinema has attempted to construct 'realities' that are quite causally implausible, if not impossible. Built into the very syntax of film (through *mise-en-scène*, montage, flashbacks and, increasingly, special effects, etc.) are specific distortions of temporality, space, causality and linearity that defy the 'laws' of physics. Do the fictional spheres of cinema have their own 'natural' laws? Is it possible to elucidate the physical logic of these worlds as a critical problem?

Certainly, the link between the traditional objective science of scientific visualisation (bound to recording techniques of mathematics, geometry, optics and, more recently, to the encoding and rendering techniques of computational modelling) and the subjective, fictional 'science' of cinema raises a number of issues related to the plausibility, objectivity, imagination, and the cultural expression of scientific principles through popular culture. Unlike science-fiction cinema, which speculates about possible sciences, cultures and futures, there is an emerging cinema that constructs worlds whose possibilities out-distance causal, verifiable, or even intelligible 'realities'. Yet the genre of science fiction, beginning just before the invention of cinema, is, in a sense, cinema's big brother, in which speculative 'worlds' have, to some extent, become legitimated as a form. As J. G. Ballard remarked: 'the fiction already exists, it is up to us to invent the reality.'

In a recent interview, George Lucas, now championing completely digitised movies, described the scenes in *The Phantom Menace* as 'immaculate realism'. Emanating from the heavenly heights of the aptly named Skywalker Ranch, this dizzying proclamation is as much a logical conundrum, as it is a tragic revelation. Surely Lucas, desperately attempting to theologise the *Star Wars* films by sanitising them of anything but hyper-prosaic mythological references, falls headlong into the traps of both mystification and universalisation. Yet, for all its sanctimony, the notion of 'immaculate realism' does pose some important issues in an understanding of the transformations of space wrought by the divine object of 'immaculate realism': computation (even as it exposes a capitulation to de-realised visual forms). No longer intent on such vulgar sentiments as correspondence, affinity or resemblance, the implication of an *'immaculate reality'* is neither redemptive nor, in the end, graven.

Of course, it cannot intend to be so. And this too suggests a troubling resonance between a sinlessly pious presumption and a condemned empirical description of a theological (even teleological) *mise-en-scène*, whose unrepresentability is confirmed by its very status as immaculate. After all is said and done, an 'immaculate reality' is neither 'immaculate' or it would not be realistic, nor 'realistic' or it would not be immaculate (we know too that Lucas is not guiltless). It recalled a remark made in an interview with Jaron Lanier, where he lamented the coining of the term 'virtual reality' by suggesting that 'intentional reality' would have been more appropriate. The relationship of the conditional with the categorical is a telling description of the era of the simulacra – even if it is not an entirely original notion. However, while the replacement of a 'virtual' with an 'intentional' reality is fascinating, it must be the topic for another discussion. But, I must say that I hope the two never meet. Can you just imagine an 'immaculate intention'!?

But neither Lucas's *immaculate realism* nor Lanier's *intentional fallacy* can begin to account for the breadth of issues raised by the substantive questions about representation. Namely: the apparatus of representation, the techniques of representation, or even the ideologies of representation, that remain largely unresolved in much thinking about the so-called 'space', now coming to pervade discussions of an electronic system, whose claims to be 'spatial' are metaphoric at best.

Virtual space inhabits the history of representation – and particularly the representation of perspective – right from the start. Emerging as much from the 'rationality' of urban Renaissance culture, as from the integration of theologised ideologies of infinity in the representation of space, perspective poses a meddlesome problem for a technological world-picture in which infinity has no fixed (perhaps calculable is better) position; in which the urban is more transactional than material, and in which sight is temporalised in the interface, rather than spatialised through the window. But the interface is more than just a portal into an illusion; it stands as the representation into a system of codes not only more complex than a sheer indexical image, but also as an algorithmic display rendered into 'visibility'. Indeed, the now vast literature on the so-called 'architecture' of cyberspace invokes immateriality, event-scenes, information atmospheres, trans-localities, forms of transitional or experiential 'space', and what might be called 'haptic' rather than 'optic' perspectives, an architecture that will, in Virilio's wonderful phrase, 'take place'.

Even William Gibson's definition of cyberspace suggested not that it is rational, not that it is an illusion, not that it is a description, but that it is a 'consensual hallucination'. This strangely conforms to a remark by a well-known VR researcher that 'psychology is the physics of Virtual Reality'.

Proposing a 'psycho-physics' of representation within the programmed terrain of a virtual reality poses some delicate issues about the link between immateriality, fantasy, illusion and cognition, while it is a bit of a confounding over-interpretation of physics. And while there is a bloated literature of the simulacra, it seems that in 'virtual space' – if we include 'intentionality' – we also might have to include Searle's 'speech acts' into the picture (literally). But, after all, the presence of the subject in VR could almost be considered not 'intentional' but incidental – perhaps even unintentional. Location mapping, anticipatory space, a frame of variables: the discourse of VR posits not a fixed position, but attenuated (or potentially attenuated) indexical locations programmed into finite boundaries. In this sense we can understand the 'space' of VR as trumping *trompe l'oeil*; the 'real' world, as Peter Weibel suggests, with a *sign world*, in which 'the eye is the swindler of the brain.' It would also be useful to recall, in this regard, Virilio's remark that 'we are programming our absence.'

Of course, these phrases come as signifiers of a relocated sense of visuality that has emerged, as the interests of scientific visualisation and mental representation intersect in the technological discourses of image synthesis, cognitive science, and, increasingly, in the digital cinema. Add to this a psychoanalytical discourse, turning its attention to the experiential forms of electronic media, and we are suddenly faced with an extraordinary issue in which the bifurcated subject/object position of modernist reception theories comes 'eye-to-eye' with a kind of 'field theory' in which cognition and representation are processes within systems. In this sense, the intelligible perception of 'reality' is posed less as verificatory or merely sensible and more as intelligible, logically possible in a milieu that is (as Jameson once remarked) 'triumphantly artificial'. Coupled with the temporalisation of computable or renderable experiences, the chrono-sensual extension of the rendered image poses striking new possibilities for a generation of so-called 'new media artists' immersed in reconsideration of the flow of experiences, rather than their mere non-linearity.

Certainly the wild speculations about immersive cinematic experiences, unfolding in multilayered post-cinematic narratives, have largely proved futile. Predicated on the elusive spectacles of the 'cinema of attractions' and the flawed subjectifications of programmed variables as unimpeded potentials, most of the attempts have succumbed to suggest grand hypertextual forms ornamented with filmed sequences, often banal effects and the alienation of an audience in favour of single users.

So instead of the now nearly defunct cross-referencing (or fancy-footnoting) strategies of hypertext, the works emerging in the reconfigured strategies in this book collapse many of the boundaries between narrative, text, and sound and image. They situate the user in the midst of experiential variability and computational feedback – a differentiated 'space', that allows the interleaving of interactions in complex post-narrative forms.

These forms exist as a melding of the practices and histories of montage (with its colliding significations), cinema (from the exploration of pre-cinema technologies to the re-conceptualisation of immersion in electronic environments), experimental literature (that broke the normative sequential drive of narrative), television (that shattered temporal continuity), and video (that reframed the observer/observed roles), with the evolving potentials of post-cinematic productions that assimilate and outdo cinema by shattering the restraints of the fixed temporality of cinema, the spatial fixity of montage, or the linear broadcast metaphor of television, or the simplistic subject/object relations of video. In these works, sequential, or arrayed, information is created in forms that suggest that traditional cinema cannot serve events that are themselves complex configurations of experience, intention, interpretation and interaction.

In the last weeks of the cinema millennium a long text appeared in the *New York Times Magazine*, hailing George Lucas and the coming triumph of digital cinema ('The Movies' Digital Future is in Sight and it Works', 26 Nov. 2000). Among the many hyperbolic remarks in the text, one came from George Lucas himself: 'When we take the digital images we see and translate them down to film, it's just down … It's less of an image – less clear, less than what we shot or created.' To this I would like to juxtapose a remark from the thoughtful theorist of cinema, Raymond Bellour:

> So the point would rather be to make this commonplace but necessary observation: there is no visual image that is not more and more tightly gripped, even in its essential, radical withdrawal, inside an audiovisual or scriptovisual (what horrid words) image that envelops it, and it is in this context that the existence of something that still resembles art is at stake today. We are well aware, as Barthes and then Eco have been pointing out for some time now, and as was so admirably reformulated by Deleuze with an extraordinary emphasis on the image, that we are not really living in 'a civilisation of the image' – even though pessimistic prophets have tried to make us believe that it has become our evil spirit par excellence, no doubt because it had been mistaken for an angel for such a long time. We have gone beyond the image, to a nameless mixture, a discourse-image, if you like, or a sound-image ('Son-Image', Godard calls it), whose first side is occupied by television and second side by the computer, in our all-purpose machine society.

Foreword

An Age of Narrative Chaos?

Martin Rieser and Andrea Zapp

I resolved to shun storytelling. I would write about life. Every person would be exactly as important
as any other. All facts would also be given equal weightiness. Nothing would be left out. Let others
bring order to chaos. I would bring chaos to order, instead, which I think I have done. If all writers
would do that, then perhaps citizens not in the literary trades will understand that there is no order
in the world around us, that we must adapt ourselves to the requirements of chaos instead. It is hard
to adapt to chaos, but it can be done. I am living proof of that: It can be done.

Kurt Vonnegut, Breakfast of Champions

We are entering an age of narrative chaos, where traditional frameworks are being overthrown
by emergent experimental and radical attempts to remaster the art of storytelling in developing
technologies. As media artists and theorists ourselves, we feel this book gives long overdue recognition to the maturation of new media art into a major innovation in screen narrative form and
genres. This collection of essays by leading cultural theorists, critics and artists using new media,
seeks to establish a clear overview of this changing territory. It does this by outlining the challenge
interactivity and new media pose to the future of cinematic and broadcast formats of story. It
specifically describes emerging narrative types in hypermedia, installation and video art, the internet, computer games, interactive television and interactive film and relates them to classical film and
drama theory. By introducing a mixed economy of reflection around attempts to accommodate
these new media forms of narrative, this book intends to look closely at issues of audience engagement in recognised works of various genres. The reflective self-critique of practitioners tests the
challenge and inspiration afforded to the user both by new navigational concepts and by sensual
encounters with shifting virtual and fictional worlds. The papers trace the development from pre-
mapped hyperlinked stories, to current examples of the audience as an editor of parallel data-
streams or even as inhabitants of virtual worlds, as well as anatomising the altered function of the
viewer using two-way connectivity and the, consequently, changed nature of authorship.

Traditional narrative has been augmented by the advent of new media, not just through the revolutionary distributive aspects of the technology, but principally through the changed relationship

between audience and author. New media forms offer both a convergence of narrative vehicles and a fragmentation of understood forms: the genesis of broadband, virtual and immersive technologies, together with the development of Artificial Intelligence (AI) and autonomous agency in interactive drama, will inevitably change current screen broadcast and Hollywood models of cinema. But we are also aware that the acceleration of technical development tends to ensure that the evolution of dramatic language can often be overlooked in the pursuit of a 'better' interface. The new narratives sometimes seem to be dependent on the speed of engineering, rather than on a developing conceptualisation of possible genres.

Therefore, given these premises, we attempt to unwrap the experimentation and critical discourses that have grown up around the realisation of interactive narrative during the past two decades. These are varied in both their diversity of approach and form, but they are all part of an incredibly inspiring and challenging field of media development. The practitioner-participants in this work were chosen by the editors for their strong reconfiguration of screen media linked to narrative content or fiction, although some of the artists themselves might deny the connection. The idea was to provoke a new discourse concentrating on content rather than interface. We also aimed, with the accompanying DVD, to provide visual examples of the discussed state-of-the-art media projects, which had previously only been accessible to the public on the global exhibition circuit. We specifically identify these as forming a rich territory for exploration precisely because of the failure of the mainstream media industry to properly engage with the non-formulaic (and risky) adventure of narratives cut free from linearity of delivery.

The recognised problematic of applying such long-established terms as 'narrative' and even 'interactivity' simultaneously to new media works is one of the motivations which drove us into conceiving the book in its present state. The new narrative forms are traced back to their historical origins in the early experiments of film-makers and the radical movements in post-war art. The transfer from classical narrative moves us into a new, more fragmentary culture of drama. As Sean Cubitt puts it:

> The themes critiqued here – of universal narrative, the end of grand narrative and anti-narrative –
> share the paradox that narrative analysis produces a static and spatial model in place of a dynamic
> and temporal one. Is it possible or desirable for narrative to regain a place in the critical and practical
> vocabulary of the emergent media? I believe so, but under a new guise that takes account of the fact
> that narrative is no longer – if indeed it ever was – the central mode of modern communication.

Critics of cinema are also deeply cynical about the hype surrounding poorly formulated claims for interactivity as *the* new narrative. Paul Willemen sharply points out:

> There is no need to dwell on silly notions such as the digital media's alleged development of some form
> of non-linear narrative: narrative constantly loops back and branches out, condenses and proliferates

uncontrollably, which is precisely why the 'meaning' of a story can never be fixed once and for all. Narrative never was linear, so to proclaim the discovery of non-linear narrative is absurd.

In the same vein, interactivity has always been a feature of any representational media, from religious rituals to painting, novels and cinema.

We are hoping that this book will provoke a fertile dialogue between these opposing viewpoints, through its combination of innovative practical experiments and critical approaches. We also hope that the reader will conclude that new media marks a major watershed in the development of screen forms of narrative.

Structural Overview

Cinema, Art and the Reinvention of Narrative

A number of identifiable themes run throughout the book, which can be regarded as major issues across all the models of narrative described. These put into question traditional analyses of narrative modelling and reception and can be seen as transitional pointers to a new grammar and aesthetic of story. They could be summarised as follows:

- Time montage and the spatial mapping of story;
- The rediscovery of the body inhabiting telepresent and immersive spaces;
- The matrix as a natural structure for the digital to define irreducible units of narrative;
- Generative fiction as 'liquid narrative' or 'the floating artwork';
- The changing nature of audience: from passive viewer to active and nomadic participant.

Inevitably a compilation of this nature throws up repeated discourses and terminology, which cross-reference frequently. We see this as a necessary side effect in the establishment of a common language by which to describe the forging of these new theories of aesthetics and structure. The uniqueness of this language will eventually allow both artists and theorists to move on from the thematics and ontologies of earlier media forms and encourage discursive readings to be shared.

While the text is well-illustrated within the body of the book, it has always been our intention that the DVD-ROM would form the primary source of still colour illustration, moving image and interactive visual material, and allow the reader to experience work at first hand, which has hitherto been mainly accessible through isolated museum exhibitions. We see the DVD as an essential component of the book and would encourage the reader to examine simultaneously both text and digital samples. Where a cross-link is involved, the reference in the book to the DVD is underlined in the text and flagged in the margin with a logo (⊙). The navigation structure of the DVD mirrors that of the book, and access to relevant websites has been automated throughout the disk itself. Texts on the DVD are simply intended as short introductions to its individual sections.

We have organised the material into a hierarchy mirroring the evolutionary processes involved in transferring old media practice into newer forms. Both the book and the DVD are divided into two major sections: **Part 1 Orientations**, examining issues of theory and history (where the past prefigures the present convergence of forms and anticipates future developments); and **Part 2 Explorations**, examining practice (where we give space to the personal voice of the artist).

PART ONE: ORIENTATIONS: HISTORY AND THEORY

In **Definitions** Cubitt redefines the narrative as a form of social exchange and communication, relating this to philosophical and political frames of reference. He speculates that in the new aesthetic dialogues thereby generated, we may yet find a valid form of narrative interaction. Willemen examines the politics of new media and globalisation, noting the disenfranchised margins, the monopolies of power and control, and the resultant politicised interface, proposing highly critical approaches to the claims of interactivity.

In **Origins** Dinkla gives a historical overview of different strategies of narration from early Victorian panoramas to multi-perspective literature and interactive storytelling. The article draws attention to the social and political implications of changing strategies of narration. Conditions of production and reception are put into a historical as well as visionary context by Weibel. He outlines a broad panorama of post-war development of media art in contrast to traditional cinema, by drawing a line from the activities of the artistic avant-garde in early multiple screen and projection experiments to the 'happenings' of the 1960s, through multi-narrative experiments to the naissance of video art. He further envisions the nature of a 'future cinema'. Following on, Blunck unpacks the history of interactive or 'expanded cinema', and its antecedents such as the experimental group clustered around Fluxus. In these early experiments in expanded and synaesthetic cinema, she tracks their relation to traditional film theory. Manovich identifies the loop as an irreducible component of moving image media, regardless of platform or genre, and speculates on the primitive nature of interactivity in relation to 'spatial montage'. He further describes the social basis of the transition from linear to spatialised narrative:

> It is not accidental that the marginalisation of spatial narrative and the privileging of sequential mode of narration coincided with the rise of a historical paradigm in human sciences. Cultural geographer Edward Soja has argued that the rise of history in the second half of the nineteenth century coincided with the decline in spatial imagination and the spatial mode of social analysis. According to Soja, it was only in the last decades of the twentieth century that this mode made a powerful comeback, as exemplified by the growing importance of such concepts as 'geopolitics' and 'globalisation' as well as by the key role analysis of space played in theories of post-modernism.   .

In **Convergence** Zapp investigates the potential of distributed web narratives as a platform for an audience's direct collaboration in fiction development. She discusses the relation between the body and its representation and identity in online visual and theatrical environments. Wyver and Butterworth examine their recent experiments building 3D worlds and avatars in 'Inhabited TV' (immersive interactive TV). From this practical background they draw conclusions on possible future transformations of mass broadcast media. The success and failure of the cinematic interface, transformed through interactivity, is narrated by Hales. He identifies essential artistic and dramatic components in relation to audience reception:

Narrative scriptwriting of the sort which has been propagated in the movie industry for 80 or more years no longer plays a role, and even the concept of what constitutes a 'story' must be re-evaluated. Whereas the popularity of the Hollywood 'style' of film has pushed the experiments of structural, abstract and non-narrative film-makers into a niche, the addition of interactivity could continue to demonstrate that there are other uses of filmic communication, based on concepts of time and space, which are at the very least equally valid.

In **Beyond Narrative?** Feingold relates narrative to an embodied experiential model, and questions the validity of goal-driven modes of interaction with their predetermined meanings. He argues for sufficient space, complexity and open-endedness in interactive works, so that they gain richness by varying contexts of display. The audience's reception of accidental changes in a work can assign new meaning to the artefact. Dovey addresses the problematic of hypertext theory in dealing with the cinematic, positing a spatial analysis of narrative as a possible solution. Rieser investigates alternative strategies for navigation, orientation and design, using the fluidity of language as compensation for the breaks in diegetic coherence through interaction. Wand juxtaposes the audience's relationship to the traditional performer or narrator with the interrupted world of the interactive, identifying the limits of that interactivity in real-time and in improvisational situations. The practical questions of design in such pieces are further illustrated and he expands the question of rule-based development for complex narrative. Weinbren considers orders of authorial and audience control mediated by the computer game, researching particularly its cinematic aspects. The individual and the machine are trapped in a competitive struggle for mastery, which becomes an end in itself.

PART TWO: EXPLORATIONS: A NEW PRACTICE

In the section **Restructuring Time** the new forms of temporal engagement, made possible through interactivity, are held up to the light. Scott explores socialised interaction, which is characterised by crossing and fusing levels of time, in her historically-influenced artworks. She explains her use of audience dialogue with characters, virtual social models, analogic means to move through story-time, role-playing and subjective memory. Dove creates fictional worlds using interfaces correlating to orders of imaginative depth and the interior spaces of character, using temporal shifting, related to the intensity of audience engagement.

Redefining Space covers the new notions of spatialised narrative. Legrady examines the effect of different presentation environments and validating modes of display, both public and private, and how these alter the reception of works in relation to his particular approaches to content. Le Grice describes VR as an alternate existence, where body perception and the search for form create a distinct break with the past. Seaman's 'Recombinant Poetics' engages virtual reality with audience-directed modes of access, coining the phrase 'vuser' to describe the active participant in virtual space: 'The technologies of virtual environments point to a cinema that is an immersive narrative space wherein the interactive viewer assumes the role of both cameraperson and editor.'

Beyond the Screen opens out our understanding of new screen forms. Courchesne sets the definition of spectatorship against the evolution of early antecedents of cinema, in particular panoramas. He denies the central role of narration as an intrinsic attribute in interactive works. Narrative is seen here more as a reconstruction of the 'visitor's' unique experiential route. Shaw contrasts the potentials of new media technology with the stereotypes of Hollywood cinema. He argues that immersive spaces liberate the choice of the spectator, and augmented reality joins to the real world in a way which supersedes passive cinema. His is a constructed and architectronic model, allowing individual creative engagement. Mirage is intensely concerned with the world on the other side of the screen, a frustrating and liberating space, in which a love affair can grow. A bifurcation of reality, dubbed 'the accident' by Paul Virilio.

> A place where one can dream. For more than three years I have been sitting behind the computer
> screen, acting and reacting in parallel worlds, all running at the same time …

In **The Personalised Interface** artists are given a chance to explain the unique forms they have devised for specific projects. Beloff examines her own intimate and self-performative digital cinema, through changing ideas of perception and psychology, using the supernatural as a virtual model.

> Central to my work is this theme of death and artificial resurrection. The machine mediating
> between these two states. I believe that this legacy, so often forgotten, of the suppression of death,
> continues to haunt the creation of virtual reality.

Buckley describes 'restlessness of the mind' as a conceptual model for his own work: a fluid fragmentary and repeating structure mapping out the sleepless contradictory reveries of his protagonist, explored through a multimedia environment. Harwood extends this conceptual mapping into the specific territories of racial stereotyping and marginalisation, explored through web and installation art. In a radical and provocative manifesto he describes the uncompromising working methods of the Mongrel collective, allowing different voices to surface in their angry reactions to racialism.

PART ONE

ORIENTATIONS: HISTORY AND THEORY

Spreadsheets, Sitemaps and Search Engines

Why Narrative is Marginal to Multimedia and Networked Communication, and Why Marginality is More Vital than Universality

Sean Cubitt

I

Media Studies both benefits from and is overdetermined by its double origin, among sociologists increasingly convinced of the centrality of communication to modernity, and among literary schools diminishingly persuaded of the relevance of past literatures to the lived experience and likely futures of their students and themselves. The clash of cultures has been immensely fruitful. But the dialectic of humanities and social sciences approaches has occasionally broken down: one critical example is the failure of 'ethnographic' audience studies to square off with qualitative and statistically-based analysis of audiences (though see the forthcoming work of Andy Ruddock), leaving a yawning gap between micro-studies of 'real people' and macro-studies of whole populations. Studies of the new media are beginning to bridge the gap through the wide-scale interactive dialogues that have begun to break down the impasse. A second unfortunate effect has been the felt necessity to preface any methodological proposal with a diatribe against whatever the author perceives as the previous dominant discourse in the discipline (see Gauntlett's introduction to his otherwise useful *web.studies*).[1] One thinks here of Barry Salt's attack on *Screen*, maintained long past its polemical sell-by date in the second edition of *Film Style and Technology*,[2] or Bordwell and Carroll's assault on interpretative criticism. The vitality of the field – since this is a necessarily interdisciplinary zone – depends, on the contrary, on the recognition of what has been achieved to date, even as we test and contest the premises, principles and, increasingly of late, the objects that constitute it. In this vein, I do not want here to decry the achievements of narratological analysis, or to claim that it has no place in critical understandings or creative dispositions in computer-mediated communications. Rather, I want to suggest that narrative is only one among several modes of organisation characteristic of new media, that this has an impact on certain universalist claims for narrative analysis, and that one crucial measure of value, the relation to narrative models, therefore does not hold good in assessing new media texts and practices. On the other hand, I also want to point up the importance of narrative's temporal imagination in a spatialised world of communication, and insist that its very marginality allows it a special role, which otherwise it could not occupy.

There are three particular discourses of narrative that need to be reassessed if we are to grasp the nettle of new media's temporalities. The first is the notion that almost any mode of human culture can be understood as narrative. In this discourse, we read of the essentially narrative form of memory, of history, of myth, of news, of psychology, of politics and of science. While such literary readings of non-literary discourses can be illuminating (for example the analyses offered in *In Dora's Case* by Bernheimer and Kahane),[3] the claim underlying this discourse is that all human activity is fundamentally structured like a story. Yet some key narratological analyses demonstrate that even apparently narrative forms (the myth and the western among them: see especially Lévi-Strauss and Wright) are better understood as structures, spatial rather than temporal formations.[4] This spatialisation of narrative analysis anticipated the spatial turn of cultural analysis, prominent in the work of geographers like Lefebvre, and Harvey in cultural studies.[5] At the same time, however, the geographical imagination altered the terms under which narrative could be deemed central to human experience. A journey, for example, may be recorded in a more or less picaresque narrative, but it may also be transcribed as a map or a geographical information system.

A second objection to the universalist claim for narrative analysis is that it restricts itself to a more or less strictly chronological model of temporal experience. There is only an apparent contradiction between this chronological critique and the criticism of spatialisation. The chronological narrative proposes to us a protagonist who always occupies a perpetual present (without which such effects as suspense and expectation would be impossible) as a point moving along a line whose dimensions have however already been mapped: the protagonist of the chronological narrative is caught in a story whose beginning and end have already been determined, and which therefore constructs story time as the unfolding of destiny rather than the passage from past certainty into an uncertain future. This sense of preordination constructs narrative as timeline, as a spatial organisation, and its protagonists as variants moving through rule-governed moves, as in a game of chess. That this is in itself a specific and historical expression of Western culture is only one aspect of its imperialist gesture. The other lies in its negation of the plurality of modes of consciousness and discursive formations through which we experience the present. As I hope to show, alternative modes of temporality are particularly important in the study of digital media.

The second discourse in which narrative takes a central position derives from Lyotard's critique of the *grand récit* or 'master narrative' as that characteristic of modern culture whose loss marks the entry into the post-modern.[6] Lyotard and his later acolytes make three critical errors. Firstly, there is a failure to register the most significant political and communicative discourses of the late twentieth century: post-coloniality, feminism and the green movement. More forgivably, Lyotard wrote too early to confront the emergence of 'techno-boosterism' as a worldwide cultural discourse running directly counter to his thesis. Nonetheless, discourses of technology, anti-imperialism, gender and ecology pose an empirical challenge to the observation that the 'narratives' of progress, emancipation and truth have ceased to exercise the political and social aspirations of contemporary society. Born of the betrayal of such aspiration by the Parti Communiste de la France in 1968, the bitter anti-Marxism of key post-modern theorists like Lyotard, Baudrillard, Virilio and Deleuze does not validate the attempt to ascribe to modernity an exclusively and uniquely narrative foundation, nor the insistence on the failure of the form.

The third weakness of the argument, again crucial to the critique offered in this chapter, is the confusion surrounding the definition of narrative as a necessarily teleological form. Certainly, Marxism has historically pointed towards the future as the site of the 'realm of freedom', which the third volume of *Das Kapital* moots as the beginning of history after the 'pre-history' of class war.[7] Equally, certainly Stalinism (and to a lesser extent Leninism) posited a definite content for the realm of freedom. But both Trotskyism and the new political movements of the late twentieth century paint a picture of the future without definite content, even when the future is imaged as the result of a stark and immediate choice, as so often is the case in the more impetuous shades of green. The difference is that between faith and hope, teleology and eschatology. In this way, the critique of the *grand récit* misinterprets progressive politics as Aristotelian narratives with a beginning, a middle and an end. Not only do such political movements not define themselves in terms of conclusion: their goals are not even necessarily conceived of as states of equilibrium. Instead, the discourse of the End is peculiar to post-modernism itself, and to post-structuralists like Barthes, Baudrillard and Lyotard, with the only difference being that each awards himself the Hegelian privilege of reading history from the vantage point of its (successful or unsuccessful) conclusion. By thus deploying a narrative strategy to emphasise the twin issues of narrative's centrality and its conclusion, the critique of the *grand récit* entered a circular logic that defeats its attempt to present itself as a philosophical account of the social world.

The third discourse significant to the current analysis belongs at once to avant-garde critiques of narrative and to the implicit evaluative frameworks of media studies. Vanguardist criticism received an immense fillip from the writers associated with *Tel Quel* in the late 1960s and early 1970s, those associated with *Cahiers du Cinéma* and *Cinéthique* in the same period and the translations that became available in the pages of *Screen*, *New Left Review*, *SubStance* and other small journals in the mid-1970s. In common with earlier avant-gardes, the poststructuralists around Boulez, Sollers, Resnais and Godard instigated an attack on the dominant culture. Identifying narrative as a characteristic of the dominant, they proposed anti-narrative, alongside anti-illusionism, as a key strategy for radical art practice. As vanguardist strategy this was fruitful. But as the language in which it had been couched became accepted as the basis for North Atlantic 'theory', the terms of the narrative/anti-narrative distinction became normative. On the one hand, narrative was assumed to be dominant, while on the other opposition to dominance has been taken as an assumed but rarely explicit criterion of evaluation. Production practices, texts and reading strategies are praised for being oppositional, resistant or subversive. Yet all these terms not only assume domination but also define themselves exclusively in relation to it. Thus, oppositional practices become dependent on the dominant they oppose. In the immediate context, anti-narrative defines itself through its dependency on narrative. This has two consequences. Firstly, narrative once again becomes universal by assimilating all aberrations from itself as merely oppositional. Secondly, the possibility of alternative forms, rather than simply oppositional ones, is elided. Put more formally, narrative/anti-narrative is a binary opposition incapable of producing a new term beyond their polarity. The emergence of alternative media forms, by contrast, demands not dualism but a dialectical understanding capable of producing something new. The themes critiqued here – of universal narrative, the end of grand narrative and anti-narrative – share the paradox that narrative analysis produces a static and spatial model in place of a dynamic and temporal one. Is it possible or desirable for narrative to regain a place in the critical and practical vocabulary of the emergent media? I believe so, but under a new guise, that takes account of the fact that narrative is no longer – if indeed it ever was – the central mode of modern communication.

II

The very universality claimed for narrative indicates the poverty of the category as a historical tool. Although, as Williams observes, the rise of the popular press, film, radio and television has led to the proliferation of narrative texts way beyond the experience of earlier generations, the larger history of modernity is better traced through its more fundamental innovations.[8] The remarkable persistence of narrative in twentieth-century media can only be apprehended as remarkable if we apprehend the environment in which it is now performed: a landscape of other modes of documentation and dissemination. Crucial among them are forms of data storage and retrieval that are not structured in time, as is the narrative, but in space. Modernity's key social formations – capitalism, the state and imperialism – cannot be imagined without the data systems on which they depend: book-keeping, record-keeping and cartography.

In their digital forms, spreadsheets, databases and geographical information systems are core facets of new media usage, an importance underlined by their significance to the history of workplace computing. Moreover, the convergence of these three core systems in popular packages like Microsoft Office and AppleWorks indicates a far higher degree of integration than that claimed for sound, image and text in multimedia and networked communications. The lack of emphasis on workplace media is a legacy of the division of labour executed between sociology and cultural studies in the late 1960s and early 1970s; largely motivated by the slogan 'the personal is the political'. Feminist criticism of the exclusivity of class analysis derived from work as object of study led the turn towards the more gender-oriented, less class-defined politics of the domestic and of leisure. But that emphasis on the media as home- and leisure-based has become misleading in a period in which the same machines occupy similar spaces at home and work, or are physically carried between them, while the very distinction between work and leisure is becoming increasingly blurred. The emphasis on narrative derives in part from a failure to address instrumental media techniques like databasing into hobby culture, spreadsheets into voluntary culture and cartography into the life experience of an increasingly mobile population.

One factor which is particularly germane to this discussion is the way in which digitisation adds a certain additional dimensionality to the existing physical media from which digital forms derive. Not only multiple drafts but also multiple linkages become available whereby a single mode of ordering and retrieval – alphabetical, chronological or co-ordinate for example – is supplemented by others. A database can be searched through any of its fields, a property leading towards the highly-integrated forms of contemporary informatics. At the consumer end, these might look like geo-positioning systems accompanied by a gazetteer of hotels and restaurants, service stations and retailers. At the industrial end, it might involve combinations of loyalty-card data from superstores with credit card transactions and postcode- or zipcode-based market research. In between lie specialist services like geo-ecological surveying for prospective house buyers. These processes and many others help to build the impression we have of the computer screen as a window or even a doorway into a complex and multidimensional space.

The critical metaphors applied to this newly three-dimensional interface – navigation, search, surfing – have incidental and contingent connotations of some specific narrative genres, but they are neither purely nor only narrative, and this for two reasons. Firstly, as already emphasised, they are spatial rather than temporal metaphors; and secondly they are eschatological, not teleological. If we take the example of record-keeping, the move from the ledger to the filing cabinet not only introduces an important division of labour allowing great intensification of bureaucratisation in the imperial state, but also introduces a new criterion for data storage: ease of retrieval. By contrast, during this same period the gigantism of narrative from *Don Quixote* and *Tom Jones* into the nine-teenth century, along with the eclipse of verse as the natural medium for epic, indicate that narra-tive was in the process of losing its oral role as popular memory, and that novels and plays ceased to function as repositories of popular memory. That task was remitted to either the imperial bureaucracy, guardian of genealogies and associations with the land, or to the almanacs and other popular compendia of herbal, meteorological, astrological and similar traditional lore. That authors of the calibre of Calvino and Borges could 'experiment' in the twentieth century with forms which were already entrenched throughout Europe and the Americas in the seventeenth is testimony to the remoteness of literary and narrative cultures from the actualities of life.

Parallel with the demands of bureaucracy, the accumulation of knowledge in books began to demand a radical overhaul of library design. The introduction of classified catalogues led directly to the first designs in the 1930s for taxonomies based on semantic principles, origin of the familiar key-word search. Boolean operators, providing for inclusive or exclusive searches, depend on a logical rather than narratological sense of what constitutes the semantic domain, and 'invisible' elements of documents, like HTML (hypertext mark-up language) metatags, are as determining of the seman-tic value of a page as its apparent content, narrative or otherwise. Even within sites the use of graphical or textual sitemaps, navigation bars and selection buttons indicate that to some extent the retrieval mechanism internal to the book, the index, has taken over from narrative as the key relay of textual organisation from the literary to the digital.

Two facts need to be noted about the prevalence of search, retrieval and three-dimensionality in this key formation of digital media. Firstly, they derive from a model of efficiency associated since Weber with the bureaucratic-rationalist ethos, and in the conceptualisation of the Frankfurt School with the instrumental reason typical of late capitalism. This efficiency model, mercifully, has plenty of loopholes to allow for serendipity in searching. The circumscription of that serendipitous con-nectivity in enclosed domains like AOL (America Online) or Microsoft Network in some ways approximates even more closely to the fully bureaucratised form of the library in which stacks and reading spaces have been separated and retrieval of books from shelves professionalised. Nevertheless the instrumentality of the logico-semantic models deployed in spreadsheets, search engines and GIS systems (Graphical Information Systems) to some extent defines the landscape in which the new media narrative must operate, if it is to operate at all.

The second outstanding fact is that this logico-semantic model of information storage is explicitly and consciously designed to facilitate the mechanised retrieval of data. It stands therefore diametrically opposite the humanism implicit in normative or universalist accounts of narrative. Machines clearly do not have an innate predilection for narrative form. Despite having been developed for imperialist, bureaucratic and capitalist (Virilio would add endo-colonial and militaristic) interests, the digital media need to be understood in an evolutionary sense as the first new mode of communication (with the possible exception of the cinema film) to propose that mediation might imply not representation, but communication, and that it might demand communication not despite or via our machines, but communication *with* them. In this light, the burden of efficiency appears as a counter-evolutionary attempt to restrict the human-computer interface (HCI) solely to those functions that suit the requirements of contemporary capital.

Key among these is the capacity to document the present in order to stabilise the future. The restrictive design of the HCI in such modes as the browser window's ever-present frame or the single-user desktop and laptop design of the physical machine, is then itself a product not of the acceleration of progress, but of the attempt to stabilise such social formations as individualism and advertising (with its underlying separation of audience and producer) at the precise point, in the meeting of human and machine, at which the evolutionary potential is highest and least controllable. The spatialisation tendency belongs to contemporary capital's need to plan the future in terms of its stability: to preserve the status quo. This is where narrative's residual and now marginal position in the new mediascape becomes once more a vital component of the culture. From its position at the margins, narrative can once more rethink itself, not as a binary system of dominance and resistance, but as a dialectical agent given the task of reintroducing time, while at the same time embracing the possibilities of human-computer communication broached and betrayed by the spatialised media. As so often in contemporary culture, the margin is the site of cultural innovation.

III

One example of the kind of work that can be imagined in this frame is an apparently linear single-monitor video work by the American artist Daniel Reeves, now resident in Scotland. *Obsessive Becoming* uses an array of digital techniques to manipulate still and moving images from the artist's family archive, gradually unearthing a history of abuse, criminality and abandonment.[9] If this were all Reeves undertook, the work would have the literary structure of a Freud case study or a detective novel. But Reeves' view of this family is neither accusatory nor aetiological. Nor is it an attempt to erase or forget the images or their implied histories. Instead it undertakes an always difficult and, in the most tangible sense of the word, responsible act of forgiveness.

Narrative here serves neither to consign history to the past, nor to project a perfected moment of closure into the future, but to enact the present – of the artist's making and the audience's view-ing – as a moment fully informed but at the same time charged with a task, in this instance not quite of healing, but of acceptance. However, where the artist intends, it appears, recognition of the appalling difficulty of life under all and any circumstances, what makes the work transcend mere apology is the commitment it exhibits to forgiveness as something akin to Heidegger's duty of care.[10] The tragedy of bigamy, desertion and casual cruelty cannot be denied or placed in paren-theses, but must be acknowledged. At the same time, the piece appeals to the sense that any life, no matter how fucked up, is worthy of respect and even love, especially of love, of an unconditional offer of understanding based on shared humanity.

It is this which takes *Obsessive Becoming* beyond the Heideggerian towards another mode of temporal awareness. Heidegger's care is essentially spatial: a reaching out and gathering in. Levinas' ethical 'first philosophy' also thinks of this ethical imperative spatially, in terms of the face-to-face encounter where, in its meeting with the Other, the I is bound to recognise its own finitude and the limitations to its freedom.[11] Reeves however comes closer to what my mother used to call 'con-sideration'. When Mum asked us to show some consideration for others, the call was first of all for a kind of environmental awareness: to notice the world and especially the other people around us. However, stepping beyond this first spatial alertness, the being considerate asked us to anticipate – to put together the baby-buggy and the crowded escalator into an ordinary act of kindness. Thus, this alertness was not only to the present but also to the future states toward which it tended. That motherly advice that illuminated my growing years today strikes me as the common wisdom that anticipates Bloch's post-Heideggerian formulation of the Not-Yet as the typical configuration of the realisably utopian in human affairs.[12]

When, in the 1880s, Pissarro took to painting peasant girls and women in moments of idleness, he was deliberately attempting to capture such an immanently realisable utopia, a world of leisure achieved after you have done enough work, not the excess demanded by the extraction of surplus value or the pursuit of consumerism in the emergent society of the spectacle. These quiet moments of still and thoughtless contemplation, as in the *Jeune Fille à la Baguette* (an image of a young girl tapping idly at a bank of rich vegetation with a loosely dangled stick), have been expropriated sub-sequently by an art market concerned to ideologise Impressionism as a love affair with the actually existing moment of perception. Pissarro's letters reveal, and Renoir's most sociable canvases like-wise, rather a sense of the unrealised but realisable, exactly the Not-Yet of Bloch's mid-twentieth-century philosophy.[13]

At its most regressive, as in Monet, the ephemerality of the moment appears as loss, and enters the predominantly nostalgic sense of beauty that so enthrals the constructors of art in the twenti-eth century. At the brink of the twenty-first, ephemerality need no longer be understood as loss, but as becoming. The much-vaunted sublime, as post-modern icon, stands across the possibility of the future, setting its ahistorical finality athwart the trajectory of emergence. What makes today's post-narrative, temporal, historical, eschatological creation so singular is neither nostalgia nor sublimity but becoming, as adumbrated in 'divisionisme', and so triumphantly realised as a new mode of thinking, being and creating in the cinematograph a hundred years ago.

And though individual artists like Daniel Reeves can open the doors to such perceptions, the cultural objects that define what we are becoming are no longer driven by individuality and objectality, by who we are, but by collaborations, conflicts, negotiations and the transgression of the subject-object divide still sacrosanct in Heidegger, Levinas and even Bloch, not to mention Vattimo[14] and Virilio.[15] Our understandings of interrelation and temporality today derive from what is characteristic of our time – the urban, the global, the networked: the environmental. Any sociologically persuasive theory must today be profoundly ecological.

In this sense, I suggest that rather than narrative as such we need to understand how it is we inhabit our twenty-first century as temporal beings: the question asked and asked again in Reeves' video piece. Three modes of being present themselves in the cybercultural discourse: the search, the journey and the ocean. The search engine presents the world as a landscape and itself as a vehicle capable of instantaneous travel to precise positions: an efficiency model. The journey is announced in the words Navigator and Explorer, which propose metaphors of colonisation of an alien world. The oceanic, precisely tuned from Reich to Goldie, articulates contemporary cultural experience as immersion, and so points towards the (progressive) indifferentiation of subject and object. The weakness of this least-worst metaphor is that it remains rooted in spatiality and the denial of time.

When we confront the World Wide Web, as distinct from the discrete or quasi-discrete objects (websites) we may identify within it, we enter a certain, as yet inchoate, mode of time. For all the boast of instantaneity, our actual relations with one another in cyberspace are mediated and as such subject to delays: slow downloads, periodic crashes, cache clearances and software uploads. Where there is something approaching communication, the processes of interpretation, misinterpretation, reply or intellectual or emotional response occupy physiologically measurable timeframes. It is this temporality that we need to adopt in order to reinvigorate the oceanic vision of cyberspace.

Obviously the least teleological or imperialistic, the oceanic thought, in its most widespread form (for example in Kelly's 'new biology of machines' or Negroponte's *Wired* column), has become the justificatory ideology par excellence for the legitimisation of free-market economics in savagely deregulated – and as a direct result fiercely monopolistic – globalised trade.[16] This misunderstanding of complexity theory rests on what should by now be a familiar trope, the narrative universalism that sees the present as the end of history. Because the present is uniquely actual in comparison with past and future, it is presumed to be final, the sum of all preceding interactions. What is rendered opaque and written out of possibility in this account is the likelihood of a future state unlike the present. For the present only presents itself as a structured system from the point of view of its beneficiaries, who form by far the minority of the human population. For the majority of the world's inhabitants, and especially from the perspective of non-human phyla, organic and mechanic, the present presents itself only as meaningless chaos and devastation.

The consciousness of what is Not-Yet, and indeed the Not-Yet-Conscious, in the light of the connectivities that increasingly regulate our waking and even our dreaming lives, must be understood firstly as hybrid, imbricating human, ecological and technological domains. The three phyla are as mutually interdependent as the members of the human alone. In that interdependence, and in its collapsing of boundaries, there begins to flare the light of another temporality, a complex emergence from the chaos of the present. It is the task of narrative consciousness, now from its newly marginal position, to reconfigure itself as the possibility of change.

This means that narrative can no longer assume its old certainties – the spatial figures of binary opposition and semantic rectangle, or the linear progression from beginning, via middle, to end. The paradoxes indistinguishable from platitudes that haunt the mid-period of this transition ('In our end is our beginning') can no longer help, indeed hinder the vision of a mode of being which is not caught in the stasis of geometrical (space) or geographical (place) metaphors. We might even begin to take seriously the Einsteinian thesis that the old Kantian division of space from time no longer holds good, if indeed it ever did beyond metaphysical speculation and the interests of the imperial bureaucracies of the enlightenment.

Thus the understandings we must obtain – and the quest is of a form and isomorphic with its object, incomplete and future-oriented – concern not only the shapes of our new media but their proximate and distant interactions with the world, from the phenomenology of the slumping body in front of the VDU to the impacts of digital trading on the fauna of the High Andes. Nowadays, ontologically as well as epistemologically indistinguishable from communication, e-cash is our dominant form of planetary intra-species communication, not storytelling. However, e-cash, though its movements may be narrativised in the daily press, is essentially non-narrative. Though we speak of its movements, we are always aware that the global stock market is a zero-sum game that always balances the books, its ceaseless trading a mask for the stasis of the break-even bottom line. Worse still, if we have any consideration at all, we must acknowledge that what temporality persists in all this fullness is the temporality of decline, punctuated only by moments of panic.

If we take Wittgenstein's starting point, that the world is all that is the case, we have to argue that the world is not nothing, as Baudrillard argues in later works like The Perfect Crime, but that the world is stuffed to overflowing.[17] Rather than propose nihilism as the solution to the superflux of spectacle, and beyond Adorno's negative dialectics, we need to commit ourselves to positivity, the increase in connectivity in the interests of emergence, against the nihilism, which is no longer oppositional, but the very form of the dominant itself.[18]

The old narrative models become dangerous when they support the enclosure of narration as object apart from both the subject that reads and the world that embraces. The discrete model of narratives as a plurality of whole and distinct entities has become the cultural type of the escapist experience pursued because it has nothing to do with the world – because, in Kant's terms, it is without interests. But today the discretion of the object and the disinterested activity of aesthetic appreciation have become very precisely sublime, removed from the hurly-burly of a life-world in which narrative has been buried under and marginalised by the sheer mass of spreadsheets, databases and GIS.[19]

Thus narrative, as it emerges blinking into the digital age, can no longer afford to be whole, entire and complete. Neither closure nor the concept of a middle defined by its terms can hold good of the new temporal arts. We have known since Lévi-Strauss that the study of origin is a futile pursuit: no archaeology will ever reconstitute the 'beginning', for every moment is the concretion of a hundred intertwined, contradictory, even contingent determinants in nets, which only become more overdetermined over time. Moreover, chaos theory stems from the observation that no possible knowledge of initial conditions is accurate enough to predict the unforeseeable unfolding of turbulence and emergence. Thus beginning is not a self-defining term. Nor is the concept of the end, since as ethical principal and thus as aesthetic axiom it is not possible to imagine the world as already complete and unchangeable. Even were it possible to define the human by its origin and conclusion, the middle remains an infinity, and it is that infinity which we inhabit. What distinguishes ethical communication is that it seeks to open up the branching possibilities of what is Not-Yet, rather than to control, define and determine them. In this perspective, new time-based media must take responsibility for the emergence of the future. Certainly, no single actor or action can, on the principles just voiced, be the sole determinant of what next ensues. But equally no one apart from those of us who are living in this very hour can have any influence whatever on the becoming of the future in this present which is ours alone.

By way of conclusion, an apology. There should be more examples and cases in a chapter like this. But since my subject is a historical 'narrative' of what emerges next, what is Not-Yet, it defines for its purposes the 'new' of 'new media' as those media and their forms that have yet to be invented. The conceptualisation of newness not as what has already been achieved (as everybody knows, the new media, if by that we mean the digital and the networked, are already 30 to 60 years old) but what waits unachieved and unimaginable, though only just around the corner. It is that immanence that today sparks the most remarkable new 'narrative' sense we have: the phenomenology of the click. It is not that any hyperlink we have already visited has taken us where we want to go, but that the link is the narrow gate through which the future could arrive at any moment.

NOTES

1. Gauntlett, David, ed. *web.studies: Rewiring Media Studies for the Digital Age*. London: Arnold, 2000.

2. Salt, Barry. *Film Style and Technology: History and Analysis*. London: Starword, 1983.

3. Bernheimer, Charles and Kahane, Claire. *In Dora's Case. Freud – Hysteria – Feminism*. Columbia University Press, 1985.

4. Lévi-Strauss, Claude. *Structural Anthropology*. Claire Jacobson and Brooke Grundfest Schoepf, trans. Harmondsworth: Penguin, 1972 and also Wright, Will. *Six Guns and Society: A Structural Study of the Western*. Berkeley: University of California Press, 1975.

5. Lefebvre, Henri. *La Vie Quotidienne dans le Monde Moderne*. Paris: Gallimard, 1968, and Lefebvre, Henri. *La Production de l'Espace*. Paris: Anthropos, 1974. See also Harvey, David. *The Condition of Postmodernity: An Enquiry into the Origins of Cultural Change*. Oxford: Blackwell, 1989.

6. Lyotard, Jean-François. *The Postmodern Condition: A Report on Knowledge*. Geoff Bennington and Brian Massumi, trans. Manchester: Manchester University Press, 1984.

7. Marx, Karl. *Das Kapital: A Critique of Political Economy. Vol. 3*, Friedrich Engels, ed. Moscow: Progress Publishers, 1962.

8. Williams, Raymond. *Television: Technology and Cultural Form*. London: Fontana, 1974, p. 59.

9. Daniel Reeves. *Obsessive Becoming*. 1995, a collection of old 16mm-films taken by Reeves' stepfather and family photographs gathered over a five-year period.

10. Heidegger, Martin. *Being and Time*. John Macquarrie and Edward Robinson, trans. Oxford: Blackwell, 1962, pp. 235–44.

11. Levinas, Emmanuel. *Totality and Infinity: An Essay on Exteriority*, Alphonso Lingis, trans. Pittsburgh: Duquesne University Press, 1969.

12. Bloch, Ernst. *The Principle of Hope. Vol 1*. Neville Plaice, Stephen Plaice and Paul Knight, trans. Cambridge: MIT Press, 1995, pp. 142–7.

13. Pissarro, Camille. *Letters to his Son Lucien*. John Rewald, ed. Lionel Abel, trans. 4th edn. London: Routledge, 1980.

14. Vattimo, Gianni. *The Adventure of Difference: Philosophy after Nietzsche and Heidegger*. Cyprian Blamires, trans. Baltimore: Johns Hopkins University Press, 1993.

15. Virilio, Paul. *Polar Inertia*. Patrick Camiller, trans. London: Sage, 2000.
Virilio, Paul. *A Landscape of Events*. Julie Rose, trans. Cambridge: MIT Press, 2000b.
Virilio, Paul. *Strategy of Deception*. Chris Turner, trans. London: Verso, 2000.

16. Kelly, Kevin. *Out of Control: The New Biology of Machines*. London: 4th Estate, 1994.

17. Baudrillard, Jean. *The Perfect Crime*. Chris Turner, trans. London: Verso, 1996.

18. Adorno, Theodor W. *Negative Dialectics*. E. B. Ashton, trans. London: Routledge, 1973, and also Adorno, Theodor W. *Aesthetic Theory*. Gretel Adorno and Rolf Tiedemann, eds. Robert Hullot-Kentor, trans. London: Athlone Press, 1997.

19. Lyotard, Jean-François. *The Postmodern Condition: A Report on Knowledge*. Geoff Bennington and Brian Massumi, trans. Manchester: Manchester University Press, 1984.

Reflections on Digital Imagery: Of Mice and Men*

Paul Willemen

On a BBC Radio 4 programme in early 1999, some cyber-nut claimed, in all seriousness, that Dante had invented cyberspace, or, at least, that the Divina Commedia was a prototype for it. With all the hype, often only interrupted by imbecilic nonsense, that infests any discussion of the accelerating digitalisation of most media, it is worth reflecting on some aspects of digital technologies in the visual media which do point to the emergence of new concerns or which, to say the least, appear to accelerate existing trends. Two such concerns meriting, even requiring further thoughts are the waning of the indexical dimension of the image and the consequent changes in its relation to the subjectivity, implicating both the narrator and the reader/viewer of the image, which animates and supports the publication of images. There is no need to dwell on silly notions such as the digital media's alleged development of some form of non-linear narrative: narrative constantly loops back and branches out, condenses and proliferates uncontrollably, which is precisely why the 'meaning' of a story can never be fixed once and for all.

In the same vein, interactivity has always been a feature of any representational media, from religious rituals to painting, novels and cinema. Indeed, pen and paper constitute an 'interactive' medium, and interactivity has been a significant feature from classical Chinese poetry to the call-and-response structures of gospel and jazz music, to Surrealism's 'exquisite corpses' and to just about all forms of commercial verbal and imaged discourses in which feedback mechanisms have played a determining role for at least a century. For instance, the tried and (de)tested Hollywood practice of the sneak preview, with its audience response cards, which then form the basis of modifications to the film, has been routine since the 1930s. At most, one could argue that inter-activity previously operating via telephony and the post office has been speeded up. To refer to interactivity as a new feature characteristic of 'new tech' discursive forms is, again, nonsense. Indeed, in many respects, the digitalisation of information has rendered interaction between reader/viewer and text-production more restricted in that the protocols governing interactivity have become tighter, narrower, more inflexible and more policed. The expansion of opportunities for interaction has been accompanied by reductions in the scope for action, which now has to be conducted according to rigorously policed protocols, by a trivialisation of the fields where inter-

---

* An earlier version of this essay was published in *292 Essays in Visual Culture*, Andrew Patrizio, ed., Edinburgh Projects, Edinburgh, 2000.

action is encouraged, such as games and bulletin boards, and by the increased isolation of the allegedly interacting individuals as kids lock themselves into separate spaces to play with their computers, as office workers are separated from their sociable places of work or are reduced to the condition of ciphers in call-centres reminiscent of the surveyed spaces of 1920 typing pools. Open-plan office spaces reduce self-selected interactions by increasing the surveillability of employees.

Whenever some new tech high priest intones about the non-linear or the interactive, you can be absolutely certain that you are listening to a confidence trickster trying to sell you some snake oil.

However, what does seem to require some extra thought is the apparent change in modes of address deployed by 'new media' and, in that context, the fact that new media seem tailor-made for modes of address most suitable for authoritarian and advertising discourses. A second aspect of the digitalisation of information, which includes images, has been raised, but all too rarely, as a problem by a number of intellectuals: the consequences of the disappearance of the indexical dimension of the photochemically-obtained image and the correlative spread of iconic and symbolic imagery, which is easier to manipulate and administer, a development that also accelerates the trend towards authoritarianism and advertising, two modalities of the same discursive procedures involving what the linguist Roman Jakobson identified as the conative function of discourse: a way of addressing the reader/listener/viewer in a manner that brooks no challenge or dissent. The most characteristic grammatical form of the conative function is the imperative or the vocative. The choice given to the addressee in such cases is exceedingly limited: either you obey or you ignore the statement, the latter not always being an option that can be safely exercised. These are the only two forms of 'interactivity' allowed by a discursive form in which the conative function dominates.

One of the twentieth century's greatest artists as well as theorists of art, Sergei M. Eisenstein, whose most important writings have recently been published in new translations by the British Film Institute, had interesting things to say about such discursive features. It is fairly common knowledge that Eisenstein's approach to editing and composition was animated by a desire to reduce ambiguity and to exert greater control over the way image discourses are received by viewers, even though he was equally concerned to expand the range of the viewers' intellectual engagement with cinema. It has been suggested, perhaps even established, for instance, by Bernard Eisenschitz at an Eisenstein Conference at Keble College, Oxford, in July 1988 (although the remarks were not included in the book of that conference, Ian Christie and Richard Taylor's *Reconsidering Eisenstein*, London 1993),[1] that Eisenstein dreamed of being able to 'play', through devices of composition, the synchronisation of the senses and other modalities of montage, the intellect and the emotions of an audience like one plays a keyboard. In that respect, Eisenstein's somewhat authoritarian dream (it must be acknowledged that this was not his only dream) survives today most prominently in the world of advertising, including the world of pop promos with their emphasis on mood manipulation to stimulate specific thoughts such as: I must buy this record.

Variants or, perhaps more accurately, negative applications of Eisenstein's approach can be detected in contemporary club culture and some shops which seek to extinguish thought altogether by imprisoning people in authoritarian sound bubbles, extending Eisenstein's principles not in the direction of synaesthesia, but anaesthesia, acknowledging that if montage practices can be deployed to synchronise the senses and to guide the formation of intellectual associations, they can also be deployed to synchronise the senses by obliterating intellectuality, drowning it by way of an extreme example of 'overtonal' montage: turn up the volume of 'the beat' until its vibrations are physically felt rather than aesthetically perceived, abolishing the distance constitutive of representation and cognition.

This development, now also increasingly deployed in Hollywood cinema as well as in other signifying practices seeking to eliminate thought – a report in *Variety* in August 1998 noted that from year to year, Hollywood blockbusters have turned up the decibel levels of their soundtracks – seems synchronised not only with a growing trend towards authoritarianism in politics, but also with the increased authoritarianism of the modes of address characteristic of the computer monitor with its plethora of imperatives (file, cut, copy, paste, format, print, etc.) and extensive rule books stating the obligatory protocols which have to be obeyed by all except those blessed few who have the skills to reprogramme their computer software packages. Perhaps the starkest indication of the authoritarian desire that speaks through the way a computer package addresses us is some form of the phrase: 'This program has performed an illegal operation and will be shut down', which appears on the computer screen when the obligatory protocols have been transgressed. To call such a mistake 'illegal' speaks volumes.

Such developments prompted me to return to Eisenstein's writings, to clarify some ideas about what has changed in regimes of signification through the shift towards digital imaging. A second reason for going back to Eisenstein was the suspicion that sooner or later, some techno-fetishist is bound to invoke, abusively, Eisenstein's name in a celebration of the internet or computer-based art. I suspect that for this abuse of Eisenstein, his particular notion of mimesis, commented upon by Misha Lampolsky in *Reconsidering Eisenstein*, will be invoked. Lampolsky quoted Eisenstein's speech to the film-makers of La Sarraz in 1929: 'The age of form is drawing to a close. We are penetrating behind appearance into the principle of appearance. In doing so we are mastering it.'[2] Lampolsky then went on to argue that for Eisenstein, the issue was to represent 'the essential bone structure' underpinning and shaping reality rather than its surface appearance. No doubt, some techno-fetishist will latch onto that formulation to claim that this is precisely what digital imaging and 'new media' enable. This claim may be further elaborated with references to Eisenstein's emphasis on drawing, painting and the iconic quality of the cinematic and the photographic image.

My argument here is mainly a pre-emptive one: Eisenstein's theories do not allow any such conclusions to be drawn, mainly because his entire theory of aesthetics and of art practice is based, not on the image as an icon or even a symbol, but on the presence of indexical elements in both, especially in the icon. Here I am using Peirce's triadic division of signs in which the index, as opposed to the icon and the symbol, retains within itself traces of the physical connection between sign and reality. Indeed, in Eisenstein's writings, this physical connection is mostly presented as a bodily connection, as in his often quoted remark, made as a young man, that *mise-en-scène* is to be regarded as 'the lines of an actor's movement in time'. Significantly, Lampolsky's concluding image, which he claims conveys 'the essence of Eisenstein's concept of mimesis', is very close indeed to one of

Peirce's favourite examples of an indexical image: the death mask, 'both the face like a skull and the skull like a face … one living above the other. One concealed beneath the other.'[3] Penetrating to the skull beneath the face is what Eisenstein means by penetrating 'behind appearance into the principle of appearance'. Lampolsky concludes his argument by criticising interpretations of Eisenstein's writings on montage which concentrate on the strictly semantic dimension of juxtapositions, pointing out that this goes against Eisenstein's own conception of the main, fundamental issue he was trying to address, his *Grundproblematik*.

Naum Kleiman noted, in an introduction to the mature Eisenstein's writings about animation and Disney, that, for Eisenstein, this *Grundproblematik*, this fundamental, core problem of art practice, was the orchestration of two diametrically opposed registers of experience: intellectual cognition relying on logical thought as well as on pre-logical, sensuous perception, the former associated with conceptual consciousness, the latter with infancy and what he calls, sensuous thinking.

Kleiman quotes Eisenstein's remarks to the 1935 *Conference of Soviet Film Workers*:

> The dialectic of works of art is built upon a most curious 'dual unity'. The effect generated by a work of art is due to the fact that there takes place within it a dual process: an impetuous progressive rise along the lines of the highest conceptual steps of consciousness and a simultaneous penetration by means of the structure of the form into layers of profoundest sensuous thinking. The polar separation of these two lines of aspiration creates that remarkable tension of unity of form and content characteristic of true art works.[4]

Here we have a characterisation of art practice as a way of orchestrating the combination of conceptual thinking and pre-logical, sensuous forms of perception. Translated into Kristevian terms, Eisenstein proposes a definition of art as the orchestration of a mix between the symbolic and the semiotic, between the kind of symbolic network of which the language system is the supreme example and the protean world of the Freudian drives, what Kristeva calls 'the chora'. In this context, Eisenstein does not, of course, use Kristeva's Platonic terminology. He uses a term on the interface between science and mysticism: plasma, and describes animated beings as beings which behave like 'primeval plasma' without any stable form.

For Eisenstein, as Kleiman notes, Disney's animation constitutes evidence of the productivity of this regressive tendency in art, which necessarily accompanies, in a dialectical relationship, the progressive tendency constituted by the stimulation of conceptual thought. Kleiman comments:

> Disney provided direct grounds and material for an analysis of the 'survival' of animism and totemism in modern consciousness and art [with] the 'animation' not only of animals and plants, but of the entire objective world. … In Eisenstein's view, the very mechanism of a flowing 'omnipotent' contour was an echo of the most concealed depths of pre-memory.[5]

What has to be remembered in this context is, that for Eisenstein, the protean, pre-logical sensual dimension of the artwork was connected with the body and manifested in the act of drawing. He notes the connection between Disney himself as a graceful body, comparing him to a dancer, and the flexibility of the body and gestures, the gracefully modulating lines of Mickey Mouse's body, describing the indexical link between Disney and his famous mouse. Eisenstein then waxes lyrical about animation in general:

> How much (imaginary!) divine omnipotence there is in this! What magic of reconstructing the world according to one's fantasy and will! A fictitious world. A world of lines and colours, which subjugates and alters itself to your command. You tell a mountain: move, and it moves. You tell an octopus: be an elephant, and the octopus becomes an elephant.[6]

Here we have a direct celebration of what we now call the virtual world, the cyberworld. Or do we? Is this divine omnipotence not exactly what computers and digital imaging packages promise us? Well no, actually. Eisenstein is evoking a world of representational freedom in which we are not likely to come up against the dictatorial 'Illegal operation. This program will be shut down.'

In the very next section of the essay I am quoting, Eisenstein goes on to contrast this divine creative freedom of the animator (or the Photoshop operator) with the world of Henry Ford's assembly line and the rule of bankers, which he characterises as the 'grey, grey, grey world' of those who are:

> … shackled by hours of work and regulated moments of rest, by a mathematical precision of time, whose lives are graphed by the cent and the dollar. … those who are forever at the mercy of a pitiless procession of laws, not of their own making, laws that divide up the soul, feelings, thoughts, just as the carcasses of pigs are dismembered by the conveyor belts of Chicago slaughter houses, and the separate pieces of cars are assembled into mechanical organisms by Ford's conveyor belts.[7]

One of the interesting aspects of this characterisation of American modernity is the implied contrast between montage (the orchestration of the fusion between the intellectual and the sensual) and assemblage, the latter leading to this curious thing called 'mechanical organisms': cars. The difference between the divine omnipotence of the animator and the grey oppressiveness of the assembly line is the elimination of the sensual, of the physical, of the body in the process of production. The rules and laws of production, if not of your own making (as they are in animation), generate merely 'mechanical organisms', organisms from which any trace of the 'indexical' has been eliminated.

One of the characteristics of digital imagery is that the technology is caught up in two separate but related dynamics, each leading towards a very specific, as yet still slightly utopian – in my view dystopian – horizon. The first dynamic projects the ability to construct an image pixel by pixel according to the rules and codes imposed by computer language, the programme. This is already possible, but prohibitively expensive in time and resources. Hence my characterisation of it as still slightly utopian. The second dynamic is the fantasy of plugging bodies directly into electronic gadgetry, or vice versa. This leads to the more chilling speculations about projecting films on the inside of one's eyelids by plugging chips into the parts of the brain which control the optical nerves.

The significant shift to be noted in relation to the image is the abolition, the reduction to zero of its indexical dimension, so that the film image and the still photograph become iconic, just like drawing or painting. Dai Vaughan cites a report about David Hockney carried in the *Independent on Sunday* of 21 October 1990, where the painter apparently used a digital photo camera and talked of 'the end of chemical photography'.[8] In a recent interview after the showing of his 'Grand Canyon' painting, Hockney changed his view, bemoaning the loss of the indexical dimension in image making. Dai Vaughan writes at some length and very pertinently on the drastic implications of the shift from the photochemical to the digital image:

> What concerns me is that we shall wake up one day and find that the assumption of a privileged
> relation between photograph and its object, an assumption which held good for 150 years and on
> which ciné-actuality is founded, will have ceased to be operative. And when that happens, it will not
> be because some thesis has been refuted but because the accumulation of countervailing experiences
> – of the simulation of the photographic idiom, of the electronic recombination of photographic
> elements, of 'photographic' processes where intervention between registration and reproduction of
> the image is not only easy but inescapable – have rendered null that 'trust' for which the idiom has
> simply been our warranty. And once we have lost it, we shall never get it back.[9]

Vaughan went on to illustrate his point with an example from a 1991 BBC *Arena* programme in which Laurie Anderson's face 'morphs' into that of a baboon:

> I assumed this to be a bit of electronic jiggery-pokery … until I read … that for this sequence
> Anderson had had to spend fourteen hours in makeup, unable to eat, drink, or scratch her nose.
> There was a time – not so long ago – when the implications of this, in terms of discomfort and
> endurance, would have remained present for us in the sequence; now they did not. A sense of the
> effort and impediment of the represented world is one thing lost when we cease to see that world
> as necessary to its representation. This is the price of *Terminator II*.[10]

With the gradual loss of that 'believability' which keeps image makers more or less honest and which has the annoying – for authoritarians – ability to show that situations are often not at all the way governments or other authorities would like to represent them to us, our ability to 'make sense' relatively autonomously and democratically, is irrevocably diminished. To quote Vaughan one last time: Photography and cinema have

> always represented an impediment to the word of authority by virtue of its ultimate appeal to some-
> thing prior to that word. It is surely not fortuitous that the age of the chemical photograph has
> broadly coincided with that of mass democratic challenges to entrenched power.[11]

The draining away of the indexical dimension of the image through digital manipulation is anti-democratic because it makes the administrative control of 'meaning' easier by facilitating the control of the flow of information (literally: the control through pre-programmed software packages of the bits that are combined to construct images), transforming images to the extent that even ordinary snapshots come under suspicion of having been 'configured'. An image of a person in a room need no longer mean that the person was in that particular room, or that such a room ever existed, or indeed that such a person ever existed. Photochemical images will continue to be made, but the change in the regime of 'believability' will eventually leech all the resistance that reality offers to 'manipulation' from even those images.

One answer to this process is obvious: it is necessary to put the emphasis on the process of reading itself and education must concentrate, not on the transfer of information nor on the reproduction of value systems, but on the urgent task of equipping people with the necessary 'thinking tools' to make sense of historical processes so that individuals may become better at assessing the 'likely' verisimilitude of any account or representation of the world. Unfortunately, and perhaps again not coincidentally, this is also the time of 'dumbing down', of training rather than education, and of the proliferation and aggressive celebration of anaesthesia (the above-mentioned sound prisons designed to obliterate thought, the promotion of films as physical sensations rather than as complex emotive-intellectual experiences, and so on).

Eisenstein's writings draw attention to a more subtle, but equally important, aspect of digitalisation: in digital imagery, the icon no longer registers the presence of the body. It removes the dancer's elegance of gesture and movement from Mickey Mouse by severing the link between the animator's body and the graphic line. The digitally-constructed death mask has lost any trace of the dialectic between the skull and the face, any trace of the dialectic between index and icon. In this respect, and probably in this respect only, some value may be attached to something with which Baudrillard's name is associated: the digitally-made, pixel-constructed image of a death mask still combines elements of both logical and pre-logical, sensuous thought, but it does so only as a simulation of that connection.

A recent film, *I Could Read the Sky* (Nicola Bruce, 1999), shows that what is at stake in the increased reliance on digital imagery in the film industry is far more than simply the deployment of labour-saving technique. The film appears to be about Irish labourers whose physical energies, whose very physical existence have been ruthlessly exploited by British industrialists with the connivance of governments. The film presents itself, with all the hallmarks of an avant-gardist discourse, as a narration by an Irish worker recalling scenes from his life. These memories are then made to stand for the collective experience of Irish emigrant labourers in Britain. In fact, though, besides liberally indulging in imagery recalling 'typical Ireland', not to say, stereotypical Ireland, the narration of the film dispossesses the labourer even further as the narrator of the film constantly, and contrary to the statements made in the subjective voice-over, usurps the place of the labourer and installs itself very ostentatiously as the film's real subject. The images and recollections triggered by the labourer-speaker are transformed, digitally, in such a way as to disconnect the memories from

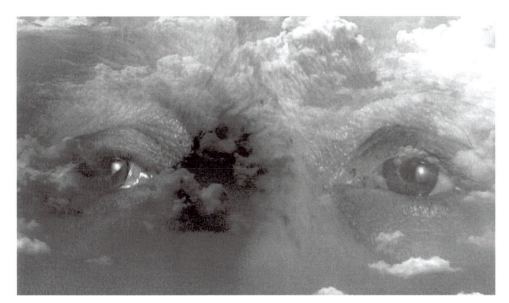

I Could Read the Sky,
Nicola Bruce, 1999

the remembering character: distances, framings and other image manipulations autonomise the recalled images, removing them from any position that can be construed in relation to a body in actual, historical space (which is something cameras cannot avoid doing in the course of registering scenes photochemically), taking them away from the speaker in the story and monopolising them as signifiers of 'with-it-ness' of the speaker of the film, designated only by a name in the credits.

These digital manipulations often give the film the appearance of a first person narration, with, for instance, direct address of the camera as if it were a character. Except, of course, that the first person in question is manifestly not attributed to the character, which says 'I' on the soundtrack. Instead, the speaking first person is neither the speaking character nor the image of that character we see in the diegesis, because their relation to what is shown does not connect with the image-track. Instead, the cinematic narrator credited as director slips into the place of the enunciator of the memory images. This act of expropriation, ostensibly in the service of a protest against the exploitation of Irish workers' physical energies, in effect (probably unintentionally, but that is irrelevant) further expropriates the Irish worker by leeching away the character's personal memories, his mental energies. In this film, memories are no more than raw material, mere triggers for the demonstration of the cinematic narrator's skill at packaging and selling the suitably transformed and 'digitally enhanced' memories of anyone incautious enough to make the results of their mental labour publicly available. The resistance of the real pointed to by Dai Vaughan is in the process of disappearing in this film, admittedly a first, still primitive and under-financed effort exploring the 'potential' of digitised narration. The film is a genuinely avant-garde product in the sense that it shows us 'things to come'. And it is not Spielberg's ode to advertising (*Saving Private Ryan*, 1998, showing us how to sell a war), nor Lucas's computerised versions of infantile 'cowboys and Indians' games, which show most directly how to expropriate whatever personal possessions exploited people may have left at the end of their lives. While bemoaning the old-fashioned industrial exploitation of physical labour power, *I Could Read the Sky* demonstrates how to exploit the 'mental' residues of people's lives, the things industrialists did not find it easy to turn into a profit. This demonstration emerged from the independent film sector sponsored, appropriately, by the state and one of the 'innovative' sectors of private enterprise, commercial television.

Some aspects of *I Could Read the Sky*, especially the way the digitised images look, might remind some viewers of a classic of the British independent cinema, the Berwick Street Collective's *The Nightcleaners*, Part 1 (1975), in which one of Britain's best and most imaginative film-makers, Marc Karlin, refilmed documentary footage, slowing it down to the point where images become grainy and highly contrasted. At the time, this was regarded by some as an unwarranted, overly aestheti-cised use of images, which 'objectified' the women nightcleaners. And yet, in spite of the reframing involved, the images in question never dispossessed the women of their bodies, their spaces or their gestures. On the contrary, these were the very dimensions of the image which the film's aesthetic devices managed to highlight. The shift in mode of address from 'documentary' footage to the slowed-down images was real enough and regarded as too intrusive an intervention by the film's narrator/director. Here we had the narrator of the film directly addressing the viewer, saying: 'Look at this. Look at these women, their lives, their emotions, their gestures. Look at them closely.' This was a far cry from the disappearance of the indexical dimension of the image. On the contrary, the aesthetic effect, although superficially not unlike the look of a digitised image, was precisely to draw attention to the indexical dimension of the filmed image.

Peter Delpeut's latest film, *Diva Dolorosa* (1999), resorts to similar strategies, although using dig-ital techniques rather than the more elaborate refilming done by Karlin, for his scrutiny of images from early Italian melodramas featuring the great 'divas' Lydia Borelli, Francesca Bertini, Pia Menichelli and others. Again, the mode of address shifts. The scenes of the films in which the women performed are transformed. As with *The Nightcleaners*, the director/narrator directly addresses the viewer, cranking up the film's conative function: 'Look at this! Look at it closely, and you will see something emerge that an ordinary viewing of the film allows you to 'overlook'.' What the scrutinised images of the emoting divas reveal is itself quite complex. By treating the photo-chemically-obtained images in this manner, Delpeut reveals something of the underpinnings of our desire for cinema, he draws attention to the very cinephilia that keeps these images alive, thus stitching the viewer's desire together with the film-maker's desire around the very 'figuration' of emoting women in melodramas. In addition, the scrutinised images change from images in a melo-drama to images in a documentary about the actresses themselves: it is the actresses themselves, their facial gestures, their way of looking, their gestures rather than the characters' which come into focus. One of the aspects *Diva Dolorosa* allows the viewer to engage with is the very problem of female subjectivity, its coming to expression within narrative, dramatic and social conventions designed to obliterate or negativise female emotion. The grandiose aspects of the diva slowly begin to make sense as a kind of exaggeration resulting from the very energy, not to say violence, required for their subjectivity to fray its way through the stories, through the melodramatic *mise-en-scène* deployed in the service of stories which are meant to contain them and to force women into the straitjackets of bourgeois behavioural and emotional codes. Again, the mode of address has shifted away from the axis between story and viewer to the actualisation of the relationship between narrator and viewer, but at no time in Delpeut's film is the indexical dimension of the actresses' images lost. On the contrary, the indexical aspect, the very trace of these precise women having 'existed' and acted in front of a camera which caught something of their 'presence', increases as it becomes the very 'ground' of the film.

In *I Could Read the Sky*, the opposite happens: the bodily presence of the Irish labourer becomes marginalised as the narrator's flashy techniques displace 'his' memories and his presence from the film and install, to the exclusion of almost everything else, the flashy celebration of the narrator/director's delight in appropriating the discourse of the movie for him-herself. Here, the mode of address is no longer: 'Look more closely at the images of these people's lives', but: 'Look at me being artistic with digital techniques.'

The key issue here is that by shifting the connection between the physical and the symbolic into the realm of the digital, into the realm of simulation, the image practices are simultaneously shifted out of the domain of the artist and into the domain of the administrators, the 'packagers' of images. Henceforth, artists will gather images which will then be brought to publishers and broadcasters and advertising agencies where they will be digitised and submitted to bureaucrats and adminis-trators who will subject them to the required computer protocols, marked by a plethora of imper-atives (do this, do that …) in order to make these images fit specific sales strategies, and, of course, the ideological strategies associated with the celebration and maintenance of 'market forces'. The narrator's mode of address that emerges from such a strategy is: 'Never mind what the images are about. Just buy my services as an expert image manipulator willing and able to deliver any discourse tailor-made to the current market requirements.'

Eisenstein's authoritarianism, demonstrated in his dream of control over the viewer's processes of conceptualisation and emotion, does not extend to the removal of the artist's body from the process of art production. If you do this, then you get merely assemblages, mechanical organisms. And yet, that is precisely what digital imagery promises us: not just the liberation of the image from its connection with 'nature', with the physical world, but the removal of all traces of the body in favour of the protocols controlled through computer codes and software packages. That is the dif-ference between digital icons and other iconic imagery such as painting, etching or drawing. Here, the divine omnipotence of being able to tell mountains to move or octopuses to become elephants must be mediated through keyboard commands and clicks of mice. The distance between the digi-tal icon and Eisenstein's celebration of the iconic image can be measured in terms of the difference between two kinds of mice: the computer mouse and Mickey Mouse. The difference is one between the transmutation of aspects of Disney's body into the drawing of a mouse, and images created by mice. It is too tempting to resist pointing out that in the latter case, the mice are manipulated by rats.

This is not an unfortunate side-effect of digitisation, it is in the very dynamics of the thing, one of the main reasons for the relentless hyping of 'new media': whereas Fordism allowed for the intensification of the exploitation of the physical energy stored in the body's musculature, digitalisation is the Fordism of mental labour, of thought work. Computers are to mental labour what the conveyor belt was to physical labour.

The implications of that change are only now beginning to be addressed. The transformations in institutions of higher education as described by Frank Noble are the tip of the iceberg. In many universities administrators are dreaming (and beginning to implement the dream) of a luxurious 'university' headquarter free of students and teaching staff, paying cheap, casually-employed young graduates to whack courses onto the net which can then be sold to a 'service provider' and marketed to 'students', for a fee, of course. Interactive contact between teaching staff, employed for a few hours only, and students can then be reduced to a couple of weekends per year.

A further implication of digitisation is only beginning to dawn on us. The historian Giovanni Arrighi, in a persuasive account of the history of capitalism, showed that the currently globalised triumph of capitalism has reached an important limit making a further developmental stage difficult to imagine because it would require an expansion of territory beyond the earth in order to mobilise and control further resources for exploitation.[12] Arrighi ends his book with scenarios involving not only the end of capitalism, but the end of human history with it as systemic crises and escalating chaos generate ever-greater levels of violence. The digital offers an alternative scenario not envisaged by Arrighi, who concentrates on the economics of extracting profit from the activity of joining physical energy, that is to say, labour power in the conventional sense, with raw materials. Digital information management and administration opens up a whole new continent: it makes it possible to harness and exploit intellectual energy, the 'other half', so to speak, of human beings which hitherto could not be industrialised effectively enough and which prompts people such as the then British Minister for Trade and Industry Stephen Byers to deliver incantations to 'the knowledge driven economy which is where our future lies' (BBC's *Today* programme on Radio 4, 13 September 1999 around 8.20). It will take a long time of determined collective action to prevent his ilk from subjecting us to such a future.

What such a knowledge driven economy means to the venerable caste of clerics, transmuted in the eighteenth and nineteenth centuries into 'intellectuals' (teachers, artists, journalists, doctors, lawyers and so on) is nothing less than the promise of radical proletarianisation, that is to say, the formation of a new working class alongside the 'traditional' physically labouring working class, each assigned its particular geographic territories, preferably at some distance from those who control the electronic information platforms.

Should this strike one as a fanciful or paranoid notion, it may be helpful to remember Joan Collins' trial a few years ago in the United States. Her publisher sued her for having delivered an unpublishable manuscript. She won the lawsuit because the judge confirmed that writers were supposed to provide a specified quantity of words relating to an agreed menu of themes. To shape this quantity of words into a publishable commodity was the responsibility of the publisher, not the writer. Similarly, the BBC has taken to commissioning raw footage from 'independent' film-makers, with the BBC staff reserving to themselves exclusively the right to select and shape the harvested images and sounds into broadcastable commodities. Joan Collins' trial gave new life to the term 'wordsmith', while the BBC is busy transforming film-makers into image peasants who, like the peasants contracted to supermarkets or to United Fruit, bring their tailor-made produce to 'the company'.

When we realise that the digitisation of the image involves, by reducing – even absenting – the role of 'the physical', the 'sensuous' (by reducing and eventually absenting the indexical aspects of the image), the redefinition and reformatting of intellectual labour as an industrially administerable process, the stakes in discussions of the digital become clearer. A process started in the mid-nineteenth century, the industrialisation of literature, is finally beginning to extend itself to all cultural production. In the notes to *The Arcades Project*, Walter Benjamin cited Friedrich Kreysig's 1865 assessment of the success of the French playwright Eugène Scribe (1791–1861), identifying him as the exemplary cultural administrator-entrepreneur, a figure analogous to contemporary publishing and television's commissioning editors, newspaper editors and all those responsible for the Saatchification of the arts, including gallery directors:

> It did not escape [Scribe's] eagle eye that, in the last analysis, all wealth rests on the art of getting others to work for us. So, the groundbreaking genius that he was, he transferred the principle of the division of labour from the workshops of tailors, cabinetmakers and manufacturers of pen nibs to the ateliers of dramatic artists, who, before this reform, working with only their one hand and one pen, have earned merely the proletarian wages of the isolated worker. An entire generation of theatrical geniuses were in his debt for their training and development, their awards, and, not infrequently, even their riches and reputation. Scribe chose the subject, sketched out the main lines of the plot, indicated the places for special effects and brilliant exits, and his apprentices would compose the appropriate dialogue and verses. Once they had made some progress, their name would appear on the title page (next to that of the firm) as a just recompense, until the best would break away and begin turning out dramatic works of their own invention, perhaps also in their turn recruiting new assistants. By these means, and under the protection afforded by the French publishing laws, Scribe became a multimillionaire.[13]

In other words: the real cultural 'producers' are the ones who determine and provide the 'templates' for marketable cultural production, the rest of us, artists and intellectuals alike, merely 'play' (i.e. produce) within the virtual parameters specified for us by the cultural bureaucrat-entrepreneurs. In addition, the digitisation of the means of production ensures that, where 'our' productive efforts are deemed not quite in line with what those bureaucrat-entrepreneurs decide the market to be, the cultural administrators now have the means to modify and re-style, relatively cheaply and efficiently, the cultural products in question. That is what is meant by 'interactivity' by the promoters of the digital: 'we' are allowed to interact with specific, preformatted templates, and 'they' will interact further by 'restyling' and polishing the resulting cultural 'software' before putting it on the market. Increasingly, the people who used to be called artists and/or intellectuals come to be seen for what they are: employees in what Adorno called 'the culture industries' or what politicians now call 'the knowledge industries'.

By way of a postscript to this argument, I would like to add that, of course, there are some posi-tive aspects to computers and digitisation as well: it is nice, at times, to be able to afford electronic servants to take some of the drudgery out of some activities involved in mental labour. But that is a trivial benefit. The real benefit, perhaps, of the proletarianisation of the intellectual is that com-puters may well enable us to distinguish more clearly between intellectuals and the kind of cut-and-paste people still far too often described – and employed – as intellectuals. Take any catalogue issued by an academic publisher, not to mention essays in magazines or newspapers or radio or television broadcasts, and you will see that the vast bulk of what passes for intellectual production is, in fact, simply cutting and pasting, recycling selected bits of existing texts according to a limited number of ideological protocols. Perhaps digitisation may be able to help us distinguish between those people and real intellectuals: the former deserve to live in a future shaped by the corporate control of the 'knowledge economy' which they are so assiduously helping to bring about; the latter are the people who are able to discern connections which are not available in any preformatted archive and who remain alive to the project of trying to figure out how the complex dynamics of a multilayered history actually work.

As every silver lining has its cloud, we may grant that the 'knowledge industries' enabled by the management of the digitisation of 'thought work' could help to differentiate between cut-and-paste clerks and intellectuals, but a more likely scenario is that it will help to identify and expose intellec-tuals, leaving them to struggle, in Yeats' words, like a fly in marmalade.

NOTES

1. Christie, Ian and Taylor, Richard. *Reconsidering Eisenstein*. London: Routledge, 1993.

2. Ibid., p. 177.

3. Ibid., p. 187.

4. Kleiman, Naum, in Leyda, Jay, ed. *Eisenstein on Disney*. Calcutta: Seagull Books, 1986, p. ix.

5. Ibid., p. xi

6. Ibid., p. 3.

7. Ibid.

8. Vaughan, Dai. *For Documentary. Twelve Essays*. Berkeley: University of California Press, 1999, p. 185.

9. Ibid., pp. 188–9.

10. Ibid., p. 190.

11. Ibid., p. 192.

12. Arrighi, Giovanni. *A Persuasive Account of the History of Capitalism. The Long Twentieth Century*. London: Verso, 1994.

13. Benjamin, Walter. *The Arcades Project*. Howard Eiland and Kevin McLaughlin, trans. Cambridge/London: The Belknap Press, 1999, pp. 671–2.

The Art of Narrative – Towards the *Floating Work of Art*

Söke Dinkla

Throughout the centuries the art of narrative, which traditionally has been understood as the depiction of a sequence of real or imagined events, has not only made social and political alteration one of its major themes, but has also expressed this social change through changing technical means, as well as being an expression of this change.

The art of narrative has gone through significant processes of change, especially in the twentieth century, during which it has experienced various crises and its death has been predicted many times. And yet, despite all such fractures and ruptures, since the 1990s, narrative has been experiencing a renaissance. Surprisingly this renaissance is taking place not only in literature and film, but also, with particular intensity, in electronic media. The internet as a new mode of communication has reached the status of a mass medium and urgently requires more adequate ways of communicating arts-based content. The already established medium of video is also utilising literary models to make narrative possible within the scope of new media.

In the following essay different historical narrative strategies – visual, literary and multimedial – are examined, emphasising the aesthetic methods used to reformulate our conception of reality. Every depiction of reality is formed through our own ideas of reality, and every depiction, in turn, influences those ideas. In the course of a historical review it is not always possible to distinguish whether the novel aesthetic method has caused changes in our perception of reality or whether it was itself an expression of those changes. However, it is certainly possible to describe in detail the current social situation and the role played in it by the art of narrative.

I would identify significant historical moments, where narrative constituted an indicator of radical social and political change (particularly with a view to the current situation of media art strategies). They are the emergence of the panorama in the late eighteenth century, the novels of James Joyce in the early twentieth century, and the experimental films of the 1940s and 1950s. Since the late eighteenth century the current heterogeneity of narrative forms and their expression in the digital have been developed on different stages and media.

THE PANORAMA – A SCHOOL OF PERSPECTIVES

Stephan Oettermann describes the panorama as 'a school of perspectives'.[1] The first generic change of perspective caused by the panorama was Robert Barker's application for a patent on his invention in 1787, which had consequences, not so much for narration itself, but for the way media art views itself. This new art form was simultaneously understood as a scientific and a technological innovation.[2] This simultaneity of aesthetic and technical innovation points straight to the ongoing discussion about the value of technical art, a discussion that did not begin with the invention of photography, but was already in process with the panorama.

In the late eighteenth century the invention of the panorama was already in the air, as its simultaneous emergence in England, France, Germany and the United States proves. The word 'panorama' was first used in 1792: it is a composite of *pan*=all and *hórama*=to see. The panorama is a circular painting, which encompasses the whole field of vision of the observer, its 360° angle conveying the illusion of a wide horizon. Theorists and contemporary reporters pointed to the perfect illusion of space as its distinguishing characteristic. Apparently, at the time, the audience was unable to distinguish between painting and reality.[3] At first, landscapes depicting distant or ideal places were common; later on depictions of political events, as well as views of cities, were added.

The tradition that brought forth the panorama is a matter of controversy. While Kemp regards baroque painting, and especially theatrical painting, as the origin of the panorama, Oettermann decisively rejects this tradition with some good and, in the context of this essay, important arguments.[4] He regards the panorama as an expression of the break with the history of painting:

> The panorama was the bourgeois answer to the already obsolete and decrepit forms of feudal art.
> […] Therefore the panorama is certainly not a direct descendant of baroque theatrical painting.[5]

In the panoramic image the web of relations between things changes, and with it the way an event is narrated. The panorama led to the discovery of the horizon as art form – as a school of seeing which conveyed a new image of the world, an image where many things can enjoy the same status. The details depicted no longer referred to a vanishing point established by central perspective, but instead they were restructured and held together by the horizon. This is one of the most important contrasts to the concerns of baroque theatrical painting, and it carries aesthetic as well as political implications. The central perspective of the baroque assumed a single correct point of view and therefore a single ideal observer. In the theatre this exclusive perspective was reserved for the privileged position of the monarch in the royal box.

The panorama changed this form of reception: it did not address an individual, but a large audience of up to 150 people, who could all observe the painting at the same time. It could be observed from a variety of perspectives and in any number of different parts. The panorama thus presupposed a 'democratisation' of the observer's point of view. This point of view is not fixed but mobile, the audience chooses and decides the parts to which it is going to pay the greatest attention. Above all the panoramic gaze constituted *access*. In a certain sense this selectivity of perception contradicted the oft-praised illusionistic qualities of the panorama. As the observer was never able to see the whole picture, he was forced to increase the level of his attention. The German journal *London und Paris* wrote of the Strand panorama: 'The observer enjoys the panorama to the extent that he is capable of bringing it to life with the help of his imagination.'[6]

There are lessons, therefore to be learned. We can assume that it was not only the illusionism (that is the realism of the painting) but also, to a significant degree, the necessity of actively completing what one could see that constituted the fascination of the panorama.

The involved observer does not place himself in front of the picture, but is surrounded by it, actually as well as imaginatively occupying a space inside the image. This shrouding is intended to resemble as closely as possible the experience of being surrounded by or being inside nature in reality. The basic idea of the panorama is founded on a historical and cultural concept, whose aim it was to deliver such a skilfully artificial image that the observer had the impression of experiencing not painted, but real nature.[7] The boundaries between real space and natural space were shifted. Today, this historical and cultural concept is being updated in the capabilities of digital CAVE technology (automatic virtual environments), where the imitation of an outer reality is linked to the illusion of an active experience of space.

THE *DISSOLVING* OF SUBJECT IN THE PANORAMA

The panorama satisfies the human desire to take possession of nature. The dissolution of the boundaries of space enables man to *incorporate* nature. The physical experiences he has are comparable to those of a CAVE. In his handbook of aesthetics, Johann August Eberhard describes the effect of the panorama in the following way:

> I vacillate between reality and non-reality, between nature and non-nature, between truth and illusion. My thoughts, my spirits experience a swinging, vacillating, fluctuating movement, which causes the same effect as going round in circles or the rolling of a ship. That is how I explain the dizziness and nausea that strikes the steadfast observer of the panorama. […] I feel as if I were entangled in the webs of a contradictory dream world.[8]

Both concepts – the CAVE and the panorama – are based on strategies of dislocating the subject, who experiences the sensation of being in two places at the same time. In this way the first aesthetic attempts at a later *telematic art*, such as those Paul Sermon has been developing since the 1980s (see also Andrea Zapp's chapter in this volume), are testing the scope of human empirical perception. The panorama imaginatively transfers the observer to a different place. The illusion of this telepresence is so intense that in the course of the nineteenth century a number of panoramic city views were created to save the educated middle class from arduous travel.[9]

The last sentence from the above quote by Eberhard is crucial in this context: 'I feel as if I were entangled in the webs of a contradictory dream world.' The panorama is perceived as a world between worlds, where unique aesthetic experiences are possible. It is not a world determined by the familiar temporal order, but is instead perceived as a web in which it is difficult to achieve one's customary orientation. This destabilisation of perception is a phenomenon that runs through the entire avant-garde art of the 1920s – from Impressionism to Cubism to Futurism.

This instability of perception characterises the novels of James Joyce, in particular *Ulysses* (1922) and *Finnegans Wake* (1939). In *Ulysses*, which took Joyce seven years to write, the experiences, thoughts and feelings of the Jewish advertising clerk Leopold Bloom, his wife Marion and young Stephen Dedalus are depicted in 18 epic or dramatic episodes. All the scenes are related to certain passages in Homer's *Odyssey*. Joyce includes in his work almost all the types of human experience and opens up new areas of consciousness through language.

NON-LINEAR NARRATIVE STRATEGIES AND THE PERSPECTIVISATION OF THE SUBJECT IN JOYCE

Joyce's language creates images that are characterised by extreme ambiguity. In its structuring and use of metaphors, Joyce's language is closer to visual artistic statements than literary models. In *Ulysses* especially, the category of visual perception assumes an unusually important role within the context of literature. Ambiguities and semantic resistances demand a restless, active reader.[10]

With Joyce, two strategies, introduced into the visual sphere by the panorama, become important to literature, albeit in different forms: Joyce develops textual strategies which both stimulate the reader's perceptions and play with his perceptive abilities. The process of appropriating the work is now the subject of the work itself and presupposes an implicit reader.[11] Now the narrative is no longer the (above-mentioned) depiction of a sequence of real or imagined events based on a sender-recipient-model, but in Joyce's work turns into an act of communication. In order to achieve this he developed a number of narrative strategies that turned out to have pioneering implications, not only for experimental film, but also for interactive media art.[12]

One of these strategies is the dissolution (*Entgrenzung*) of the boundaries of the subject, which already formed a central part of the aesthetic impact of the panorama. With Joyce this *Entgrenzung* concerns the merging of separate spheres of experience. With the help of imagination and consciousness the present sphere of experience is turned into a transitional space in which the living and the dead may interact. The process of thought itself now constitutes the topic and makes it possible to leave the linear, straightforward world of logic. Joyce here uses the stream of consciousness technique to express the merger of subject and world, of the internal and external.[13] This *Entgrenzung* of the subject is accompanied by a desire for transformation and change. Whereas in Joyce's early texts this change is brought about by the transforming power of love, later on the *Engrenzung* of the subject is caused by metamorphoses of man to animal. This *Entgrenzung* can only be fully understood in the context of that time; an important philosophical and theoretical role is played by Heisenberg's uncertainty principle, with which the physicist Heisenberg showed that the description of reality is dependent on the point of view of the observer.[14] This qualification of an objective view of the world was accompanied by an 'atomisation' of things under the influence of electricity, which caused well-defined objects to dissolve.

Another Joycean method for dissolving the subject and its distinct separation from the world of objects and to split up its uniform entity is the 'perspectivisation of the person'.[15] This method reveals a person's manifold layers and fluidity, which may change according to perspective. The multiple refraction of perspective, which is exemplified by the 'Wandering Rock' chapter in *Ulysses*, causes the fictional subject to change, depending on the perspective from which it is observed. The novel thus gives up the idea of an objective reality. Concomitant to this, the rigid relationship between subject and object is dissolved in favour of a dynamic depiction.

THE NARRATIVE STRATEGY OF 'NETWORKING'

This new experimental narrative strategy, which is often difficult to decode, is motivated mainly by Joyce's interest in *generating* reality, as opposed to representing reality. The new dimensions of reality that emerge in this way are not fixed, they remain in motion and change their constellations. This applies to characters as well as objects and events. In *Finnegans Wake*, in particular, the linear narration of the objective report repeatedly reaches its limits. The text constantly creates new constellations, which are open to changing relations and to the tying of ever new knots. Reading progressively turns into 'networking'.[16] This view of Joyce's work would be impossible without post-structuralist theory and the metaphor of the rhizome, proposed by Gilles Deleuze and Felix Guattari in 1977. They write:

> The rhizome itself can take all sorts of different forms, from the branching out in all directions on the surface to the compression into knots [...] Any point of the rhizome can and must be connected to all other points.[17]

The rhizome therefore constitutes the ideal metaphor for a narrative strategy, whose basic outlines can be witnessed in Joyce's texts, but which was only fully realised aesthetically with the development of the computer. Since the mid-1960s the narrative strategy of hypertext has been discussed in art. Since the 1970s Theodor Holm Nelson, who coined the term 'hypertext' as early as 1965, has pursued the idea of developing software which, like the library of Babel, contains all existing texts and thus enables the user, when coming upon a reference he or she would like to follow up, to call up the respective text.[18] Nelson defines 'hypertext' as 'non-sequential writing – text that branches and allows choices to the reader, best read at an interactive screen.'[19]

In contrast to hypertext and rhizome, though, whose starting and end points almost never coincide, Joyce's *Finnegans Wake* is characterized by a circular structure, that at least partially dissolves the principles of traditional logic. In this maelstrom of narrative the principles of cause-and-effect, causality and a progressive conception of history are simply inconceivable. These same structural principles of circularity can also be found in the works of Ken Feingold, Jeffrey Shaw or Grahame Weinbren.[20] They do not stand so much for an anti-modern, but for a post-modern conception of history which has lost faith in progress. With this cyclical narrative structure Joyce anticipated the cybernetic strategies of the computer: the digital machine functions as the permanent cycle of a feedback system.[21] The cybernetic principle describes a communication model which would be unthinkable without Heisenberg's uncertainty principle. It presupposes an endogenous recipient who is an intrinsic part of the system. In Joyce as well as in Shaw, Feingold and Weinbren the recipient is invited by ambiguities, non-determinabilities and blanks to create consistency and to complete the work, at least for the interim.

The experimental strategies developed by Joyce in *Ulysses* and *Finnegans Wake* were obviously very much ahead of their time. This might be the reason why these highly complex novels are regarded as perhaps the most difficult texts of world literature. However, this judgement and the partial 'unreadability', especially of *Finnegans Wake,* might also be a sign that Joyce developed aesthetic strategies for which there was no adequate medium at that time. From this point of view, *Ulysses* and *Finnegans Wake* can be regarded as convincing evidence for the impossibility of realising aesthetic strategies which have not yet found an adequate medium for developing their full aesthetic effectiveness.

THE DEPICTION OF DREAMS AS A MODEL FOR AN ALTERNATIVE ORGANISATION OF TIME AND SPACE

Joyce himself at first assumed that the (then new) medium of film would be the right kind of medium for *Ulysses*, and some Joyce scholars have identified movie techniques in Joyce's texts.[22] Indeed Joyce's work strongly influenced experimental and underground films of the 1940s and 1950s. Attempts to find alternative forms of organising space and time which were distinct from linear forms of narrative in particular characterise Maya Deren's experimental movies. Influenced by Surrealism she developed a mode of depicting dreams in which a fusion of inside and outside, of reality and dreams, takes place. Her films *Meshes of the Afternoon* (1943) and *At Land* (1944) create subjective imaginative worlds where the protagonists develop multiple personalities. Apart from these so-called 'trance movies' she also developed a procedure referred to as 'the dance with the camera': to her the camera was no longer the fixed point from which to record an action in an objective way, but was itself set in motion. With this method Deren rebelled against the objectivity inherent in the machinery of the camera; she was interested not in the external, but in internal states of the psyche, in myths and rituals. In similar ways to the novels of Joyce, she created new time-space-relations, thereby generating worlds instead of depicting them with the camera.

These methods of cinematic manipulation of time and space, however, could not obscure the fact that while film, as Joyce correctly surmised, is superior to fiction as to its synaesthetic possibilities (the combination of moving image, sound and text), it can only be partially utilised for the depiction of non-linear narrative strategies that appeal to the imagination. This circumstance is confirmed by the multi-screen installations that have been created since the 1970s, and particularly since the 1990s, in the works of Doug Aitken, Steve McQueen and Pipilotti Rist.

While Joyce prefigured some of the central aesthetic categories for an interactive art within the scope of literature, these were unable to fully develop their aesthetic effectiveness inside the medium of literature. This was only finally achieved through the medium of the computer, where action on the part of the recipient is inherent, not only structurally, but also functionally. Only the computer as a 'communication machine' can fulfil the desire for a proceduralisation of aesthetic experience. In interactive art, however, the aspect of communication soon lost its prominence; instead the new medium was used to make it possible to experience imaginative processes.

'SHIFTING PERSONALITIES'

It is likely that important pioneers of interactive media art such as Ken Feingold, Grahame Weinbren and Jeffrey Shaw were aware of the primary role James Joyce played in the conceptualisation of this new art form. In their works Joyce's narrative strategy has been, as it were, taken to its aesthetic completion.[23] For these artists, as well as for Joyce, interaction is not just active interpretation, but continuation and imaginary achievement of independence from the ur-text. Dynamic and fluctuating narrative material, which organises itself in a non-linear way, is not created by the process of narration by the author, but only in the interaction with the reader, who changes from implicit reader to *user*. An interactive media work is not only potentially open-ended, it does not exist unless there is interaction.

Joyce plays a special role in the work of Lynn Hershman. In her site-specific works, performances, videos, films, photos, interactive installations and network projects, she manages to push the *Entgrenzung* of the subject to its dissolution. Hershman's female protagonists not only possess unstable identities – they are 'shifting personalities', whose inner logic presupposes the non-existence of boundaries between different layers of reality.

If there is something common to Lynn Hershman's personae, it is their failure to acquire pre-formed social roles: their lives are characterised by futile efforts to make social contacts and to form stable relationships. Female characters such as Roberta, Lisa, Lorna as well as the most recent reincarnation of Roberta as CyberRoberta compulsively repeat the same fatal strategies.

The same happens to 'Roberta Breitmore', a portrait-performance created by Lynn Hershman in the mid-1970s.[24] Like all other protagonists in Hershman's *oeuvre*, Roberta represents the archetypal urban female. Although an active participant in social life, she is nevertheless lonely and anonymous and lives a marginalised existence. Strictly speaking 'Roberta' exists neither as a subject nor as a work of art, since hardly anybody has ever seen her. She exists only as a remnant in the memory of those that have heard of her or have seen papers documenting her existence. Only after her exorcism in 1978 was she represented in exhibitions by the many relics she left behind throughout her life.[25] Cheques, driving licence, advertisements, letters, diary, electrocardiograms, finger prints, photos, films, videos and tapes are the leftovers of her existence, and together with Hershman's stories, are used for her reconstruction in the art world. In the Mandeville Art Gallery in San Diego in 1976 Hershman showed photos of Roberta, her psychiatric report and a hologram which showed how she changed into Roberta. In the context of the construction of Roberta, the application of make-up, which for many women is an everyday procedure, does not create a disguise but an identity.

Since the mid-1990s Hershman's strategy of *generating* reality has changed. In interactive video installations such as 'Deep contact' or 'Room of one's own' digital technology is the medium that generates reality. This change of medium has also caused a change in the personae: the shy, neurotic and awkward woman, personified by Roberta and other personae, has been substituted with the forthright, short-haired Marion, who aggressively attacks the observer from the monitor. She becomes the target of the male gaze, but at the same time the observer realises that it is he who creates reality with his gaze. The artwork is no longer a manifestation of the artist, but instead it is a projection of the observer's imagination.

In each of Hershman's 'shifting personalities' there is at first the possibility for freedom of self-determined action, for example in the reincarnation of Roberta as CyberRoberta in 1998. CyberRoberta is a cybernetic mannequin who observes the real space with her camera eyes and then transfers what she has seen into the world of the internet. As a cyborg, Roberta is on the one hand an omnipotent observer who controls events, on the other hand she is also a mediator and agent for the internet users who actually control everything, who act invisibly and anonymously.

She represents the co-existence of different layers of reality, whose boundaries are also blurred in our experience of everyday life. Her defining characteristic is that she is constantly subjected to a reorganisation through multiple users. The subject blueprint underlying CyberRoberta is neither the Joycean multi-perspective subject nor the multiple personality of Maya Deren's movies, but a network of changing identities, intensities and energies which every moment manifests itself anew through the activities of multiple users.

THE FLOATING WORK OF ART

The terms 'work-in-progress' or 'open art work' (Eco) inadequately describe works of art based on such a network concept.[26] The term 'interactive art' is now established for art works that utilise the operational qualities of the digital medium in order to create spaces of experience that can be changed by the actions and interventions of the users. But nowadays this term no longer seems satisfactory since it does not describe the aesthetic qualities of this new art form. In order to close this gap I would propose the term 'floating work of art'. This term is supposed to give an idea of the way the conventional characteristics of traditional works, as well as the boundaries between different layers of reality and the various concepts of the subject, are now in flux.

The floating work of art is a phenomenon of the late 1980s. Its aesthetic characteristics were formed following a time of technological euphoria in the 1970s. The floating work of art is part of the philosophical tradition of post-modernism, although it developed new strategies of deconstruction by means of digital cultural techniques. While the floating work of art achieves its most radical form in the digital medium, it is not solely a phenomenon of digital art. Some of its central characteristics can also be found in literature or in performing arts such as dance or theatre.

Nineteen eighty-nine saw an extraordinary concentration of political and artistic events. In many ways the year 1989 marks a watershed. The reorganisation of the Eastern European political landscape, together with the fall of the Berlin Wall, led to the transformation of the then established political order. The world was no longer divided into two antagonistic camps. A new world order emerged, where conflicting powers rearranged themselves and centres of power shifted. Nineteen eighty-nine was also the year in which the *floating work of art* first appeared. Apparently its emergence was in the air, since it was during this period that artists like Jeffrey Shaw, David Rokeby, Lynn Hershman and Grahame Weinbren developed their first interactive installations. These works offered models for trying out a new distribution of roles. Because of this ability to restructure existing roles, interactive art had the chance to develop into a symbol for the basic reordering of obsolete structures.

At the same time novel artistic strategies of criticism emerged. At first sight these new critical strategies did not reveal themselves as such because they were not, as had been the case before, based on negation and exclusion. With respect to the *floating work of art* the only appropriate method appears to be to comment on the system from within its own means and so develop new critical forms. Such strategies have been emerging since the mid-1980s. Next to a McLuhanesque variant that expressed itself in models of 'artificial reality' (and found its sequel in the 1990s with 'artificial life' installations) there developed a *floating work of art* that does not indulge in cybernetic fantasies of omnipotence and connection to the machine, but instead designs models in which traditional orders are being restructured. The *floating work of art* conceives of the digital medium, not as an extension of the human sensory organs, but as an aesthetic space, which allows for the reconstruction of a changed world order.

THE NET MODEL

This new aesthetic option of reconstructing a changed world order offers the possibility of defining a new model of transformed social space. This is of even greater significance, since the process of globalisation at the end of the twentieth century has not only been accelerated by new media, but is also fundamentally questioning cultural spaces and territories defined in a nationalistic way. Frederic Jameson defines the new role of art in the following manner:

> The political art, if at all possible, will follow the 'truth' of postmodernism, that is it will cling to the essential fact, to the new world of multinational capital. [...] If there should be such a thing as the political manifestation of postmodernism, it would be called up to create a global cartography of perception and cognition and to project it into a precisely measured social space.[27]

Indeed the metaphor of cartography is important for the organisation of the *floating work of art*. The map is both abstract and concrete at the same time, and therefore permits a new evaluation of space that to a large extent abstains from customary forms of representation. The world of objects is substituted by a world of texts and signs. These signs are not perceived in a linear way, but are seen as branching out. This is common both to the map and to the structure of the *floating work of art*. Artists like Jeffrey Shaw use this metaphor to create an individual cosmology of digital space. In this cosmology the person moves through visual, textual and aural spaces, which are not structured hierarchically, but are organised like a hypertext. The *floating work of art* creates the urban space of today not just as a moving, fragmentary and non-linear order, but also as a hyper-text that can be perceived spatially and explored associatively:

Roland Barthes states

> The city of today can only be known by an activity of an ethnographical type: one cannot orientate oneself in such a city by means of the book, the address, but by walking and seeing, by familiarity and experience. Here every experience is intense and fragile. It can only be rediscovered through the memory of the trace left behind: to visit a place for the first time therefore means: beginning to write it: since the address is unwritten, it needs to create its own script.[28]

The exploration of the *floating work of art* proceeds in a similar way to Roland Barthes' descrip-tion of his experience of Tokyo: the observer turns into a traveller who structures the text/space in a new way through his decisions. The urban space as (hyper)text discloses itself differently to each user, depending on his or her experiences, associations and momentary decisions. The *float-ing work of art* creates space as a range of possibilities that allows for the physical testing of alterna-tive actions. In the process the user moves through the work. He is both inside and outside the work at the same time. This particular situation can no longer be understood in the terms of the concept of the 'implicit reader' (Iser) or the 'observer inside the image' (Kemp), since the 'being-inside-the-work' is linked to a simultaneous physical experience of the 'outside'.[29] It is not just being imagined, but created by body movement and experienced physically. In this way the *float-ing work of art* is able to negotiate between physical experience and intellectual cognition. While seemingly so familiar at first, the aesthetic method of the floating work is diametrically opposed to the approach of conceptual art: its aim is not to visualise an abstract idea, but to open up to experience a reality which organises itself in an abstract way and feeds back this reality to the body.

RECOMBINANT POETICS

In this instance the *floating work of art* faces the aesthetic challenge of creating models for a new orientation in an abstract reality without falling back on customary modes of representation, since customary modes of visual representation carry the risk that behaviour also follows established rules, instead of opening up new spaces of experiences. The *floating work of art* meets this challenge in a different way. It develops strategies of 'recombinant poetics' (Bill Seaman), where meaning is only created by the changing 'coming together' of image, text, language, sound and movement. Here Seaman speaks of 'fields of meaning'.[30] They resist the inner nature of language and the linear rep-resentation of (hi)story by creating an abundance of possible meanings, which continually collide with each other. Together with a chance algorithm, the interventions of the visitor lead to a con-tinuous recombination of the fields of meaning. In this way they create a new spatial order, resem-bling a network of associations. A floating intellectual space emerges, a space of the 'unsaid', of 'what is on the tip of the tongue'. The floating work permits the location of the logic of language in space.

In contrast to the combination games of Surrealism, the *floating work of art* does not aim at a dissolution of logic, but at its deconstruction. The way the user moves around the work resembles an aimless meander, with a freely roaming perception. The *floating work of art* allows the navigation through fields of meaning, where there is no temporal sequence and only momentary hierarchies.

The critique of logic in the *floating work of art* must be understood as a fundamental critique of the computer as a logic machine, unfamiliar with any non-logical operation. A similar deconstruction of logic can be found in the works of Simon Biggs, Grahame Weinbren, Ken Feingold and, particularly convincingly, in the most recent work by David Rokeby, *The Giver of Name* (1998). Here the computer as association machine continually creates new metaphors that reveal the limitations and regularities of everyday language.

DISSOLUTION OF REPRESENTATION

Just as the *floating work of art* develops a fundamental suspicion of logic, which is alien to it, it also regards the representational claims of the image as problematic. It offers two possibilities for dealing with images without confirming their claim to an unlimited representation of reality: it examines archetypal images with a view to their current symbolic content and forms new momentary orders on the basis of the existing collective memory of images (Jeffrey Shaw). This method is based on the conviction that we have at our disposal an enormous pool of cultural symbols, which need to be reformulated in order to enable a new understanding of (hi)story. With its second possibility the floating work practices a criticism, schooled by modernism, that completely avoids common methods of visual representation. It develops a new vocabulary of forms, which resists the temptation to transfer visual habits into the new space (Knowbotic Research). Its visual language is abstract and concrete at the same time. New metaphors emerge in the world of immaterial data: as agents the knowledge robots, or knowbots, give us access to a world which is above all technically, though hardly culturally, encoded.[31] In this variant the *floating work of art* consists of a collection of heterogeneous elements (texts/sounds/abstract signatures), which are contributed by different 'participants' and which are all connected to one another. In its web-like structure all elements are in contact with one another and influence each other. This way discursive fields or 'spaces for acting' (*Handlungsfelder*) emerge, that empower the user to interfere and to order the complexity according to personal criteria. It is particularly this ability to form personal criteria that is tested, because the user is placed in a situation of permanent insecurity (since his attempts to form representation in traditional ways fail continually). They are only made concrete through the user's active appropriation. It is in this process that the aesthetic potential of the *floating work of art* can be found, which for the first time makes possible the sensual interpretation of an abstract immaterial order.

Linked to this process is a reinterpretation of the term imagination. Imagination is no longer the creative achievement of a privileged individual, but is instead defined as the ability to organise abstract orders sensually. It is the user, not so much the artist, who is required to perform the imaginative act.

FROM AGENT TO ACCOMPLICE TO *FLOATING WORK OF ART*

Part of the authorship transfers from the artist to the user in the *floating work of art* through the imaginative act. Just as the figure of the artist in performance and body art was a sign for changing constructions of identity, it is now the role of what was formerly the observer and currently the user, that is at stake. As part of the cybernetic circle in which he spontaneously finds himself, the user feels the effects of his own behaviour, which is determined by social norms and rules, and which he is reluctant to put aside. In her work Lynn Hershman shows how the obsessive, compulsive and regulatory are vital parts of the human character. Compared to these the desire for free, self-determined action is insignificant. Man loves to surround himself with rules that relieve him of responsible behaviour. In the cybernetic circle his own gaze, which is determined by social conventions, is thrown back at him and makes him realise that it is he who generates reality with his gaze. In the *floating work of art* the user becomes conscious that he is an accomplice in a fundamental sense. However, he only seemingly occupies an omnipotent position that allows him to control events, since he is always victim and perpetrator at the same time. In a web of relations he is only one of many controllers. This becomes particularly clear when the *floating work of art* is extended directly into the internet. In this case it is possible to try out 'shifting personalities', which are capable of continually changing their appearances and adapting them to new conditions.

SUMMARY

The development of the *floating work of art* shows that our narrative strategies and our concepts of (re)constructing reality have acquired new forms. This change can already be detected in Victorian panoramas and in the experimental literature of James Joyce. It was only with the utilisation of the computer and the internet for artistic purposes that the *floating work of art* could fully develop its aesthetic potential.

During the techno-euphoria of the 1970s the connection between body and machine was tried out in the scope of 'artificial reality' environments. Since the end of the 1980s, mental, as well as functional interactions, have been developing in the scope of the *floating work of art*, which reconnects abstract processes to the body. It is only this connection between mental interaction and re-embodiment of abstract processes that makes possible a reflexive intercourse with digital cultural technology.

The *floating work of art* makes it possible to try out a new conception of the world, where there is no longer a linear relationship between cause and effect and no distanced point of view, where one participates, at the same time, in the creation of such a new conception. In order to achieve this, however, it needs to change some of the characteristics of the traditional art work: in contrast to the latter, the *floating work of art* is not an entity, but a state transformed by changing influences. The *floating work of art* is mobile and dynamic and therefore only recognises temporary hierarchies. Its uniqueness lies precisely in the fact that it is recreated with every moment of perception.

The *floating work of art* is no longer the expression of a single individual. Neither is it the expression of a collective, but it is the state of a 'connective' – a web of influences that are continually reorganised by all participants. The individual placement by a single artist or a group of artists is replaced by artistic practices that are not intended to be permanent. Their temporary nature constitutes the precondition for their intrinsic potential for continual change. Emerging from the intervention of its participants the *floating work of art* can show how to engage as many people as possible in the social processes of globalised societies.

NOTES

1. Oettermann, Stephan. *Das Panorama. Die Geschichte eines Massenmediums*. Frankfurt am Main: Syndikat Autoren- und Verlagsgesellschaft, 1980, cover text.

2. However, the protection the patent was supposed to offer was unsuccessful. The panorama became a mass medium throughout the nineteenth century in England, France, Germany and the United States.

3. Kemp, Wolfgang. *Funkkolleg Moderne Kunst*. Weinheim, Basel: Beltz Verlag, p. 97.

4. Ibid.

5. Oettermann, Stephan. *Das Panorama. Die Geschichte eines Massenmediums*, p. 20.

6. *London und Paris*, Vol. XIV (1804), p. 206.

7. Oettermann, Stephan. *Das Panorama. Die Geschichte eines Massenmediums*, p. 41.

8. Eberhard, Johann August. *Handbuch der Ästhetik*, Part I, Halle 1805, quoted in Buddemeier, Heinz. *Panorama, Diorama, Photographie. Entstehung und Wirkung neuer Medien im 19. Jahrhundert*, Munich: Wilhelm Fink Verlag, 1970, p. 175.

9. 'Finally the old list of never-ending complaints about the vicissitudes of traveling can be put aside, as well as the laments about insolent public servants, cheating landlords, robberies by bandits armed to the hilt [...] All this has now been cut short; mountains and seas, the classical valley, the antique town have been carried to us as if on the wings of the wind.' *Blackwood's Magazine*, quoted from Oettermann, 1980, p. 88.

10. Compare also Peters, Susanne. *Wahrnehmung als Gestaltungsprinzip im Werk von James Joyce*. Trier: WVT Wissenschaftlicher Verlag Trier, 1995. The importance of the visual was the incentive for Sabine Fabo to examine Joyce and Beuys. See *Joyce und Beuys. Ein intermedialer Dialog*. Heidelberg: Universitätsverlag C. Winter, 1997.

11. In the early 1970s Wolfgang Iser founded the reader reception theory of literature. See his *Der Akt des Lesens. Theorie ästhetischer Wirkung*, Munich: Wilhelm Fink Verlag, 1990. Wolfgang Kemp is convinced that in the visual arts, too, each work of art is 'designed to require the active supplementation by the observer, that is a dialogue between partners takes place.' See Kemp, 'Kunstwissenschaft und Rezeptionsästhetik', in *Der Betrachter ist im Bild. Kunstwissenschaft und Rezeptionsästhetik*, Cologne, 1985, p. 21. See also Kemp, *Der Anteil des Betrachters. Rezeptionsästhetische Studien zur Malerei des 19. Jahrhunderts*, Munich, 1983.

12. For a definition of interactive art see Dinkla, Söke. *Pioniere Interaktiver Kunst. Von 1970 bis heute*. Ostfildern: Cantz Verlag, 1997, pp. 14–16.

13. These motifs, in particular the crossing of spacial boundaries in 'The Virtual Museum', play a cen-

tral part in the oeuvre of Jeffrey Shaw. This parallelism is not by chance. To Shaw narrative strategies developed by Joyce can be transferred into physical experience in the interactive medium. There is a meeting of minds between Joyce and Shaw in other respects as well. Similar to Joyce, Shaw uses myth not as a point of reference for content, but as a higher organisational form which is capable of connecting heterogenous materials. The mythical model for Joyce as well as Shaw is the 'blank' (Iser), which is a condition for the continually different narration of the archteype. For Shaw compare Dinkla, Söke. *Pioniere Interaktiver Kunst. Von 1970 bis heute.* Ostfildern: Cantz Verlag, 1997, pp. 97–147. See also Iser, Wolfgang. 'Der Archetyp als Leerform. Erzählschablonen und Kommunikation in Joyces *Ulysses*', Hans Blumenberg, ed. *Poetik und Hermeneutik IV, Terror und Spiel*, Munich: 1971, pp. 369–408.

14. Heisenberg, Werner. 'Die Kopenhagener Deutung der Quantentheorie', Jürgen Busche, ed. *Quantentheorie und Philosophie, Vorlesungen und Aufsätze*, Stuttgart: 1983, pp. 42–61.

15. Fabo, Sabine. *Joyce und Beuys. Ein intermedialer Dialog.* Heidelberg: Universitätsverlag C. Winter, p. 17.

16. For the concept of the web in Joyce's work compare Hayman, David. 'Nodality and Infra-Structure in *Finnegans Wake*', *James Joyce Quarterly*, vol. 16, no. 1/2, Fall 1978, pp. 135–49 and Clark, Hilary. 'Networking in Finnegans Wake', *James Joyce Quarterly*, vol. 27, no. 4, Summer 1990, pp. 745–58.

17. Deleuze, Gilles and Guattari, Felix. *Rhizom*, Berlin: Merve, 1977, p. 11.

18. Nelson, Theodor Holm. *The Hypertext*, Lecture at the Congress of the International Federation for Documentation, Washington DC, 1965, mentioned in Nelson, Theodor. 'Getting it Out of Our System', in *Information Retrieval. A Critical View*, George Schecter, ed., based on Third Annual Colloqium on Information Retrieval, Philadelphia, 1966, Washington DC 1967, pp. 191–210.

19. Nelson, Theodor Holm. *Literary Machines*, South Bend, Edition 87.1, 1987, p. 2. Until the second half of the 1980s Nelson's work was known mostly to a small circle of insiders. Vannevar Bush's essay 'As We May Think' from the 1940s, which formed part of the basis for Nelson's thoughts, also received little attention until that time. In James M. Nyce and Paul Kahn, eds. *From Memex to Hypertext. Vannevar Bush and the Mind's Machine*, San Diego/London: Academic Press, 1991, pp. 85–110. (Reprint from *Atlantic Monthly*, vol. 176, no. 1, July 1945.)

20. For a detailed interpretation of Weinbren and Feingold see Dinkla, Söke. *Pioniere Interaktiver Kunst. Von 1970 bis heute.* Ostfildern: Cantz Verlag, 1997, pp. 196–216.

21. In the following years this principle above all revolutionised our theories of communication and has brought forth the system theory, the game theory, the automaton theory as well as information, message and signal theories.

22. Spiegel, Alan. *Fiction and the Camera Eye. Visual Consciousness in Film and the Modern Novel*, Charlotteville: University Press of Virginia, 1976. Deane, Paul. 'Motion Picture Techniques in James Joyce's "The Dead"', *James Joyce Quarterly*, vol. 6, Spring 1969, pp. 231–6.

23. See note 20 and note 13.

24. Roberta is a 30-year old divorced woman who in 1975 moves from Cleveland Heights to San

Francisco with her savings amounting to 1800 US dollars. She is unlucky, neurotic and behaves awkwardly most of the time. For an extensive analysis and description of Lynn Hershman's inter-active works see the author's *Pioniere Interaktiver Kunst. Von 1970 bis heute*. Ostfildern: Cantz Verlag, 1997, pp. 170–95.

25. Compare *XLII Esposizione internationale d'arte. Arte e Alchemia*, La Biennale di Venezia, Venice: 1986, p. 78, p. 118 and p. 263.

26. Eco, Umberto. *Das offene Kunstwerk*, Frankfurt am Main: 1973.

27. Jameson, Frederic. 'Postmoderne – zur Logik der Kultur im Spätkapitalismis', in Andreas Huyssen and Klaus R. Scherpe, eds. *Postmoderne. Zeichen eines kulturellen Wandels,* Reinbek bei Hamburg 1986, pp. 45–102 and pp. 99–100.

28. Barthes, Roland. *Das Reich der Zeichen*, Frankfurt am Main: 1981, p. 54 f.

29. Iser, Wolfgang. *Der Akt des Lesens. Theorie ästhetischer Wirkung*, Munich, 1976; Kemp, Wolfgang. 'Kunstwissenschaft und Rezeptionsästhetik', *Der Betrachter ist im Bild. Kunstwissenschaft und Rezeptionsästhetik*, Cologne, 1985, pp. 7–27.

30. Seaman, Bill. 'Rekombinierbare Poetik. Plädoyer für einen "abstrakten Physikalismus" ', *Tanzdrama*, vol. 2/2000, no. 51, pp. 25–7.

31. In the art work 'Dialogue with the Knowbotic South' the south polar area serves as the model for a relatively unexplored natural space with no history of civilisation in its true sense. Instead it is put on the map mainly through Antarctic research stations. With a taster the visitors move through sound and visualised data which are displayed on two projection areas. The visualised data – the knowbots – function as an interface and provide the visitor with access to the data space. Compare the exhibition catalogue *InterAct! Schlüsselwerke Interaktiver Kunst*, Wilhelm Lehmbruck Museum, Duisburg. Ostfildern: Cantz Verlag, 1997.

Narrated Theory: Multiple Projection and Multiple Narration (Past and Future)

Peter Weibel

MATERIAL EXPERIMENTS

The subversive explosion that shattered the cinematographic code during the 1960s affected all of the technical and material parameters of film.

The material character of film itself was analysed by artists who, instead of exposing the celluloid, scratched it (George Landow, *Film In Which There Appear Sprocket Holes, Edge Lettering, Dirt Particles, etc.*, 1965–6; Wilhelm and Birgit Hein, *Rohfilm,* 1968), perforated it with a hole punch (Dieter Roth, 1965), painted it (Harry Smith used 35mm material, processing it with grease, paint, tape and spray, 1947), covered it with fingerprints (Peter Weibel, *Fingerprint*, 1967) or glued moths to it (Stan Brakhage, *Mothlight*, 1963, in which moth wings and leaves were fixed between layers of perforated tape and projected). Empty frames, black film and over-exposed material were also used.

At the same time, the technical resources of film, from camera to projector, were taken apart, reassembled, augmented and used in entirely new ways. There were camera-less films, for which unprocessed celluloid, known as clear film, was inserted into the projector (Nam June Paik, *Zen for Film*, 1962), and films without film, in which Kosugi, to name one example, focused light from a projector without film against a paper screen, cutting out sections of the screen from the middle until there was nothing left of it (*Film No. 4*, 1965). In other works, the light beam was replaced with a stretched length of rope (Peter Weibel, *Lichtseil*, 1973), the conventional screen with curtains of steam, running water (Robert Whitman, *Shower*, 1964) and the surfaces of human bodies (in his *Prune Flat*, 1965, Robert Whitman projected a film onto the body of a girl wearing white clothing; the film showed her taking off the same clothing; in Andy Warhol's and Jud Yalkut's *Exploding Plastic Inevitable*, 1966, the film was projected onto the figures of people dancing in the audience to music by the Velvet Underground).

MULTIPLE SCREEN EXPERIMENTS

Many film artists carried out radical experiments with the screen itself. It was exploded and multiplied, either through division into multiple images using split-screen techniques or by placing screens on several different walls. Thus multiple projections occupied the foreground of a visual culture that was intent upon liberating itself from the conventional concept of the painting, from the technical and material restrictions of imaging technology and from the repressive determinants of the social codes. One example worthy of note is Andy Warhol's *Chelsea Girls* (1967), a mixture of split-screen techniques and multiple projections in which a number of performers discuss their unusual lives from multiple perspectives and at several different levels at the same time. In much the same way that some painters sliced up the canvas (Lucio Fontana) or used the human body as a canvas (Vienna Actionism) in search of avenues of escape from the picture, cinema artists were also engaged in a quest for ways of breaking out of the limited film screen during the same period. There were monumental mobile projections from moving vehicles onto building facades (Imi Knoebel, *Projektion X*, 1972), onto dancing people, onto forests and fields, onto the curved inside and outside surfaces of geodetic domes, onto plastic balls, hoses, etc.

These techniques of mobile projection or using the screen as a window of a moving vehicle have been taken up also in the present visual practices. *Crossings* (1995) by Stacey Spiegel and Rodney Hoinkes, is an interactive installation which simulates a train-ride between Paris and Berlin. The physical space is transformed into the virtual interactive space of the World Wide Web. *Room with a View* (2000) by Michael Bielicky and Bernd Lintermann for the Autostadt Wolfsburg uses four projectors for a perfect 360° dome projection with a touch screen in the centre of the dome to manipulate the projected images in multiple ways.

MULTIPLE NARRATIVE EXPERIMENTS

Multiple projections of different films alongside one another, one on top of the other and in all spatial directions represented more than merely an invasion of space by the visual image. They were also an expression of multiple narrative perspectives. The film-maker Gregory Markopoulos, an early master of quick cuts and complex cross-fading techniques, published a manifesto of new narrative forms based upon his cutting technique in *Filmculture* no. 31, Winter 1963–4.

> I propose a new form of narration as a combination of classical montage technique with a more
> abstract system. This system incorporates the use of short film phases that evoke thought images.
> Each film phase comprises a selection of specific images similar to the harmonious unity of a musical
> composition. The film phases determine other interrelationships among themselves; in classical mon-
> tage technique, there is a constant relationship to the continuous shot; in my abstract system there is
> a complex of different images that are repeated.

From the outset, the extension of the single screen to many screens, from the single projection to multiple projections, represented not only an expansion of visual horizons and an overwhelming intensification of visual experience. It was always engaged in the service of a new approach to narration. For the first time, the subjective response to the world was not pressed into a constructed, falsely objective style but instead formally presented in the same diffuse and fragmentary way in which it was experienced. In the age of social revolts, consciousness-expanding drugs and cosmic visions, multiple projection environments became an important factor in the quest for a new imaging technology capable of articulating a new perception of the world.

In 1965, Stan Vanderbeek published a manifesto in justification of real-time multiple projection environments, a kind of 'image-flow' in which image projection itself became the subject of the performance. In the same year he showed *Feedback No. 1: A Movie Mural*, achieving a first breakthrough for multi-projection cinema. To realise his idea, he established the Movie-Drome in Stony Point, New York; a vaulted cupola modelled on the geodetic domes of R. Buckminster Fuller. The USCO ('US' company) Group associated with Gerd Stern began working on the multi-projection shows on the east coast of the United States in about 1960 (*We Are All One*, with four 16mm projectors, two 8mm projectors, four carousel projectors, etc., 1965). Several artists also created huge multi-vision environments for Expo 1967 in Montreal (Roman Kroitor, *Labyrinthe*, 1967, for example) with the intention of developing new forms of storytelling. As Roman Kroitor asserted, *'people [were] tired of the standard plot structure.'* Francis Thompson, a pioneer in large-scale, multi-image cinematography, presented his piece *We Are Young* on an arrangement of six screens at Expo 1967. The Czech pavilion featured a huge screen on which 160 slides could be shown simultaneously (Diapolyceran screen). Milton Cohen, the leading figure in the ONCE Group from Ann Arbor, Michigan, had been at work since 1958 developing an environment for multiple projections with the aid of rotating mirrors and prisms using mobile rectangular and triangular screens under the title *Space Theatre, To free film from its flat and frontal orientation and to present it within an ambience of total space.* [1]

John Cage, Lejaren Hiller and Ronald Nameth staged *HPSCHD*, a five-hour 'Intermedia Event' with 8,000 slides and 100 films projected onto 48 windows at the University of Illinois in 1969. Between 1960 and 1967, Robert Whitman experimented with multiple plastic and paper screens onto which films were projected (*The American Moon*, 1960). In *Tent Happening* (1965), films, including a sequence filmed through a glass pane showing a man defecating, were projected onto a large tent. Beginning in 1965, Aldo Tambellini *Electromedia Theatre* worked with multiple projections (*Black Zero*, 1965) in which, to cite one example, a gigantic black balloon appeared from nowhere, blew itself up and eventually exploded. Hundreds of hand-painted films and slides were used. In 1968 Tambellini organised *Black Gate* along the banks of the Rhine in Düsseldorf, an event featuring projections onto helium-filled, airborne plastic hoses and figures by Otto Piene. Jud Yalkut created *Dream Reel* for Yukihisa Isobe's *Floating Theatre*, a gigantic parachute held by nylon threads – a portable hemispheric screen for multiple frontal and rear projections. The group 'Single Wing Turquoise Bird' (Peter Mays, Jeff Perkins, the later video artist Michael Scroggins and others) from Los Angeles put together light shows for rock concerts in 1967 and 1968. Sponsored by the painter Sam Francis, they subsequently conducted experiments in an abandoned Santa Monica hotel with constantly changing images, from video projections to laser beams. In their *Theatre of Light* (1964), Jackie Cassen and Rudi Stern projected multiple images on pneumatic domes, transparent Plexiglas cubes, polyhexagonal structures, water surfaces, etc., with their self-constructed 'sculptural projectors' during the late 1960s. Particularly impressive was a fountain illuminated by a strobe light, a technique that evoked the impression of individual falling drops of water suspended like crystals in the air.

TIME AND SPACE EXPERIMENTS

In addition to the expansion of the technical repertoire through experimentation with projectors and multiple projections, another material-oriented approach to the visual expression of the new concept of reality, the renunciation of historical social obligations and the new drug-induced, consciousness-expanding experience emerged. It involved the shifting and distortion of the conventional parameters of space and time using techniques designed to extend, slow, delay and abbreviate time. Film duration was extended to as much as 24 hours (Andy Warhol, *Empire State Building*, 1963) or to an extreme of only a very few seconds (Paul Sharits, *Wrist Trick*, ten seconds, 1966). Time dilations in film and music were favoured as primary means of expression not only because of their consciousness-expanding effects but also for compositional and formal reasons. The same applies as well to time-shortening and aggressive cutting techniques.

The contents of these independent avant-garde and underground films also strayed from the familiar terrain of the industry film in a social sense. Images from the personal sphere, psychodramatic documents of an excessive individualism, were shown publicly in uncensored form. Normally taboo sex scenes were acted out in front of the camera (Jack Smith, *Flaming Creatures*, 1962–3, a transvestite orgy that triggered a scandal even in artists' circles at the time yet became a major source of inspiration for Warhol's universe; Kenneth Anger, *Scorpio Rising*, 1963, which marked the birth of *Biker Movies* and homoerotic self-fashioning, *Inauguration of the Pleasure Dome*, 1966). The widening of material and technical parameters also went hand in hand with the dissolution of social consensus.

SOUND EXPERIMENTS

Both formal and thematic extensions of the cinematographic code were welcomed enthusiastically in the aesthetic and social revolutionary atmosphere of the 1960s and, like progressive rock music, were supported by a new, youthful audience. Indeed, a large number of such underground films were accompanied by rock (from the Grateful Dead to Cream) and avant-garde (from John Cage to Terry Riley) music. Music played a much more emancipated role in these films than in industry movies. In standard industry productions, regardless of whether they used classical or popular scores, music serves more or less as background sound and as a device for controlling mood and atmosphere – heightening or resolving dramatic tension. In many avant-garde films, on the other hand, music and sound have a determining effect upon the structure of imagery, and images are cut and composed in accordance with musical principles. The function of the soundtrack, the serial arrangement of existing popular songs and the commissioned piece known as a theme song and used to associate a certain film with a certain musical hit, clearly illustrate the tendency toward the industrial exploitation and marketing of film images through linking with music. This technique of using semi-prefabricated components in movies is reminiscent of the accelerated prefab building techniques employed in mass industrial high-rise construction. Instead of compound concrete-and-steel construction, the rapidly mass-produced industrial film made use of a compound sound-and-music construction. In contrast, the avant-garde films of the 1960s employed a highly differentiated approach to the development of new relationships between sound and visual imagery.[2]

'EXPANDED CINEMA' AND NEW VIDEO

Several avant-garde galleries promoted analytical refinements and developments ranging from the structuralist films to spatial film installations during the 1970s. This period also witnessed the emergence of video art, with viewer-oriented closed-circuit installations that anticipated the observer-relative interactive computer installations of the 1990s and time-delayed installations, which pursued further the experiments of expanded cinema. The market-induced revival of figurative painting in the 1980s put an abrupt end to the development of expanded cinematic forms and video art. Broad segments of visual culture were affected by amnesia as scandalous as it was total, for which not only the market but also institutional art historiography, which had buckled under to the power of the market, was to blame. Viewed from this perspective, the triumphant embrace and revival of the tendencies of the expanded cinema of the 1960s by the video generation of the 1990s is all the more astounding and gratifying.

This generation takes its cue less from the progressive achievements of video artists of the 1980s, since their art was subordinated to the sculpture and painting of their time. Thus, in pursuing the development of a specific video-based language, the video art of the 1990s focused deliberately on the expansion of image technologies and social consciousness of the 1960s. We find surprising evidence of parallels, sometimes extending even to the finest detail, not only in style and technique but in content and motif as well. For the most part, the video art of the 1990s is also shaped by an intense interest in multiple projection and the new approach to multi-perspective narration that comes with it. Numerous representatives of the video generation of the 1990s, including such artists as Jordan Crandall, Julia Scher, Steve McQueen, Jane and Louise Wilson, Douglas Gordon, Stan Douglas, Johan Grimonprez, Pierre Huyghe, Marijke van Warmerdam, Ann-Sofi Siden, Grazia Toderi and Aeronaut Mike, now work within the context of a deconstruction of the technical 'apparatus' outlined here. Many computer artists of the 1990s, among them Blast Theory, Jeffrey Shaw, Perry Hoberman, Peter Weibel and others, have also taken up the tendencies and technologies of the expanded cinema of the 1960s once again. In a series of interactive computer installations like *On Justifying the Hypothetical Nature of Art and the Non-Identicality within the Object World* (1992) or *Curtain of Lascaux* (1995–6) Peter Weibel realised various virtual worlds, where the observer had a pivotal role derived from his closed circuit video installations from the late 1960s and the early 1970s. The observer became part of the system he observed, articulating the immersive image system, and changed the behaviour and content of the image by his actions. *Desert Rain* (1999) by the British group Blast Theory sent six visitors onto a mission in a virtual environment of six rooms. The projection of the virtual worlds took place on a curtain made of streaming water. Each visitor had 30 minutes time to complete his mission with the help of communicating with the five other virtual environments and their inhabitants. However, video artists of the 1990s are pursuing the decon-struction of the cinematographic code in a much more controlled, less subjective manner, applying strategies that are also more methodical and more closely oriented to social issues than those of the 1960s. In the video art of the 1990s, experiments with multiple projections are employed primarily in the service of a new approach to narration. Video and slide projections onto unusual objects are used by artists ranging from Tony Oursler to Honore d'O. Projections onto two or more screens are found in the work of such artists as Pipilotti Rist and Sam Taylor-Wood, Burt Barr and Marcel Odenbach, Eija-Liisa Ahtila and Shirin Neshat, Samir and Doug Aitken, Dryden Goodwin, Heike Baranowsky and Monika Oechsler. Split-screen techniques are characteristic features of the art of Karin Westerlund and Samir. Multiple-monitor environments are employed by Ute Friederike Jürß and Mary Lucier.

MULTIPLE MONITORS, MULTIPLE PROJECTIONS AND MULTI-PERSPECTIVE NARRATION

These multiple projections take advantage of the opportunities offered by multiple perspective for a departure from familiar ways of looking at social behaviour. On three screens projected in alter-nation, Monika Oechsler's *High Anxieties* of 1998 shows the construction of feminine identity as it begins in childhood, illustrating how even girlfriends of the same age control the formation of the individual as agents of society. The changing cinematic perspective calls to mind the familiar cinematic codes of courtroom dramas involving prosecutors, defence attorneys, victims and defendants. Enhanced by the possibilities offered by triple projection and multiple viewpoint achieved through this formal montage technique, this new perspective intensifies the hidden violence inherent in the socialisation of the individual. In a similar way, the triple projection in Eija-Liisa Ahtila's *TODAY/Tänään* of 1996–7 enormously enhances the possibilities for complex linking of image and text elements independent of the narrator's perspective. Only rarely do the texts match the faces and genders. Texts and images do not identify each other; instead they distinguish each other, floating alongside one another and forming moving islands, nodes in a network of multiple relationships, which the viewer must create himself. Free-floating chains of signs, be they images or texts, are interwoven to form a universe without a centre. Yet its core harbours the catastrophe of a fatal accident that has obviously eradicated all possibility of a coherent, linear narrative. Only disparate fragments of memory are presented in strangely objective fashion by the passive, *Networked Subjects* (Elisabeth Bronfen, 1998). The story of the catastrophe no longer follows the linear track of rational thought; instead, the irrational essence of the catastrophe is released (from censorship) by disorderly, cen-trifugal, multi-perspective trajectories of narration. Only in this way can the catastrophe be experi-enced as such – through the refusal of image and text elements to merge and fit together. Narrative structures of this kind, which employ the irrational character of dream and the human psyche as plot elements, clearly reveal associations with the early films of Ingmar Bergman (*Wild Strawberries*, 1957, for example). The work *Augentauschen* (1993) (Eye Exchange) by Heiner Blum investigates the relationship of photography and face. The interactive CD-ROM *Troubles with Sex, Theory and History* (1997) by Marina Grzinic and Aina Smid analyses aleatoric, combinatoric and recombinatoric relations between images and text, based on a selection of works by Grzinic and Smid between 1992 and 1997.

Shirin Neshat presents the binary opposition of man and woman in a patriarchal society on two screens positioned facing one another. The woman has a voice but neither words nor listeners. She has only sound and her ability to scream. The man possesses the words, the culture of language and an audience, which rewards him with frenetic applause at the end. The exclusion of woman from the building of civilisation and society can hardly be illustrated more vividly than in this binary juxtaposition of projectors and positions. The device of the synecdoche (used here in the representation of the violence inherent in gender issues and the politics of identity) is typical of many of the best works of video art, which deal in a methodological-analytical manner with the eradicated power mechanisms of the social code, as opposed to the predominantly subjective approaches of the new American cinema of the 1960s. Modern society offers the real subject a number of different role models and possibilities for role behaviour.

On a scale of multiple possibilities defined by the culture industry in media ranging from popular movies to highbrow opera, from slick magazines to low-ratings TV, the subject can make its choice and position itself, as long as it can take the pressure of the respective social code. This relationship between the subject as a real possibility and the imaginary subject option is expressed as a synecdoche in Sam Taylor-Wood's *Killing Time* of 1994. Like several other artists, Taylor-Wood works with 'found sound'. Interestingly enough, her work confirms the theory of the dominance of musical structure as the determining narrative structure. It is not the visual image but sound that dictates the behaviour of the actors. The four persons shown in the quadruple projections listen to *Electra* by Richard Strauss, waiting for cues for their assigned voice parts. Like Shirin Neshat's work, the film sequence is a synecdoche for the range of available (social) roles and the role of the voice in society.[3] The theatre of sound opens a view to the theatre of subject positions. In comparison, Pipilotti Rist tends rather toward the structure of semi-prefabricated components in her work. She uses pre-recorded music, which she illustrates with her pictures, or the music illustrates her pictures according to coded schemes of the kind we see on MTV. She remains within the codes of the subject option and the industrial narrative prescribed and accepted by society. We find a similarly interesting adaptation of the relationship between sound and image at the narrative level, since remembering is one of the functions of narrative, in *A Capella Portraits* by Ute Friederike Jürß.

FOUND IMAGE AND SOUND, FOUND FILMS EXPERIMENTS

Just as artists of the 1960s made use of 'found images' and 'found footage' (George Landow and others), contemporary video and film artists like Douglas Gordon, Marcel Odenbach and Martin Arnold employ found material as well. Perry Hoberman uses in his interactive CD-ROM piece *The Sub-Division of the Electric Light* (1996) found slides and 8mm films and old projection instruments. Erkki Huhtamo uses a selection of found vaudeville rides, mostly computer-generated to imitate on a simulation platform a journey on virtual vehicles through the highlights of historic cinematographic rides in his piece *The Ride of Your Life* (1998). George Legrady in his interactive CD-ROM

piece _Slippery Traces_ (1996) uses about 200 postcards for a non-linear narration built on an algo- (DVD)
rithm, navigating through a databank. Martin Arnold deconstructs his found footage to the extreme
in order to make hidden semantic structures visible through gradual repetition. Found footage is
reassembled, looped, partially re-filmed and visually estranged in its entirety. The use of found film
is part of a general strategy of media reflection and appropriation. When Marcel Odenbach,
Gabriele Leidloff, Samir, Isabell Heimerdinger, Andrea Bowers, Burt Barr, Pierre Huyghe and
Douglas Gordon allude to familiar films, including such classics as _From Here to Eternity_ (Fred
Zinnemann, 1953) and _The Godfather_ (Francis Ford Coppola, 1972) or to popular television images
ranging from cheerleaders (Andrea Bowers, _Touch of Class_, 1998) to scenes from Diana, Princess
of Wales' funeral (Gabriele Leidloff, _Moving Visual Object_, 1997), then what we have are media-
oriented observations of a second order, in which visual culture as a whole is exposed as a ready-
made object for analysis. Consequently, observation of the world gives way to the observation of
communication. The unconscious character of the visual code becomes evident in a kind of symptomatic reading.

In Doug Aitken's installations, with multiple screens, the narrative universe is broken down into
individual, autonomous film frames and series of effects of the kind familiar to viewers schooled in
video-clip techniques: from detailed shots, blurred motion, technical modifications achieved with
the camera, digital image processing, short cuts and dilations of time. Narration is not only broken
apart spatially through projection onto multiple screens but in chronological terms as well.

Shifts and distortions of conventional parameters of space and time play a significant role in the
new narration. As in the 1960s, these experiments with time emphasise the technological time of
the cinematic order as opposed to the biological time of life. The focus is on artificial time rather
than 'rediscovered time', on time constructions as visual symptoms of a completely artificial, constructed reality. In his triple projection _L'Ellipse_ of 1998, with Bruno Ganz, Pierre Huyghe illustrates
the difference between industrial time (the use of time in the industry film) and personal time (the
use of time in Pierre Huyghe's own film). He uses found footage or found film, film as a ready-made
work of art, which he deconstructs by subjecting it to chronological manipulation: wherever Bruno
Ganz is off-screen in the industry films, the projection of his personal film begins and interrupts the
projection of the industry film. Huyghe plays with the cinematographic technique of cutting from
one scene to another by deleting the time and space in between which technique is called 'ellipti-
cal'. Douglas Gordon subjects industry films to similar time manipulations. He also works with found
films, from Hitchcock's _Psycho_ (1963) to Ford's _The Searchers_ (1956), expanding them to 24 hours
or five years, respectively.

REVERSIBLE RHIZOMATIC NARRATION
The narrative universe becomes reversible and no longer reflects the psychology of cause and
effect. Repetitions, the suspension of linear time, temporal and spatial asynchrony blast classical
chronology apart. Multiple screens function as fields in which scenes are depicted from a multiple
perspective, their narrative thread broken. The accusation once levelled at the new music that it

had cut the link to the listener, since the listener could no longer reconstruct or recognise the principles of composition, can now be applied without reservation to the advanced narrative techniques of contemporary video art. They have severed the link to the viewer, who can no longer
make out the narrative structure. Linearity and chronology, as classical parameters of narration, fall
victim to a multiple perspective projected onto multiple screens. Asynchronous, non-linear, non-
chronological, seemingly illogical, parallel, multiple narrative approaches from multiple perspectives
projected onto multiple screens are the goal. These narrative procedures comprising a 'multiform
plot' have been developed with reference to and oriented toward such rhizomatic communication
structures as hypertext, 'associational indexing' (Vannevar Bush, *As We May Think*, 1945), text-based
'multi-user dungeons' (MUDs) and other digital techniques of literary narration.[4] Gilles Deleuze's
definition of the rhizome as a network in which every point can be connected with any other point
is a precise description of communication in the multi-user environment of the World Wide Web
and the allusive, open-ended image and text systems derived from it. These narrative systems have
a certain algorithmic character. As early as 1928, Vladimir Propp demonstrated in his famous study
Morphology of the Fairy Tale that the 450 fairy tales he analysed could be reduced to 25 basic functions and narrative events, or narrative morphemes. These 25 morphemes form a kind of algorithm, which generates an endless string of new plots through new combinations. With its
audiovisual narrative techniques, contemporary video art breaks down holistic forms into their
basic morphological components. These are then reassembled using the multiple methods
described above. These new narrative techniques render the complexity of social systems lucid.
The crisis of representation, which painting averted during the 1990s by resorting to a restorative
repetition of historical figurative and expressive conditions, is being overcome in contemporary
video art through the revival of narrative conditions anticipated by the historical avant-gardes of
literature, theatre and music: from the French OULIPO (Ouvroir de Littérature Potentielle) group
to the Vienna Group. The interactive installation *Passage Sets/One Pulls Pivots at the Tip of the Tongue*
(1994–5) by Bill Seaman refers to the automatic writing techniques of the Surrealists, but acted out
by a computational random access algorithm. Texts and images are networked in this way of
aleatoric combinations. The interactive installation *Tafel* (Black Board) (1993) by Frank Fietzek
reveals a moving monitor in front of a big black-board hiding words like a palimpsest.

The banishment of narration by abstraction led to the rejection of narrative as an obsolete historical phenomenon. This modernist dictate of recognising only the purely visual and banishing the
verbal was overturned by post-modernism in favour of a more intense discursive orientation. Thus
even the post-modern visual language of contemporary media art becomes increasingly discursive,
the more it makes use of avant-garde narrative techniques. Unlike technically ponderous film art,
the video technology of today permits more complete control of cinematic resources and thus
promotes a more stable development of the cinematic code. The advantage of today's video technology over yesterday's film technology lies in the improved logistics of its technical repertoire.
What was once virtually impossible and susceptible to problems as well is now much easier to
realise and entirely reliable. Thanks to this technical stability, the possibilities for new narrative tech-

niques based upon multiple large-screen projections, perhaps the most striking feature of contemporary video art, can now be explored extensively for the first time. And so the video art of today has taken up the lance left behind by the cinema avant-garde of the 1960s and developed the universe of the cinematic code a step further.

FUTURE IMAGE DE/CONSTRUCTIONS

The artificial technology in use up to now to create an image, representing reality, imitated the natural technology of a natural apparatus, the eye organ. The decisive step in a closer representation of reality was the possibility of imitating movement with pictures. This grounded the transformation of painting and photography to cinema, as a *trompe l'oeil* technology to simulate motion with the help of an ingenious technology invented at the end of the nineteenth century but standardised and made compatible for mass-use at the beginning of the twentieth century. The next development in the progress of the image technology was the step from the simulation of movement, motion picture, to the simulation of an image as living system, the viable picture. The computer allowed virtual storage of information as electronic configuration. Information was no longer locked up magnetically or chemically as with videotape or filmstrip. The virtuality of information storage set information free and made it variable. The image became a picture field, its pixels became variables, which could be altered any time and in real-time. This caused the variability of the image content. The creation of an interface technology between observer and image technique enabled the observer to a certain degree to control with his behaviour that of the image. The picture field became an image system that reacted to the observer's movement. Moving image and moving observer moved towards a new synthesis of image and observer: the interactive image, the most radical transformation of the image since its coming into being. Since artificial systems, which behave in similarly reactive ways to living systems, have been termed 'viable' by constructivist philosophy, the new image systems can also rightfully be called 'viable'. The viability of image behaviour turns the moving image into a living image. Thus the computer is a decisive medium for perfectly simulating reality. The interactive computer-based installation _Sonomorphis_ (1998) by Bernd Lintermann and Torsten Belschner simulates the codes of evolution, giving the spectator the chance to create new species according to algorithms of recombination and mutation built on six offered optional organisms.

From this revolution of image technology follows the thesis of the technical and social deconstruction of the image. For this deconstruction of the technical dispositive of the image the artist can enlist the help of a revolution in materials, which enable a new physics of the image. The important role of the index and the imprint in modern art (especially since the 1960s, as a result of material-based artistic research) indicates that, the indexical image (which is defined through a material and physical relation between sign and object – such as smoke and fire), as a post-digital image will ultimately replace the illusionistic world of computer-based 3D simulations, which at the moment are at their ecstatic height. The indexical image is the beginning of a new culture of materiality of the image. The interactive installation _The Winds that Wash the Seas_ (1994–5) by Chris

Dodge allows the observer to blow against the screen of the monitor. The direction and power of the breath are changing the image. A second observer can interact by moving his hand in water. Both observers are transforming the image. The interactive CD-ROM piece _Impalpability_ (1998) by Masaki Fujihata has also an indexical character, as the human hand manipulating the mouse shows on the screen again close-ups of a human hand. This new culture of materiality will be especially marked by the transition from electron technology to photon technology. This transition is supported by three stages in computer development. The mainframe era of computing saw the use of a room-sized computer by a lot of people. In the PC era of computing one person was using one computer, thus the term personal computer. In the future era of calm technology and ubiquitous computing one person is going to carry and use a lot of microcomputers.

Quantum computers will replace electronic computers in the future. This new computer technology is going to enable the development of the cinematographic code from a 1:1 relation (1 spectator – 1 movie – 1 space – 1 time) into a multi-user virtual distributed environment (x spectators – x movies – x spaces – x times). In this dispersed virtual reality 100 spectators are going to act not only in front of the screen but also behind it. Internet technology already serves as a new stage for visual communication. Real and simulated worlds become models, between which connections and transformations occur which are variable and which become similar to each other (see the motion picture _The Matrix_, 1999). Just as the twentieth century has standardised and normed and thus turned into a mass industry the inventions in the image technology of the nineteenth century, the twenty-first century has to transform the advanced image technology of the twentieth century, the computer-based or net-based interactive virtual reality technology, into a mass compatible one. Today's virtual reality technology strongly reminds us of the hour of birth of the cinema in the nineteenth century, which has been characterised by singular reception. Taking the phenakistoscope as an example enables us to grasp the principle of singular reception: 1 person watches 1 film in 1 place at 1 time. Projection made a collective simultaneous perception possible: x persons see 1 movie in 1 place at 1 time. Television brought about non-local perception: x persons see 1 movie in x places at 1 time. Video and CD-ROM enable either singular or collective perception, simultaneous as well as non-simultaneous: x/1 person(s) see x/1 movie(s) in x/1 places(s) at x/1 time(s). The digital image at the end of the twentieth century starts from scratch. The head-mounted display of VR-systems again has the singular local reception as the cinema of the nineteenth century: 1 person sees 1 film in 1 place at 1 time. If VR technology wants to survive it has to appropriate the forms of perception we already know from television, radio, records, CDs, film, etc.: collective, non-simultaneous, non-local reception. _Nuzzle Afar_ (1998) by Masaki Fujihata is one of the first network-installations where observers at two distant places can interact in a common virtual space, taking up the world of online games.

The tele-technology of sound that we know from mobile phones (compare wearable ubiquitous computing) supplies the music of the future, which is going to seize the tele-technology of the image as well. Through the image technologies of the future, as I have sketched them, anybody is going to be able to see any movie in any place at any time: x persons see x films in x places at x times. Anybody, anywhere, any time is the formula for the digital image technology of the future. The decisive point about this, however, is that with this form of collective interaction (instead of the now only individual interface technology) the observer becomes an internal observer of the world. He does not stay external observer as with film but as internal observer he is going to take part in the image-worlds and thereby is going to change them. His entry into the image-world is going to trigger reactions in the sense of the covariant model not only in multiple parallel image-worlds but also in the real world. The relation between image world and reality is going to be multiple and reversible. The observer himself becomes the interface between an artificial virtual world and the real world. The events in the real world, controlled by the internal observer, are going to affect the virtual world, and the events in the virtual world, also controlled by him, are going to affect the real world and parallel virtual worlds.

The observer cuts from one narration to another. The installation replaces the classical cut by one narrator. Instead of linear narration, multiple users will create instant multiple narrations. Interactions by the observer between himself and the image world will become bi-directional. A cause in the real world will have an effect in the virtual world and, reversibly, a cause in the virtual world will have an effect in another parallel virtual world or in the real world. Observer-controlled interactions between real and virtual worlds and between different parallel virtual worlds in computer or net-based installations enable the spectator to be the new author, the new cameraman or woman, the new cutter, the new narrator. The observer will be the narrator in multiple-media installations of the future. This could happen locally or be remote-controlled through the net. The observers create, through their navigation, new forms of narration in net or computer-based installations.

Translation by John Southard and Barbara Filser.

NOTES

1. Youngblood, Gene. *Expanded Cinema*. New York: Dutton, 1970, p. 371.

2. Chion, Michel. *Les Musiques Electro-Acoustiques*. Aix-en Provence: INA-GRM, 1976; idem., *Le Son au Cinéma*. Paris: Cahiers du Cinéma, 1985; idem., *L'Audiovision*. Paris: Nathan, 1990; idem., *La Musique au Cinéma*. Paris: Fayard, 1995.

3. Silverman, Kaja. *The Accoustic Mirror. The Female Voice in Psychoanalysis and Cinema*. Bloomington: Indiana University Press, 1988.

4. Grond, Walter. *Der Erzähler und der Cyberspace*. Innsbruck: Haymon, 1999.

Towards Meaningful Spaces

Annika Blunck

INTRODUCTION

The involvement of art is of crucial importance to the work of 3D information visualisation. One way to inform such projects is to examine and explore both the current status of technologically-generated art pieces, particularly those akin to visualisations of information, and the art history which has led to today's artistic explorations.

One of the major impacts of virtual reality on the general public has doubtless been, and will continue to be, in the entertainment sector. The very nature of cinema has been, and will be, challenged by the technological combination of multimedia data, visualisation and manipulation, allowing the spectator to become an author, director, or even a protagonist, of the film. No longer are the members of the audience reduced to passive viewing, they have become an integral part of the experience, their actions affecting the way in which the story unfolds.

CONTEXT

The development of new technologies, combined with an artistic, scientific and technical interest, has not only resulted in new inventions, but has also produced new promises. The new combinations of image, film and sound, elements cinema made us familiar with, possess completely new features: the spectator is immersed in the projection; his movements influence the movement of the image; passivity transforms into activity. The idea of recombining established components in a new way, however, was not born with the rise of media technologies. At the beginning of the twentieth century, a military term was chosen to describe those movements in the arts that turned to experimentation. The avant-garde, being suspicious of traditional art forms, aimed at attacking, perforating and finally dissolving established aesthetic borders. The avant-garde sought to break down the separation between art forms to expand and synthesise them.

Adapting the spirit of the avant-garde, the artist groups of the 1950s and 1960s worked with techniques of montage in rigorous acts of expanding reality. At that time the blurring and dissolving of borders of film was pursued mainly under the heading *Action Art* or *Happening*. These artists thought that only by exceeding the borders of the classical film system, would they allow the film itself to recapture its original value. Commercialisation, monopolisation and industrialisation of film had superseded that value. Today, the conventional film forms are modified by varying and mobilising the projection and the projection screen, by diffusing the points of concentration, and integrating the audience. Through these techniques, new patterns of action are created. Those patterns nurture today's action paths of digital-driven interactivity.

A complete understanding of the artistic strategies of the interactive installation requires knowledge about the circumstances that have led to these forms of expression. Therefore, in this context, interactive installations will be examined for their closeness to the concepts and strategies of the 1960s. Characteristic similarities will be elaborated and programmatic contraries will become obvious. In the past, as now, the spectators have become actors: yet now they are absorbed by immersion into exactly that artificial world from which *Action Art* and *Happening* wanted to free them. While narration, storytelling apparatus and narrator were separated in the 1960s in order to be critically examined, the programme of the 1990s aimed at synthesising these three aspects.

CHALLENGED CINEMA

Anybody visiting the cinema, as Adorno and Horkheimer thoroughly warned in their *Dialektik der Aufklärung*, gets caught in the trap of the cultural industry. Even if one prepares with the best of intentions, one does not seem to have a chance of escaping the cinema seat without any damage. After each visit to the cinema they felt despite having been carefully vigilant 'more stupid and coarser', since being pressed into the cinema seat, isolated both from the outside world and their neighbours, lulled by the darkness and blinded by the white light, everyone follows the dictation of the projected narration.[1] Imagination and spontaneity are interrupted. Sound films are structured in such a way, Adorno and Horkheimer state, that adequate viewing demands promptness, observation and experience; yet the thinking activity of the viewer is more or less prohibited, if one does not want to miss the quickly passing facts.[2] The camera sets the beat for the spectator, who has been transformed into a perceptual apparatus. With the camera the speed is set and one has to adjust to it. The viewer has to be able to just catch up, must be able to just follow the events, in order to be under the spell of the racing images.

Criticism of film and cinema had marshalled its arguments long before the *Dialektik der Aufklärung*, and these arguments had been presented in a more diverse and much more precise manner than in the chapter on the culture industry. Here, however, the most important reservations on which the development of experimental (or underground) films since the 1950s have been based, are concentrated. This development was meant to interrupt and break the frictionless functioning of the 'machinery of fantasy'[3] and to break down the walls of the 'dream' and 'ideology factory'.[4] Rudolf Arnheim in his book, *Film as Art* (University of California Press, 1957) described the beginning of the cinema as a time in which the narrative structures succeeded, while the actual quality of the medium was reserved for experimental applications. However, it was not the goal of this campaign to paralyse and finally end the cinema as an institution, as Adorno and Horkheimer thought would be appropriate. Instead it held programmatically on to Béla Balász's belief who proclaimed in 1930 that the spirit of the film and the spirit of the movies are not identical.[5]

The spirit of the film is for Balász 'the spirit of progress', even when it is consumed by the culture industry.[6] Balász recalls the explosive force of the film and its techniques, which cannot be deactivated that easily. This force resolved the distance between a spectator and a closed-circuit art world. By switching the focus, the 'absolute and always' valid point of view was removed in favour of a relativity of meanings. As a consequence, he positions himself, with radical concretion, against 'murderous abstraction'. He argues that in the spirit of capitalism, this abstraction turns objects into products, values into prices, and human beings into impersonal workers.[7] If the technique of film is not used as a massive form of blending, but as an art form that allows a view on exactly these relations, then the film experience is able to help overcome the simple reproduction of the spirit and to introduce expanded reproduction as one that can emancipate the spirit.

Yet, for this – and this is the firm conviction of all those artists who, since the end of the 1950s dedicated themselves to experimental and underground film – the cinema needs to be expanded. The cinema of isolation has to become an 'expanded cinema', which leaves all limitations and restrictions behind, wakes up the spectator from his anaesthetisation and causes him to determine the requirements of his reproduction himself. Consequently, we can call 'expanded cinema' whatever exceeds the cinema customary film projections and which questions the conditions of the performance:

- Through varied damaging or expansion of the performing technologies;
- Through multiplying the projection apparatus and projection screens;
- Through linking the various media in order to scatter and overload the attention of the audience;
- Through destroying the inventory of the cinema;
- And most importantly, through including the so far passive spectator into the bewildering event, which only becomes clearer when he himself actively influences the designing of the screening and the course of the film.

EXPANDED CINEMA

The activists of 'expanded cinema' lit up the dark space with a big bang. Spectators, who came in September 1967 to see a screening entitled *EXIT* by the artist Peter Weibel in order to give themselves up to the beautiful gleam, found themselves unpleasantly surprised. During the performance Weibel let off fireworks, which were fired directly through the projection screen into the audience. Contemplation resolved into panic, rapt silence into furious screaming. The audience retreated and looked for what was already promised at the beginning: the exit.

When Weibel in 1969 directed a water-cannon towards the cinema audience, and when in another 'expanded cinema' action the artist Valie Export lashed the audience with a long whip, the much-maligned passivity of the spectators resolved into a new form of interaction: fights were carried out in the cinema in which also the artists were injured.[8]

If one could subscribe such actions to a pure effect of emotion, one has confirmed the calculated success of the activists, since it is only the effect that motivates immediate and unreflective activity. The intention of this effect is to get the spectator to reflect on his passivity. To achieve this, however, the spectators of the action need not always be scared away nor subjected to aggression.

In *The American Moon* (1960, one of the most original of what have become known as *Happenings* in art history), the artist Robert Whitman used sheets of plain white typing paper mounted in grid formation on translucent plastic sheets to create a theatre-in-the-round. These sheets acted as tunnel spaces for the divided audience. The tunnels were like the spokes of a wheel, where the hub of the wheel is a central, oval-shaped performance area. Each segment of the assembled audience witnessed a different aspect of the events taking place. These events included huge, view-blocking balls of paper rolled across the stage, film imagery broken into abstract facets by projection onto a screen consisting of gridded white typing paper, and finally, a man swinging upside down above an audience: now crowded at the centre, and thus brought into the climactic action. In this action, the projection light fell on the individual, rather unevenly mounted sheets of paper, or got lost in the translucent background – two dimensions turned into three. The exorbitant image of the film resolved at the margins and in the centre of the projection where the confused spectators were standing.

By destroying the projection screen, the film loses its actual scenery. Its true character becomes apparent – a pure gleam that falls into the void, as soon as no surface is offered it. In order to understand this gleam as a gleam, it is not the film that snaps in Whitman's action, but the surface onto which it is projected. Although it seems that parts of the film dissolve in the gaps between the sheets, neither the gleam nor the material are lost for the spectators. It is cut up, only to be organised anew. Even though the magical illusion of film and film recipient have evolved in the disappearance of a unifying screen, it is merged again in the perception of the spectators: they complete the projected image in order to follow it continuously and, on the other hand, to acquire it afresh. In this way, they participate in the production of this new film.

Transporting the images into the audience, or transporting the audience into the images – these are the two strategies which basically determined the actions of 'expanded cinema' in the 1960s. While Whitman resolves the images before his spectators' eyes, the audience of the 'expanded cinema' performance *Emergences of Continuous Forms* was placed, right from the beginning, between projector and screen in such a way that the spectators became part of the film plot through their shadows. Yet, this environment created by the Dutch artist Tjebbe van Tijen and the Australian Jeffrey Shaw, offered more: balloons hang from the ceiling, which could be blown up by the audience and could intersect the projector beam. The effect of this action was extremely ambiguous. The bodies moving in the space in-between interrupted the projection. On the screen, they appeared as black surfaces that could only partly inform reality, as in Plato's cave. As bodies, though, they had become themselves projection screens and through this, part of the film. Their movements permanently formed new contours – unplanned and in real-time. Consequently, this action resulted in an extremely lively play of pretence and phenomenon, of solidity and the temporary. The casting of the shadows revealed the film as a bodiless unreal play. The body of the film was the spectators themselves and the material with which they captured the light.

This piece showed clearly that the 'murderous abstraction', the transformation of the objects into appearances, which Béla Balàsz denounced as the motor of capitalism, had been exchanged by a radical concretion. Using the hands and reforming the materials again makes accessible what normally evaded access in the cinema. Balàsz's spirit of progress is additionally made visible by totally different means: he emphasised that the film and its technology had resolved the distance between a spectator and a self-contained world of art, and that by switching the focus, the absolute and always valid viewpoint had dissolved in favour of a relativity of meaning. In the actions of 'expanded cinema', this finally became concrete. The power of the projection and the narration had been broken. Only when the screen cracked and the spectators closed those gaps, and by so doing acquired parts of the screen: the distance was bridged. Only when each spectator, by himself, tried to capture his individual part of the film with the material he had acquired, did the eternally valid viewpoint resolve in favour of the numerous viewpoints of the activists of 'expanded cinema'.[9] In the resulting ecstatic union, film and life were merged and undifferentiated for the duration of the action. Though not, as Adorno and Horkheimer assumed of the cinema of the culture industry, by aligning oneself with the life of estrangement. The film consumers were supposed to change into film actors, contemplation was to be surpassed, and by itself the delivery should be accompanied and celebrated as the arrival of the new.

IMMERSIVE CINEMA

If you want to exceed all closed space, you will finally end up in the street. And if you here want to resolve art in life and life in art, you will get lost in endless space searching for the whole. 'Our action', says Tjebbe van Tijen 'all came from the spirit of the 60s. As everybody else, we were looking for strategies aiming for the *Gesamtkunstwerk*.' The most attractive prospect seemed to be the public streets and buildings, which now became the setting for the art actions. According to Allan Kaprow such a *Happening* is defined as

> an assemblage of events performed or perceived in more than one time and place. Its material
> environments may be constructed, taken over directly from what is available, or altered slightly; just as
> its activities may be invented or commonplace. A *Happening* unlike a stage play, may occur at a super-
> market, driving along the highway, under a pile of rags, and at a friend's kitchen table, either at once
> or sequentially.[10]

In such an event, the various art forms are integrated to such an extent that one cannot differentiate any more – and is not meant to be able to differentiate – whether one is confronted with dance, theatre, painting or film. Most importantly for the activists, the art forms are derived from one of the traditional artists' ghettos, that they break up their natural limitations and that they come together outside a prescribed space where they can meet with all those who also went beyond their borders.

In 1968, Valie Export and Peter Weibel expanded their cinema into the street. The so-called *Tapp- und Tastkino* (Touch and Grab Cinema) still corresponded to a classic iconoclasm: the visual senses which allowed the female body to freeze into a 'construct' of technical images, was contrasted in their cinema with the perception of the body through the tactile sense. This action involved strapping on a box that enclosed her naked breasts. The box had holes in the front so that the spectators could stick their hands through. Peter Weibel at the same time announced, 'This box is the cinema hall. The body is the screen. But the cinema is not for looking – it is for touching!'[11]

The cinema has shrunk somewhat – only two hands fit inside it. For seeing or rather feeling and touching the film, the viewer has to stretch his hands through the entrance of the cinema. At last, the curtain that formerly only rose for the eyes, now rose for both hands.

Even though *Action Art*, under the heading 'expanded cinema' had reached its limitations with the evaporation of the projection screen, it served as a starting point for the other possibility of capturing the borders symbolically. After the walls of the cinema had been turned inside out, in order to unify it with the world, now the outer skin of the world could be turned to the inside in order to form a new cinema space as an extensive cosmos.

Such a cosmos became the centre of the actions of Stan Vanderbeek. In 1963 he produced *The Movie-Drome*, an extensive cinema body, which recalled the visions of the total theatre movement. Influenced by the wide dome-constructions of R. Buckminster Fuller, Vanderbeek planned, at the end of the 1950s, a spherical theatre in which the audience was supposed to lay on their back and look up to watch multi-screen films in countless fluently moving images.

> My ideal theatre will consist of an endless space, without a limiting screen – no proscenium effect as in traditional theatre – but a totally immersive environment, which allows a sheer endless multitude of images to float above the spectator all around in the dome.[12]

In 1957, he started to produce multi-screen films for his Movie-Drome, though the building of the space did not start until 1963. In 1966, Vanderbeek's studio in Stony Point, New York, had a 9.5 metre high silo-roof-dome in which multi-screen films were shown to a small audience. This cinema strove to dematerialise the opaque, flat projection screen of the traditional cinema and exchange it for a three-dimensional volume, within which the cinematic fiction could be materialised in a new manner. The expansive characteristic of the 'expanded cinema' becomes immersive, though without giving up its energy and its claim for passing the limitations of cinema. Immersion crosses the cinema's borders to the inside, and makes the horizons of the world like the world of a film, a film, which can permanently be changed through new actions and which can be continually acquired.

SYNAESTHETIC CINEMA

At the end of the 1960s, the inflatable or steel-construction supported domes already belonged to the growing inventory of *Action Art*. In 1969, John Cage and Ronald Nameth built for their action *HPSCHD* (computer abbreviation for Harpsichord) a ring made out of polyethylene foil, which was nearly 100 metres in diameter. It was hung in the centre of the Assembly Hall of the University of Illinois, 30 metres above the heads of the audience, and was connected to the ground by polyethylene foil strips. From the inside, thousands of slides and hundreds of films were simultaneously pro-jected. The images formed a visual documentation of the development of human awareness of the cosmos. 'The visual material explored the macrocosm of space, while the music delved deep into the microcosmic world of the computer and its minute tonal separations.' (Ronald Nameth)[13]

In the action *Black Gate* that took place in Cologne in 1968, Aldo Tambelli and Otto Piene let the auditorium disappear under a huge, up-folded plastic tube, which was filled with helium. With their hands, the spectators formed a playing space, by pushing the material upward while moving beneath.

The idea of setting up numerous inflatable spheres, within which the visitors could interact with soft walls and floors, was so successful that at the start of the 1970s huge inflatables were intro-duced in leisure parks. This form of institutionalised regression with its closeness to the culture industry, seemed suspicious to a lot of artists, and consequently they continued their actions with-out helium and polyethylene and turned towards other material and temporary media on other scales.

The film has been freed from its 'window frame' – it has gained a third dimension. At the same time, it is no longer untouchable by the spectator. Instead, they participate in its construction. The spectator has become an author and even a part of the film, since projection screen and auditorium have merged. They have entered the filmic space; the cinema experience has become a full-body sensation. It becomes apparent that it was not only digital simulation and its possibilities for interac-tion that challenged artists to first question the relationship between art and spectator. Their analy-sis of the recipient's role exceeded the frame of contemplation and interpretation of the 1960s: the spectator has become a protagonist.

When, in 1970, the film critic and theoretician Gene Youngblood formulated the guidelines for the 'expanded cinema' formed by immersion, he explained that its potentiality to create new worlds outside reality as a true reality would not be exhausted for a long time. On the contrary, the breakthrough of the new cinema is still to come: 'The conclusion is that the art and technology of expanded cinema mean the beginning of creative living for all mankind and thus a solution to the so-called leisure problems.'[14]

Creative living starts, according to Youngblood, when the narration of traditional film is replaced by a cinematographic space of possibilities – when the activists present in the respective moment shape reality. '*Expanded Cinema* isn't a movie at all: life-like, it's a process of becoming.'[15]

This merges art and life together, because those who get their hands on cinema have also a grip on their own life – and the other way round. Yet, this fatefulness proclaimed by Youngblood is as technically as biologically loaded.

What he pushes within his 'expanded cinema' is no longer simply the expanded reproduction of society, but the technically supported evolutionary expansion of human awareness to an exten-sive cosmic awareness, that can keep itself present and transparent on all levels. 'When we say expanded cinema we actually mean expanded consciousness'.[16]

Because of this, Youngblood speaks of a 'synaesthetic cinema', a cinema, which includes all forms of art, all phenomena of the world and all ways of living and thinking of the human being, and makes them available. Everything that diverges in modernity through permanent differentiation is here captured again by the 'one unifying force in all of synaesthetic cinema.'[17]

Through joining the computer with the human being, who is nevertheless interpreted by Youngblood as a 'human-bio-computer', the exterior world can be abolished. In the medial protection zone, the walls will only mirror the image of the human, who has withdrawn himself. Youngblood is fascinated by the 30 metre high air-inflated dome that was set up on the occasion of Expo 70 within the Pepsi-Cola pavilion, on a base of more than 1,000 square metres. This dome was completely covered in the inside as well as on the outside with mirroring PVC, in order to capture the totality and unity of macrocosm and microcosm.

> An astonishing phenomenon occurs inside this boundless space that is but one of the many
> revelations to come in the Cybernetic Age: one is able to view actual holographic images of oneself
> floating in three-dimensional space in real-time as one moves about the environment …
> Interfaced with perpetual fog banks and krypton laser rainbow light showers at the World
> Exposition. The Mirror indeed 'exposed' a world of expanded cinema in its widest and most
> profound significance.[18]

The reflecting sphere once again makes us aware of the principle of expansion through immersion. Only through total exclusion from the outside world and feedback in the inside world (by depicting the images on itself) can the fiction of an endless space without horizons emerge. This is a space – and this is an important ingredient of the fiction – which can be completely controlled.

DIGITAL CINEMA

The action space in the cybernetic age is called 'cyberspace'. Computer-supported systems offer all those artists convinced of the 1960s' pathos of enlightenment and liberation, the possibility of emancipating the spectator's physicality and sensuality from social obligations. The practised removal of the separation between the world of real life and the projected film world; the integration of the spectator's body; the stimulation to active participation, in order to manipulate the mechanisms of projection and the automatisms of narration, can be rediscovered in the interactive installations of the 1990s. These works transported the transformation of the variables emphasised by the activists – time, projection, space and spectator – into the digital space.

Everything that was dismantled in the 1960s into its individual components in order to be critically examined can now be put together again. In these art spaces, the timeframe has finally become a changeable determinant. Multiple projection technique undergoes another development: the computer has now been inserted between projector and projection, and takes away the control over the timeframe from the film medium. The space surrounding the spectator converts from space for participating, to space for interacting, while the spectator is becoming a constructor, a performer and an observer of the work. In digital projection spaces the objective world is divided into information packages (the repertory) and is mirrored in a virtual world of illusion. The author has programmatically withdrawn. Such art pieces attempt to aim at a spatial unity between audience, intimate experience and the environment. In order to make this new experience of reality perfect, the unity is not designed to be static but floating. In real space experiences, as well as knowledge are collected linearly, since we are subjected to the conditions of our three-dimensional existence; though linearity stands first of all in contrast to the multimedia possibilities of the works, and is not explicitly given. Linearity has to be established and structured by the visitor himself, while either acting or observing.

Multimedia artists have put this repertory, and through this the information for designing the actions, at the spectator's disposal. Beyond that, the exceptional aspect of this kind of installation is located in directing the interaction. The spectator intervenes with the action via the interface. He not only directs the camera, but directs all medial forms of expression: moving and still images, text and sound. If the active viewer takes hold of the carriers of information, he automatically becomes part of the work by interacting and exploring, reconstructing and finally consuming the artwork in front of other spectators. Each decision means changing the general condition, means collecting knowledge, experiences and requirements for this perception of the piece. As performer, the viewer collects knowledge by using the interface, while simultaneously mediating knowledge to the observing spectator.

So has the body become the only real limitation to an 'expanded cinema' for the digital age? Initially 'if only' was exclaimed, in order to protest, by means of the film, against the dream factory's consumption of subject. This exclamation has transformed into a defiance against the self. The wish to liberate the body seems to have been replaced by the wish to liberate oneself from the body. What is needed now is a new expansion of the cinema. A cinema that frees itself from the suction of immersion and that goes beyond all the limitations of simulation.

NOTES

1. Adorno, Theodor W. *Minima Moralia*. Frankfurt am Main, 1976, p. 26.
2. Adorno, Theodor W. and Horkheimer, Max. *Dialektik der Aufklärung. Philosophische Fragmente*. Frankfurt am Main, 1978, p. 134 ff.
3. Fueloep-Mueller, René. *Phantasiemaschine*. Leipzig, 1931.
4. Erenburg, Ilja: *Die Traumfabrik*. Berlin, 1931. Kreimeier, Klaus. 'Das Kino als Ideologiefabrik'. *Kinemathek*, no. 45, November, 1971.
5. Balász, Béla. *Der Geist des Films*. Halle, 1930, p. 215.
6. Ibid., p. 217.
7. Ibid., p. 216.
8. Hein, Birgit. *Film im Untergrund. Von seinen Anfängen bis zum unabhängigen Kino*. Frankfurt am Main/Berlin/Vienna, 1971, p. 158.
9. This step becomes explicitly clear in Paul Lenis' film, *Happening Puzzle* (1929). Here the audience is supposed to put together the distributed fragments of a film plot themselves to form a new

story. The images of the film are carried into the audience and the audience into the images.

10. Kaprow, Allan. *Some Recent Happenings*. New York, 1966, p. 4.

11. Museum für moderne Kunst, Stiftung Ludwig Wien, ed. *Split Reality: Valie Export*. New York/Vienna, 1998, p. 10.

12. Davis, Douglas. *Vom Experiment zur Idee. Die Kunst des 20. Jahrhunderts im Zeichen von Wissenschaft und Technologie. Analysen, Dokumente, Zukunftsperspektiven*. Cologne, 1975, p. 65.

13. Youngblood, Gene. *Expanded Cinema*. New York: Dutton, 1970, p. 378.

14. Ibid., p. 42 ff.

15. Ibid., p. 41.

16. Ibid.

17. Ibid., p. 86.

18. Ibid., p. 416.

Spatial Computerisation and Film Language[*]

Lev Manovich

INTRODUCTION

How does computerisation affect our very concept of moving images? Does it offer new possibilities for film language? Does it lead to the development of totally new forms of cinema? In this article I explore three (among the many possible) new directions for film language – or, more generally, the language of moving images – opened up by computerisation. The first concerns the temporal structure of film language, the second deals with the spatial organisation of a frame, and the third addresses the amount of information presented in 3D space contained by this frame. In short, the first direction concerns time, the second – surface, and the third – space.

My examples will come from different areas where computer-based moving images are used: digital films, net films, self-contained hypermedia, and web sites. Combatting the usual tendency of new media discussions to always focus on the very latest works and not remember its own past, I selected on purpose as my examples works which were completed throughout the 1990s and which, in my view, have already became recognised as the 'classics' of new media. They include a website by Olia Lialina (*My boyfriend came back from the war!*, 1996), a CD-ROM by Jean-Louis Boissier (*Flora petrinsularis*, 1993) and digital films by Christian Boustani (*Brugge*, 1995; *A Viagem*, 1998).

NEW TEMPORALITY: THE LOOP AS A NARRATIVE ENGINE

All nineteenth-century pro-cinematic devices, up to Edison's Kinetoscope, were based on short loops. As 'the seventh art' began to mature, it banished the loop to the low art realms of the instructional film, the pornographic peep show and the animated cartoon. In contrast, narrative cinema has avoided repetitions; as do modern western fictional forms in general, it put forward a notion of human existence as a linear progression through numerous unique events.

Cinema's birth from a loop form was re-enacted at least once during its history. In one of the sequences of *A Man with a Movie Camera* (1929), Dziga Vertov shows us a cameraman standing in the back of a moving automobile. He cranks the handle of his camera as he is being carried forward by an automobile. A loop, a repetition, created by the circular movement of the handle, gives birth to a progression of events – a very basic narrative which is also quintessentially modern: a

---

[*] This text is adapted from my book, *The Language of New Media*. Cambridge: MIT Press, 2001.

camera moving through space recording whatever is in its way. In what seems to be a reference to cinema's primal scene, these shots are intercut with the shots of a moving train. Vertov even re-stages the terror which the Lumières' original film supposedly provoked in its audience; he positions his camera right along the train track so the train runs over our point of view a number of times, crushing us again and again.

The early digital movies of the 1990s shared the same limitations of storage, as did nineteenth century pro-cinematic devices. This is probably why the loop playback function was built into the original QuickTime interface, thus giving it the same weight as the VCR-style 'play forward' function. So, in contrast to films and videotapes, QuickTime movies were *supposed* to be played forward, backward or looped. Computer games also heavily relied on loops. Since it was not possible to animate every character in real-time, the designers stored short loops of a character's motion – for instance, an enemy soldier or a monster walking back and forth, which would be recalled at appropriate times in the game. Internet pornography also relied heavily on loops. Many sites featured numerous 'channels' which were supposed to stream either feature-length films or 'live feeds'; in reality they would usually play short loops (a minute or so) over and over again. Sometimes a few films would be cut into a number of short loops, which would become the content of 100, 500 or 1,000 channels.

The history of new media tells us that the hardware limitations never go away: they disappear in one area only to come back in another. As the CPU (Central Processing Unit) speed increased and larger storage media such as CD-ROM and DVD became available, the use of loops in stand-alone hypermedia declined. However, online virtual worlds such as *Active Worlds* came to use loops extensively, as they provide a cheap (in terms of bandwidth and computation) way of adding some signs of 'life' to their geometric-looking environments.

Can the loop become a new narrative form appropriate for the computer age? It is relevant to recall that the loop gave birth not only to cinema, but also to computer programming. Programming involves altering the linear flow of data through control structures, such as 'if/then' and 'repeat/while'; the loop is the most elementary of these control structures. Most computer programmes are based on repetitions of a set number of steps; this repetition is controlled by the main loop of the programme. So if we strip the computer from its usual interface and follow the execution of a typical computer programme, the computer will reveal itself to be just another version of Ford's factory, with a loop as its conveyor belt.

As the practice of computer programming illustrates, the loop and the sequential progressions do not have to be regarded as being mutually exclusive. A computer programme progresses from start to end by executing a series of loops. Another illustration of how these two temporal forms can work together is *Möbius House* by the Dutch team UN Studio/Van Berkel & Bos.[1] In this house a number of functionally different areas are arranged one after another in the form of a Möbius strip, thus forming a loop. As the narrative of the day progresses from one activity to the next, the inhabitants move from area to area.

Traditional cell animation similarly combines a narrative and a loop. In order to save labour, animators arrange many actions, such as movements of characters' legs, eyes and arms, into short loops and repeat them over and over. Thus, in a typical twentieth century cartoon a large proportion of the motion involves loops. This principle is taken to the extreme in Zbignev Rybczynski's film *Tango* (1982). Subjecting live action footage to the logic of animation, Rybczynski arranges the trajectory of every character through space as a loop. These loops are further composited together resulting in a complex and intricate time-based structure. At the same time, the overall 'shape' of this structure is governed by a number of narratives. The film begins in an empty room; next, the loop of a character's trajectory through this room is added, and so on, one at a time. The end of the film mirrors its beginning: the loops are 'deleted' in a reverse order, also one by one. This metaphor for a progression of a human life (we are born alone, gradually form relations with other humans, and eventually die alone) is also supported by another narrative: the first character to appear in the room is a young boy, the last one is an old woman.

The concept of a loop as an 'engine', which sets the narrative in motion, became a foundation of an interactive TV programme, *Akvaario* (aquarium), created by a number of graduate students at Media Lab at Helsinki's University of Art and Design (1999).[2] In contrast to many new media objects, which combine the conventions of cinema, print and HCI (Human-Computer Interface), *Akvaario* aims to preserve the continuous flow of traditional cinema, while adding interactivity to it. Along with an earlier game *Johnny Mnemonic* (Sony, 1995), as well as the pioneering interactive laserdisc computer installations by Grahame Weinbren in the 1980s, this project is a rare example of a new media narrative which does not rely on the oscillation between non-interactive and interactive segments.

Using the already familiar convention of such games such as *Tamagotchi* (1996), the programme asks TV viewers to 'take charge' of a fictional human character.[3] Most shots which we see show this character, engaged in different activities in his apartment: eating dinner, reading a book, staring into space. The shots replace each other following standard conventions of film and TV editing. The result is something, which looks at first like a conventional, although very long, movie. In fact the shots are selected in real-time by a computer programme from a database of a few hundred different shots.

By choosing one of the four buttons, which are always present on the bottom of the screen, the viewers control a character's motivation. When a button is pressed, a computer programme selects a sequence of particular shots to follow the shot, which plays currently. Because of visual, spatial and referential discontinuity between shots typical of standard editing, the result is something which the viewer interprets as a conventional narrative. A film or television viewer does not expect that any two shots, which follow one another, have to display the same space or subsequent moments of time. Therefore, in *Akvaario* a computer programme can 'weave' an endless narrative by choosing from a database of different shots. What gives the resulting narrative a sufficient continuity is that almost all shots show the same character.

Akvaario is one of the first examples of what I would like to call a 'database narrative'. It is, in other words, a narrative, which fully utilises many features of a database's organisation of data. It relies on our abilities to classify database records according to different dimensions, to sort through records, to quickly retrieve any record, as well as to 'stream' a number of different records continuously one after another.

In *Akvaario*, the loop becomes the way to bridge between linear narrative and interactive control. When the programme begins, a few shots keep following each other in a loop. After users choose a character's motivation by pressing a button, this loop becomes a narrative. Shots stop repeating and a sequence of new shots is displayed. If no button is pressed again, the narrative turns back into a loop, i.e. a few shots start repeating over and over. In *Akvaario*, a narrative is born from a loop and it returns to a loop. The historical birth of modern fictional cinema out of the loop returns as a condition of cinema's rebirth as an interactive form. Rather than being an archaic leftover, a reject from cinema's evolution, the use of loop in *Akvaario* suggests a new temporal aesthetic for computer-based cinema.

Jean-Louis Boissier's *Flora petrinsularis* (1993) realises some of the possibilities contained in the loop form in a quite different way.[4] This CD-ROM is based on Rousseau's *Confessions*. It opens with a white screen, containing a numbered list. Clicking on each item leads us to a screen containing two windows, positioned side by side. Both windows show the same video loop made from a few different shots. The two loops are offset from each other in time. Thus, the images appearing in the left window reappear in a moment on the right and vice versa, as though an invisible wave is running through the screen. This wave soon becomes literally materialised: when we click inside the windows we are taken to a new screen, which also contains two windows, each showing a loop of a rhythmically vibrating water surface. The loops of water surfaces can be thought of as two sine waves offset in phase. This structure, then, functions as a 'meta-text' of a structure in the first screen. In other words, the loops of water surface act as a diagram of the loop structure which controls the correlation between shots in the first screen, similar to the ways in which Marey and the Gibsons diagrammed human motion in their film studies at the beginning of the twentieth century.

As each mouse click reveals another loop, the viewer becomes an editor, but not in a traditional sense. Rather than constructing a singular narrative sequence and discarding material which is not

1 *Flora petrinsularis,* Jean-Louis Boissier, 1993.

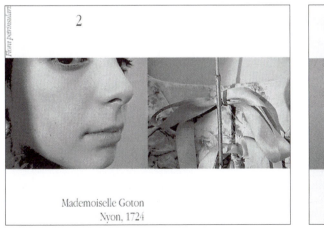

Mademoiselle Goton
Nyon, 1724

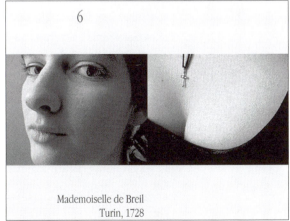

Mademoiselle de Breil
Turin, 1728

2 *Flora petrinsularis*, Jean-Louis Boissier, 1993.

Reine des prés
Couvet, 21 juillet 1993

used, here the viewer brings to the forefront, one by one, numerous layers of looped actions which seem to be taking place all at once; a multitude of separate, but co-existing temporalities. The viewer is not cutting but re-shuffling. In a reversal of Vertov's sequence where a loop generated a narrative, the viewer's attempt to create a story in *Flora petrinsularis* leads to a loop.

It is useful to analyse the loop structure of *Flora petrinsularis* using montage theory. From this perspective, the repetition of images in two adjoining windows can be interpreted as an example of what Eisenstein called rhythmical montage. At the same time, Boissier takes montage apart, so to speak. The shots which in traditional temporal montage would follow each other in time, here appear next to each other in space. In addition, rather than being 'hard-wired' by an editor in only one possible structure, here the shots can appear in different combinations, since they are activated by a user moving a mouse across the windows.

At the same time, it is possible to find more traditional temporal montage in this work as well – for instance, the move from the first screen, which shows a close-up of a woman, to a second screen, which shows water surfaces and then back to the first screen. This move can be interpreted as traditional parallel editing. In cinema, parallel editing involves alternating between two subjects. For instance, a chase sequence may go back and forth between the images of two cars, one pursuing another. However, in our case the water images are always present 'underneath' the first set of images. So the logic here is again one of co-existence rather than that of replacement, so typical of cinema (see my discussion of spatial montage below).

The loop, which structures *Flora petrinsularis* on a number of levels, becomes a metaphor for human desire, which can never achieve resolution. It can also be read as a comment on cinematic realism. What are the minimal conditions necessary to create the impression of reality? As Boissier demonstrates, in the case of a field of grass, or a close-up of a plant or a stream, just a few looped frames become sufficient to produce the illusion of life and of linear time.

Steven Neale describes how early film demonstrated its authenticity by representing moving nature:

> What was lacking [in photographs] was the wind, the very index of real, natural movement. Hence the obsessive contemporary fascination, not just with movement, not just with scale, but also with waves and sea spray, with smoke and spray.[5]

What for early cinema was its biggest pride and achievement – a faithful documentation of nature's movement – becomes for Boissier a subject of ironic and melancholic simulation. As the few frames are looped over and over, we see blades of grass shifting slightly back and forth, rhythmically responding to the blow of non-existent wind, which is almost approximated by the noise of a computer reading data from a CD-ROM.

Something else is being simulated here as well, perhaps unintentionally. As you watch the CD-ROM, the computer periodically staggers, unable to maintain a consistent data rate. As a result, the images on the screen move in uneven bursts, slowing and speeding up with human-like irregularity. It is as though they are brought to life not by a digital machine but by a human operator, cranking the handle of the Zoetrope a century and a half ago …

SPATIAL MONTAGE AND MACROCINEMA

Along with taking on a loop, *Flora petrinsularis* can also be seen as a step towards what I will call a spatial montage. Instead of a traditional singular frame of cinema, Boissier uses two images at once, positioned side by side. This can be thought of as the simplest case of a spatial montage. In general, spatial montage would involve a number of images, potentially of different sizes and proportions, appearing on the screen at the same time. This by itself, of course, does not result in montage; it is up to the film-maker to construct a logic which drives which images appear together, when they appear and what kind of relationships they enter into with each other.

Spatial montage represents an alternative to traditional cinematic temporal montage, replacing its traditional sequential mode with a spatial one. Ford's assembly line relied on the separation of the production process into a set of repetitive, sequential and simple activities. The same principle made computer programming possible: a computer programme breaks a task into a series of elemental operations to be executed one at a time. Cinema followed this logic of industrial production as well. It replaced all other modes of narration with a sequential narrative; an assembly line of shots which appear on the screen one at a time. A sequential narrative turned out to be particularly incompatible with a spatial narrative, which played a prominent role in European visual culture for centuries. From Giotto's fresco cycle at the Capella degli Scrovegni in Padua to Courbet's *A Burial at Ornans*, artists presented a multitude of separate events within a single space (be it the fictional space of a painting or the physical space of architecture), which can be taken in by the viewer all at once. In the case of Giotto's fresco cycle and many other fresco and icon cycles, each narrative event is framed separately, but all of them can be viewed together at a single glance. In other cases, different events are represented as taking place within a single pictorial space. Sometimes, events, which formed one narrative, but were separated by time, were depicted within a single painting. More often, the painting's subject became an excuse to show a number of separate 'micro-narratives' (for instance, works by Hiëronymous Bosch and Pieter Bruegel). In contrast to cinema's sequential narrative, in spatial narrative all the 'shots' were accessible to a viewer at once. Like nineteenth-century animation, spatial narrative did not disappear completely in the twentieth century; but just like animation, it came to be delegated to a minor form of western culture – the comics.

It is not accidental that the marginalisation of spatial narrative and the privileging of sequential mode of narration coincided with the rise of a historical paradigm in human sciences. Cultural geographer Edward Soja has argued that the rise of history in the second half of the nineteenth century coincided with the decline in spatial imagination and the spatial mode of social analysis.[6] According to Soja, it was only in the last decades of the twentieth century that this mode made a powerful comeback, as exemplified by the growing importance of such concepts as 'geopolitics' and 'globalisation', as well as by the key role analysis of space played in theories of post-modernism. Indeed, although some of the best thinkers of the twentieth century such as Freud, Panofsky and Foucault were able to combine historical and spatial modes of analysis in their theories, they probably represent an exception rather than the norm. The same holds true for film theory, which, from Eisenstein in the 1920s to Deleuze in the 1980s, focused on temporal rather than spatial structures.

Twentieth-century film practice has elaborated complex techniques of montage with different images replacing each other in time; but the possibility of what can be called 'spatial montage' between simultaneously co-existing images was not explored as systematically. (Thus cinema was given a historical imagination at the expense of a spatial one.) The notable exceptions include the use of split-screen by Abel Gance in *Napoléon* in the 1920s and also by the American experimental film-maker Stan Vanderbeek in the 1960s; also some other works, or rather, events, of the 1960s 'Expanded Cinema' movement, and, last but not least, the legendary multi-image multimedia presentation shown in the Czech Pavilion at the 1967 World Expo. Emil Radok's *Diaolyektan* consisted of 112 separate cubes. One hundred and sixty different images could be projected onto each cube. Radok was able to 'direct' each cube separately. To the best of my knowledge, since this project, nobody has tried again to create a spatial montage of this complexity in any technology.

Traditional film and video technology was designed to completely fill a screen with a single image; thus to explore spatial montage a film-maker had to work 'against' the technology. This in part explains why so few tried to do this. But when, in the 1970s, the screen became a bit-mapped computer display, with individual pixels corresponding to memory locations, which can be dynamically updated by a computer programme: the one image/one screen logic was broken. Since the Xerox Park Alto workstation, GUIs (Graphical User Interfaces) used multiple windows. It would be logical to expect that cultural forms based on moving images will eventually adopt similar conventions. In the 1990s some computer games such as *Golden Eye* (Nintendo/Rare, 1997) already used multiple windows to present the same action simultaneously from different viewpoints. We may expect that computer-based cinema will eventually have to follow the same direction – especially when the limitations of communication bandwidth disappear, while the resolution of displays significantly increases. I believe that the next generation of cinema – what I will call macrocinema – will add multiple windows to its language. When this happens, the tradition of spatial narrative, which twentieth century cinema suppressed, will re-emerge once again.

Looking back at visual culture and art of the previous centuries gives rise to many ideas of how spatial narrative can be further developed in a computer; but what about spatial montage? In other words, what will happen if we combine two different cultural traditions: information-dense visual

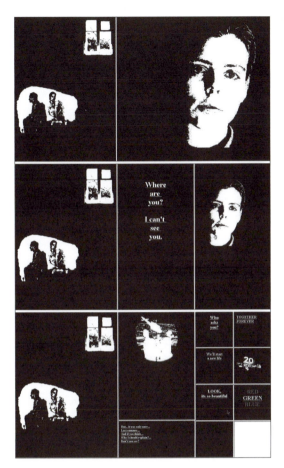

3 *My boyfriend came back from the war!*, Olia Lialina, 1996.

narratives of the Renaissance and baroque painters with the 'attention-demanding' shot juxtapositions of twentieth century film directors? *My boyfriend came back from the war!* (1996), a web-based work by the Moscow artist Olia Lialina can be read as an exploration of this direction.[7] Using the capability of HTML (hypertext mark-up language) to create frames within frames, Lialina leads us through a narrative, which begins with a single screen. This screen becomes progressively divided into more and more frames as we follow different links. Throughout, an image of a human couple and of a constantly blinking window remain on the left part of the screen. These two images enter into new combinations with texts and images on the right side, which keep changing as the user interacts with the work. As the narrative activates different parts of the screen, montage in time gives way to montage in space. Put differently, we can say that montage acquires a new spatial dimension. In addition to the montage dimensions already explored by cinema (differences in images' content, composition, movement) we now have a new dimension: the position of the images in space in relation to each other. In addition, as images do not replace each other (as in cinema), but remain on the screen throughout the movie, each new image is juxtaposed, not just with one image that preceded it, but also with all the other images present on the screen.

The logic of replacement, characteristic of cinema, gives way to the logic of addition and co-existence. Time becomes spatialised, distributed over the surface of the screen. In spatial montage, nothing is potentially forgotten, nothing is erased. Just as we use computers to accumulate endless texts, messages, notes and data, and just as a person, going through life, accumulates more and more memories, with the past slowly acquiring more weight than the future, so spatial montage can accumulate events and images as it progresses through its narrative. In contrast to the cinema's screen, which primarily functioned as a record of perception, the computer screen functions as a record of memory.

As I already noted, spatial montage can also be seen as an aesthetic appropriate for the user experience of multi-tasking and the multiple windows of a GUI. In the text of his lecture *Of other spaces* Michel Foucault wrote:

> We are now in the epoch of simultaneity: we are in the epoch of juxtaposition, the epoch of near and far, of the side-by-side, of the dispersed (…) our experience of the world is less of a long life developing through time than that of a network that connects points and intersects with its own skein …[8]

Writing this in the early 1970s, Foucault appears to prefigure not only the network society, exemplified by the internet ('a network which connects points') but also by GUIs ('epoch of simultaneity … of the side-by-side'). GUIs allow the users to run a number of software applications at the same time and use the convention of multiple overlapping windows to present both data and controls. The construct of the desktop which presents the user with multiple icons which are all simultaneously and continuously 'active' (since they can all be clicked at any time) follows the same logic of 'simultaneity' and of 'side-by-side'. On the level of computer programming, this logic corresponds to object-oriented programming. Instead of a single programme, which, like Ford's assembly line, is executed, one statement at a time, in an object-oriented paradigm, a number of objects send messages to each other. These objects are all active simultaneously. Object-oriented paradigms and multiple windows of GUI work together; the object-oriented approach was in fact used to programme the original Macintosh GUI, which substituted the 'one command at a time' logic of DOS with the logic of simultaneity of multiple windows and icons.

The spatial montage of *My boyfriend came back from the war!* follows this logic of simultaneity of modern GUIs. The multiple and simultaneously active icons and windows of GUI become the multiple and simultaneously active frames and hyperlinks of this web artwork. Just as the GUI user can click on any icon at any time, changing the overall 'state' of the computer environment, the user of Lialina's site can activate different hyperlinks which are all simultaneously present. Each action either changes the contents of a single frame or creates a new frame or frames. In either case, the 'state' of the screen as a whole is affected. The result is a new cinema where the synchronic dimension is no longer privileged to the diachronic dimension, space is no longer privileged to time, the simultaneity is no longer privileged to sequence, montage within a shot is no longer privileged to montage in time.

CINEMA AS AN INFORMATION SPACE

What is cinema, seen in the context of computer technologies and their accompanying concepts such as the Human-Computer-Interface (HCI)? If HCI is an interface to computer data, and a book is an interface to text, cinema can be thought of as an interface to events taking place in 3D space. Just as painting before it, cinema presented us with familiar images of visible reality – interiors, landscapes and human characters – arranged within a rectangular frame. The aesthetics of these arrangements range from extreme scarcity to extreme density. The examples of the former are paintings by Morandi and *Shots in Late Spring* (Yasujiro Ozu, 1949); the examples of the latter are paintings by Bosch and Bruegel (and much of Northern Renaissance painting in general), and many shots in *A Man with a Movie Camera*.[9] It would be only a small leap to relate this density of 'pictorial displays' to the density of contemporary information displays such as web portals which may contain a few dozen hyperlinked elements; or the interfaces of popular software packages which similarly present the user with dozens of commands at once. Can contemporary information designers learn from the information displays of the past – particularly films, paintings and other visual forms, which follow the aesthetics of density?

In making such a connection I rely on the work of art historian Svetlana Alpers, who claimed that in contrast to Italian Renaissance painting primarily concerned with narration, Dutch painting of the seventeenth century is focused on description.[10] While the Italians subordinated details to the narrative action, creating a clear hierarchy of the viewer's attention, in Dutch paintings particular details and, consequently, the viewer's attention, are more evenly distributed throughout the whole image. While functioning as a window into an illusionary space, the Dutch painting is also a loving catalogue of numerous objects, different material surfaces and light effects painted in minute detail (works by Vermeer, for instance). The dense surfaces of these paintings can be easily related to contemporary interfaces; in addition, they can also be related to the future aesthetics of the moving image, at least when the digital displays move much beyond the resolution of analogue television and film.

The trilogy of computer films by Paris-based film-maker Christian Boustani develops such aesthetics of density. Taking his inspiration from Renaissance Dutch painting as well as from classical Japanese art, Boustani uses digital compositing to achieve unprecedented (for film) information density. While this density was typical of the old art he draws on, it was never before achieved in cinema. In *Brugge* (1995) Boustani recreates the images typical of winter landscape scenes in Dutch seventeenth-century painting. His next film *A Viagem* (The Voyage, 1998) achieves even higher information density; some shots of the film use as many as 1,600 separate layers.

This new cinematic aesthetics of density seems to be highly appropriate for our age. If, from a city street to a web page, we are surrounded by highly dense information surfaces, it is appropriate to expect from cinema a similar logic. (In the same fashion, we may think of spatial montage as reflecting another contemporary daily experience: working with a number of different applications at once on a computer. If we are now used to distribute and rapidly switch our attention from one programme to another, from one set of windows and commands to another set, we may find multiple streams of audiovisual information presented simultaneously more satisfying than the single stream of traditional cinema.)

It is appropriate that some of the densest shots of *A Viagem* recreate a Renaissance marketplace. This symbol of emerging capitalism was probably responsible for the new density of Renaissance painting (think, for instance, of Dutch still-lives which function as a kind of store display window aiming to overwhelm the viewer and seduce her into making a purchase). In the same way, in the 1990s the commercialisation of the internet was responsible for the new density of web pages. By the end of the decade all home pages of big companies and internet portals became indexes containing dozens of entries in small type. If every small area of the screen can potentially contain a lucrative advert or a link to a page with one, this leaves no place for the aesthetics of emptiness and minimalism. Thus, it is not surprising that the commercialised web joined the same aesthetics of information density and competing signs and images, which characterise visual culture in a capitalist society in general.

If Lialina's spatial montage relies on HTML frames and actions of the user to activate images appearing in these frames, Boustani's spatial montage is more purely cinematic and painterly. He combines mobility of camera and movement of objects characteristic of cinema with the 'hyper-realism' of old Dutch painting which presented everything 'in focus'. In analogue cinema, the inevitable 'depth of field' artefact acted as a limit to the information density of an image. The achievement of Boustani is to create images where every detail is in focus and yet the overall image is easily readable. This could only be done through digital compositing. By reducing visible reality to numbers the computer makes it possible for us to literally see in a new way. If, according to Benjamin, early twentieth-century cinema used close-up 'to bring things "closer" spatially and humanly', 'to get hold of an object at very close range', and, as a result, destroyed their 'aura', digital composites of Boustani can be said to bring objects close to a viewer without 'extracting' them from their places in the world. (Of course an opposite interpretation is also possible: we can say that Boustani's digital eye is super-human.)

Scrutinising the prototypical perceptual spaces of modernity – the factory, the movie theatre and the shopping arcade – Walter Benjamin insisted on the contiguity between the perceptual experiences in the workplace and outside of it:

> Whereas Poe's passers-by cast glances in all directions which still appeared to be aimless, today's pedestrians are obliged to do so in order to keep abreast of traffic signals. Thus technology has subjected the human sensorium to a complex kind of training. There came a day when a new and urgent need for stimuli was met by the film. In a film, perception in the form of shocks was established as a formal principle. That which determines the rhythm of production on a conveyer belt is the basis of the rhythm of reception in the film.[11]

For Benjamin, the modern regime of perceptual labour, where the eye is constantly asked to process stimuli, equally manifests itself in work and leisure. The eye is trained to keep pace with the rhythm of industrial production at the factory and to navigate through the complex visual semiosphere beyond the factory gates. It is appropriate to expect that the computer age will follow the same logic, presenting the users with similarly structured perceptual experiences at work and at home, on a computer screen and outside of it. Indeed, as I already noted, we now use the same interfaces for work and for leisure, the condition exemplified most dramatically by web browsers. Another example is the use of the same interfaces in flight and military simulators, in computer games modelled after these simulators, and in the actual controls of planes and other vehicles (recall the popular perception of Gulf War as 'video game war'). But if Benjamin appears to regret that the subjects of an industrial age lost the pre-modern freedom of perception, now regimented by the factory, modern city and film, we may instead think of the information density of our own work spaces as a new aesthetic challenge – something to explore rather than to condemn.

Indeed, while computerisation opens up many new possibilities for film language, the three directions on which I focused here share the common 'heritage': they all borrow from everyday use of a computer. Put differently, I have tried to speculate on how people's everyday, 'non-aesthetic' experience with computers can be extended into the realm of digital aesthetics. How can we bring the information density of web portals into a cinematic space ('Cinema as an Information Space')? How can our experience of multitasking be used to redefine such basic mechanisms of cinema as montage ('Spatial Montage and Macrocinema')? How can the loop function – standard in all multimedia players – become the organising principle of cinematic narrative ('The Loop as a Narrative Engine')?

Similarly, new media artists, including digital film-makers, should systematically explore the aesthetic possibilities of all aspects of a user's experience with a computer, this key experience of modern life: the dynamic windows of GUI, search engines, databases, navigable spaces, spreadsheets, online chats, e-mail, and so on. Rather than resting on its already significant achievements, cinema should address new perceptual and cognitive experiences, offered by computers, head on. Only this will ensure that it will remain a vital cultural form in the twenty-first century, rather than a leftover monument from the twentieth.

NOTES

1. Riley, Terence. *The Un-private House*. New York: Museum of Modern Art, 1999.

2. Pellinen, Teijo, and others. *Akvaario*. http://www.akvaario.net/ (11 Jan. 2001).

3. My analysis is based on a project prototype, which I saw in October 1999. The completed project is projected to have a male and a female character.

4. *Flora petrinsularis* (1993) is included in the compilation CD-ROM *artintact 1*. Karlsruhe, Germany: ZKM/Centre for Art and Media, 1994.

5. Neale, Steven. *Cinema and Technology*. Bloomington: Indiana University Press, 1985, p. 52.

6. Soja, Edward. Keynote lecture at the 'History and Space' conference, University of Turku, Turku, Finland, 2 Oct. 1999.

7. Olia Lialina. *My boyfriend came back from the war!* http://www.teleportacia.org/war (11 Jan. 2001).

8. Foucault, Michel. *Dits et Ecrits. Sélections, vol. 1*. New York: New Press, 1997.

9. Anne Hollander's *Moving Pictures* presents parallel compositional and scenographic strategies in painting and cinema, and it can be a useful source for further thinking about both as precursors to contemporary information design. See Hollander, Anne. *Moving Pictures*. Reprint edition. Cambridge: Harvard University Press, 1991. Another useful study which also systematically compares compositional and scenographic strategies of the two media is Aumont, Jacques. *The Image*. Claire Pajackowska, trans. London: British Film Institute, 1997.

10. Alpers, Svetlana. *The Art of Describing: Dutch Art in the Seventeenth Century*. Chicago: University of Chicago Press, 1983.

11. Benjamin, Walter. 'On Some Motives in Baudelaire' in Hannah Arendt, ed. *Illuminations*. New York: Schochen Books, 1969, p. 175.

net.drama://myth/mimesis/mind_mapping/

Andrea Zapp

'Interactive narration' at first sight appears to be a very interesting contradiction. Interaction codifies a post-modern aesthetic slogan, which describes a technical condition as 'dynamic hands-on-experience'. Narration seems somehow to be the very opposite because of its mainly classical and archetypal interpretation in the field of storytelling or, as Sean Cubitt points out in his contribution to this book, the fact that almost any code of human culture (and communication) can be understood as narrative.

Therefore I shall reflect on the digital format as something which is still evolving. Deriving from film studies, my own research as well as artwork has always been influenced by an interdisciplinary and convergent interest in new media, so that I am mostly experimenting with parallels and redefinitions of so-called 'old' and 'new' media to achieve a more unique form of digital scenario.

> Television, film, computer graphics, digital photography, and virtual reality – our culture recognizes and uses all these technologies as media. This cultural recognition comes not only from the way in which each of the technologies functions in itself, but also from the way in which each relates to other media. We offer this simple definition: a medium is that which remediates. It is that which appropriates the techniques, forms and social significance of other media and attempts to rival or refashion them in the name of the real. A medium in our culture can never operate in isolation, because it must enter into relationships of respect and rivalry with other media.[1]

The open structure of the digital network offers the most appropriate configuration by which to examine audience participation as an alternative form that can enrich our concept of 'story'. Interactive platforms can be designed as accessible environments for the viewer. Content systems can be set up that are filled, shaped and further developed through the influence and contributions of various participants from different locations.

Depending on the idea and interactive potential of the technical interface, the viewer is usually required to take on a certain function and this has become one of the catchphrases in the fiction-orientated art experiments with new media. The former audience is lifted out of their seat of distanced contemplation and placed in the limelight of subjective physical involvement: addressed as a storyboard controller, co-author, actor or self-performer. In any case, the flow of content in the actual artwork is made directly interdependent through these personal interventions of the participants.

DEFINING CLASSICAL NARRATIVE

With the help of the following examples of telematic art projects and internet artwork, I want to probe these shifts of role-play more deeply since they comprise a fundamental basis of new types of story.

A quick glimpse of the basic model of character-driven narrative might be appropriate before structuring a new classification of narrative grammar and will provide a better understanding of artistic motivations. The majority of dramatic forms follow the (Aristotelian) idea of mimetic narration: the presentation of a dramatic action is understood as a copy or imitation (mimesis) of reality, in which the author talks through the figures that are the actors. The fictional action is represented by these personae, being either a character as an individual being or a type as a representative of a certain social group. They are put into a constellation, in which their specific and characteristic attributes are arranged in opposition to each other to show the different dimensions of the conflict and story. Protagonists, antagonists, main and sub-characters lead to a personification of story content and also of representative social behaviours. Most importantly they are all the author's creatures. The viewer is taking on the role of a voyeur, witness or emotional judge. He or she is immersed in the story by emotional means of identification, as the plot aims to provoke sympathy or antipathy with the characters or draws possible parallels to the viewer's subjective reality.[2]

VIRTUAL HEROES – MIMICKING VERSUS BEING

How is this fundamental model now being reconsidered and re-formed in networked digital experiments? Is it possible to establish a performative, content-responsible role for the viewer in the new media space? Can the virtual be treated as a stage for user narrative?

Some of these questions can be answered by looking at specific examples of telematic performances. The British artist Paul Sermon makes use of an open network structure to offer direct real-time interaction and coexistence of multiple participants in a visual/virtual environment. The user actively takes part in initiating as well as processing a story, within a sensory meeting space.

> The basic principle used in all the telematic installations I have produced since the beginning of the
> nineties involves a form of video-conferencing telepresence. By using systems of cameras, video
> mixers and projectors, two remote participants are combined and framed within the same
> screen/image. With the help of virtual studio chroma-key effects (the video mix of two identical
> scenes) the geographically distant users/performers appear in the same room, sitting at either the
> same table, on the same sofa, or on the same bed. All these works embody open systems of interac
> tion, involving two or more remote locations and participants, linked together via computer data net
> works. All technology is a development of language – a means of construction and interpretation of
> an environment. The definition of the virtual and real are all part of the same linguistic construct.

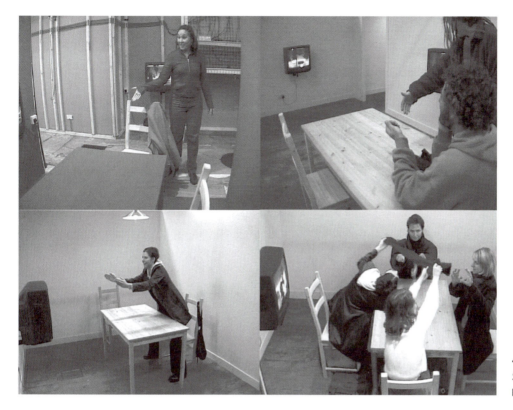

4 *There's No Simulation Like Home*, Paul Sermon, 1999.

Technology/language is not an apparatus or attachment to the body, but rather an extension of it. The marriage of the terms 'tele' and 'information' (informatic) encompasses many fields of research, including telepresence – the ability to be in more than one place at one time – ultimately a quantum physics model of teleportation.[3]

The screen as the common border, which divides the real world from the spectacle, has actually disappeared and the viewers rediscover their bodies in a disorienting copy-world, now located inside the monitor. The telematic interface throws people from remote sites into the same space of experience, and their motivation in handling the resulting confusion unfolds the narrative. The scenery reminds one of an improvised theatre and the potential for conflict becomes very subjective. The viewers have to accommodate to the unfamiliar space and redefine their accustomed behaviour in this set, as everyday objects like a simple bed or table are now located in the virtual to be shared with unknown visitors – so the viewers are put into a confusing turbulence of senses and emotions. The interface determines the rules of the social game and sets the initial moment of communication, from which the participants develop their own sequences. Instead of presenting a role or a character, they act themselves. Through the interactive narrative origin, they have to invent and actively direct their own episodic story in the media environment. The similarity to early silent movies and their typical exaggerated gestures and mimicry is very obvious and the viewers instinctively adopt this. As a digital extension of the narrative model described above, the actor as a type is replaced by the participant's own personal complexity, which fills the media space with content. The more the viewer develops pantomimic and creative skills and ideas, the more he or she motivates their partners and the more the story can mature as an episodic play of cause and effect. A shift and acceleration in perception and action takes place: from distant viewer to emotional participant, being forced into a role within a spontaneous episodic play. (In retrospect it would even be possible to assemble the sequences and their different characters as types and figures familiar from the film experience: So we find the bossy one, the shy or the crazy one, we can trace back the sequence of the loving couple …) Mimesis as a copy of reality is replaced by self-defined and reinvented reality. The narrative prototype is structured as an empty room and it is not until the viewer physically enters this room that the dynamics of the story can

(DVD) unfold.[4]

> Technical visions are social fiction (…) Technical visions are directed towards correspondence of the
> body and towards co-ordination of behaviour. They are daydreams born out of social connections
> directed towards other social connections.[5]

NET.DRAMA – OWN FIELD STUDIES

To establish a decent strategy of audience involvement and participation, my work is based upon these major aspects of research. Through defining the media space as a user-conducted and inhabited environment, I am trying to achieve a metaphorical symbiosis of real personae and virtual figures. The virtual then operates as a personal projection field that allows an open narrative construct and story-flow in a self-dynamic context system. It configures a virtual social milieu and community in which visionary identities and incidents can grow, as an extension of the authentic background of the (former) outside viewer.

The internet is at present the most open and most productive format for this, as exchange of data and alteration of information is continuously possible. It still seems to be in a state of permanent narrative flux and through the collaborative aspect of my work I am exploring this territory.

> The unpredictability of what will happen next is one of several features by which narration lives. The
> narrative threads a network between events and people without immediately revealing and making
> visible the interconnections. Narration per se is a voyage of discovery, therefore, and the main figure
> in a novel acts as a kind of guide. (…) Narration is chaotic and viable in structure, neither mechanical
> nor dead, owing its life less to the objects and characters described than to the dynamic links estab-
> lished, elaborated and made accessible between them.[6]

My first experimental work of this nature was *Last Entry: Bombay, 1st of July … a Travel Log through Time, Space and Identity*. This work was running between 1996 and 1998 as a collaborative project on the internet. The starting point was a kind of virtual soul, crossing the time and cultural zones of the internet and becoming tangled up in different events. The project was inspired and based upon

Virginia Woolf's novel *Orlando,* written in 1928 as a witty biography of a character oscillating between male and female gender, an eccentric vagabond wandering not only between the sexes but also through epochs, centuries and various cultural and historical backgrounds. Looking at the novel in the light of digital time-travel, it revealed many obvious parallels to the actual state-of the-art of the internet and its possibilities for masking and reinventing personal representation in a timeless connection of locations and cultures.

5 *Last Entry: Bombay, 1st of July … .* Index page of the website http://residence.aec.at/lastentry/, Andrea Zapp, 1997/8.

And when one departs, when one sets off, one looks wide-eyed at everything one had seen before and yet never seen. In order to be able to recount these things, to tell of the sea and its waves, to tell of the earth and its scent. This gazing face is then weighed down by stories that make it beautiful, and soft.[7]

Consequently, Orlando enters a second span of existence, now becoming the digital wanderer and *flâneur,* whose gender and further personal attributes are unknown. The novel itself served only as an exposition, as the metaphorical reference to give some basic understanding of the intended headlines of possible story development. The net figure Orlando develops his or her very own digital identity. Her destiny was only fragmentarily made visible, in fact she was only ever present through incoming documentation and letters to the project website from internet users, artists and other interested participants around the globe. They were requested to involve Orlando in their personal backgrounds and describe their experiences and thoughts during meeting, observing, or exchanging roles with this figure (using many different kinds of media, be it video, text or sound). The collaborative scenario was classified by individual story spaces, contributed as HTML documents, playing with the notions of gender shifting while using the main character Orlando as an avatar. The participation becomes a play using imagination, real existence, virtual sketches and personal dreams located within a carefully-designed scenario. Different styles and content were juxtaposed – poetry, snapshots, graphics or home videos visualised anecdotes, diaries, parodies and mysteries.

… and I had never recognised the flawless, fertile beauty of an old person until the first thing I saw at the end of my thousand journeys was my radiant, now aged, self, radiant in front of an antique glow in the mirror of the horizon. Look at me, every wrinkle tells a story, everything my eyes have seen and heard and felt flows constantly on my face, and on your own.[8]

WHAT'S ON A PERSON'S MIND? – 'INTER-FACIAL' DESIGN

The entry window simulates a turning dice, with a male and female face on either side. Through the circular movement they seem to melt together and be torn apart at the same time, to refer to the splitting of identity in the game. The following main navigation page shows a head formed by empty faces, like placeholders, to be filled with the participants' visions. As a consequence the map structure of the central interface is not only used because of web design practicality, but also to refer to a topology of 'mind-mapping' as a general idea of the work. The different entries form a multi-inhabited virtual body, in which the boundaries between real and virtual presence are melted together. The head functions as a mental travel log, a point of start and return, to document the paths of Orlando into the (net) world. It invites us to cruise inside the persona's multiple minds – as the growing membrane of the participants' reflections, plans and déjà-vu's encompassing past, present and future.

The project refers strongly to elements of legend, especially in its references to ancient techniques of storytelling like the letter, diary or travel report, nowadays replaced by home video or e-mail. It intends to mix archetypal forms with digital stereotypes to draw a connecting line into a discussion of poesis. In relation to Aristotle, a 'true' narrative always starts by rumours, by word of mouth, in this case by the collected digital gossip, which follows Orlando through the network.

Though *Last Entry …* is playing with a highly metaphorical level of immersion as identification, the technical interface is rather simple. The project belongs to the collaborative hyperfiction genre, which means material is assembled from outside to keep the content in motion, but all the contributions are laid out as flashbacks. Looking backwards, it functioned as a successful sketchbook of user-embedded narrative to prepare the way to my next project. As a further step towards a unique narrative model, live user action and performance was to be implemented with parallel video streams in a timeless and circular montage system.

(DVD) *Little Sister – a CCTV Drama and 24 Hours Online Surveillance Soap* went online in Spring 2000. *Little Sister* is a daily internet soap, combining live webcam images and surveillance cameras. The narrative strategy is based on the discovery of random routine and live action in public and private locations. An ironical play with expectations is created. The piece addresses the voyeuristic networking technology as an acute and ongoing media phenomenon.

The work was developed at a time when CCTV and surveillance cameras were questioned more and more critically as an issue in mass media society. During the set-up of the work the growing success of the TV Show *Big Brother*, which is based on the live observation of an isolated group of volunteers sharing a sealed flat, added some more actuality to the topic. So the project (and especially its final title) in general satirises the popularity so-called 'reality TV' is gaining because of its voyeuristic peeping-tom methods.

KEY HOLE PERSPECTIVES

The *Little Sister* interface relates to the closed circuit system in various ways. It shows snapshots of a local town area and its corners, shops, flat entrances and inhabitants, referring to the typical spatially limited set-up as a unique code of the TV dailies. The images are arranged in a circular hemisphere, to remind one of a surveillance mirror as found in a department store. By dragging the mouse over the image fields, a focus effect appears on every single picture, to symbolise a focusing camera shot. Hidden behind are over 20 online links to webcams spread all over the world, observing private and public locations. They open in small non-resizable windows, which can be arranged parallel or opposite to each other on the screen. *Little Sister* experiments with the interface of the split screen, in which different live actions are streamed in parallel or associative modes in the same time span, although the cameras are often operating in different time zones. The user is allowed to choose his or her personal casting in this timeless virtual drama by opening the different webcam connections. This open control of dramatic display is set in contradiction to the rigidly designed interface.

Suspense arises from the live character of the webcam images and videos as they are in con-

6 *Little Sister* index page, Andrea Zapp, 2000.

stant motion. They establish further links to the soap opera genre, as they also show the characteristic venues such as the shop, the office, the bar, the hairdresser or the kitchen. It is intended to
familiarise the viewer with these locations so that he/she can identify with their residents and guests.
In other words to stay tuned and return often. The webcam itself contains a strong narrative motif
in its voyeuristic effects. *Little Sister* plays explicitly with this notion of curiosity by addressing the
user's wish to find a very personal story acted in front of these cameras or to find at least something a little bit scandalous and obscure. But one is simultaneously aware, while watching images
slowly dripping onto the screen and freezing only seconds of visual information, that it might be
very hard to catch one of these rare and precious moments. Some of the webcam links parody
this issue by, for example, showing a fire station with the engines just being maintained or a basin
with frogs paddling quietly along. Several shoplifting incidents can be observed, but after a while the
viewer has to realise that it is just a fake, looped QuickTime movie.

We can trace back two stages of involvement in this work:

1. The performative action control and
2. The combinatory action editing.

The online sources depend only by conception on the author. There is no influence on the live-
streamed content, on the focus points and when (and also whether) the camera is switched on. As

7 *Little Sister* screen
showing live webcam
images, Andrea Zapp,
2000.

a consequence, the project forms its own virtual social system, where the webcam space itself directs the flow of time, image and action. The shop is closed at night, while the bar is open; the students are having a party, while the classroom is locked up for a holiday.

Yet this fictitious narrative frame is shattered at the same time, as the user is confronted with authentic surveillance material. One of the most frequently asked questions about the project was how I came to find the spaces for setting up the cameras. To some people it seemed to be quite disturbing that I am actually just linking to IP (Internet Protocol) numbers which already exist and which are beyond my control. So the user is turned into a spy and secret witness and some felt rather unwillingly dragged into the events. This was accentuated in the first phase of the project since the webcam URLS (Uniform Resource Location) weren't defined. But now there is a link list attached to the site, which makes a clear cut between the performance in the soap and the real identities and locations. By linking to private cams and live CCTV in one context, *Little Sister* draws a very thin line between the free choice of self-exhibitionism on the net and the limitations of movement through visual registration in media society. It is intended that the user vacillates between feelings of curiosity and oppression. It leads to a subordinated change of role and perception: the virtual observer could also possibly be the detected one and vice versa. The circle is closed back on the narrative impulse itself: a *24 Hours Online Surveillance Soap*.

AUGMENTED REALITY

In conclusion, the projects are trying to mirror the net in one of its most significant modes: as a pool of private and puzzling (home) spaces, laid open on the global networked stage. They are motivated by the given inner structure of the net as an enormous amateur theatre arena with plenty of possible character casts to be discovered. They can not only be found on the homepage as the visiting card itself, but also in the wide range of virtual playgrounds such as chat rooms, CU-See-Me groups or MUDs (Multi-user Domains) and MOOs (object-oriented MUDs). One could also say, the stories are just out there to be highlighted and as a consequence the described projects are merely providing a framework and platform for this.

At the same time, they try to research the users' way of expressing and defining their personal inner projections. The interface remains rather simple, as in *Last Entry* ... for instance. No rules about design were given, to make it as easy as possible to enter the story process from all levels. In *Little Sister* I just linked to the webcam location set up by the users themselves. The general idea is therefore to constitute a seamless portal to the net itself as the main source material, making the borders between the individual and the theatrical room less obvious. My projects recognise contemporary mass media as easy to access, open and changeable from your own private space. But the isolated social space is linked by the new media into a shared creative realm.

> Face to face interaction and verbal communication is losing primacy, while at the same time the complex heterogeneous computer transmitted, telemedial presence is increasing. Identity and physical integrity become an art form since understanding one's own individuality through the anonymous,

hetero-anonymous and pseudo-anonymous, the body has become a style through which to deal with media environments.[9]

Another work which illustrates these criteria very clearly is the website *Distance*, by the New York-based artist Tina LaPorta, which was produced in 1999 as a commission of New Radio and Performing Arts, Inc. for its Turbulence website.[10]

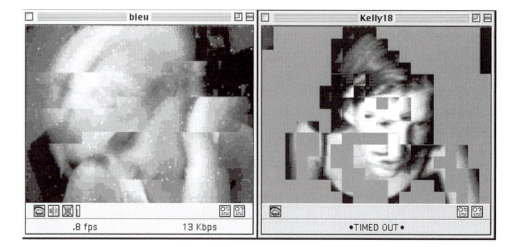

8 *Distance*, Tina La Porta, 1999. http://turbulence.org/ Works/Distance

Distance explores our desire for communication, through connection and disconnection, via fluctuations in transmission and reception between geographically separated participants mediated by the surface of the screen. This work investigates the disembodied and dislocated nature of online communication through a re-combination of images and text as a continued exploration of presence, absence and the desire for connectivity within a global networked environment.[11]

The site shows a very reduced interface, as there is just a follow-up of screen shots of different anonymous CU-See-Me chat members, sitting in front of their terminals. The shots are placed in the middle of the screen as black and white images, mostly worked on with digital effects, to either blur, pale or fragment the image. So many of the persons documented appear like rather ghostly shadows of themselves caught in the virtual room. Underneath the images are placed single phrases that read like the participants' thoughts, the artist's vision or just simple elements of talk extracted from the chat. They are linking to the next image and by browsing through these different levels of real questions and virtual answers they cause a very immersive effect. The user is dragged into an online date, but at the same time is kept on hold as the text jumps from tangible desire and longing to reflection and critique.

Ready to make a connection, she logs on … Authenticating Remote Access … Her social network is dispersed, connecting through wires … Her desire to communicate to an other is met online … Each encounter occurs in real-time … Interaction is immediate … Leaving traces on her screen … There is a sense of intimacy here … Without touch … He asks: when will you be on again? … He waits for her response … She imagines his surroundings … He imagines her voice … Is technology a veil? … Reflecting back … He contemplates the nature of her presence … She is afraid he will not reply … her mind begins to drift … She returns to herself … Extending her presence … He appeals to her gaze … Who are you? He is a stranger to her … She wants to know more … He disappears … logging off for a while … Time unfolds … Time runs out … Where do we go from here? … Searching … She thinks about her future … She asks: is the virtual, real? … She considers her response … He reappears … Are we getting closer, or further apart? She thinks of him in the abstract … Processed through technology … She feels out of place … Detached from the outside world … Everything is split in two now … Fragmented … Slipping out of focus … and inverted … We are artefacts in motion … Becoming pixels on the screen … [12]

The effect of drifting between the two worlds of presence, between inside and outside, is strongly reinforced by the simplicity of navigation and editing, being arranged like a walk into the depth of the different rooms behind the screen. The scenario is further based on a time model – the virtual players log on, find each other, lose each other, log off and back on again. The design of the images underlines this by either showing explicit gestures or expressions of curiosity, thoughtfulness or reaction or by showing faces vanishing, exploding into pixels or fading into oblivion.

Through the space and time orientated montage and the mimesis of real personae *Distance* opens up a parallel to the cinematic process. But as in *Little Sister* it is extended into the essence of the digital scenario. The cast is put together from web users and rearranged as a fictive meeting, to illustrate telepresence (or inter-subjectivity as the artist calls it) as an emotional and confusing reallocation of existences.

THE STORY, THE MEDIUM AND THE MESSAGE

Linking back to the mimetic model I referred to earlier on: we now have a definite shift from the pre-mapped storyboard (finding its expression in controlled acting) to a loose connection of user destinies becoming the major storyline; where suspense arises from observing *and* sharing these destinies, since accessing the same room is made possible. A condition that could be best described as digital docufiction or docudrama (compare on this term Butterworth and Wyver in this book), in which subjective, immediate, random and constantly changing content is displayed through flashes of intimate behaviour. These create a timeless space of action, as the continuum of story is disrupted by opening and actively reshaping the dramatic setting and environment.

Different narrative worlds will probably coexist. The new type of author changes from the omniscient author to the 'travel guide' in artificial interactive environments, who leads the active navigation through thematic rooms and offers orientation through tableaux of possible events. They are combined in the head, though as a story, but as a personal event. Maybe a new cultural orientation, at least for one part of the world, can be read from this, moving away from a retrospective historical told (single) story towards an (omni) present simultaneous 'Parallel World', in which different cultural spaces are connected.[13]

As there is no closed narrative complex in this kind of interactive framework, the author occupies more the role of a host offering a room for pluralistic dramatic action and animating multi-authorship. In fact the interactive media work would just be an empty technical frame without the viewer's activity. Narration and story has to be redefined under these conditions. In the classical discourse, story stands for the most advanced and detailed description of the incident. Dealing with open interactive attempts at narrative, it seems necessary to concentrate on the highest level of narrative compression, whereby the 'theme' becomes the basic question of conflict in the work. The main philosophical problem now appears as a matter of design. We are also very close to the 'idea' as a narrative fragment, or, to paraphrase Aristotle, to the 'mythos', - in modern narration regarded as a 'timeless story, which mirrors the central circumstances in human lives'.[14]

… staring, staring far away, into the distance. The horizon constantly creates new stories one should listen to, learn by heart, carry in one's soul and leave them lying there. Stories of fog, of wet swamps, slow rivers, unmoving trees and meadows under a grey sky, stories of people … Stories demanding respect, and silence.[15]

NOTES

1. Bolter, Jay David. 'Networkings of Remediation'. Quoted from the website: http://www.lcc.gatech.edu/~bolter/remediation/book.html, on the book: Bolter, Jay David, and Grusin, Richard. *Remediation. Understanding New Media.* Cambridge: MIT Press, 1999.

2. On character and author compare here: Hickethier, Knut. *Film- und Fernsehanalyse. VI.2: Zur Analyse des Narrativen: Figurenkonstellationen.* Stuttgart/Weimar: Verlag J. B. Metzler, 1996, pp. 120–1.

3. Sermon, Paul. Unpublished manuscript. 2001.

4. The DVD includes a project I developed together with Paul Sermon in 1999, A Body of Water, commissioned by the Wilhelm Lehmbruck Museum Duisburg for the exhibition *Connected Cities – Processes of Art in The Urban Network*. It integrates the telematic interactive communication into a water-based interface and projection screen, within a very site-specific narrative, questioning the influence digital technology has on the former industrial coal-mining area in Germany.

5. Fassler, Manfred. 'Stile der Anwesenheit', Brigitte Felderer, ed. *Wunschmaschine Welterfindung.* Vienna: Springer Verlag, 1996, p. 260 (trans. A. Zapp).

6. Weibel, Peter. 'The Post-Gutenberg Book' in *artintact 3. Artist's interactive CD-ROMagazine.* Karlsruhe: ZKM Centre for Art and Media, 1996, pp. 21–2.

7. http://residence.aec.at/lastentry/massi/fenster.html (1 Jan. 2001).

8. http://residence.aec.at/lastentry/massi/2frauen.html (1 Jan. 2001).

9. Fassler, Manfred, 'Stile der Anwesenheit', p. 271 (trans. A. Zapp).

10. http://www.turbulence.org (2 Jan. 2001).

11. http://www.turbulence.org/Works/Distance/statement.html (2 Jan. 2001).

12. Quoted from the website http://www.turbulence.org/Works/Distance.html (2 Jan. 2001).

13. Neuhaus, Wolfgang. *Die Vernetzung der Fiktionen*. Telepolis 2000
    http://www.heise.de/tp/deutsch/inhalt/sa/4245/1.html (12 Nov. 2000) (trans. A. Zapp).

14. On the topic of this narrative hierarchy compare here: Hickethier. *Film- und Fernsehanalyse. VI.2: Zur Analyse des Narrativen: Story, Fabel, Thema*, pp. 110–11.

15. http://residence.aec.at/lastentry/massi/see.html.

Interactive or Inhabited TV

Broadcasting for the Twenty-first Century

Alex Butterworth and John Wyver

There once was a time, known only anecdotally to the generation who are now rising to guide broadcasting into the new millennium, when television was a true prism of national communal life. In those golden days crowds would convene spontaneously on the terraced streets of our industrial heartlands the morning after a *Wednesday Play* or *Play for Today* had been screened, thrilling with vicarious passion and eager to discuss the personal and political significance of what they had seen. Debate would rage, government policy would be changed and broadcasting would be seen to have performed its public service, or so we have heard.

For the beleaguered few who still harbour such memories it is little wonder that inter-active TV sounds frighteningly like the last trump for their ideals: heralding a bleak dystopia, where the suckered mass of lonely viewers will be so narcotised as to commune exclusively with the shopping channel's hotbots. Indeed, judging by the initial forays into interactivity by some broadcasters, one might consider these fears well founded, though the kind of material so far produced only echoes the tendency towards the lowest common denominator found in broadcasting more generally. But is it just possible that interactivity may not only rise above these concerns, promoting the creation of worthwhile and intelligent new experiences, and may at last even incarnate that very dream of communal participation?

Convergence is the catch-all name given to the myriad processes by which the media, telecommunications and computing industries are becoming ever more closely entwined. The creative challenge facing producers is to manage the ever-changing combinations in which users will be able to engage with a cornucopia of media, while the responsibility is to ensure that the activities in which they are empowered to participate do not promote solipsism. Rather, the experience should be shared through communities of interest in ways which might at best even compensate for some of those communal functions lost through the fragmentation of our society: a sense of mutual support, a data resource of life experience, a collective wisdom.

Any approach to bringing together broadcasting with network systems must then in part involve seeking new, deeper and different relationships with those we have traditionally thought of as audiences. At one level, these relationships can simply provide feedback to assist us as producers to make better, more effective and more useful programmes. Yet, beyond this, the new media conjunctions offer the potential for re-inventing and perhaps re-invigorating, far more radically, a number of the more intellectually weighty programme forms. This can be achieved by assimilating the audience into parts of the actual process of producing the programme content; a fairly familiar notion in forms such as the quiz show, but rare until recently in the narrative forms of drama and documentary.

Fundamental to any discussion of the questions explored here is an understanding of the paradigms on which the current communications systems are founded. Telecommunications is essentially a one-to-one system that is distributed across an extensive network of nodes, each of which can connect directly to each of the others. It is also non-hierarchical, i.e. no node has an inherent superiority or advantage when it comes to offering information to one or many other users of the system. Broadcasting by contrast is a one-to-many system, which is highly centralised with communication being essentially one way, from the centre out to the periphery. Such a structure is inherently hierarchical, with the power concentrated at the centre, and with the 'receivers' having little or no opportunity to contribute to the communication process.

As currently configured, and largely because of its historical development, the internet remains closer to the telecommunications paradigm. But there are powerful corporate forces which would be pleased to see its present, many-to-many structure, shift more closely towards a one-to-many framework in the future – not least because the revenue models for such a system are clearer and longer established. Our hope is that by focusing a creative interpretation of convergence on forms, which combine the open and egalitarian paradigm of the internet with the potential of broadcast to provide a sustained, and editorially structured narrative for an audience, it might be possible to move towards a situation where less monopolistic models may be negotiated.

In one sense, this is to say that the software mechanisms needed for mediating interaction and participation should editorialise only to the extent that they represent the wishes of the participants in good faith. However, while this must be accepted as a basic duty, the linear presentation will unavoidably be shaped by editorial decisions to as great a degree as in any traditional broadcast, while the design of the interactive environment entails still further editorial manipulation. The issue must really be defined by artistic choice: granted a window of freedom from expectation, in what kind of activity is it interesting for us to encourage the usually passive audience to become complicit and how can this complicity be achieved?

Free will underwrites all dramatic narrative: those moments of choice, which encapsulate inner conflict or catalyse it in the outer world. In conventional, statically authored drama, the audience are led to identify with certain characters on the stage or the screen and to be carried with them through the choices they make, gauging their own ethical inclinations against the consequences for the characters and their world. Only at moments of extreme transgression are the audience likely to recoil and attempt to dissociate themselves, and it is in these instants of perplexity and vulnerability that the skilful dramatist can confront his or her audience with their own complicity. They are moments of true reckoning when the audience must wrestle with a choice of their own: to justify or recant their previously held position. To bring our participants to this kind of self-recognition, its impact intensified by the knowledge of their own determining praxis, might then be a worthwhile demonstration of the social potentials of the new form.

So how might this simple narrative structure of a causational chain followed by a revelatory rupture translate into a form in which the audience members become emotionally engaged interactors or participants? For more than a decade now a received opinion has been gathering momentum, fomented by the medium's Cassandras who proclaim either the impossibility of interactive narrative or the undesirability of participatory experiences, which carry forward the torch of conventional narrative. Their arguments in essence are familiar from twentieth-century theory: that the world is a complicated place and intractable to the normative effects of narrative structuring without hideous and dishonest deformation. But a cynic might suspect this attitude to be simply tracing a path of least resistance in the face of challenges, such as how to guarantee a participant the cumulative, dynamic experience of causational logic and concomitant responsibility in their choices without imposing osten-sible constraints.

The creation of structured interactive dramatic experiences and the narrative representation of those experiences seems to us an entirely legitimate activity. The addition of tele-matics to the interactive media mix now provides an author with a vastly greater array of possible means with which to shape narrative experience than were available even a few years ago. Between the decisions which structure a static hyperlinked dataspace with its textual or multimedia representations and those which inform online chatrooms, through the imposition of certain rules of etiquette, there is a wide spectrum of approaches which the creator of an interactive experience can adopt to communicate his or her vision.

Our lives are so suffused with media noise that the distractions render us resistant to becoming immersed participants in any collective media experience unless the experience itself can provide us with an alternative and more coherent media reality. Narrative in a media-saturated age must adopt methods which reflect this dispersed and parallel system if it is to be accepted as a valid simulation of real world experience. It is our contention that only an author with the functional flexibility to adopt multiple strategies from across that spectrum, from moment to moment, as the status of the developing narrative changes, can hope to support an experience of sufficient coherence to qualify as a compelling participatory narrative. But that flexibility and those strategies are dependent on the software tools which are to hand.

For several years interactive television has been a buzzword for broadcasters, though their quest for the grail has been a history of inevitable and sometimes excusable failures, not least in the awkward area of finding suitable commercial models to exploit. Investment in the brief CD-ROM boom proved misplaced, while others were quicker to see the commercial potential of the internet and, to compound their confusion, there has been prolonged uncertainty about the roll-out schedule for broadband services. Furthermore the cost of software development for digital projects almost inevitably translates into a requirement for a mass audience and in this new field, even more than any other, the market is hard to predict.

Sadly, their efforts were also usually marked by a lack of daring, often simply repackaging old media material fractured into advent calendar boxes with presentation prioritised over what was intrinsically interesting about the interactive medium. What was more, television itself got little more than a walk-on part as the charitable donor of cast-off 'content': to all appearances convergence was not even on the horizon. At the start of the twenty-first century it would seem that broadcasters are rediscovering an appetite for experimentation in the interactive arena, scenting that there is an audience whose tastes are becoming more sophisticated and who are more alive to the pervasive and intriguing presence of the new communication media.

Ironically this recent stimulus to television probably came from the internet: the infant daringly donning the old lady's stolen clothes as retro chic and reawakening dim memories of her own carefree youth when anything seemed possible. Online game shows like *You Don't Know Jack* are explicit about their derivation from broadcasting. Online soaps such as *The Spot* and *East Village* have explored how one of television's most durable forms can be transferred to the kind of scrapbook media which the web currently facilitates, although the journey to this new medium has yet to prove very profitable either creatively or commercially. Narrative web-based documentaries are also being created, although again, convincing templates of the form have yet to appear.

In the United Kingdom recently an internet 'movie' was scripted in instalments and distributed on the net, with plot development influenced by audience feedback. Masterminded by the screenwriter of the hit comedy *The Full Monty*, Simon Beaufoy, it was apparently based on an underlying arborescent structure of bifurcating choices, but is still noteworthy for the illusion it gave of aggregating the opinions of remote participants to effect a basic choice of narrative direction. Unsurprisingly for a conventional thriller, the audience willed their expectations to fulfilment in a rosy ending: closure being perceived as the final validation of the experience's 'cinematic' status.

Online Caroline was also exclusively an internet project which made extensive use of the technique of drawing participants into its story world by means of fictionalised e-mail, originated by the authors of the infamous 'Dysson' scam, which convinced recipients of supposedly misdirected e-mails that they were witnesses to corporate murder. Screening on the BBC, as the internet bubble burst, Island World's *Attachments* was a drama series set in a dot com start-up company and accompanied by a website which purported to be that of the fictional company itself, the fortunes of which were mirrored in the site's development. By making the story's representation in the two media not only complementary, but also organically related, it marked an advance on the extension of television narratives into original content for the web, such as the series *Homicide* ventured with its 'Second Shift' pages.

Where these projects are interesting is in their attempt to concatenate different modalities of communication to augment the illusion of narrative verisimilitude and encourage credulous immersion on the part of their audiences. But there is still no suggestion of this being taken to the next stage at which the audience can themselves become present within the drama, not merely as a shaping influence but as fully expressive participants. The resources required to support this kind of form are far from trivial and so it is encouraging that the BBC's Fiction Lab is currently pursuing at least one project of this kind. We shall later return to a brief consideration of their stated aims in light of our own pioneering and emphatically experimental investigations into some of these areas.

Illuminations Television first became engaged with the problems of convergence through our magazine series *The Net*, created for the BBC in April 1994. Within hours of the first programme being broadcast and at a time when e-mail use was far less widespread than it is today, some 600 messages had streamed in, and this despite the fact that the e-mail address we had given in our closing credits was incorrect. Most television programmes attract at best a dozen inconsequential letters, but these were thoughtful and engaged, knowledgeable, concerned and even passionate. It was the beginning of what for us was a unique and influential dialogue with the viewers of the programme.

As *The Net* evolved, more and more online components were used to enhance the transmission of the programme. A website provided extensive further information, including extended interviews with those featured in the programmes, additional resources, competitions and detailed feedback. Viewers were engaged in chat and forum dialogues. Such services helped the production team shape *The Net* in significant ways and the show improved directly because of this rich feedback.

The form we have called 'Inhabited Television' was first developed for the third series of *The Net* in early 1997, when Illuminations collaborated closely with British Telecom Laboratories at Martlesham, with Sony and with the BBC to extend the online elements of the project in an original way. Developing their own extensive work with shared virtual spaces, BT Laboratories built *The Mirror*, six inter-linked virtual worlds, mostly in VRML 2.0, for operation with Sony's Community Place server and browser software. Each of the worlds related to one of the themes of the six programmes in that series of *The Net*, such as Space or Play, and took its visual style and its activities from the theme.

Viewers of the programmes registered for *The Mirror* across the web and received through the post a CD-ROM containing the graphics for the worlds and also the Community Place browser. Using this the viewer could connect with the server running the shared components of *The Mirror* and participate in collective discussion and collaborative activities, while *The Net* television programmes carried occasional recorded reports on these events. During its seven weeks of operation, *The Mirror* attracted more than 2,000 registered users and the party to celebrate the end of the worlds was inhabited by approximately 80 users simultaneously.

The Mirror was a fascinating experiment and valuable addition to the media mix, which now comprised the audience experience of *The Net*, establishing a more sustained and more flexible rhythm than the routine of weekly broadcast. This, at least, was what we recognised as its potential. What we had learnt very quickly though, as have many others in the business, was that the 'Field of Dreams' principle (after the Kevin Costner movie: 'If you build it, they will come') is not in itself sufficient. However attractive the space, however engaging the collaborative activities, entry and social use will remain at a relatively low level unless a programme of activities is organised to provide a focus for social interaction.

The provision of regular 'hosts' was to be a key element in achieving this. These hosts would greet new entrants, introduce people to each other, point out activities and generally help people around. More than this, however, over time they would become the core of the community of the world, encouraging people to return and beginning to develop the particular culture of *The Mirror*. It was their presence, which enabled the creation of a real community, which even resulted in one real world marriage and one very real baby.

In the aftermath of *The Mirror* we were uniquely privileged among television production companies to be involved at the inception of the *eRENA* project with some of our old partners and a number of new ones, who brought additional skills and knowledge to the enterprise. The project's aim was to produce 'Tools for the Art of Tomorrow'. In total, the consortium brought together academic institutions in Germany, Sweden, Switzerland and England, a major corporate partner in the form of British Telecom as well as Illuminations Television as sole commercial practitioner. Collaborators also contributed from many other cultural worlds, including the traditional theatre, avant-garde performance and puppetry.

Several of the strands of this project either developed directly out of our Inhabited Television work or else promised to be complementary to it. Among the myriad projects successfully undertaken during the three years were: *ViCrowd* for simulating virtual crowds; *BFinder* which traces movement in physical space to aggregate group feedback; camera control within virtual worlds; and the round table control device for supporting event management in potentially large-scale virtual environments. For us this was a unique opportunity to set about redefining what interactive entertainment and particularly drama might be in the context of television, looking not at what was possible at the inception of the project but attempting to predict what might just be feasible on its completion in 2000 or still later.

The research was to be phased around demonstrator productions and it was decided that each of these should initially focus on individual areas of technical and creative challenge, while building towards an integrated vision. It seemed clear to us that remotely inhabited virtual worlds should be the conceptual foundation of every phase. However, the lack of appropriate software to support the kind of nuanced interactions for which we were aiming would necessitate certain compromises while the University of Nottingham developed its *Massive* system to meet the required specifications. How then to frame each of these phases?

A single programme construct seemed to encapsulate the initial technical challenges we would face with Inhabited TV: how was it possible, not only to support remote participation in virtual worlds, but also to broadcast in real-time from within those worlds, so that the participants could experience events simultaneously at first hand and in an editorialised form. In seeking to confront these challenges directly the basic terms of the project's first production were decided: a project whose results would prove highly instructive.

Called *Heaven and Hell Live*, it was a single live broadcast in a late-night slot on Channel 4 in 1997. Aiming to use familiarity with a linear precedent to acclimatise its audience to the interactive element, the programme took the form of a quiz show in which two lead competitors in the studio were advised by a number of 'lost souls' who participated through an online virtual world.

Technically successful, with the broadcast staying on air for a full 50 minutes and with some 150 users in the space pretty much throughout the broadcast, the fundamentally anarchic and chaotic transmission was also apparently watched by an extraordinary 200,000 viewers. Aside from the familiar underlying quiz structure, which in any case became almost imperceptible beneath a welter of bemused voices, there was insufficient coherence to the experience of the participants and almost nothing to make the transmission intelligible to viewers. A very busy web forum for comments and complaints accompanied the broadcast!

The production of *Heaven and Hell Live* gave us a powerful lens on our ultimate ambition of creating participatory community-based dramatic narratives for broadcast. What became immediately clear was that the aspiration of transmitting such events live was perhaps an unnecessarily strict and debilitating stipulation to impose on ourselves. While it would remain an aim throughout, providing very valuable insights and prompting the creation of tools with serendipitous applications, we recognised that even multi-camera studio dramas, whose live broadcast was part of the proud tradition of British television, had been tightly scripted and blocked, as well as being performed by highly experienced actors.

Of more general significance it also brought into focus one of the great problematics in producing participatory drama for television: how to tally the dual functions of entertaining participants with simultaneously eliciting performances which are sufficiently legible to underwrite a spectator's experience. What is simple to achieve in real-world interactions between skilled actors is far from simple between untrained participants in a virtual environment. The issues are manifold: deprived of the subtle clues implicit in face-to-face group communication, how can speakers sequence their contributions to avoid cacophony? How prohibitively great is the dexterity required to use a keyboard interface to trigger expressive gesticulation? What explicit rules of etiquette need to be known to effectively legislate the interactions, which redefine even a very familiar activity when it is transposed into virtuality?

The first two of these questions are part of a wide ongoing debate concerning the modalities of communication online, and it was partly with an exploration of this in mind, that the ideal specifications of the *Massive* system were conceived. By 1998 though, the capabilities of the system were such that an experimental production aimed at progressing audience legibility had to look instead at the third of these questions. In considering suitable conceptual models for interactive television, we had first looked to the public participation quiz show, not only for its familiarity to viewers, but because it seemed necessary to provide a tight temporal structure for the broadcast. In retrospect, it was primarily the choice of a form dependent on very specific information being communicated which had limited its legibility to an audience. So might it not have been more effective to build more on a sporting analogy where skill in manipulating objects to a designated end was the unmistakable indicator of success?

With this in mind *Out of this World* (1998) concentrated on ensuring that the participants were well enough prepared to understand and enjoy their experiences in the virtual world, which this time consisted of a games arena, apparently marooned in outer space. Two teams of four, each

with a leader, competed against each other to be the first to reach a spaceship, which would take them away from this arena before it exploded. The intention was that their own demonstrable competence would translate into audience comprehension.

9 *Out of This World,* 1998.

The other important development made in this project was the introduction of systems for controlling both the movement of the characters (taking away their autonomy for limited periods of time) and the four virtual 'cameras'. Each of the cameras was still controlled by a cameraperson, but he or she could pre-programme smooth movements, find particular vantage points or lock on to an avatar and follow it through the space. These new controls facilitated a much more coherent 'broadcast' to a theatrical audience: coherent enough for them to criticise it harshly on its own terms. With the technical groundwork covered, the challenge was now to produce compelling content.

Although establishing narrative forms had always been the intended destination of the project for us, it was not until halfway through the third year of research that we felt prepared to make a decisive move in this direction. Following our experiences with *Heaven and Hell Live,* it had been felt that future projects should attempt to work with less of a 'top-down' model (i.e. rules imposed from outside) and more of a 'bottom-up' understanding in which the participants are properly involved in conceiving and developing activities for broadcast.

It was with this agenda that we returned to the ground earlier covered in *The Mirror,* although unfortunately Nottingham's powerful *Massive-2* collaborative virtual worlds platform was still not engineered to run over modem connections. Of the commercially available alternatives we opted for Microsoft's Virtual Worlds which while limited to graphics and text was, we thought, capable of supporting relatively large numbers of users over modem connections. With four worlds, reduced from the seven planned to represent the Ages of Man, the inherent narrative of the worlds' design remained vestigial in the project's title: *Ages of Avatar* (1999).

The objectives of the *Ages of Avatar* phase were two-fold: to build a community over the three month life-span of the online environment and to intermittently film crucial moments in the drama of the participants' relationships and their development of a microcosmic society. This observed material would then be edited into short interstitial programmes of 'a virtual world docusoap' for broadcast on dottv, the Sky technology channel that was also promoting the project to potential participants. It was the tension between different conceptions of community building, under pressure from the conflicting demands of narrative, which proved the most instructive aspect of this phase of research.

One of the authors of this chapter, Alex Butterworth, was recruited at this point as the author. He approached the project from a background as a writer and dramatist with improvisational theatre companies and more recently as a researcher into participatory forms of drama using complex and dynamic virtual environments, populated by autonomous characters. In these environments, both environment and characters would respond to the user's behaviour to produce an emergent narrative across the space of the story world while a monitoring system would unobtrusively reconfigure the options accessible to the user at any time, in order to guarantee that his or her free-willed linear experience would nevertheless conform to certain formal constraints.

In reapplying this expertise to evince viable narrative from virtual communities, the chosen strategy was to actively shape the community by encouraging participants to coalesce in diverse but overlapping groups of interest. The thesis was that external conflicts of an interesting nature would arise out of the divergent interests of the society's members, while the individual's own divided loyalties would give rise to internal conflict expressed as inconsistency of behaviour or confessional dialogue.

Participants were to be invited to nominate themselves for official positions and to accept some different ongoing responsibilities. A legislature should develop, and alongside it agents of enforcement, while those with a more spiritual inclination would offer moral guidance in the paths of higher enquiry: the 'what are we here for' questions which were at times so pertinent. The hope was that by providing the means for participants to record their experiences and feelings, and by perhaps obliging them to do so as a pre-condition for receiving certain rights, the community would become more self-aware and ultimately its narrative become self-generating.

Far from our ideal array of multiple media tools, the instruments of social engineering with which we had to work were quite blunt (even had they been fully operational). The software platform did not support object manipulation or persistence of any user-preferences between areas (or 'worlds') let alone persistence between sessions. Participants would constantly appear in different guises, using different names and in different virtual costumes, making identification or profiling practically impossible. And the only means of enforcing the collective will was by granting access to 'spells' of rather clumsy effect: changing the appearance of a character's avatar, for example, or spinning them around. These are not the most fearsome of sanctions in a virtual world, where if authorial manipulation is to be used for story-shaping purposes it requires real legerdemain and must impact not externally, but on the psychological and emotional condition of the participants.

It was unavoidable then, that our efforts as social engineers had to be directed at the participants rather than their avatars, in the hope that they would enter into the spirit of the narrative enterprise and maintain Chinese walls between their multiple personae. In a virtual, even more than in a physical world, knowledge is power and knowledge was the commodity which we planned to ration, apportioning it exclusively at times to certain social groups. In doing so the social infra-structure, which the participants were themselves expected to organise as they saw fit (by means of elections and delegation of administrative functions) would be validated by the creation of functional specialisms among the community.

The means of demonstrating these functions would additionally serve to elaborate the already implicit narrative of the worlds: since powers of transformation or punishment would refer to the mythic 'prehistory' of the worlds, which was implicit in the design of the environments. Trading and competition in this knowledge between participants would provide leverage for the emerging conflicts. The practical means of catalysing and then supporting the creation of clandestine subgroups, and providing access to this information, presented the next challenge.

It was decided of necessity that the mechanisms for shaping the community and seeding dramatic conflict would not be automated. Instead, we would exploit the auxiliary functions, which were already available to the *Ages of Avatar* community: the discussion forums, e-mailed flyers and newsletters alongside certain facilities for leaving messages within the virtual worlds. A list of subscribers' e-mail addresses was available, but plans to use them were stymied because of certain ethical concerns, which would ramify throughout the project.

One of the most disputed areas for the production crew concerned the relative emphasis on narrative-directed or organically developing community and in particular how far participants should be informed that an experiment in story development was underway. Should it come as a complete surprise to them, or should they be forewarned, or, most radically, should admission to the worlds even be dependent on an undertaking to engage with narrative? In retrospect, the latter option would have avoided much confusion, but at the time the implicit decision was that the narrative agenda would be hinted at to participants while any story construction should remain non-coercive. Paradoxically, this proved to be the one strategy which could not work since, unless primed to expect that they were taking part in a dramatic event of some kind, the participants tended to misread the contextual signals with which we seeded the environment. The result was that ultimately coercive imposition became the only means available in which to create material with a strong enough narrative through-line to edit into even brief interstitial programmes for broadcast.

In light of all these difficulties, the original composition of the worlds' populace was a crucial determinant of how likely the participants were to come into conflict as individuals when isolated together. In the case of *Ages of Avatar*, an accidental self-selection mechanism was in operation. The first stage was that those aware of the project were almost certain to be Sky television subscribers, who would indicate a preference for certain socially normative genres of drama, while the likelihood was that they were also viewers of the dottv channel and hence technophiles. The likely profile of those entering the worlds for the first time was filtered further, as a consequence of the combination of technical expertise and sheer bloody-minded persistence required to log on to the virtual world browser, which, reports suggested, could require up to six re-installations, as well as fundamental repair to the host computer's operating system. And, for those who eventually did make it in, patience and a fondness for end-of-pier games were prerequisites for paying more than a brief visit; while having many spare evenings to spend online was the final requirement for admission as a regular member of the community.

The result was a group of participants who appeared homogeneous in their docility and conservatism and whose desires were more than fulfilled by the themed party nights, quizzes and games that were organised on a nightly basis. This was compounded by the presence of a hostess, whose function was somewhere between that of a Butlin's Red Coat and a boarding school matron, which the previous phases of the project had indicated as necessary for nurturing a sense of security and community. A very charismatic, kind and imaginative figure who quickly became known as 'Queen Mimmy', the hostess was unfortunately a major symptom of the confusion in agendas: necessary for supporting community development, but antipathetic to drama being so effective in stabilising any disturbance. Loyalty to the Queen was absolute and a consensus immediately formed against any challenge to her moral authority: the possibility of leading the participants to confront the moral consequences of their choices did not exist, since those choices were consistently delegated.

10 *Ages of Avatar –* 'Nirvana' section, 1999.

To the extent that the objective of *Ages of Avatar* was to create a community we were moderately successful: a small but robust group formed but did not evolve into any form of society. Furthermore, to all appearances this community was utopian: almost entirely devoid of meaningful conflict and characterised by a kind of obsequious gratitude for the chance to be there at all. It provided very little material with which the author could work. Indeed, at times the population seemed so similar in occupation and outlook that one was reminded of the sequence in Douglas Adams' *Hitchhikers' Guide to the Galaxy* where all the hairdressers from Earth find themselves marooned on a distant planet, having been deceived that the rest of humanity will be following shortly.

Fatally compromised, the narrative ambitions of the project degenerated into a one-avatar-stand

11 *Ages of Avatar* –
'Egeria' section, 1999.

by our invented comic book villain Arnold de'Ath, whose rather impotent interruptions of the smooth running of the worlds were universally recognised as irritating. Perhaps because the frequent crashes of the Microsoft Virtual Worlds client software had sensitised everyone to the desirability of continuous service. Nevertheless, Arnold, played at different times by members of the production team, did unify the nascent community still further and the hostess was provided with spells to combat Arnold's malign influence: which she allocated to inhabitants as a means of drawing them into the margins of the narrative.

Ages of Avatar was to be the penultimate phase of the research, and in deciding what should be our next and concluding step it was important to assess thoroughly what we had learnt, as well as taking into consideration overall project related issues. Among these was the preparedness of Nottingham University's *Massive-3* platform for use in supporting full audio, object manipulation and 'temporal link' recording and playback (but only over a LAN, Local Area Network) and the desire to test audience responses to virtual world narrative material in Jeffrey Shaw's *EVE* dome at the ZKM, another of the consortium partners.

The experience of *Ages of Avatar*, in spite of the functionality for the planned narrative being only partially implemented, made us confident that, given time, and resources it would be possible to create and sustain a diverse virtual world society into which narrative elements could be seeded. But, in addition to those aspects of the experiment mentioned above as being unsatisfactory and in need of reassessment, it was at this point that we became convinced of the necessity for the inclusion of several other major features which would depend for their success on all the subscribers being aware that they were inhabiting a narrative space.

Among these was an automated auxiliary system, which could track and profile the participants and co-ordinate personalised e-mail communication with them, integrated with a database for inhabitants to record their own experiences, a database where they could themselves write the folklore of their society. The justification for this was the perceived need to provide a critical mass of information to reassure inhabitants that untoward events were not simply to be ignored, as one might ignore irritations in real life, but rather a coherent weave of authored material inviting them to suspend their disbelief and immerse themselves unself-consciously in the ebb and flow of the story world. And it was in order to provide persistent foci for emotional investment on the part of the group, that some form of constructionist functionality was required which could allow inhabitants to leave evidence of their activities: artefacts which, ideally, should in themselves be of subsequent use or significance to the community members.

12 *Avatar Farm*, testing through an immersive performance, 1999.

However, while confident that with these provisions we could seed narratives, which would be entertaining for the inhabitants involved, we remained uncertain of how we could ultimately harvest legible audiovisual drama, which was suitable for broadcast. In the absence of audio-communication such as that available in *Massive-3*, the options for gestural communication remained very limited – with the result that participants were so concentrated on typing their dialogues that there was little meaningful movement of their avatars within the virtual space. In *Ages of Avatar*, even scenes of supposed animation such as a party, would often appear absurdly static, with participants abandoning their avatars as empty shells while they used the environment as a marginally enhanced text-based chatroom.

Avatar Farm (2000), the final demonstrator of the project, was explicitly addressed to achieving narrative engagement and character empathy from an audience in three different circumstances. These were a live web cast; a group interaction in an immersive environment (the *EVE* dome, which controlled the temporal and spatial editing of the 3D playback), and a television broadcast using high-resolution post-produced graphics. The *Massive-3* platform would be used: its tools for multi-camera virtual direction fully tested and its unique 'temporal links' technology put through its paces, not only for recording generated material in full 3D and synched audio suitable for post-production, but also by nesting three-dimensional flashback sequences within the live arena.

At a weekend event, four public participants, selected from the online inhabitants of *Ages of Avatar*, were situated in a virtual environment with nine actors, all of whom doubled their roles. Sizeable technical and direction teams worked both to manage the dramatic improvisation itself and the live web cast, while human 'helpers' were deployed to emulate the functionality of the planned 'simulation engine', allowing us to test its design for future implementation. Communication within the worlds was by means of audio links, each of which was lightly distorted to conceal the participants' identities, augment their vocal performance, and alleviate any self-consciousness.

With hands freed from typing, the potential for avatars to display a wide range of gestures was available and the ritualised use of some of these gestures was integrated into the story at particular points: to provide formal recognition of the events in question and to familiarise the participants with gestural operations. Immersive interfaces were used by some of the actors to create highly expressive, nuanced and at times almost balletic virtual performances.

The drama was located in the four worlds for which we had 'virtual sets' left over from *Ages of Avatar*, the style of which was interpreted by the author as a kind of post-*Magic Roundabout* cyber-neo-classicism. In the context of the rather pantomimic style of performance, possible via desktop workstations, this aesthetic suggested a variation on an archetypal pastoral drama of decadent gods and their mortal servants vying for influence in the dying days of Arcadia. The four-part story was loosely structured around objectives, information to be provided and parameters for performance and, in a further nod to the *Commedia dell'Arte*, scenarios were also provided as scaffolding for the actors' performances.

The success of *Avatar Farm* exceeded all our expectations and marked an exciting step forward for Inhabited Television. With the exception of technical problems with the web cast, the stability of the software platform when supporting a hugely ambitious project was an extraordinary achievement for Nottingham University and holds out great promise for the future. A concerted effort on the part of the directors and world managers ensured that improvised story events were tightly co-ordinated and much was learnt about the tools which would enhance communication and execution in this area. What is more, the virtual camera crew were able to operate with almost as much facility as would have been possible in a real-world multi-camera studio. Experiments in graphical post-production to benefit further from the exceptional gains in audience legibility, which derived from the use of more gesturally expressive avatars, have been very fruitful and post-synch facial animation is quite possible. In all, by the end of the project we finally had at our disposal the resources needed to properly test our creative ambitions.

So what now for Inhabited Television? After four year of experimentation, what configurations of the different approaches seem most promising? It is ironic that in the time since we conceived of an online digital experience, which would put communities of public participants on the television screen as narrative entertainment, new forms of real world participatory television have become hugely popular. From *1900 House*, which transposed a millennial family into the domestic circumstances of a century earlier and observed their hardships over several months, to the worldwide craze for voyeurcam pseudo-anthropology in the *Big Brother* franchise, we seem to love to watch our peers put through the mill on screen.

In a virtual world, by comparison, there does not exist the possibility for direct empathy with an expressive human face on the part of the audience; nor is it possible to impose such an intensity of physical or psychological pressure on the participants, as will cause them to confess their inner selves. The strengths of virtual world communities are rather different: they can be far larger and more complex in their social structures, while participation can be a more considered and cerebral experience. In addition, they can present circumstances for the imaginative existence of their inhabitants, which are quite impossible in the real world, whether for absolute or budgetary reasons: from a world which simulates the absence of spatio-temporal continuity, to the first colony on Mars.

It is these possibilities which the BBC Fiction Lab seemed to aspire to exploit with its putative and hugely ambitious multi-user virtual world project *The Block*, inspired by Perec's *Life: A User's Manual*. Within an infinitely extensible virtual built environment, the design of which is to be provided by one or more of the world's leading architects, 200 apartments are to be inititally inhabited by professional writers who will sow the seeds of drama and intervene, in character, to shape the narrative development. Beginning with an e-mail fiction in early 2001, the environment will go online six months later and within a year of its launch it is intended that the public community, which has formed in *The Block*, will be large enough and sufficiently committed for the narrative to become self-generating and the writers gradually to withdraw. A full range of auxiliary services will be available, as will cutting edge technology for the graphical representation of the participants: with such resources the broadcast reports on events within the world should define a new standard for Inhabited Television. While the team behind the project are reluctant to reveal the full scale and sophistication of their technical infrastructure, it would indeed be exciting, as well as a source of some envy to us, if their community reaches that indefinable critical mass where it can transform into a genuine society.

Our own current developments are focused more pragmatically on an educational form of semi-Inhabited Television: the virtual docudrama *Pompeii*. Using high end graphical and animatronic post-production of an inhabited 3D reconstruction of the ancient city we will aim to provide the most detailed imaginative recreation of daily life during the Roman Empire that television has yet attempted. The backbone of the dramatic narrative, which explores certain key social issues in the city, will be scripted and performed by professional actors. Inhabitants, selected from an online multi-user version of the environment, will participate in task-based activities on the periphery of this story. Subsequently, academics will contextualise the decisions made by the participants, who will themselves reflect in interviews, on the unforeseen ramifications of their actions within an unfamiliar, but pre-defined society.

In future it may perhaps be possible to go a step further, confidently dispensing with the actors and placing at the heart of a virtual environment a simulation engine of such simple perfection that it nurtures a communal narrative, a narrative so vivid and richly focused that inhabitants learn to see their own real lives and communities with fresh eyes. Certainly there can be no doubt that the new formulations of media offer opportunities for a profound redefinition of public service broadcasting, which is truly inclusive and, perhaps, democratic. Now, in a manner impossible within the rigidly controlled and unresponsive structure of traditional broadcasting, the audience is embraced, drawn in and encouraged to create its own meaning. Inhabited Television holds out the prospect of true 'bottom-up' developments, and from such a notion, it is to be fervently hoped that a renewed understanding of public service media may emerge.

New Paradigms <> New Movies

Interactive Film and New Narrative Interfaces

Chris Hales

INTRODUCTION

Attempts to link together narrativity and interactivity, in both theory and practice, cover a very wide and well-trodden ground.[1] My own practice, for quite some time, has been specifically formulated around digitised 'live action' video clips. I have been experimenting with ways in which movie scenes can be combined under computer control, such that the viewer, interacting with the work, can experience something which might be considered new and different from the well-known experience of cinema-going. For want of a better word, I use the term 'interactive movie' because these works could only be conceived of in the context of audience interaction (I have never made a video or cinema film). These works can currently be seen at art galleries or on CD-ROM, and like true experiments, each new movie tests out a different mode of interaction or a visual interface metaphor. The questions I try to resolve are: In what ways can an audience interact with a movie? In what visual ways can interactive movies be made that are instinctive and meaningful for as wide an audience as possible?

Such preoccupations are not unusual now, with artists, authors and manufacturers all taking an active interest in the possibilities of making movies interactive. From the manufacturer's viewpoint, the product might be considered as a new kind of special-format movie (i.e. in the same category as IMAX), whereas the artist might want to use interactivity simply as a means of closer engagement with the audience. As would be expected, many scriptwriters and film-makers with traditional backgrounds also investigate the possibilities of digital and non-linear movie-making. More often than not their discussions revolve around 'narrative' and 'story' as if these seemingly precious items – although they may indeed be cornerstones of cinematic entertainment – really are prerequisites to making interactive movies, or indeed any kind of movie. In this case, the technology is not leading to a change in thinking: simply a way of getting things done more efficiently and more economically. It is certainly true that dramatic story-based interactive movies/games can be made (and some will be discussed later), digital special effects can offer new visual thrills, and websites such as Atom Films offer new possibilities for distribution, but can the technology be applied to make something different?[2] This has become my occupation: research through artistic practice into the development of meaningful and engaging works structured from interactive video segments.

This chapter first presents a non-exhaustive overview of the history and potential of interactive movies. Then follows a more personal discussion of some of my own works and my observations concerning the audience's reaction to them.[3]

THE HISTORY

Interactive movies are neither unusual nor a by-product of the new digital age, and to contextualise my own work it will prove instructional to review what sorts of products have already been produced. Just like trying to classify movie genres themselves, there are numerous ways in which such a survey could be carried out, and interactive works are notoriously difficult to categorise.[4] In very broad terms of approach, three areas have proliferated: documentary and information (for example, training videos), entertainment (filmic computer games, or drama with the addition of full-motion video), and artworks of self-expression. For our purposes, this overview will be rather arbitrary, and will highlight the variety of technological platforms that can and have been used to show that the idea of interacting with moving images is neither recent, nor technology dependent, and that both film and television have experimented with it.

CINEMA

An often-discussed forerunner which used film as its display medium was called Kino-Automat, shown at Expo 67 in Montreal.[5] The problem of choice was overcome by having the actors appearing 'live' in front of the projected film which would stop in split-screen form at the end of the reel while the protagonist/actor (actually appearing on stage) would ask the audience to make moral judgements upon which direction the plot should take. Lamps around the screen would light up to show each viewer's selection (each seat had a button offering two choices), and the majority vote determined which reel would be shown next.

Filming multiple endings is a much simpler model and one suitable for detective-style narratives where skilful writing (and enough red herrings) can make a variety of outcomes seem equally possible. The British-made horror movie *The Beast Must Die* (Paul Annett, 1974) was reputed to have been filmed with three possible endings (reels) – the poster proclaiming 'One of these eight people will turn into a werewolf. Can you tell who it is when we stop the film for THE WEREWOLF BREAK?' Towards the end of the film the action would stop and a clock would be shown for 30 seconds, during which time the audience could decide for themselves the identity of the werewolf, choosing from the three characters still alive at that point in the film.

The concept of audience voting as a group experience was resurrected in the early 1990s when a number of small cinemas were equipped with pistol-grips by the United States company Entropy Entertainment Inc. (in association with Sony), which showed 30-minute movies such as *Mr Payback* (Bob Gale, 1995) and *I'm Your Man*, which had been shot on film but transferred to laserdisc for instant random access. There were frequent three-way choice points in the plot, which would be determined by majority vote, the audience being predominately teenage males, who would shout loudly to canvas, voting for their preferred option. Following the demise of the company, ChoicePoint Films revived some of the original material more recently. The original stories were re-marketed, but this time targeted at the domestic DVD environment with interaction by a single person rather than a group.

PRE-INTERACTIVE

Apart from the novelty of the voting and interface, the Kino-Automat film had all the usual elements of a quality cinematic release: well-defined characters, a beginning, middle and end, relationships, dilemmas and crises, good cinematography. Other film-makers, although not necessarily embracing interactive technologies, have attempted to break free from this formulaic version of cinema. The Hollywood film *Short Cuts* (Robert Altman, 1993) is often cited as having a hypertextual non-linear structure, even though the business of this movie is out-and-out storytelling and to all intents and purposes, it is a conventional Hollywood product. Whether the scripting of *Short Cuts* has been influenced by, or been an influence on non-linear hypertextual writing, is open to discussion. Moving further from established cinema, we might look at the work of Peter Greenaway, who puts it quite succinctly:

> Why has the cinema associated itself with the business of storytelling? Could it not profitably exist
> without it? My cinema experiments with numerical systems, alphabetical sequence, colour-coding, have
> all been attempts to dislodge this apparently unquestioned presumption that narrative is necessary
> and essential for cinema to convey its preoccupations.[6]

A personal inspiration is the innovative Polish film-maker Zbigniew Rybczynski, described by the Polish critic Ryszard Kluszczynski as being

> one of the most important artists deserving merit for delinearising the cinema … *New Book* (1975)
> and *Tango* (1980) in particular, when seen from today's perspective, seem to be an extremely
> important stage in the development of non-linear film poetics.[7]

The author describes this stage as 'pre-interactive'. The rarely shown split-screen movie *New Book* used multi-scene film editing in a *tour-de-force* of spatial representation and choreography, whereas the Hollywood product *Timecode* (Mike Figgis, 1999) appropriates a similar format without innovation, simply to show four strands of a conventional drama, filmed with the freedom and economy of single concurrent takes using digital video cameras.

BROADCAST

Terrestrial television as an experimental interactive medium has been established for some time using stream switching, which essentially means running a drama over two or more channels simultaneously and using the viewer's regular channel-changing button as the interactive interface. An example would be the simultaneous broadcasts on Danish television channels during New Year's Day 2000 of partially improvised dramas shot in the streets of Copenhagen the previous night by some of the well-known 'Dogme' directors. Many countries have experimented at least once with this format, another example being *Noodles and 08* which was an eight episode pilot for a 'soap', broadcast simultaneously on Sweden's SVT1 and SVT2 in August 1996, each channel showing the same story from two different characters' perspectives. The show's creator Steven Bawol outlined the benefits of this type of programming:

> The really neat way [to watch] is to put two TV sets side by side, since there are some good visual tricks, such as a condom being passed from one screen to the next. Another way is to flip between channels using the remote control, or you can just watch one channel and maybe discuss each episode with someone who watched it on the other channel. With a VCR you could even edit your own version.[8]

This type of synchronised multi-stream drama is more suited to cable or satellite systems, where greater channels are available. The Canadian company Videotron experimented with this in the early 1990s, a notable example being the murder mystery *A Vous l'Enquête: L'Affaire Landreux,* which was delivered simultaneously over four channels. In certain scenes viewers could choose point-of-view while at other key points there was a choice of which suspect to interrogate (there were four possible endings, only one of which was the correct supposition). More recently, Sky Sports have packaged up several channels and made them appear like a single so-called 'interactive' channel, by offering the audience the possibility to watch a football match from the camera angle of their choice.

A different interactive narrative model using television is the Finnish programme *Akvaario* (Aquarium).[9] Aimed at an insomniac audience, it was broadcast on Finnish national TV throughout March 1999 during the early hours of the morning for six nights a week, and revolved around the lives of two sleepless urban 'singles', Eira and Ari. They are portrayed as being awake at night in their homes and, almost like tamagotchis, can be influenced by a voting system of telephone calls from the viewers: the four predefined telephone numbers would satisfy the character's needs for food, drink, to party and to be cared for. If nobody calls, the character becomes upset and melancholic. The technology behind *Akvaario* is essentially a computer, which composes the show on the fly according to the moods of the virtual Ari and Eira from a media database with 5,000 different videoclips (which include some dreams). A linked website provides information on the voting, and a forum for comment. Interactivity is collective rather than directly personal and the responses from the Aquarium back to the viewers reflect their own collective feeling and mood. The essential principle is that *Akvaario* is NOT meant to be watched as a normal serial, from beginning to end, although some rapprochement between the two characters does develop during the month. Instead it is conceived as a place to drop by, to see how Ari and Eira are doing, and to help or disturb their lives.[10]

HOME COMPUTERS AND GAMES CONSOLES

Using CD-ROM, or more recently DVD, has proven to be a most suitable delivery medium for interactive movies both because it has a very broad user base and because technically it offers a workable compromise between quality and performance. A consequence is that it is conceived of as being a solitary medium for the home or workplace, and has been widely used by the gaming industry in their attempts to liven up gameplay by the addition of full-motion video, or by the entertainment industry eager to produce interactive dramas. Although these two approaches are perhaps fundamentally different (many writers discuss the basic conflicts between game and narrative), some manufacturers experiment with actual products, which attempt with greater or lesser success to unite the two very different entities. *The X-Files Game* by Hyperbole Studios has a strong appeal for fans of the cult television series of the same name because it features a familiar cast and storyline.[11] It is composed almost entirely of video sequences, linked together using the manufacturer's patented VirtualCinema® (an interactive engine and interface for interactive media) – but the use of video does not disguise the formulaic gaming paradigms upon which the product is built. The opposing approach is to emphasise that the product is a film, with all its intrinsic qualities such as a big name cast, great acting, and high production values – but with some interactivity added on to make the experience even better. In these cases, the publicity would still suggest that the drama is good enough to be enjoyed passively in its own right, without the need to interact. Shooting on 35mm film adds further kudos. One example from many would be *Tender Loving Care* described by its manufacturer's website as a

> provocative, psychological thriller designed to take full advantage of the stunning capabilities of DVD technology, while lifting CD-ROM to new heights. Starring two-time Oscar-nominee John Hurt, and based on a novel by Andrew Neiderman (*The Devil's Advocate*), *TLC* provides all of the pleasures of a traditional motion picture while satisfying the voyeuristic and self-analytic interests engaged by its unique interactive elements. *TLC* is not like other so-called interactive movies; its design is unprecedented in that the viewer's psyche is the invisible director of the tale, determining both character and plot development every step of the way.[12]

VIDEODISC FOR GALLERIES

The rather outdated 'videodisc' (or 'laserdisc') technology has been pivotal in the development of interactive movies, simply because it was one of the first to offer non-linear video access capabilities, and at reasonable full-screen quality. Artists and research establishments were the early adopters of these features, although (as discussed earlier) the entertainment industry has also experimented with videodisc.

One of the earliest works was the much-documented *Aspen* project made by a team from the MIT's Medialab in which visual journeys on all streets in the rectilinear gridplan of this town were documented and put together such that the user of the system could make their own tour.[13] This type of system came to be called a 'moviemap', characterised by an organised network structure of video segments.

Moving to the gallery environment, Lynn Hershman's *Lorna* (1979–84) has been described as the 'first autonomous work of interactive media art' and portrays

> a woman whose world has shrunk to the size of a television. Using a remote control device, the viewer calls up various channels from an interactive videodisc, and is thus able to observe Lorna

engaged in various activities in her insulated living space. Depending on how the viewer moves through the channels, three different endings to Lorna's story are possible: Lorna switches off her television, Lorna kills herself, or Lorna leaves her prison and sets off for Los Angeles.[14]

Grahame Weinbren's *Sonata* also used a videodisc gallery installation to weave together threads of filmed drama and associated imagery, putting

the means of summoning/interpreting the work firmly into the hands of the user, who, by pointing at a central computer-controlled display, can interrupt the course of the action, explore the past (or future) fate of a character, or, most interestingly, view pivotal events from another protagonist's perspective.[15]

The critical success of this artwork later led to the artist's *March II* in which the interaction is governed by the position and movement of the audience watching the movie on a special ramp.

The video artist Luc Courchesne has connected together banks of computer-controlled videodisc players to create multi-movie installations that are at the same time interactive for the audience and aware of each other's behaviour. From the four movie-characters comprising *Hall of Shadows* (1995) (each responsive to the actions of the other three as well as the audience) to the contiguous panoramas of *Landscape One* (1998), these internationally exhibited works explore the possibilities of an interactive dialogue with the characters portrayed, and a digital reinterpretation of the historical concept of a panorama.

13 *Landscape One*, Luc Courchesne, 1998.

In fact, just as Apple's proprietary 'QuickTime VR' opened up new possibilities in the mid-1990s for still images, so a sub-genre has come to exist of panoramic interactive movies, based around the use of a spherical lens such as the one produced by Be Here Corporation. Courchesne's own Panoscope system, in which the gallery visitor places their head inside a special screen and physically rotates their body, and the internet streaming of so-called 'immersive movies' (see below) are two manifestations of this phenomenon.

INTERNET

Increases in speed and bandwidth, and technological advances in digital video streaming have seen the internet become a more recent arena for interacting with moving images. Some movies are predicated on technological developments, others rely on the capability of websites to respond to mass audience voting.

In the former category the 360° movie makes a reappearance, this time streamed over the internet, but again using a proprietary lens to create video scenes which can be panned around at will (while the movie plays in the browser) by each audience member visiting the website. Significant action in these movies might be missed if the viewer does not actively spin the scenes around. *The New Arrival*, a four-minute film written and filmed by director Amy Talkington and made exclusively for the internet using this technology, was presented at the 2000 Cannes Film Festival.[16] Whether something new and substantial can be made from this genre of 'immersive' movies or whether it will remain a curiosity, remains to be seen.

One trend for interacting with movie segments using websites is towards empowering a mass vote (in a return to the fundamental concepts of Kino-Automat), since this is something that the internet does very well. Another movie promoted at Cannes 2000 was called *Running Time*, in which the movie script itself is written and filmed weekly in response to the most popular vote from the website's audience.[17] Each episode would generally finish with three fixed alternatives, and the plot would be elaborated according to the weekly vote. The team's follow-up entitled *Get a Life, Harry* allowed even more flexibility with the evolution of the story and characters, and also allowed suggestions to be entered on a 'chat' page, which would be curated by the team making the weekly episodes. The essential characteristic is that this system is dynamic, as opposed to most of the movies we have reviewed in which the content – although choosable – is ·entirely pre-recorded by the movie-maker onto a storage medium. Like a 'soap opera' the audience must watch weekly in order to enjoy and affect the development of the plot.

EXPERIMENTS IN INTERACTIVE FILM ART: A PERSONAL APPROACH

In many respects, the techniques behind my movies are deliberately simple. Since my work is made entirely of linked or combined digital video segments, I refer to it as 'interactive movie-making' or 'interactive film art', and the resultant artefacts can be experienced in two different ways by the audience. To enable some sort of distribution of my work I use CD-ROMs which can be viewed on a personal computer, in whatever environment the computer is situated in – possibly a home or workplace – and presuming an audience of one. The second possibility (more immersive) is a generic touch-screen projection installation, which I have set up in public galleries as far apart as Australia, South Korea, Iceland, San Francisco and Poland. As discussed above, videodisc has historically proved an excellent non-linear medium for delivery of interactive movies, and broadband offers the requisite bandwidth and response time, but I have not had the opportunity to experiment with either of these delivery systems to date.

There are two unavoidable fundamental structures that I use. The first presents the viewer with a single screen of video narrative all the way through, whereas the second offers multiple stories all going on at the same time. The former therefore tends to be a hard-wired branching system in which highly interlinked pathways are pre-authored into the video material. The other is more algorithmic and potentially different at each viewing since much of the behaviour of the video material is controlled by computer programming as well as by interaction from the audience. Regardless of structural intricacies these are attempts at producing engaging works that reward the viewer's manipulation by offering provoking, satisfying or inquisitive responses, and in general utilise the visual field of the movie itself. They are certainly (and most deliberately) not games, and not really dramas either, but could incorporate many elements from these genres. The playfulness inherent in interacting directly onto the surface of the movie itself is used to compensate for complexities of plot or high drama.

Although Bertolt Brecht once reproached cinema itself as being *'the result of a production that took place in the absence of its audience'*, interactive movies require a special dynamic between filmmaker and audience.[18] They must be judged through feedback from the users and for this reason I developed my interactive touch screen installation as a generic 'canvas' on which I could exhibit a larger and larger selection of movies as I completed them. The same installation has travelled around galleries since 1995, although its digital movie content has been in continual expansion.

One of the important issues raised when making a movie interactive is whether to design for a single person or for many. Cinema designs its product for theatre audiences, where a shared viewing contributes to the experience, and in my own work I find this analogous to designing interactive movies for a gallery installation. Watching rented movies at home on a video recorder would equate to using a CD-ROM or DVD on a home computer. Even so, the fact remains that only one person at a time can actually trigger the gallery interaction while the remainder of the audience can observe the changes made, and are often quite happy to remain 'observers'. (I frequently notice that certain individuals are too shy to interact in front of a crowd, because they believe they might make a mistake and embarrass themselves in front of others.)

When analysing the success (or otherwise) of my interactive movies, audience feedback tends to be subjective and there are many variables involved. I do however consider the observation of the audience in front of my gallery installations to be an important element of my research. I try to conceal myself in the space and watch how different cultural and demographic audience members come to terms with what they are experiencing, and if possible I document video footage of what is happening. Video taken in Reykjavik (for example) would show a crowded gallery space at the opening of the exhibition, with the majority of the audience quite content (and seemingly happier) to simply watch the screen being controlled by another person. The bolder or younger members of the audience willing to work out how to interact with the movie show expressions of concentration and captivation, and the time they spend at the piece confirms a definite engagement with the work presented to them.

The interaction I implement is nearly always pitched at a simple, visual and intuitive level, and this has been learnt through empirical observation. The viewer usually only needs to make a touch on the movie screen (or click with the mouse) in the right place at the right time to cause a change, a technique sometimes known as spatio-temporal linking. There are no complicated menu systems or on-screen buttons to get in the way.

An overview of the movies themselves would logically start by analysing a work that has the easiest structure to comprehend and in which the results of interaction are immediate and visual. *Jinxed!* (1993) is a short drama-based slapstick comedy that fits the classic model of joining video segments together in a branching system.[19] It is also episodic, in that there is no ultimate beginning or end. We are battling against the protagonist who has a goal to achieve and we try to hinder him in achieving it by selecting 'jinxed' objects at the right moment. There is a certain element of gameplay, but a humorous satisfaction at the hero's misfortune is the most engaging goal. The interaction is simple: parts of the house become 'jinxed' hotspots for four seconds and the viewer must 'click' at these hot spots to achieve the movie's goal of malicious enjoyment and laughter. Feedback and critique from this movie suggested that viewers enjoyed both the visual sight of the protagon-

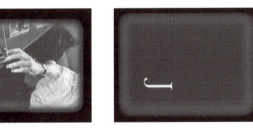 

14 *Jinxed!*, Chris Hales, 1993.

ist being 'inconvenienced', plus the need to react quickly to the jinxed items. The audience appeal seemed universal – and effective when the screen was projected to a larger audience of passive viewers who could share the laughter. Although culturally the movie is clearly set in a London apartment, there is little use of language and the comedy is visual, conscious decisions, which have clearly helped to make this a popular work. A suggestion from a viewer was that the protagonist could also receive 'lucky breaks': a long-lost five pound note hidden under the carpet, or some good news received in a surprise letter, for example. But audience feedback clearly showed that there would be a lack of interest in any interaction that ran to the benefit of the 'loser', since quite simply it would not be funny – so such sequences were never inserted.

The non-fiction work entitled *The Twelve Loveliest Things I Know* (1996) is a personal documentary-based work resulting from research into the elementary things that children find fundamentally satisfying.[20] Twelve areas of childhood recollections are accessible from a single, looped clip and each

of these thematic areas can be dipped into and explored in a playful and reflective manner. The density of the information – much of the piece consists of split-screens – and the dynamic, colourful 'hotspots' engage the viewer's concentration and produce a moving and immersive effect. The musical soundtrack changes with the predominant mood of each individual scene. In this movie, the interaction is truly intuitive – things within the film that catch the eye: generally moving or colourful items such as a rolling red marble or a blue coat in the snow. The audience's motivation is curiosity and emotional response from the subject matter, and visual appreciation of the images and music. Feedback from this movie showed me that the structure was a useful reference for the viewer to orientate himself or herself, though a criticism was that it was hard to work out what was happening in the structure and some of the 'hotspots' were very eclectic. However, the main goal of aiming to produce an emotional and intense piece was achieved (one viewer reported 'now I feel I can give so much more to my son having seen your film'). The average viewer spent much time exploring the work. Though aimed squarely at adults, the work has been popular with children who try to find the 'fun' moments. Again, although an English childhood is portrayed, the nostalgia and subject matter that underline this film have widened its international appeal.

A short work which highlights my interest in the visual aspects of interaction is entitled *Sketchbook* (1996/7) because it came about as a vehicle to try out certain ideas, in the same way that a traditional artist might use a paper sketchbook. It was also an attempt to make something engaging simply by filming within a 100-metre radius in the countryside, in which an interactive world is revealed. Scenes of nature will loop indefinitely until the viewer touches the interactive key point, which in most cases is instinctively obvious. This will trigger a denouement, such as the sun setting quickly over the horizon. There are 30 different sketches called up purely at random without any suggestion of an ongoing story, although they could easily have been re-sequenced to portray a dawn-to-dusk sort of narrative. As a pedagogical experiment, a variation of *Sketchbook* brings up the first letter of the word representing the key image (e.g. S for Spider) and the word is completed only upon interaction from the user. The images of a dandelion being blown always caused a strong positive reaction, inspiring me to develop a 'selection menu movie' composed of ten dandelions in a field overlaid with text, from which the viewer could select any of my works (when they are shown together on the touch-screen installation).

Spring, Summer, Autumn, Winter (1998) is an experiment in which the viewer, by inter-action, can reconstruct the traces left in a landscape by the film-maker in his own movie and as such it plays with the concept of cinematic time. There are four scenes from the different seasons, conceived as tableaux, each with its own internal 'dramatic structure'. It is possible by touching the screen at the right place at the right time and in the right sequence, to reveal the film-maker's path at the time of recording the movie. There are no cues or visual clues to indicate where to touch (or click): this must be found by exploration. There is a definite 'ending' to each of the tableaux. Video of a gallery audience in Poland shows two ladies, neither of whom appears to know much about interactive art, coming to terms with how this piece works. Clearly demonstrated is the learning process by which they decode the visual language of the piece, step by step discovering that it is possible to advance in the tableau by consistently touching the screen in the right place in the right sequence. Failure to do this sees the footsteps disappear one by one.

I made *Bliss* (1998) as a contribution to an eponymous CD-ROM funded by the Arts Council of England, featuring different personal artistic expressions inspired by the short story *Bliss* by Katherine Mansfield. Nine movie streams are displayed simultaneously, and these conceptually represent nine scenes in a blissful domestic interior, with (for example) a baby at peace, a hot bath running, a gramo-

16 *Bliss,* Chris Hales, 1998.

phone playing. By skilful interaction within each scene, it is possible to maintain a blissful state of order, but each scene has a tendency to go out of control – a lack of attention and interaction brings about chaos and destruction. The baby starts to cry, the bath overflows, and the gramophone record scratches and breaks. Different screens are interlinked: for example from the top left scene the overflowing bath water drips onto the scene directly below it. The viewer can click different scenes to maintain order: calm the baby, close the book, stop the dog, lift the iron, etc. Again, although the interior portrayed is a 1920s domestic middle class English one, the visual concepts behind the piece seem recognisable to all and there is no use of spoken language.

17 *The Tallinn People's Orchestra,* Chris Hales, 1998.

The Tallinn People's Orchestra (1998) also experiments with multiple video streams, or at least non-synchronous multiple items controlled by both computer and user. Activities are portrayed in the main square in the old town of Tallinn (Estonia), showing local residents going about their business, children playing, tourists, pony rides, car traffic. Thirty-seven different elements of the scene have been isolated and each assigned a short musical 'leitmotiv'. The

computer chooses up to five elements at a time to place in the empty square, which becomes animated again with the same people as during the original filming. However, they now appear in any order and with a musical motif, to produce a kind of deconstructed jazz-ballet based entirely upon real-life activity. This piece shows the beauty inherent in day-to-day activities, many of which are repetitive. The computer does the work in generating the Tallinn people and in its own right, this has aesthetic value and pleasure, but the audience CAN interact by clicking on any of the moving elements of the screen. This simply makes the chosen element disappear instantly, allowing new musical and visual combinations to be put in place by the computer and sometimes enabling the larger characters to appear when they may not otherwise be able to. Although a specific location is represented, the visual and musical aspects of this piece seem immediately understandable by all audiences that I have observed, whether or not they fully appreciate the aesthetic behind it. An unexpected audience reaction (from all types of audience member) was the clear satisfaction gained from removing the characters in the square by touching them with the finger. Like the all-powerful hand of God able to change destiny (rather than the artistically creative control that I had envisaged), this pleasure was not the one I expected – rather like the experience of *Jinxed*, the strong link between interactivity and destruction appeared to have been established.

Like *Bliss*, the experimental basis behind <u>Grandad</u> (2000) is to create a cinematic space by combining separate moving image streams (commonly referred to as 'split-screening'). However, whereas the cinema or TV can show pre-composed split-screens, the nine simultaneous screens that are portrayed in these movies are asynchronous. This means they are not permanently linked together and each screen can show autonomous behaviour. The film was conceived as a documentary portrait of the closed life of an elderly retired watchmaker, whose wife died some years earlier and who relies on the friendship of his ageing dog Jack for company. The nine spaces – from which he can never break free – represent the limited horizons of his life in a northern mill town: his backyard, his bedroom, the stairs, an alleyway, his couch in the living room, etc. In the movie,

Grandad falls asleep and his disobedient dog decides to run away. When Grandad wakes up, he proceeds to look for his dog – which always seems to manage to evade him. The film is a spectacle, which is different every time, yet has very little interaction. It is possible to click on any of the nine spaces and select it as a destination for the dog, which will eventually try to reach that space while avoiding its pursuer. Other events can happen: a cat appears, a little boy hides to scare Grandad, Grandad visits the toilet, Grandad rests in bed for a while (among others). The programme investigates how events in space can be mapped out in an interactive movie, in a way that is almost – but not completely – representational. In addition, how an unsynched soundscape can add to the enjoyment of a movie, which is constantly changing. Audience feedback showed that as a conceptual 'portrait' the piece was effective, but its value as entertainment was limited and the audience seemed surprised that the level of interactivity was so low.

18 *Grandad*, Chris Hales, 2000.

CONCLUSION

Although we have reviewed the history of interactive movies and used this to put my own experimental works in context, the difficulty of quantifying anecdotal observations makes it impossible to make sweeping conclusions. Many products and artworks have come and gone in transient fashion, seldom attracting more than a passing excitement from the public.

Assessing my own attempts more qualitatively, I can at least try to compare the same movies under interaction from different audiences and different cultures, then employ a feedback loop to reuse the features that are clearly effective and abandon techniques that are confusing. By keeping the same technological level across all my works, the comparison is at least made fairer since there is a controlled environment. Not producing movies for commercial gain has afforded me the luxury of being able to analyse and adapt my work in this manner.

My practical experimentation has led me to believe that when movie sequences are linked together non-linearly, under computer control and with possibilities for user interaction, new forms or paradigms can potentially emerge. Links in space and time between specially art-directed movie sequences can be orchestrated to produce something that seems unique. My personal rule is that narrative structure and content can be successfully subjugated in favour of a visual linking system through time, space, colour, object and point of view. Narrative scriptwriting of the sort which has been propagated in the movie industry for 80 or more years no longer plays a role, and even the concept of what constitutes a 'story' must be re-evaluated. Whereas the popularity of the Hollywood 'style' of film has pushed the experiments of structural, abstract and non-narrative film-makers into a niche, the addition of interactivity could continue to demonstrate that there are other uses of filmic communication, based on concepts of time and space, which are at the very least equally valid.

NOTES

1. There will be no endless discussion here of the definitions of what interactivity and narrative could or do actually mean. Such wonderful arguments seem to be perpetuated *ad infinitum* between rival camps and fuel many a conference agenda. Similarly, I use the word 'movie' generically, to mean a sequence of moving images whatever format they may be in (film, video, digital, etc.).

2. http://www.atomfilms.com.

3. For another reading of the subject, see my chapter: 'The Interactive Filmmaker's Challenge', Fullerton, John and Söderbergh Widding, Astrid, eds. *Moving Images: From Edison to the Webcam. Stockholm Studies in Cinema.* Luton: John Libbey, 2000, pp. 187–92.

4. As an example, see the difficulties of classification encountered by the 'Interactive Art' jury at the *Prix Ars Electronica 1996*, as detailed in Perry Hoberman's article: 'Free Choice or Control', Leopoldseder, Hannes and Schöpf, Christine, eds. *Prix Ars Electronica 96.* Vienna/New York: Springer, 1996, pp. 53–7.

5. A small custom-made cinema showing a film entitled *One Man and his World*, made by a group of Czechoslovakian film-makers and directed by Radusz Cincera.

6. Greenaway, Peter. *The Stairs.* Geneva/London: Merrell Holberton, 1994, pp. 12–13.

7. Kluszczynski, Ryszard W. *Film-Wideo-Multimedia.* Warsaw: Instytut Kultury Warszawa, 1999, p. 210.

8. As reported in: Millichip, Jane. 'Two Sides to Every Story.' *TV World*, Feb. 1996.

9. A co-production of YLE (Finnish National Television) and the University of Art and Design, Helsinki. Directed by Teijo Pellinen. Producers Raimo Lang and Kari Paukkunen.

10. From Teijo Pellinen: 'The program divided its viewers radically into two opposite parties; the haters and the lovers. From our website we got a lot of encouraging feedback of how sleepless people were not feeling lonely any more. And one young woman quit swallowing tranquillisers. I met a man that told that he fell asleep, watching evening news on the sofa and woke up at night because somebody was staring at him from the TV.'

11. *The X-Files Game* by Hyperbole Studios, Seattle. http://www.hyperbole.com.

12. *Tender Loving Care* by Aftermath Media. http://www.aftermathmedia.com.

13. ZKM, *ZKM Centre for Art and Media*, Karlsruhe. Compiled by Sibylle Peine (Prestel-Museum Guide). Munich/New York: Prestel-Verlag, 1997, pp. 38–9.

14. See for example: Lippman, Andy. *Moviemaps: An Application of the Optical Videodisc to Computer Graphics*. Siggraph Proceedings 1980.

15. Steven Bode, from the exhibition brochure of the United Kingdom tour of *Sonata*, 1993.

16. Uses iVideo™ technology developed by Be Here Corporation: http://www.behere.com. Other companies also offer 360° movie technology, such as Remotereality: http://www.remotereality.com.

17. Produced by a company called the Interactive Motion Picture Corporation: http://www.itsyourmovie.com.

18. Diary entry, originally in Brecht's 'Arbeitsjournal' for 27 March 1942. Willett, John, ed. *Journals 1934–1955. Bertolt Brecht*. Hugh Rorrison, trans. London: Methuen, 1993, p. 214.

19. Made with Mike Williams and Toby Inwards during 1993.

20. Hales, Chris. *LAB002 Twelve* (Mac-only CD-ROM). London: Research Publishing, 1996.

The Interactive Art Gambit*

Ken Feingold

Emerging from a peculiar concatenation of sculpture, experimental cinema, automata, arcade machines, shrines and computer technology, the interactive work of art holds an equally peculiar status in a nether-world between Fine Art, what has come to be called media art, and electronic entertainment.

The cover that Marcel Duchamp made for the catalogue of the 1947 exhibition titled *Le Surréalisme*, organised by Duchamp and André Breton, is a fake breast. The catalogue has a reverse side, which bears the inscription, in French, 'Please Touch'. I thought about this work almost instantaneously when I first saw a computer touch-screen positioned over an image, wherein one was coaxed to 'touch' the image, touch the object of desire. It seemed to me that this link between looking, wanting and touching connected quite directly to these very fundamental urges – to touch the breast, or, more autonomously, to play with faeces. To touch, to acquire, to investigate, to examine the results of one's production … to affirm one's own existence in the world – the earliest and most durable forms of agency. Freud writes in *Three Contributions to a Theory of Sex:*

> At least a certain amount of touching is indispensable for a person in order to attain the normal
> sexual aim. It is also generally known that touching of the skin of the sexual object causes much pleas-
> ure and produces a supply of new excitement.[1]

The same holds true in the end with looking, which is analogous to touching. This statement is clear and not at all surprising in this context that touching is analogous to looking. And it is these two senses which dominate the field of interactive art, and immediately transform an audience member of these works from a passive viewer to something of a performer in an eroticised field of interaction.

The gesture of the hand as that which 'opens-up' the work, so that we might perceive and thereby decipher and interpret its inner qualities, can be connected to the fundamental technology of the moving image itself. Cinema, from the beginning, was involved with performance and the physical gesture – the hand-cranked camera, mutoscope, projector, the gestures which mark the moment of the exposure, the interruption of the light by the shutter – the cutting of time by the

* Based on a lecture originally presented at *Technology in the 90s*, the Museum of Modern Art, New York, 7 April 1997.

clock crystal in the circuit that shifts the flow in an interactive work. And these were also present in the basic reception and way of selecting early radio and TV – adjusting the antenna, tuning the dial, the remote control … This intervention of the hand is reproduced again and again, marking our ever-ambivalent relationship to time: we use it, it finishes us …

It has been some time since art practice first pointed towards becoming interactive. There is, for example, a painting by Jasper Johns, titled *Tango*, from 1955. In the lower right there is a small key protruding from the painting – the key of a music box. Something to touch, to turn, to activate another dimension of the work, hidden within. Johns is quoted in Michael Crichton's 1977 book (referring to *Target with Plaster Casts* and *Tango*):

> I wanted to suggest a physical relationship to the pictures that was active. In the targets, one could stand back or one might go very close and lift the lids or shut them. In *Tango*, to wind the key and hear the sound, you had to stand relatively close to the painting, too close to see the outside shape of the picture.[2]

Crichton goes on to say:

> In other words, Johns was already aware of trying to influence the observer – in this case, to influence the observer's physical position in relation to the painted surface. And he did it by providing a temptation, a source of curiosity, a reason to move closer and then to step back. The painting provokes an interaction with the viewer: it takes two to tango.

Johns' most well-known work which overtly evokes physically interaction was his 1960 *Target*, a framed, unfinished watercolour of a target, below which are some small tins of colour and a brush. The obvious suggestion is that the painting itself is to be physically completed by another, unknown to the artist. In this work, the interaction is conceptual, meta-interactive. The physical interaction is essentially irrelevant, as it is simply the idea of the action, which is enough to carry the meaning of the work. Here it is clearly *the idea* of a viewer participating in the work, which is significant, and this piece was often discussed in art schools during the early 1970s as a proto-conceptual artwork.

Going back even farther in time, looking for cultural formations, which are now familiar aspects of interactive art, I was struck early on by the essentially interactive nature of shrines and other somehow consecrated public places. What differs there from the contemporary interactive artwork which relies on, as Crichton said, temptations and sources of curiosity is the fact that the encounter is ritualised and made into theatre. It is performative, highly prescribed, and passed on from generation to generation. In the ritualised encounter, there is quite often an actual physical exchange, which is also a symbolic exchange. One leaves something, in a certain way, and takes something away – usually as a mark upon the body. It is generally performed by simultaneous actions of touching and looking, but here, very importantly, and in most cases completely absent in interactive art, the voice of the participant plays an important role.

The orchestration of the body's movement through space plays an important role, too, in the framing of the interactive encounter. A path, such as those found at most approaches to shrines, not only makes one highly conscious of each footstep taken, but also clearly has a destination, and unfolds in time, like cinematic works, leading to a cathartic moment which itself is located in another place of exchange, where the 'real' meets the magical. Reaching the destination, one knows what to do. For example, a wishing-well reveals a trace of what is expected – clearly, 'someone else has been here'. It is the prescribed, known actions, which carry one's gesture forward – and improvisation is at a micro-level. 'Real' money is exchanged for the fulfilment of a wish – so it is, in a way, a kind of time-extended vending machine. Put in the money, the wish comes true, in some other time and place.

(DVD) I made my first computer-controlled interactive artwork in 1991, titled <u>The Surprising Spiral</u>. It utilised a computer-controlled videodisc, computer graphics, digitised sounds and texts, and synthesised voices, embedded within sculptures. The work responds to the form of the viewer-participant's engagement. There are two sculpture/interface objects through which a viewer can interact with the work. One is a large, hollow, hand-made book in which are encased replicas of human hands. In a cut out in the centre of the cover is embedded a transparent touch-screen, which appears to be a glass 'window' into the book. On this touch-screen are fingerprints, placed above the fingertips of the larger hand within the book. When a viewer touches any of the fingerprints, various things can happen: there are always sound responses to these touches, usually speech; the video can change to another location in the world, or an animated text might be evoked. In any case, a turn is taken in the labyrinth. The viewer's ability to interact and direct the

19 *The Surprising Spiral*, Ken Feingold, 1991 (collection ZKM/Center for Art and Media, Karlsruhe) – shown here at ZKM's 'Bitte Berühren (Please Touch)' show, 1992.

flow of images and sounds allows him or her to 'play' the piece, to seek or escape from finding a destination, or to enjoy its labyrinthine paths. The work has a complex cause and effect structure, and a touch that the viewer makes might have an immediate visual response, happen a short time later, or much later. I wanted these to mirror our daily cause and effect experiences. That is, sometimes we see the results of an action immediately, very soon, much later, etc. No two viewers will see the same flow of images or hear the same sounds in the same sequence, and the actions of previous viewers will also affect the structure found by another viewer.

On the spine of the book is the title *La Espiral Sorprendente*, the title of the work in Spanish. It is an homage to Jorge Luis Borges and Octavio Paz, the writers whose work inspired this piece. The other interactive object is also a book, an actual copy of Paz's *The Monkey Grammarian*. Embedded in the cover of the book is a casting of a man's lips, and between the lips a faint red light glows. When a viewer-participant holds their fingertips upon the lips, one hears texts from the book spoken aloud. When the hand is removed, the text ceases, the mouth falls silent again. If no one does anything to interact with the work for a length of time, it follows a path of images, which lead to one of the looped 'nature' images. At this point, the work will also clear its memory of the touches previous viewers have made, and it begins anew when touched again. These objects are set upon furniture sculptures, which I made, and these stand upon a painted wooden platform. From a narrative point of view, the work is about the simultaneous sensations of ecstasy and emptiness which arise from the labyrinthine nature of travelling, of being in motion; the mind reflecting upon itself and upon the organisation of languages, thoughts and perceptions. Images flow from one place in the world to another, a continuous movement of the passenger, the one walking through, passing through; the view of the world along the path, with no end in mind. These are images, which I recorded from 1979 to 1991, in the United States, India, Japan, Argentina, Thailand, Scotland, Sri Lanka, utterly without any conception of cinematic *mise-en-scène*. They are the remains, the visual and auditory residuum of what has been passed by, moved through. As a reverse side, moments of the camera's fixity with which we have observed what we think of as 'nature', that is, time outside of our own determination, events unfolding oblivious to human purposes, the temporal order which marks our own passage through time, whether we are in motion or not.

Because it connects to known forms, such as the shrine or the vending-machine, the circuit described between the desire to 'get something' from the work and the expectation of a 'return' informs the basic drive in the interactive encounter. *The Surprising Spiral* brought this to my attention quite clearly. The structure of the work is such that the viewer-participant cannot know what effects their actions will produce. What I learned was that many who encountered this work were frustrated by their inability to 'get what they wanted', to control the work. Interactivity is, in many ways, about affirmation of the human action by a non-human object, a narcissistic 'it sees me'. But beyond that, there is the desire for control, for mastery over the non-human entity. I also learned that it is a rare viewer who feels comfortable in the role of public participant in an interactive work, which has no clear 'goal'. People always seem to ask the same questions when the 'destination' of the interaction is unclear – 'How is it structured?', 'Is it random?', 'How can I get what I want (or see what I want to see)?', 'Am I doing it right?', 'What will happen if I do "this" or "that"?'. Most will come to the conclusion that, if they cannot perceive the structure, then it is 'random'; an interesting, but in the case of my work, largely incorrect conclusion.

But one of the things I was after in that work was to take away the possibility of 'control' so that people have to abandon the idea of having a goal, a destination. Why? Centrally, it is one of the main subject matters of this work, relating to the idea of travel, as a medium for the experience of the 'going-along' itself. But also, I wanted to be quite clear that I was not offering people 'choices', 'menus', or any of the other fare well known at that time from commercial kiosk applications and training videodiscs.

Watching audiences engage in this work pointed something out to me very clearly – that people expected unambiguous interaction. It actually disappointed me tremendously, as I expected the audience, and audiences turned into participants, to bring to interactive works the same capacity for abstraction, metaphor and ambiguity that is well-deployed and comfortable when viewing painting, or other artworks.

The mainstream audience, trained on cash-dispensing computers and information kiosks, wishes to affirm the qualities Regina Cornwell says are valued in mass culture forms of interactive media: efficiency, simplicity, logic, clarity.[3] The essential negativity, the rebellion or break so central to any notion of the avant-garde, formulated in the twentieth century, is no longer at work in a world where artists talk or care about 'users', where curators measure 'hits' on their websites and where audiences want our so-called 'interfaces' to be 'friendly' or 'intuitive', efficient, simple, logical and clear. When works strive to be completely understandable, they cannot produce any sort of break, and cannot create any new meanings. And the effect makes it is easy to forget that even those media forms which appear efficient, simple, logical and clear are expressions, constructions, ideologies which reinforce known structures of economics, power and agency.

This is a territory I have explored in my work for a long time: the area where cultural fragments are redirected into collision courses in order to precipitate new meanings; and to foreground the process in which we become aware that we are actively giving meaning to what we see and hear. Like subatomic particles thrown together in an accelerator, their collisions bring new, multivalent meanings to light, only partially under the control of the author.

My videotapes and films (such as *5dim/MIND*, 1983 and *The Double*, 1984) used juxtaposition and collision to create complex meanings across the point of the edit, multivalent possibilities riding the edit as the line of the world, inside the mind of the viewer. I was keenly aware of this as a kind of interaction, but was often frustrated by the convention in cinema of releasing a single, finished version of a work. Later, I became involved with computer-controlled image playback, allowing random access to image and sound fragments, and another dimension could be added, that one could create editing which was changeable within certain specific, written parameters, that within the creation of the subjective narrative of the work (whether non-narrative or explicitly story-oriented) one could deploy a logic of the sort 'if the viewer-participant does "this", the playback does "that". So part of what became interesting for me within these technological possibilities was a way to extend, in a significant way, an investigation with which I had already been involved for some time. But though the technology is one of random access and points to the possibility of restructuring fixed relations, as long as the sequencing of images and sounds are not random, which they are not in these interactive video works of mine, they are still written. And though the complexity is substantially increased, the particular sequences and possibilities remain highly determined.

In 1993 I completed a work titled *Childhood/Hot & Cold Wars (The Appearance of Nature)*. At the centre of this work, I undertook a search for my childhood TV memories, a kind of archaeology of those images and sounds which I remembered, or saw later, as having been formative in my personal understanding of what was 'going on' in the world. I grew up watching television. Some of my earliest and most vivid sensory and emotional memories are of television programmes I saw in my first years. The themes of my childhood emerged amid ever-present references to World War II, the atom bomb, the Communist threat and the domino theory, intersected by the emergence of suburbia, Sputnik, the Space Race and promises of endless progress in a fantastic technological future, a future in which I would be visiting other worlds. These recurring themes were played out through TV characters, news, advertisements, science-fiction films, children's programmes and Civil Defense films: a strange mixture of cartoon violence, sci-fi monsters, cowboys and Indians, and 'air raid drills', in which we spoke with equal ease of 'Nazis', 'Communists', 'the end of the world', 'aliens' and 'space-stations'. We only had to say or hear the names 'Hiroshima' and 'Nagasaki', 'Auschwitz' or 'Dachau' to feel a surge of fear, and a thrill at being 'the winners' of that war. In school and at home, we practised for nuclear attack, and watched people, monsters and cartoon animals killing each other on TV. It seemed natural, the way things were. I was learning, in a way, to learn violence as the language of the world, as a kind of entertainment.

The work has interactive aspects. It has been organised in such a way that a viewer who becomes physically involved with the work by turning a globe affects the ways in which clips of TV images and sounds are played, and may move through them forwards and backwards in time. The circuits and software I have made respond to gestures and types of movements, rather than simply following the participant's spinning (as a trackball might). Like fragments of early memories, disconnected, crystal-clear, momentary, the 'seconds, minutes and hours' in this work are stretched to infinity, going around over and over (as in my mind) with the hands of the clock, changing through the interaction of a viewer-participant, or going along without them.

The point of temptation here is a globe. It is hard to resist spinning any globe, and I relied on that impulse to create a way to interact with this work. But beyond that, I had to write a computer programme, which would play certain images and sounds in certain ways, depending upon how people turned the globe. I was interested in a kind of nervous interaction, one which had more of a response to the type of gesture evidenced by the way a person turned the globe, than the actual position of the globe itself. Careful and rather slow forms of turning allow people to dig around in the 200,000 fields of highly structured image-sequences stored on the laserdiscs. But if someone begins to spin the globe wildly, the images and sounds also reflect that, go out of their control, become nearly delirious, so that there is a relationship in the way in which someone interacts with the work to the facets of the work which are revealed.

In each interactive work, one initially has to put oneself in the position of the one who will encounter this work in a public place, if that is its destination. In the same way that a designer will anticipate and design for the ways in which a person will interact with a functional object, artists creating interactive works think about the ways in which people will encounter and try to manipulate their work. This aspect, of imagining oneself as another, adds a layer to the creative process, which is highly problematic. Can I imagine myself as another, or do I imagine them as myself? Is there a loss of integrity when the artist tries to imagine his or her audience, as if targetting a product for a market? Does one need to know to whom one is speaking? To paraphrase Paz in *The Monkey Grammarian*, am I the same one as the one who writes when I read what I have written?

In 1979, I showed an installation titled *Sexual Jokes* at the Whitney Museum in New York. According to my idea, this work was supposed to be only barely interactive, and it was not computer-controlled. There was a microphone near one of the chairs, with which one could throw one's voice across the room to a speaker near another chair – a kind of projection that I would revisit in another work with robot-puppets. The work was chaotically organised – not only were the chairs and monitors at skewed and disorienting angles to each other, but so were the images inside the video. The true interaction in this work was supposed to be at the collision-point of the title and the complexity presented by the objects and images in the room. But what shocked me was that people moved the chairs around as they pleased. I was utterly at a loss for what to do to stop it, short of fastening them to the floor, which was impossible. The positions of the chairs, making it difficult or impossible in many cases to look at a video monitor, were very carefully structured, yet people did not give a moment's thought to moving them about. Chairs, in the context of art museum, remained chairs, as long as one was allowed to sit on them, and therefore, also could be moved to a spot where they were most useful in the ordinary way – here, offering a good view of the television.

Duchamp's idea of the art coefficient says that every work of art can be evaluated, in part, as a ratio between that which is intended by the artist and not expressed in the work, and that which is unintentionally expressed by the work. In other words, recognising that each work finally escapes, to some extent, from its maker's intentions, and these are the two main factors, which come between the original intention of the artist and the understanding of the work by the audience.

But I have realised that in making interactive artworks, we have to add a corollary to Duchamp's equation, and also say that we have to look at the ratio of what unexpected things the audience does when they become participants, and which expected things they do not do at all. It is one thing to draw a viewer into a role of participation, but quite another to clearly anticipate their actions. Like Johns' *Target*, what the work finally looks like is left to that participant, and the artist has to give up their control, the ultimate sacrifice for those whose art is one of careful aesthetic manipulation. Duchamp said,

> All in all, the creative act is not performed by the artist alone; the spectator brings the work in con-
> tact with the external world by deciphering and interpreting its inner qualifications and thus adds his
> contribution to the creative act.[4]

Interactive artworks go beyond 'deciphering and interpreting … inner qualifications' and also draw
their audiences into actual, physical participation in the final materialisation of the work itself. But
for me, such materialisations must themselves be complex, and finally, if the work is successful the
audience is left, still, to decipher and interpret.

Complexity is a key factor in my work. What I find so extraordinarily compelling about using
computers to control interactive works is that it is possible for me to write software, which has the
ultimate result of creating works which behave complexly, and in many cases, unpredictably. It is
because of this unpredictability and the fact that the works must have real limits that I find myself
able to remain interested in my own work after it is completed. I assume that, for a critical viewer-
participant, extended or repeated encounters with the work will also result in some further vari-
eties of experience, and that new meanings will continue to emerge from the work as a result. Not
because they are endless, but the opposite – because they are finite, because they are written.

My work _Interior_ (1997) was a direct investigation of this idea. As a way of thinking through the
question, I made a work which was organised into repeatable 'scenes', and one could easily relo-

20 _Interior_,
Ken Feingold, 1997 –
shown here at
Postmasters Gallery,
New York, February
1999.

cate oneself within its episodic structure. It is a room with a human medical torso standing in front of a very large projection. Talking organs and puppets enact a delirious masked theatre within a shifting virtual landscape, changed by the way that the torso is touched. Along the spine, small sensors are embedded. Each organ of the human body appears as a speaking, puppet-like entity, offering aphoristic puzzles. Stroking the nervous system stirs up the cast of characters; while scenes can be entered by keeping one's hands in the same place for some time. Some scenes can only be found if more than one person is touching. In the sound landscape distant voices, many drawn from radio-scanner recordings, circle before backdrops which create a stage like *mise-en-scène*.

Interacting with a complex artwork is something far more unknown than interacting with a well-oiled functional machine. While the computer-driven work is not truly unpredictable, the subjective experience of it is that it is unpredictable, complicated, mysterious. As Edmund Jabès has written, '*Complexity is a game of the visible to attract the invisible*', and here we can get back to the real import of Duchamp's statement ('*All in all, the creative act is not performed by the artist alone*').[5] The complexity in these works provides the path upon which a participant can find these inner qualifications, in a dialogue between the work and their own subjectivity. Art is a social form of the imagination. Whether audiences can perceive value in works depends on the extent to which their own imagination can intersect with the work, the way in which their experience of the work is constructed on their own subjectivity, and the ways in which the work moves towards and relates to their prior experiences. It is not enough for interactive works to simply respond: vending machines and home appliances can do that. I try to think about and to write computer programmes as complexly determined traces of a self – obviously, myself. They have 'behaviours' and respond as traces of a personality might, oscillating between disguising their inner identity and revealing glimpses of it, an erotics of meaning created through this play of disguise and disclosure, interacting, more than anywhere else, in the mind of the viewer. This is still, for me, the primary site of interaction with art. The goal is to get beyond the vending-machine menu-driven forms of interaction. The efficient, simple, logical, clear work – 'if viewer does this then computer does that' – is too fixed, and as a result lacks mystery, complexity or paradox, which I consider to be essential qualities of a good work of art.

But I have been disappointed to learn that, to a large extent, audiences and critics expect to find the same formats in these artworks as they do in popular culture. For some reason, the 'difficult' artwork is now resisted by many audiences, who prefer to be guided and rewarded as they are in games of the common variety, with obvious metaphors and off-the-shelf mysticism. That the most widely accepted works traffic in the obvious is almost a foregone conclusion. This earnest spirit of so-called 'understandability and functionality', is, in my opinion, the most limiting and conservative notion of art that has emerged in recent times, because it does not raise questions. Many artists, too, champion this kind of 'user-friendly' work, this frightening spirit of 'happy-happy good citizenship', of 'artist-as-designer' or 'techno-populist' or 'here's-my-gift-to-you-mystic', of art having to have a moral code which equates responsibility with *not* breaking from the constraints of commercially-driven forms. Rather, with a kind of new age entrepreneurial 'Media-R-Us' sensibility, it

has no chance to offer any alternative to a status quo increasingly dominated by a globalised consumer's fascination with electronic technology and products.

I made _Jimmy Charlie Jimmy_ rather early on in my experimentation with spoken inter-action – around 1992. Basically, it speaks all the time. But it doesn't speak in a very loud voice, and getting really close to it causes it to stop speaking, because it has sensors which detect someone standing close to it, and these trigger circuits and software I made to shift it from one state to another. As it also happens, if one speaks to it while it is silent it will repeat what you have said to it in your own voice. So it is pretty obviously about the vain desire to have some electro-mechanical device, whether computer-driven or otherwise, become truly like a person. It is

21 _Jimmy Charlie Jimmy_, Ken Feingold, 1992.

incapable of a real conversation, but what it has to say might be worth listening to … so why interact? Why force the issue? At this moment, my interest was to draw the viewer-participant into a joke, in which they were mocked by the artwork for their desire to make it say something other than what it 'planned' to say.

In 1994, I was invited by the publication _artintact_ to make a work for their third CD-ROM. What really was the critical problem here for me was that a CD-ROM presumes that interaction will be via the familiar computer interfaces – mouse and keyboard, which I had avoided in my other works altogether. I came back to the _Jimmy Charlie Jimmy_ piece, but took it even farther. I decided to make a play on the idea of the button-driven work, the familiar computer icon that acts as a guide in interacting with the software and hardware – the psychic point of focus. There is this ever-changing whirlwind of buttons and icons, obviously compelling one to try to click on one of them. What happens is that the notion of the icon or button as a sign representing a particular choice is destroyed – one simply will go after anything at all, in a rush to succeed on the terms set by the piece. And what happens when one catches one of these buttons – not an easy job – is that the puppet starts to speak a phrase, and repeats it endlessly. So, almost immediately you realise that, having gotten what you wanted, you don't really want it any more, and in order to get rid of it, you have to catch another one. So you're pulled into a manic frenzy of undifferentiated button grabbing. There are no other levels, no score, no final outcome, no narrative except how you are behaving. Actually, all of the buttons and sounds in this piece were scavenged from the internet, and this is why the work is called *JCJ-Junkman*, completed in 1995 and published in 1996. It is a kind of network parasite. I put together some software, which, each time you hit a button, would go to websites and FTP (file transfer protocol) servers, and download images and sounds, transform them to a certain size, make button-like effects on them, and put them into the game. What I imagined originally was that the CD-ROM you owned would be able to connect to the internet, and that the person using it would eventually fill up their computer with these buttons and sounds. The more they used it, the more the files accumulated: a computer tapeworm rather than a virus. But it was decided that the published version would be self-contained – and what is in *artintact*, as it was published, is a politely fossilised and harmless version.[6]

Anyway, when I made the first version of *Jimmy Charlie Jimmy* I was also beginning research for another project, one which went off in another direction altogether, later titled <u>where i can see my house from here so we are</u> (1993–4). When I thought about 'interactivity', I also had to think about earlier notions of an interacting audience from performance art. *Claim* by Vito Acconci (1971) was an extremely important work in this regard. He described it as follows:

> A two-level loft – at street level, next to a stairway door, a TV monitor records my activity and functions as a warning to viewers (a viewer decides whether he wants to open the door and come down). I'm in the basement, blindfolded, seated on a chair at the foot of the stairs – I have at hand two metal pipes and a crowbar – I am talking aloud, to myself – talking myself into a possession obsession.[7]

In this kind of interactive work – which, for the artist, was clearly not theatre – there is obviously another dimension which is not shared with computer-driven artefacts. One is not interacting with the traces of the artist's gesture, as left in a mechanical device or a computer programme, but rather, with the artist, a person, directly, or (unwilling to interact), observing at a distance. Interacting through the video, with the clear awareness that what one sees in the video is happening at that moment, in real time, elsewhere, person to person. And because it is only one flight of stairs away, this form of telepresence had yet another dimension to it still, the possibility of moving from the virtual to the real and back, in the traversal of that flight of stairs.

But the point, for me, was that computer-driven 'interactive art' had to stop short of being interactive in the way that conversation, playing music, dancing, making love, or confronting a blindfolded artist swinging a crowbar are interactive – and admit to computer-driven 'interactivity' as a figure of speech … But this is not something to be disappointed about! On the contrary – it is a relief! It is just a critical step in seeing that the writing of the work, what it is about, is of greater significance than the formal innovation, or what the technology might promise in the way of other developments. What I also wanted to explore was the idea that this real interaction, whatever that might be, was still always within a specific frame of experience, and that an artwork was, to some extent, about creating that conceptual frame, not only the 'experience' itself. So, although I have described *where I can see my house from here so we are* as a 'telerobotic, telepresence, Internet-based interactive installation', this description says nothing at all about the specific nature of the experience created by the work, nor of its subject, the conceptual frame.[8]

The work creates an immediate sense of dislocation, a making-ambiguous of the sense of 'here' and 'there', qualities which I value more in this work than the more hypeable aspects of 'connecting over the internet' or 'taking on new personalities'. It is definitely a kind of hell in cyberspace, and obviously, this work is no simple chatroom on America Online, no utopian telematic embrace. One sees, at very low resolution and with much time-lag, into a life-size hall of mirrors, where it is nearly impossible to distinguish between the puppet who is 'you', its reflection, and the other puppets and their many reflections. So in this state of mind, conversations tend to expressions of 'where am I?',

22 *where i can see my house from here so we are*, Ken Feingold, 1993–4 – shown here at the Interactive Media Festival, Los Angeles, June 1995.

'is that me or you?', 'which way am I going?', etc. And I have to admit that, to a great extent, I was aiming a critical jab at this notion of purely open interaction, at online sentimentality, and at the kind of conversation that I was finding online up to those days when I began working on it. It also addresses, in a rather overtly dystopic way, the new possibility at that time of sending real-time video over the internet (using the Mbone, a live audio and video streaming in the internet), which was still dominated entirely by text. And I was also thinking about radio: ham radio and CB radio, and the experiments I had made with these. After all, what would three people who don't know each other and can't see each other's faces have to say to each other? If I gave people a means to communicate, it was overwhelmingly mediated by the qualities of the work I had devised and the technology was both medium and subject, in a way. What I have really imagined for this work from the beginning in 1993 is that it needs to be a permanent installation somewhere, in order for a very particular sub-subculture to develop around it. I do imagine it as a kind of public space, a kind of public hell.

I had a wonderful surprise in exhibiting the work for that very crowded week in 1995, when, after thousands of people, in an unbelievable, intense heat, which was magnified even more by the mirrors, the robots (really still quite hand-made and very much classifiable, by industrial norms as prototypes) began to turn what I could only call 'insane'. They would break down, and at first, I would fix them again, every few hours. But after a while, I began to enjoy the personalities they developed when they were 'broken', not working as they were 'supposed to'. One would only go in circles. Another would confuse left and right, front and back. Gearboxes began to strip, making noises and making some movements impossible. Another, though it could move properly, had lost its voice, but was instead, due to a crossing of wires, able to project its voice into one of the other puppets, which then had a split personality when occupied by two of the unwitting visitors. As they devolved further and further, their pathos was hilarious, perfect, like a Beckett play. It was in the breakdown of the technology that these puppets began to differentiate themselves, rebel against demands made on them, find a form of irrationality and unpredictability, and resist attempts at interacting with them, and it seemed to me that in a really successful piece, whether it is working or not is not very important.

A later work, *Head* (1999–2000), approached both the questions of creating 'real inter-action' and this fascinating dys-functionality. Utilising speech recognition, pseudo artificial intelligence, and synthe-sised speech, it presents to its audience a life-like animatronic human head with which one can have conversations, or

23 *Head*, Ken Feingold, 1999–2000; collection Kiasma Museum of Contemporary Art, Helsinki; photo by Pirje Mykkanen, The Central Art Archives, Finland.

24 *Séance Box No. 1* (detail), Ken Feingold, 1998–9; photo by Franz Wamhof.

something like conversations … It not only has hearing problems due to the still primitive nature of continuous speech recognition, but also the artificial intelligence aspect of the work was written in such a way as to create a 'personality' for Head which is insane, and almost completely incapable of paying attention to a subject matter. It does, from time to time, give quite direct and relevant responses, often enough to make it seem that it really is possible to have a conversation. Here, as I had done in *where I can see my house from here so we are*, participants are drawn into spoken inter-action. In speaking, the aesthetics of the initial subjective experience are transformed and overwhelmed by a making-public of oneself, it is not possible to remain silent and have any partic-ipatory role at all, except that of an observer. So the one who steps forward, who turns him/her-self outward to engage the work, also becomes a performer in front of all the others who are there. Contact with the work as an 'other' is made by way of the voice, a drawing out of the inner narrative produced by the work within the viewer-participant. Not everyone is willing to engage in such a performance, some find it excruciatingly uncomfortable, even antithetical to their notions of experiencing art. But others have discovered that there is a certain pleasure to be found in talk-ing back to art, in breaking the silence of the white space. As one member of the curatorial staff at the Kiasma Museum of Contemporary Art in Helsinki, where the work lives, wrote to me, 'It is driving people crazy and they love it.'

In other recent works, such as *Séance Box No. 1* (1998–9), these embodied conversational fig-ures also come to have an image world, and like the figure in *Interior*, act as the physical gateway for ordering the episodic image-sound narratives. But these works also, like the earlier *where i can see my house from here so we are*, use the pathways of computer networks as a means to get inside them, to interact with, as well as to take possession of, the 'minds' of these figures. They are also marked by the appearance of other characters – like *Head* in that they have conversational abilities, but purely virtual projections – and the only way to communicate with them is to get inside of the network through one of the physical figures and speak with these *agent provocateurs* through the puppet-medium. The screen is the projection *of* these figures, video inside-out; that is, the inner 'imaginary' workings of these figures, and how people interact with them, control what is seen. Image and sound are 'emotions', here, signs and symptoms emitted by the work. The means through which the viewers come to determine their own possible forms of agency, and to gather meanings from the work, are through these dialogues in which the inner qualities of these figures and scenes are discovered through that drawing out of the inner narratives of the visitors themselves.

NOTES

1. Freud, Sigmund. *Drei Abhandlungen zur Sexualtheorie*. Vienna 1905. *Three Contributions to a Theory of Sex*. A. A. Brill, trans. New York: Modern Library, 1938.

2. Crichton, Michael. *Jasper Johns*. New York: Harry N. Abrams/Whitney Museum, 1977.

3. Cornwell, Regina. 'Touching the Body in the Mind.' *Discourse* 14.2, Spring 1992.

4. Duchamp, Marcel. *The Creative Act*. Text of a talk given April 1957, American Federation of the Arts, Houston. Published as a phonograph recording by Aspen Magazine. New York, 1967.

5. Jabès, Edmund. *The Book of Questions*. Paris: Editions Gallimard, 1963.

6. CD-ROM Magazine, *Artintact 3*. ZKM Center for Arts and Technology, Karlsruhe, 1996.

7. Acconci, Vito. *Avalanche Magazine*. New York, Fall 1972.

8. Feingold, Ken. CNN news interview. Los Angeles, June 1995.

Notes Toward a Hypertextual Theory of Narrative

Jon Dovey

One of the effects of the development of cyberculture is a kind of retro-technological imagining, in which our media histories are remapped from the new vantage points of the digital domain. So, for instance, experimental literatures from Sterne's *Tristram Shandy* to the stories of Borges are reassigned as proto-hypertexts: multilinear, fractured and deeply reflexive.[1] Similarly, cinema history is rewritten as a teleology of the virtual, in which immersive VR is the end to which film has always been heading.[2] The narrative of media history is itself being amended by the present.

I want to comment on a similar reappraisal, a retro-retheorisation, of some elements of structuralist narrative theory, that seems to me to have also been occurring. In particular I will apply an approach based in hypertext theory to thinking about narrative and narrative theory, in the hope that this may make some contribution to the development of interactive narrative forms (in both literary and visual cultures). This will perforce be a recursive contribution, in which thinking about theoretical perspectives feeds back into production practice. I hope it might also be able to suggest a way in which a theoretical problem might be readdressed. This problem is formulated through the argument that interactive narrative is a contradiction in terms, that because existing attempts to create such a hybrid do not fit into any existing definition of narrative, they therefore cannot be narrative. This problem has resulted in a number of useful attempts to define this new formation.[3] I want to work from these new vantage points to retrospectively comment on some more traditional understandings of narrative.

Strictly speaking, 'hypertext' refers to works which are made up from discrete units of material, each of which offer the user a number of choices as to which unit is next encountered. That is to say: pieces of text which carry within them paths to other texts. The work itself is made up from discrete bodies of representational content, linked together in a web of connection, which the user must navigate. Each block of content in a hypertext is commonly referred to in literary theory as a 'node'; to progress to other nodes the user must make choices from the 'links' embedded within it by the authors.

This simple facility – call it the jump-link capability – leads immediately to all sorts of new text forms: for scholarship, for teaching, for fiction, for poetry.[4]

The potential of the instant 'jump-link' to create a very different kind of 'text' has been envisaged throughout the history of the development of computer media. The hypertext origin myth locates Vannevar Bush's 'As We May Think' piece from 1945 as the beginning of the idea that science and technology might be applied to the management of knowledge in such a way as to produce novel methods for its storage and retrieval. Already in 1945, Bush was writing about the problem of the sheer volume of knowledge that specialists have to access and manipulate – the idea of hypertext here arises from the problem of knowledge management. Bush suggested a machine, the 'Memex' in which information could be stored not through the conventional alphabetical and numerical indexing methods, but by association. 'The human mind . . .' observed Bush, '. . . operates by associ-ation. With one item in its grasp, it snaps instantly to the next that is suggested by the association of thoughts, in association with some intricate web of trails carried by the cells of the brain.'[5] All items in the Memex could be coded so that they could be called up using the associative links entered by its user,

> It [the Memex] affords an immediate step, however, to associative indexing, the basic idea of which is a
> provision whereby any item may be caused at will to select immediately and automatically another . . . .
> The process of tying two items together is the important thing.[6]

Using this customised series of trails or links through data, the user would be able to edit and com-bine documents into entirely new formations – formations determined by the associative trails themselves.

What is critically important to us now, looking back on this visionary proposition, is that it rests upon a particular model of cognition that has continued to inform and support both the develop-ment and the claims of hypertextuality. The idea that the mind functions principally through associ-ation underpins the whole appeal of hypertext as somehow a 'natural', transparent and empowering method for the organisation of knowledge (in its widest rather than text-specific sense).

The microfiche technologies envisaged by Bush never delivered his vision. However, by the time the computer had begun to establish itself as a data storage and retrieval system in the 1960s, Bush's vision was revived by Ted Nelson in a paper called 'A File Structure for the Complex, the Changing, and the Indeterminate' (Proceedings of the ACM national conference, 1965). Since that point Nelson has become the most persistently quoted hypertext visionary, continually searching for and developing new systems to support or augment the human intellect through hypertextual navigation and retrieval methods. His 1982 paper 'A New Home for the Mind' references both the literary and industrial trajectories of the hypertext claim.

> The link facility gives us much more than the attachment of mere odds and ends. It permits fully non-
> sequential writing. Writings have been sequential because pages have been sequential. What is the
> alternative ? Why hypertext – non-sequential writing.[7]

The idea of non-sequential writing (and reading) is central to the debate about the implications of hypertext for our understandings of textuality as we have received them to date. What has appealed to me in this account is the relation of hypertext to associative patterns of thought. This is undoubtedly because I come to the field as both teacher/writer and practitioner – in this instance it is the experience of production that grounds my approach. Making video, writing or producing multimedia have for me always been processes that begin with what we now may call a hypertextual association of possibilities; a pattern of images and ideas which gradually, through the process itself, takes on a more or less linear form, a time-based arrangement of material with a narrative structure or argument.

So the process is what shapes an essentially hypertextual experience of the subject matters into a linear form. This process is of course both painful and essential, since it has been, to date, precisely where the artifice of the narrative artist is at its most pointed, the point at which the multiple connections that bind the material together have to be separated out and reconstituted in a linear form. Editing film or video tape for instance, is a process in which the physical and structural elements of the work are rearranged in many different possible combinations, each weighed, viewed, tested before rearrangements and final orders are settled upon. Each of these elements (in hypertextual terms each 'node' or 'lexia'), has potential connections with other elements on the basis of space (what is represented), time, colour, sound quality and verbal content. The process of editing is about selecting out all those qualities not deemed functional in the narrative construction of the finished piece. Editing is not just about cutting out material (in the sense of leaving shots on the cutting room floor), but far more importantly about limiting and directing the possible range of significance within each element to a regime determined by a narrative structure. Having spent much of the 1980s editing and re-editing video tape on various Scratch Video projects, I encountered hypertext for the first time as an opening out of the possibilities of montage with which we were experimenting.

Equally, my understandings of narrative theory were informed by creative experience with editing and with multimedia. By the beginning of the 1990s narrative theory had already become a simultaneous and overlapping collection of methodologies. Linguistics, literary formalism, structuralism and post-structuralism had contributed to a protean and competing field in which any sense of linear historical progress had been lost (if it ever existed), rather:

> It would be more realistic to see the new criticisms of the 1980s and 1990s as approaches that were enabled and resourced by narratology – as the products and not the successors of narratology.[8]

It is beyond the scope of this article to review the relative merits of the various methodologies for theorising narrative. My perspective is informed by the structuralist accounts of narrative that continue to inform production practice and its pedagogy. (See Parker below.) In the most general terms: structuralist narratology offered an attempt to denaturalise narrative, and to see it as a culturally-specific and historically-contingent structural device for the ordering of material so that it makes sense. I want to argue that within the differences embodied in these analytic approaches, there is in structuralist accounts of narrative a common attempt to struggle with fundamental problems, which hypertext theory is able to throw into relief. This central problem concerns the process described above in my account of film editing.

How are we to understand what happens when a series of narrative events, a linear time-based process of action is represented, becomes for the reader an experience that is always so much greater than its linear succession of parts? How do narratives manage to work as both linear events and yet also exist for the audience as a rich experience that remains with the viewer, felt as a web of association and meaning? While simple successive linearity is clearly the spine of the cinematic or novelistic event, its extended body is what we remember. The success of the film or story in this formulation would therefore depend upon the skill of the makers in controlling the web of associative meaning set in play by narrative events. It is as if, for the reader, the text always exists simultaneously: as a linear experience and as a non-linear understanding.

Narrative theories have sought to explain this process by systematising the kind of events, or lexia, that make up the action represented. These attempts have been characterised by a common taxonomy in which represented events are defined as either those which move the action on in time or those events which primarily have another function or significance to do with theme, tone, form or patterning. It is as if narrative is always said to exist in two axes, one horizontal, based in time progression (or fracture and reassemblage) and the other, a vertical axis, which calibrates events on a different set of scales.

Evidence of attempts to explain this duality of narrative by reference to linguistic forms of criticism can be found throughout narrative theory. For instance for the novelist E. M. Forster:

> A plot is … a narrative of events, the emphasis falling on causality. 'The king died and the queen died'
> is a story. 'The king died and then the queen died of grief' is a plot.[9]

Here the 'story' is made of events linked in successive causality, while the 'plot' colours, thematises and patterns those events – indeed it is the 'plotting' of the narrative that makes it a satisfying experience for the reader/user.

Within the Russian Formalist tradition we encounter a not dissimilar distinction between *fabula* and *sjuzet*, the former being the material of the narrative itself, its events and 'theme', the latter being the arrangement and pattern of the material.[10] In this interpretation the success and operation of narrative depends crucially on the *sjuzet* as an organising principle of linkages and 'architectonic' patterns achieved through juxtaposition.[11] The object of literary criticism here becomes the illumination of the patterns and refractions that structure the narrative plot. This process already begins to offer a way into conceptualising narrative as a navigational experience for readers.

Similarly Roland Barthes begins his introduction to the 'Structural Analysis of Narrative' by distinguishing between two orders of narrative event. 'Functions' that correspond to 'a functionality of doing', and 'indices' which correspond to 'a functionality of being'.[12] A narrative function operates for Barthes primarily in time, it is a 'distributional' moment in which an action points the way forward to a further action. Barthes' functions operate within the field of consequential linearity, one thing happens after another, one event causes or presupposes a successive event and so on. Barthes' indices on the other hand (or axes) have a metaphorical relation, *referring to a more less diffuse concept which is nevertheless necessary to the meaning of the story'* for example, psychological or atmospheric. Barthes goes on to suggest that certain kinds of narrative such as the folktale are heavily functional, whereas the psychological thriller, in which very little might actually 'happen' are heavily 'indicial' or indexical. For Barthes, in this essay at least, the attempt to establish a method for the structural analysis of narrative *begins* with an understanding that he has to explain and account for the text as time as well as the text as metaphor.

> The form of narrative is essentially characterised by two powers: that of distending its signs over the length of the story and that of inserting unforseeable expansions into these distortions.[13]

Barthes' indexical, symbolic, metaphoric, events are 'inserted' and lead to 'expansions' of meaning, to the text suddenly (they are 'unforseeable') opening up levels of meaning that are other than the immediately signified.

In each of the above cases we can see that there is a fundamental distinction being made between two orders of narrative activity, one of which is primarily concerned with time, action and event structures, the other with character, atmosphere, feeling and theme.

From a different perspective it is also possible to argue that Eisenstein's carefully elaborated theories of montage can be read as attempts to explain the simultaneous action of these funda-mental axes of narrative. Certainly it is possible to see how Pudovkin's and Kuleshov's early mon-tage experiments relied upon the kind of cognitive assonance drawn upon by Ted Nelson in his arguments for hypertextual reading and writing practices. The mind makes meaning by associating different data inputs together to form relational patterns that are significant or useful. Where early montage experiment and hypertext differ is precisely around the issue of successive linearity or more complex patterns of cause and effect that have more in common with networked models. For early advocates of montage there is almost an assumption that the process is mechanical; par-ticular kinds of juxtaposition will produce particular meanings for an audience. Although Eisenstein is often thought of as a proponent of this 'montage mechanics', his later attempts to bring all film production within the aegis of the idea of montage recall other attempts to explain narrative on the basis of linguistics.[14]

For Eisenstein the act of montage, of putting one shot next to another, is seen as progressively more complex, subtle and ambiguous as he talks about the different classifications of montage: intel-lectual, overtonal, rhythmic, culminating in the musical analogy of polyphonic 'vertical' montage.[15] It seems to me that he is also attempting to explain how his linear succession of shots can produce a richly aesthetic experience. The linear horizontal axis of the film of course also operates within a vertical axis of symbolism that can be structured through montage. In an excellent introductory

essay from 1995 Ted Friedman makes the claim that Eisenstein 'hoped that the technology of montage would make it possible to film *Das Kapital*'. This never happened but, observes Friedman, '*A
computer game based on Das Kapital* (…) is easy to imagine.' This is because,

> escaping the prison house of language that seems so inadequate for holding together the disparate
> strands that construct postmodern subjectivity, computer simulations provide a radically new quasi-
> narrative form through which to communicate structures of interconnection.[16]

Similar structuralist patterns of opposition between horizontal and vertical axes of narrative are
also apparent in the literature of screenwriting which are driven by explications of how to link 'deep
structure' to narrative construction. Solutions are offered in the basis of script formulae by Syd
Field or Robert McKie in his internationally successful screenwriters' workshops.[17] More interestingly Christopher Vogler suggests ways in which script structure can be made to relate to mythic
structures that pre-date either the novel or Hollywood.[18] Drawing upon the rediscovery of Joseph
Campbell's work by Lucas and Spielberg in the mid-1970s, Vogler elaborates a formula that will
work both as a series of actions as well a vehicle for deep-seated heroic myths. For the purpose of
this essay Phil Parker's recent critique of what he calls these 'new structuralist' prescriptions for
script construction is crucial.[19] Parker argues that the existing approaches to thinking about script
construction are too narrow, in part because of their insistence on linear dramatic structures that
fail to explain either the startling variety of narrative form in existing film and TV or the complex
levels of engagement which the audience may have with them. Instead he argues for an understanding of narrative as a matrix whose points are genre, style, plot, theme, story and form. In other
words, for an understanding of the way that narrative works that is based upon a spatial rather than
a linear apprehension.

It is this sense of narrative as a space rather than as a succession of events that I have argued
above struggles to emerge from many of the classic structuralist accounts of narrative and cinematic form. Hypertextual ways of working, of course, invite us as both as authors and users to
experience information as a spatial arrangement. We are called upon to navigate the database in
order to make sense of what is stored within. Knowledge that may once have been transmitted in
narrative form, as story, novel, report, essay or article, can now be accessed through a network
of links in which a spatial relation between component parts can be preserved.

I want now to turn to how this recent understanding might be applied to narrative analysis.
What might a 'spatial' analysis of narrative begin to look like? Is there a way in which we can make
use of the insights gained from working in hypertextual forms to make a map of narrative structures ?[20] Let us take Wilder's 1944 film *Double Indemnity* as an example. One of the reasons for
looking at this film for narrative analysis is that the usual linearity of a cause-and-effect story structure is in part decentred by the fact that we know at the outset how the film will end. The opening sequence features the hero (played by Fred MacMurray) hurtling through the dawn streets in
an out of control car before staggering, bleeding, into an office building. He sits down at this point

to tell the story into a dictaphone. So we know from the outset that whatever the action about to unfold, it will have a bad outcome for the narrator and central character – we are immediately less concerned with the ultimate 'what will happen ?' (at the end) than 'how will it happen'?

Because of this flashback narrative structure the film already has a cyclical *pattern*: from leaving off MacMurray's dictation we dissolve through to live action of the events he describes before, as it were, 'catching up with ourselves' at the end of the film when Keyes (the Edward G. Robinson figure) enters the office building to find MacMurray dying at the end of his story. The dynamism that drives the viewer through this cycle is at an immediate level based in anticipation of the sexual relationships between MacMurray and the *femme fatale* played by Barbara Stanwyck. This is followed by our dawning understanding that the consequence of their consummation is to be the death of Stanwyck's husband and their discovery by the indomitable Keyes, MacMurray's father figure.

However, the tragic dimensions of the story are orchestrated by the complex patterning of theme and character that enrich (or in Barthes' terms 'expand') the event sequence. What a scriptwriter might call the 'deep structure' is the struggle between good and evil, dark and light, innocence and knowledge, in the character of MacMurray himself. This pattern is then heavily gendered through the opposition of Stanwyck (sexuality, knowledge, evil), to Keyes (masculine, fatherly, superior, 'rational' scientific, knowledgeable). Stanwyck's daughter additionally fits into this pattern, not in any way to advance the action, the events of the film, but I would argue, purely as a signifier of innocence to throw into relief the 'scheming' sexualised step-mother, Stanwyck. So the narrative structure of the film might be represented by a diagram with light/goodness/virtue at the top and dark/sexuality/knowledge at the bottom; each of the events could be identified on such a diagram and the progress of the characters through the moral structure plotted. The tragic element of the film derives entirely from this structure, without it the MacMurray character would simply be a venal opportunist, when in fact, through his relationship with the father figure Keyes, we are encouraged to identify with him as a morally complex figure making the wrong choices.

Christopher Nolan's 1999 *Memento* offers an even more interesting example of a narrative structure that might respond to a spatial analysis. This seems to me a film that is itself *of the cultural moment* of hypertext. This has something to do with the film's disregard for a conventional narrative timeline in favour of a complex time structure that instead of inviting the viewer on a journey in time, invites us instead to contemplate the static reality of a number of events that have already occurred and then to try and make sense of them. The ostensible 'story' of the film is of a man who has lost his short-term memory and is trying to track down the murderers of his wife. However most of the film is told backwards, that is to say the first scenes the audience witness in the film text are the final scenes in the chronological events of the story. Each sequence runs 'forward' in conventional cinema time and space but the end of each sequence actually links chronologically with the end of the sequence before. The audience has a sequential experience of the story in the sense that each sequence runs as coherently cinematic time and space, as well as in the sense that each sequence is chronologically juxtaposed to the next. However the familiarity of this sequential experience is a profoundly dislocated one, since the sequence is not linked by cause-and-effect – the removal of this causal logic has the effect of forcing the viewer to constantly update his/her state of understanding on the basis of a 'back link' to the end of the previous sequence. The Ariadne's thread of cause-and-effect is withheld: as a viewer I found myself of course trying to reconstruct it, but in the process having to move back and forth in time, having in fact to inhabit a web of connection that becomes the only way of 'making sense' of the text. This structure is additionally complicated by the inclusion of a black and white sequence in which the hero sits on a motel bed talking on the telephone narrating Sammy's story – in which we see the story of another man with the same short-term memory loss. However this intercut sequence preserves a conventional chronology, it moves forward through time in the opposite direction to the events that surround it. This overtly experimental time structure supports a 'theme' that is as much concerned with ontological uncertainty as the solution to the murder mystery – if indeed such a mystery even exists.

The story of a man with no short-term memory is perforce a story about precisely the kind of fragmented and chaotic account of social reality presented in literary hypertexts such as Michael Joyce's *Afternoon – A Story* (Eastgate Systems 1987). Janet Murray has identified a genre of hypertext stories to which *Afternoon* and *Memento* might both claim allegiance.[21] She calls it a 'violence hub' structure in which a violent and disruptive event lies at the heart of a story web that the user explores. In the case of a hypertext this exploration might be from the point of view of different characters' perspectives, or within different time frames. (For instance in the mystery game *Seventh Guest*, Trilobyte 1993, what we discover about the murder will depend on what time of the weekend we choose to visit a particular room in the country house where the events occur.) What is common to both the hypertext and the cinematic here is that both forms represent events that have clearly already happened and address the reader/user with the task of understanding how and why they happened on the basis of the available textual evidence.[22] The experience of trying to make sense of *Memento* is altogether one of piecing together and revisiting contradictory pieces of evidence, of navigating a web of information that stubbornly refuses conventional narrative resolution and instead offers a commentary on knowledge, identity and memory. Rather than being taken on a journey, as the conventional linear model of narrative might suggest, we are invited instead to explore a space.

When we design a piece of work for a hypertextual interactive environment it is necessary to think of the work in fragments, to break it down to constituent nodes or lexia. Each of these is then embedded within a linked network in which the author chooses a number of associated links. These could take the user to further definition, background information, alternate points of view, poetic resonances or formal equivalences. When we dispose of our material in this fashion we are working with a map that I am arguing has striking similarities with the kind of 'maps' that a spatial analysis of linear narratives might yield. These mapping processes have already been at work within narrative construction of all kinds, however they have been obscured by a reliance upon linguistically-derived textual criticism. The cultural moment of hypertextuality allows these qualities of narrative to be brought more sharply into focus, to emerge not as an 'unforseeable expansion' of language but as a central aspect of the method of narrative construction and analysis.

This re-emphasis on the spatial aspect of the shape of narratives might be the contribution that hypertextual modes of analysis makes to narrative theory. However I want to argue finally that my analysis of narrative as existing on horizontal and vertical axes also has some value for artists and producers working with interactive media. For the hypertextual producer making a spatial arrangement of materials is in fact hardly the problem, as I have hinted above the initial experience of not having to shoehorn one's material into a linear succession is seductively liberating. However the producer soon discovers that limiting the links to those that actually make sense or create meaning and value for the reader is harder. Freed from the task of having to decide which single juxtaposition, between shots or nodes, is *just* the right one does not necessarily produce better work, indeed it more often merely produces frustration for the user who has to pick their way through all the links. In other words precisely the *lack* of editing required in hypertext causes its own problems.

There are a number of strategies open to the producer facing the promiscuous possibilities of the hypertext environment. The first is to think through the registers of juxtaposition to be made available to the user. What quality of montage do I want to set up for the user? What are the thematic links and echoes that I want my users to be able to experience? The second is to reintroduce limitations on the user, to limit the number of routes through the web. Hence the art of the use of 'guard fields' in a hypertext authoring software like Eastgate Systems' *Storyspace*. Guard fields are a way of guiding the author through the hypertext by limiting the number of choices that can be made, by reintroducing a degree of linearity into the hypertextual field of possibility. Finally the creator of the hypertextual environment has to relinquish the kind of control over the text by which producers have traditionally defined themselves. This fundamental condition of the digital artwork is well summarised by Pierre Levy,

> The established differences between author and reader, performer and spectator, creator and interpreter become blurred and give way to a reading writing continuum that extends from the designers of the technology and networks to the final recipient, each one contributing to the activity of the other – the disappearance of the signature.[23]

Paradoxically however the aspect of my notes that I think is more useful as far as producers are concerned is not the spatial aspect of narratives but their temporal aspect. From the users' point of view the pleasure of narratives in time is of profound significance – we want to be taken into another world where quotidian time is suspended. We want to be 'transported', and for this to be possible the text has to work in time. Linear succession, cause-and-effect, is what allows the reader/user to 'relax' into the tale without having to fuss about making choices, finding key words or clicking on dialogue boxes. For all these reasons interactive producers have to bear in mind that successful narratives occur when the spatial and the temporal axes are *both* functioning. In this formulation then the successful interactive narrative is likely to develop out of the experiments of an artist like Grahame Weinbren, who ensures that the interface for his work is always time-based. The stories are always progressing, moving along, whether seen/read by the user or not. The piece will come to an end, to find another reading we have to return to the start and find an alternative way through the plot on the same timescale. The user is left with the satisfaction of an experience with beginnings, middles and ends, of an experience in which the storyteller is at least fulfilling some of their traditional role without relying upon the user to do it all. It seems unlikely that the traditional role and skills of the storyteller can be completely abnegated in the new environments offered by interactive media.

The compelling question that drives this volume is precisely what kind of narrative forms are emerging in these new environments. Given that narrative has become the dominant form of cultural activity in the past 200 years, it is unlikely to disappear. Indeed it is already clear that Hollywood and Tokyo are equally fascinated by what a mature form of narrative-based entertainment might be. It may not be pushing this fascination too far to argue that the computer game and its associated narrative forms may turn out to be as significant a part of twenty-first century popular culture as film has been of the twentieth century. Given this possibility we will have continual recourse to an understanding of narrative that is historically-grounded, to a continual reworking of the resources that narrative theory has already established.

NOTES

1. Aarseth, Espen. *Cybertext – Experiments in Ergodic Literature*. Baltimore: Johns Hopkins University Press, 1997, p. 22.
2. Bolter, Jay David and Grusin, Richard. *Remediation. Understanding New Media*, Cambridge: MIT Press, 1999, p. 161.
3. See e.g. Aarseth above on 'ergodic' literature; Martin Rieser on narrative as space, 'Interactive Narratives: A Form of Fiction?', *Convergence*, 3.1, Spring 1997, pp. 10–19; Bob Hughes on narrative as landscape, *Dust or Magic?* Boston: Addison Wesley, 1999.
4. Nelson, Ted. 'A New Home For the Mind'. P. Mayer, ed. *Computer Mediated Communications*. Oxford: Oxford University Press, 1999, p. 121.
5. Bush, Vannevar. 'As We May Think'. P. Mayer, 1999, p. 33.
6. Ibid., p. 34.
7. Nelson, Ted. 'A New Home for the Mind'. P. Mayer, 1999, p. 121.
8. Currie, Mark. *Postmodern Narrative Theory*. London: Macmillan, 1998, p. 10.
9. Forster, E. M. 'Aspects of the Novel', Murray, Janet H., ed. *Hamlet on the Holodeck. The Future of Narrative in Cyberspace*. Cambridge: MIT Press, 1997, p. 185.
10. Erlich, Victor. *Russian Formalism. 3rd Edition*. Yale: Yale University Press, 1981, p. 240.
11. Ibid., pp. 241–5.
12. 'The Structural Analysis of Narrative', Barthes, Roland. *Image – Music – Text*. London: Fontana, 1977, pp. 92–3.
13. Ibid. p. 117.
14. See e.g. Rhode, Eric. *A History of World Cinema*. London: Allen Lane, 1976, p. 100.
15. Eisenstein, Sergei. *The Film Sense*. London: Faber, 1943, p. 64.

16. Friedman, Ted. 'Making Sense of Software'. Steven G. Jones, ed. *Cybersociety*. London: Sage, 1995, p. 86.

17. Field, Syd. *The Scriptwriter's Workbook*. New York: Dell, 1987.

18. Vogler, Christopher. *The Writer's Journey*. London: Michael Wiese, 1992. Janet Horowitz Murray in *Hamlet on the Holodeck* also draws attention to this heroic myth structure, p. 196.

19. Parker, Phil. 'Reconstructing Narrative', *Journal of Media Practice*. vol. 1 no. 2. Intellect 2000, pp. 66–74.

20. This idea of mapping narrative is not original. Formalist criticism approached something very like it and Brenda Laurel calls attention to the work of Gustav Freytag in 1894, that offered the idea of narrative as the apex of a triangle on a graph made from axes of 'time' and 'complication': Laurel, Brenda. *Computers as Theatre*. Los Angeles: Addison Wesley, 1991. However these metaphors see narrative as a route, a line, rather than as a web of connection.

21. Murray, Janet Horowitz. *Hamlet on the Holodeck*, p. 135.

22. Of course all representation is historical, its events are always in the past. However the distinction here is between narrative structures that present a timeframe, in which the reader is positioned in a present tense that develops throughout the story, and structures, in which the reader is positioned outside the timeframe and enabled to move back and forth within it.

23. Levy, Pierre. 'The Aesthetics of Cyberspace'. Timothy Druckrey, ed. *Electronic Culture*. New York: Aperture, 1997.

The Poetics of Interactivity:
The Uncertainty Principle

Martin Rieser

Negative Capability, that is when man is capable of being in uncertainties, Mysteries, doubts, without any irritable reaching after fact and reason.

John Keats (letter to his brothers, December 1817)

The discovery of ambiguity in the sub-atomic world was the essential catalyst for the twentieth century's abandonment of hierarchical Newtonian science, with its omniscient privileging of the observer.[1] Quantum mechanics, revealed through Heisenberg's Uncertainty Principle, provided definitive proof of the ultimately unknowable and unpredictable nature of the universe – all versions of reality were thereafter tied to the subjectivity of observation. As the ambiguity of fundamental particles raised a conundrum for particle physicists, so for artists, writers and film-makers (engaged in the experimental discovery of appropriate form and language for interactive story and drama), the rediscovery of ambiguity in the language and structure of narrative still poses a primary challenge, although it is the omniscient privileging of the author, as opposed to audience, which is now under contention. In this chapter, I hope to demonstrate some of the means by which interactivity and narrative can utilise the interpenetrative power of language to collapse the distance between subject and object, and between interior and exterior spaces.

The frequent assertion that interactive narrative is 'a contradiction in terms' centres on the argument that the diegetic space of narrative is compromised or destroyed by interactive engagement with the story; as I hope to show, this argument is based on a misunderstanding of narrative mechanisms. The active participation of audience is not new nor is it disruptive of narrative diegesis; it is merely incompatible with certain narrative conventions, which have become unduly emphasised by historical accident.

LANGUAGE AND 'DEEP STRUCTURE'
Writers frequently use complex strategies to manipulate the engagement of audience with content. These strategies often fall outside the normal complexities of the Aristotelian model of drama. Dickens, for example, was an episodic writer by practice and his plots are often thin or incredible

to the critical eye. What we value in late Dickens, apart from his characterisation, is the vividness, energy and *ambiguity* of his language; and it is through such language that the darker symbolic sub-texts of his narrative worlds can reach an audience.[2] These affinities of language have been remarked in many great writers and form a secondary 'deep structure', which creates the uncon-scious mood of the work. We can also find equivalents to such literary devices in various cinematic genres such as *film noir*, where complex plots have very little to do with the powerful unconscious effect of the imagery on audience mood, and may even defy logical analysis.[3] It seems to me that language is the perfect tool for overcoming the discontinuities and schematic thinness brought about by sudden shifts of timescale or viewpoint, typical of interactive narratives. The very flexi-bility of language allows both for a compression of meaning and a proliferation of association, which can simultaneously lend rich ambiguities of meaning and organic unity to a new media work.

NARRATIVE FRAMING

A second literary-derived tool available to control audience engagement is the 'framing' of the work. There are also many examples in literature of the 'nesting' of narrative framing to ensure that the diegetic illusion is not compromised by violent shifts in time or viewpoint. *Wuthering Heights*, for instance, uses three frames of narration to achieve this: Lockwood relates the narra-tive as recounted by Nelly Dean who recounts the reported speech of the main protagonists. This simultaneously maintains a distance from the extraordinary melodrama of the book and reinforces the impact of that melodrama, as well as the dream-like quality of the story. Curiously, the com-plex framing falls away when we engage with the work and we see and hear at first hand the vivid life of the story. This is not altogether surprising when one thinks, for example, of cinema where the musical score also comes from beyond the diegesis of the film narrative, yet enhances the audi-ence engagement with that world. Similarly, strategies for maintaining the diegetic coherence of interactive media works have often relied on spatial mapping to provide a secondary framing device to keep the audience within the narrative world. Modern literature has become secure enough to add the frame of the real world itself to multiple internal framing of the narrative. It is typical of the post-modern writer to call attention to the artificial nature of the very devices which have hitherto sustained the diegetic illusion.

We are in a period where emergent grammars are continually being invented and these in turn are feeding back into the fixed conventions of 'old' media.[4] The nature of digital media is such that the fossilisation of narrative forms which has occurred in the development of cinema since the late 1920s – partly through the influence of Hollywood, and partly through the unchanging nature of the medium itself – is unlikely to occur with new media: the digital matrix is simply too indetermi-nate a structure to dominate emergent forms. The very linearity of film stimulated a number of conventions to counteract its effect. Flashbacks, jump-cuts, etc. reintroduced fluidity to a rigid medium. New media has the reverse problem: that of coherence. Interactive narratives demand a certain minimum 'granularity' of material, which can be assembled or reassembled in multiple com-binations by an audience. This modular structure can easily become shallow or incoherent, unless temporality remains uncompromised and the potential for poetic ambiguity and therefore richness is enhanced.

MULTILINEAL VERBOSITY

The multilinear possibilities of new media are not in themselves of any advantage in developing narratives. Economy and compression usually are hallmarks of successful artistic work, and cinematic conventions are based on its powers of visual shorthand and suggestion, with the audience filling in the details (witness the montage theories of Eisenstein). Imagine the artistic disaster, if a film like *Groundhog Day* (Harold Ramis, 1993) were spatially mapped as an interactive story, in such a way that the audience could live through all the repeated days and detail of the hero and his discovery of community. A tale of redemption would become a circle of hell – and the audience would empty the cinema. Multilinearity then demands two things: compression and precision. Only the relevant is useful to art.

> For cinema already exists right in the intersection between database and narrative. We can think of all the material accumulated during shooting forming a database, especially since the shooting schedule usually does not follow the narrative of the film but is determined by production logistics. During editing the editor constructs a film narrative out of this database, creating a unique trajectory through the conceptual space of all possible films that could have been constructed. From this perspective, every filmmaker engages with the database-narrative problem in every film, although only a few have done this self-consciously.[5]

The frustrations of a multilinear approach and the resulting non-hierarchical equivalence of all the material are anathematised by many critics. As this quote from the press shows, with new media narrative, the cup can be either half-full or half-empty.

> For every path taken, there is the path not taken. In frustration, we re-read the story, trying to exhaust all the possibilities in the search for the satisfying tale that surely must lie somewhere within. No wonder interactive fiction is such a troubled domain. That search for the 'right path', after all, is heresy to the interactive evangelists. There is, to them, no right way to read an interactive story, just as there is no right way to explore a new city. Each person, the argument goes, is both reader and writer, creating by his choices a unique story of his own. And no version is more right than the next.[6]

AUDIENCE AND INTERACTIVITY

As we move, as it were, from the interactive digital equivalents of the Lumières' spectacle to the appearance of the first work of D. W. Griffith or Sergei Eisenstein, the need for a better understanding of audience 'interaction' becomes all the more pressing. My own observations of the popularity of an experimental interactive video piece by Chris Hales at a German short film festival illustrate the case.[7] The users continually returned to torment an interactive character, who was struggling to wake up and dress for a vital interview. Doors could be opened by the user, soap spilt on the floor and alarm clocks switched off. The generated 'cause-and-effect' gave endless amusement and satisfaction to this supposedly sophisticated elite. In terms of audience, interactivity seemed stuck at the slapstick stage (significantly the predominant form of early cinema).

STRUCTURE AND MEANING

How then to tackle this problem of content and meaning pushing against the constraints and trivia of form? A re-examination of formal structuralist analysis makes it seem obvious that most interactive hypertext fictions and interactive movies tend to be a collection of what Barthes terms 'cardinal functions' or narrative hinge points, without the necessary 'indices' and 'catalysers' which add depth and flow to the narrative:

> These (nuclei) are both consecutive and consequential (…) a catalyser (…) accelerates, delays,
> gives fresh impetus to the discourse (…) the catalyser ceaselessly revives the semantic tension of
> the discourse, says ceaselessly there has been, there is going to be, meaning (…) A nucleus
> cannot be deleted without altering the story, but neither can a catalyst without altering the dis-
> course …[8]

The schematic dominance of the structure at the expense of content (of 'nodes' over 'indices' and 'catalysers') in most hypermedia narratives is vividly critiqued by Gareth Rees, the absurd reductionism of many such an approach is satirised in his version of an imaginary interactive Hamlet:

> 1. [the battlements of Elsinore Castle] HAMLET: To be or not to be, that is the question. If Hamlet
> takes up arms against a sea of troubles, go to 3; if he shuffles off this mortal coil go to 2[9]

Unfortunately, this was precisely the model adopted by the majority of early hyperfictions and computer games narratives.

In many ways drama differs from narrative fiction through the freedom of interpretation given to the performance. There are as many versions of Hamlet as there are directors; music is even more vastly dependent on the interpretive. The composer's original coding is given new 'interactive' life with each performance – in this we seem but one step away from Barthes' conclusions about authorial authority and the primacy of the reader:

> We know now that a text is not a line of words releasing a single 'theological' meaning (the message
> of the Author-God) but a multi-dimensional space in which a variety of writings, none of them orig-
> inal, blend and clash. The text is a tissue of quotations drawn from the innumerable centres of culture

(…) but there is one place where this multiplicity is focussed and that place is the reader (…). The reader is the space on which all the quotations that make up a writing are inscribed without any of them being lost; a text's unity lies not in its origin but in its destination.[10]

COMEDY AS INDEX

As a member of the Ship of Fools group,[11] my first creative encounter with the branching model of interactive narrative was in the early 1990s through authoring our production of _Media Myth and Mania_.[12] Here we struggled with the intrinsic problems of the tree form, which forces the participant to repeat a part of the logic branching on each replay and constrains any true freedom of choice in the development of narrative. The strategy we adopted was primarily an 'indexical' one, to compensate for the reductive constraints of structure. We extensively employed pastiche and humour coupled with hard documentary facts, rapidly switching position and viewpoint to encourage the audience towards a critical handling of the material.

Designed as an interactive spoof game, using digital sound and photographic sequencing, it examined issues of power and control of the mass media by a multi-choice biographical journey through the life of a media 'mogul'. The individual player identified with the protagonist, through use of anarchic humour in various parodies of contemporary biography. The player made moral choices based on absurdly limited visual data at various life stages, viewing the consequences in dramatised photo-romance style tableaux.

Photo-realistic image-based adventure games were, at the time, a growing section of the computer games market and were spearheading the penetration of interactive CD-ROMs into the domestic environment. Our game was an attempt to subvert this process by demystifying the use

25 _From Silver to Silicon: Media, Myth and Mania_, Ship of Fools, CD-ROM Artec, 1995.

of representation within the genre, through both form and content. Density was achieved through themes related to the role of public media and their relation to the domestic sphere. Media verities were continually questioned via hidden quotes and layered juxtapositions of media facts, embedded behind the tableaux. Since photo-romance magazines and adult comics provided the inspiration for the visual 'feel' of the piece, actors were posed for various life situations and placed digitally against computer-generated photomontage backgrounds. In a sense this updated the *Citizen Kane* idea of rooting the public figure in the personal depths of childhood. Biographical parallels to the lives of such contemporary 'moguls' as Maxwell and Murdoch were explored.[13] Here language was used ironically, the layering of media facts clashing uncomfortably with the over-simplistic form of the moral choices forced on the audience by the structure itself.

STORY AS RITUALISED LANDSCAPE

Unhappy with the experience of the branching 'tree' structure, where huge amounts of overlap and determinism are the obvious drawbacks, we moved on to another strategy altogether. Ritual and myth appeared to offer a route for 'deep' story. Narratives where actor and participant are one and the same, where the proscenium arch is dissolved, where landscape takes on symbolic significance, and where the usual hierarchies of temporal sequence, plot and sub-plot are suspended. In other words, the same model as early Greek theatre, carnival and religious ritual.

In the *Dreamhouse* project, Ship of Fools was seeking to bring such an experience up to date, combining spatial, ritualistic and dream-like elements.[14] As in many other 'games' the user finds themselves in a house. A walk through the *Dreamhouse* offered access to a number of rooms or experiences; each designed by an artist, reworking traditional storytelling structures. Various rooms were appropriately matched to the different psyches of those involved in authoring the piece. So the house became an interactive theatre, where different tales are triggered by audience exploration. The bland domestic environment of a real suburban house (in fact a real Barrett's 'Show Home' in a suburban estate at Bradley Stoke, the negative equity capital of the United Kingdom) became the main interface.[15]

In my own contribution, _Labyrinth_, various devices – doors, windows, mirrors and other objects – opened gateways into the mythological world.[16] The themes of intimacy and alienation were explored through such devices as multiple talking heads, each with their particular poetic fragments, or through a hall of sleepers who could be individually awakened. I sought to employ the resonance of poetic verse drama to unpack a number of thematics around fatherhood, overwhelming passion and 'Real Politik' suggested by the original Theseus and Daedalus legends. The transition in Greece from the worship of the Goddess to Apollonian religion is explored in the myth, where the Frankenstein-like quest for knowledge has equally dire consequences for the inventor. Daedalus commits murder, loses a son, and creates the monstrous Minotaur through his overweening pride in science. The piece explores these themes through dramatised video and a verse structure, which utilised parallel monologues (or duologues), set in dialectic opposition for each linked pair of protagonists. The verse is con-

26 Scenes from
Labyrinth,
Martin Rieser, 1999.

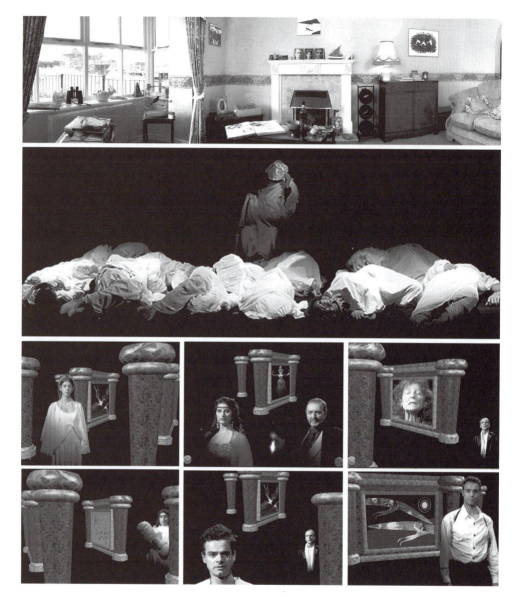

structed so that cross-counterpoints occur with every phrase. The verse reads vertically for
the individual speaker and horizontally for each pairing. The freedom to switch video streams
at any time allowed the audience to reconstruct meaning somewhere between the two opposing narrations. The development of irony and pathos demanded that no single monologue is
privileged. Writing for such an interface involved a new and precise multilinear approach to
scripting:

The arrival of Theseus and the sudden love sparked by him in the king's daughter Ariadne is notated
here. The Minotaur is her brother and Ariadne lends him the thread and sword by which he kills
the Minotaur and returns safely from the labyrinth.

Theseus	**Ariadne**
Crete is full of olives and laughter	*Careless, smiling*
	You stood askew
Minos keeps a good table	*Watching me*
Amphora clutter the Palace stores	*Brushing my hand as I poured*
Cicadas compete with lyres	*Breaking the stream*
Between the kitchens and the stables	
	In a moment we can turn
	In a minute burn
	As I do
Calcined, grouted	*A thread connects*
Clayed in water – twisted reels	*Souls, surely as*
The cavern drips	*A wedding vow*
In several corners	*Think, think and listen*
Ghosted by shadows	*To the whisper*
Echoing to the vaults	*Of your full heart*
Thank your heart	*Grace in your step*
For this Nadir	*Steel in your hand*
Walking on bone	*Remember*
Walking on stone	
Nothing connects	*We shall live as one*
In this nightmare	*After my brother's release*
Soundless	
Hollow as an ear	
Engulfing nothing	
In the cold Labyrinth I turn	*In a moment we can turn*
And turn, choked by carbon dark	*In a minute burn*
Stumbling on bones	*As I do*
Spooling Ariadne's thread	
Frail as cobweb	
Thin as breath	

Here Daedalus arrives in Cumae Italy after the flight from Crete, where Icarus has died in his climb toward the sun. He visits the Sibyl for guidance, who counsels that he erect a temple to Apollo to atone for the death of Icarus.

Daedalus	**The Sibyl**
Wings and rain	*Under sea*
A slow pageant spiralling to madness	*A body rolls and shifts*
I remembered falling:	*In strong currents*
Stars or something worse	*Ambition and ecstasy curled in rictus*
Smoking to the sea	*Picked by fishes*
I connect nothing	*Your care, your mind*
On the shore	
The god's eye blank,	*The god turns away*
vengeful	*Ashamed*
The Sibyl spelled in signs	*Locate your heart*
Hissing, urgent	*Open your armoured closeness*
Engraved in madness	*Locate a centre*
At Cumae I raised	*Build around the flame*
an architecture of atonement	*In tender stone*
For my deep neglect	
At Cumae I wept	*And calculate its beauty*

RESPONSIVE MACHINES AND BELIEVABLE AGENCY

Grahame Weinbren proposes an alternative model both to branching narratives, like that of *Media Myth and Mania,* and the parallel video streams of *Labyrinth*: a two-way transaction between computer and audience, only partially achieved in his own interactive cinema piece *Sonata* which also uses multilinear streaming.

> The ideal is a responsive representation machine, responsive in its capacity to change according to how the viewer responds to it. With such a machine, a new language of cinematic communication will be possible and a different type of narrative can unfold.[17]

In his *Sonata* the viewer can only control certain aspects of the narration – moving from the murderer of Tolstoy's *Kreutzer Sonata* telling his story in the railway carriage, to the events themselves,

27 Toybox: *Desktop Theatre of Amnesia*, Jon Dovey, Video Positive, 1995.

which can in turn be overlaid with the mouth of Tolstoy's wife berating the author, references to Freud's Wolfman case, the story of Judith and Holofernes, etc.[18] These indexical elements continually qualify and requalify each other. *Sonata* is linear, with time's arrow pointing forward, but it never reads the same way twice.

In Jon Dovey's piece on The Toybox CD-ROM, *The Desktop Theatre of Amnesia*, these techniques of parallelism were tested out on a grid structure.[19] The emotional transformations of an unhappy love affair and its visually equivalent symbolic analogues are mapped over a matrix of QuickTime minimovies. A simple click on symbolic arrays of objects reveals the underlying talking heads, each one narrating a separate epiphany. Like multiple personalities locked inside one mind, but still aware of the other's presence, they reinforce poetic resonance by proximity and association.

This approach has also been employed by practitioners such as Malcolm Le Grice[20] and Bill Seaman[21] as a way of neatly side-stepping the straitjacket of articulated narrative, allowing the audience to set the selection criteria of matching components: thereby creating a form of associative narrative flow. Turning up a particular image forces the computer to turn up a matching narrative fragment, as in a card game. Here we begin to approach Weinbren's 'responsive representation machine'.

ALTERNATIVE STRUCTURES – TOWARDS THE MATRIX

As we have noted, the technology of digital media has virtually no grain, no resistance. The lack of linearity in the medium itself, coupled with its ability to simultaneously reintegrate representations of all forms of 'old' media, means that it can pretend to be all things to all people. This is manifestly not the case in cinema. As a consequence, a taxonomy of hypertextual systems supporting narrative could be said to range from the completely 'open' matrix of certain multi-participant web-art projects to the completely 'closed', predetermined, single author mode of a CD-ROM. My next project was an attempt to explore an open matrix, where the text itself became not simply an adjunct of the work, but the central formative agent, altering the structure and the indexical quality of the piece at one and the same time. Thus the work would be in continuous flux, but would retain an overall shape or architecture.

One of the earliest British multi-participant web art collaborations was the ArtAids project, conceived as a series of artists' images available for transformation by a global web audience. New variants could be posted on the website and the resultant image 'family trees' explored. In *Screening the Virus* I tried to expand the concept to fully utilise the unique potentials of the web.[22] I sought to develop a far looser approach to narrative, exploring an open structure: a self-curating and evolving website, based

28 *Screening the Virus*, Martin Rieser, 1997.

on the theme of viral infection, investigating issues around HIV/AIDS, through contributions in both text and image from web users and artists. The project website attempted to create an analogue of a viral organism in all its stages of development. This was to be achieved by the self-curation of the site by a special programme that recognised keywords in the user's textual contribution. Image and text submissions were to be placed on a strictly temporal rotation into whichever space was most appropriate for the text. Displays would change quickly as new contributors logged on. This process involved developing a visual database to store the contributions and Perl scripting routines to link to the HTML of the interface, including keyword search routines. Thus socially-weighted contributions, containing both text and imagery, were to be

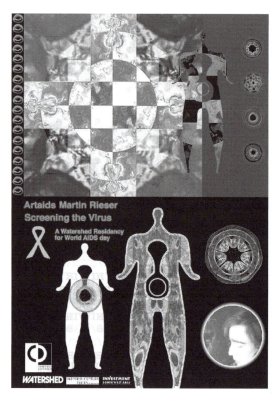

assembled by neutral machine judgement. In partnership with artificial-life programmers it was further intended to develop evolutionary algorithms to constantly change the visual appearance of the interface, through generative mapping, based on the data from the table of keywords. The more positive the attention given by callers, reflected in affirmative words, the 'healthier' the images would appear (primarily through colour changes towards red), thus acting as a 'barometer' of the climate and nature of the attention the site received.

The theme of viral infection was further reinforced by the way in which users logged their contribution, placing a viral icon onto a map of the human figure. This gave each user a unique identity. The site reflected four stages of AIDS from early HIV infection through to full-blown AIDS and its aftermath: symbolising these areas of experience as four 'worlds' based on the elements of Earth (the body), Water (early stages of HIV), Fire (full-blown AIDS) and Air (aftermath and reflection). Although still work in progress, the site sought to create open thematic narratives on a matrix of changing cross-referenced responses. The database-narrative trajectory, referred to earlier by Manovich, is here at once navigated and renewed by the same audience.

PHYSICAL SPACE EMBODYING DIEGETIC SPACE

The main direction of my recent work has been in examining the nature of theatrical and interactive installation spaces where poetry can be re-imagined as part of a hypertextual universe. In pursuing this direction I was attempting to synthesise aspects of cinema, video art and more primitive and associative spaces, to create a narrative form based in a physical environment, rather than on a virtual one. While in *Labyrinth* a more directly theatrical route was chosen, the *Understanding Echo* [23] installation was an attempt to root interactive narrative in a magical space (DVD) corresponding to part of the audience's 'collective unconscious' where 'memory, dreams and reflections' could rise to the surface.[24] Language once more played a central role, one indexed directly onto a physical space.

In a darkened room hung a number of translucent panels, displaying large digital photographic montages. In the centre space of these images was a shallow circular pool of water. In the silence of the installation the audience could make out the drip of water. Flickering in the pool was the image of a woman's face, submerged below the surface. From time to time she rose from the depths and talked slowly in short poetic fragments or aphorisms. The audience may not immediately have realised it, but the form of these spoken fragments became ever more personal as they approached the pool. (A similar strategy had been successfully used in earlier interactive works such as Lynn Hershman's *Lorna*.) The large, changing digital montage projections around the pool represented combinations of memory.

The figure rising from the waters loosely corresponded to the nymph Echo, in myth forced to forever repeat the last lines of her lover Narcissus's speeches, trapped in a pool for all eternity. The form of the work also alluded to the female spirits that inhabit wells and rivers in various folklores, such as the Lady of the Lake in Arthurian Legend as well as the drowning Ophelia in *Hamlet*. The woman reviews her life and the sense of powerlessness her situation has brought. The poetic frag-

29 Scenes from *Understanding Echo*, Martin Rieser, 2000.

ments were intended to resemble a mix of colloquial musings and the timeless incisiveness we associate with poetic aphorism. They ranged from the general to the intimate. The woman is by turns embittered, flirtatious and coquettish, disillusioned and enthusiastic: ignoring the audience one minute; hectoring it the next. Her character moves through a wide emotional range, returning obsessively to her situation and the unhappy love affair which caused it. The woman inhabits the present, but lives only in the past. Onto the audience she projects her loves and fears. We are immersed in her longings and become her blank screen: the spatialised narrative and the poetic monologues were fused together in the environment of the piece.

Once an audience enters the installation room, it becomes part of the diegetic space of the narrative and is continually addressed directly or obliquely by the character of Echo. The precise sequencing or order of the fragments is irrelevant. There is no linear temporal curve involved. The more a visitor interacts, the more intimate the knowledge they gain of Echo's character. Thus the narrative is embedded in every experienced fragment. The difference between conventional literary narrative and this interactive form could be compared to the difference between a conventional photograph and a hologram. While in a photographic fragment we see a part of a single perspective view, in a hologram each fragment of the photographic plate carries the total waveform of light generated by the original object. This holistic potential is what attracts me both to poetry and to interactive work. The immanent form is not only manifest in each part of the work, each fragment attains further resonance, meaning and 'negative capability' from the collection of other fragments and that meaning is subtly altered with each viewing.

Zone 1 (Distant)	**Zone 2 (Intermediate)**	**Zone 3 (Intimate)**
This is what I can remember From our past: A single thought Expanding to fill the Universe Like the mind of God.	Sometimes I think I am really all alone With my fictions And the world is A mirror suspended over me Like a small sky.	Please move closer. I have so much to tell you – Last night I saw a star Right above me like small jewel So perfect, it changed me Into a better person.
•	•	•
I can see the clouds Passing over Like airships And the stars opening out Burning.	It's all very well for you Tramping around out there I feel so cold … And the lights keep coming and going	I recognised you At a distance. Didn't we meet Last year? I remember your face So vividly, so clearly …

AI AND IMMERSION

The move from the physical narratised space of the interactive video installation to that of the fully realised virtual environment is one I have so far avoided. I am sure it has something to do with the acute travel sickness I felt on my first encounter with a CAVE at the University of Illinois, where the 'pilot' was late for an appointment and 'drove' too fast! But it is probably only within a truly virtual space we might reach the equivalent of Weinbren's 'responsive representation machine'.

In speaking of the pleasures and engagement within VR environments, Janet Murray of MIT Media Lab identified '*Immersion, rapture and agency*' as the key requisites of interaction in virtual space.[25] While these certainly identify the pleasures of the medium, they do not of themselves create the complexity of meaning found in the fixed structures of traditional forms. Char Davies's VR piece *Osmose* is a case in point, where an audience could float through a semi-transparent virtual world, viewing natural processes, gliding effortlessly through trees, following rising sap into the leaves, etc.[26] The user's breathing controlled their descent into the world and, because of this trance-like immersion, many came out of the installation in a deeply emotional state. This direct physical relationship between the audience and the content seemed to have been the most telling aspect of the project.

In the search for narratives without predetermined scripting, the use of artificial life algorithms is increasingly leading towards the granting of autonomous agency to individual VR characters. Only a few years ago, the state of the art in artificial life seemed to be at the level of MIT's attempts at programmed behaviours, exemplified by Bruce Blumberg's virtual dog Silas in the Artificial-life Interactive Video Environment, where a computer-generated ball-fetching creature was mapped onto a mirror image of the real user's environment.[27] Since then artificial life creatures have become common-place, from the dreadfully primitive Tamagotchi to the unstoppable Furby. Norns are even more sophisticated entities, evolving and breeding in virtual environments through genetic coding embedded in software, they have even been known to evolve independently patterned behaviours such as playing collaborative ball games.[28]

The Oz project (and the Virtual Theatre project at Stamford University) have engaged for many years with the problems of 'interactive drama' and 'liquid narrative'.[29] Oz is a computer system developed to allow authors to create and present interactive dramas (Bates 92). The architecture includes a simulated physical world, several characters, an interactor, a theory of presentation, and a drama manager. A model of each character's body and of the interactor's body are in the physical world. Outside the physical world, a model of mind controls each character's actions. The interactor's actions are controlled by the interactor. Sensory information is passed from the physical world to the interactor through an interface controlled by a theory of presentation. The drama manager influences the characters' minds, the physical world, and the presentation theory. The goal of the Oz project at Carnegie Mellon University was to build dramatically interesting virtual worlds inhabited by believable agents – autonomous characters exhibiting rich personalities, emotions and social interactions. In many of these worlds, the player is himself a character in the story, experiencing the world from a first person perspective. Typically, the player's representation within the world – the avatar – is passive. The avatar performs actions as fully specified by the player and reports events (by, for example, rendering a 3D scene or generating descriptive text).

MACHINES ARE NOT POETS

More recently Naoko Tosa and Ryhohei Nakatsu at ATR research Labs in Tokyo have created *Play Cinema*, where controllable avatars act under the audience's direction, creating new scenes from *Romeo and Juliet (in Hades)*, as the characters journey through the Underworld.[30] The dialogue and plot are unconvincing and by no means free-form. But at least here gesture-recognition and speech-synthesis, as well as facial and emotional-state recognition software, have been fused to create a variety of responses and variations on the basic plot. The neural net software is about as adept as a human observer at detecting emotional nuance in audience response. In an earlier experiment, *Muse*, a software agent spoke poetry to which the audience responded in preset phrases or in their own words. The animated *Muse* responded in turn with emotional expressions controlled through a neural network, that also recognised emotional nuances in the audience's own phrases. Most of Muse's words were previously developed by programmers, as were many of the dialogues in *Romeo and Juliet (in Hades)*. There is obviously a long way to go before machines can properly attempt the precise art of poetry, and it is a moot point whether machine consciousness will ever have any affinities with human consciousness, let alone poetic sensibility!

CONCLUSION

The responsive nature of such systems opens up a potential new craft for the writer, where the encoding of mood, emotion and their syntax takes precedence over plot and and traditional forms of narrative technique. In the experience of any serious work of art, the audience must invariably map narrative onto a whole range of cultural and historical references and resonances (a process conflated by Barthes as the 'death of the author'). This process seems to be independent of whichever medium is involved. Interactivity by itself may never introduce closer engagement than that achieved by traditional art forms, even when autonomous agents in immersive environments conduct the narrative. Words alone are clearly not enough, but if used intelligently within such models they can, as I hope I have demonstrated, move us nearer to the serious works of art new media has the potential to deliver. And, just as in the great religious debates around First Movers and Free Will, the author remains the architect, no longer a direct voice or manipulator of plot, but a creator still.

NOTES

1. I am referring to Heisenberg's theory of Quantum Mechanics, outlined in the Uncertainty Principle Paper 1927:

    I believe that the existence of the classical 'path' can be pregnantly formulated as follows: The 'path' comes into existence only when we observe it.

2. Witness Alan Shelston, University of Manchester, writing on *Our Mutual Friend*:

> The convoluted plot, involving its central character in not two, but three, separate identities, all involving disguise, outdoes anything its author had contrived before; we are asked to accept concealed evidence, simulated behaviour and hidden secrets as part of the day-to-day processes of existence … *Our Mutual Friend* seems at times like a vast and somewhat decaying baroque structure, threatening at any moment to collapse.   <http://www.lang.nagoya-u.ac.jp/~matsuoka/CD-Shelston.html>

3. For example *The Big Sleep* is notorious for its illogical and convoluted plot:

> The most famous loose end in the story concerns a chauffeur, one Owen Taylor, who turns up dead in a water-logged Packard, 'washing around off Lido Pier.' Questions on the set arose as to who, in the carnival of conflicting motives that made the film a Chinese box of mayhem, actually did kill Owen Taylor? Hawks realized he didn't know, and successive calls were put in to screenwriters Leigh Brackett, Jules Furthman, and William Faulkner; they didn't know, either. Finally, Chandler himself was reached; no, he said, he guessed he didn't know, either. (…) Hawks realized it didn't matter who killed Owen Taylor, and the film went ahead, its atmosphere of treachery somehow improved by the ambiguity.

> Hagopian, Kevin Jack, *10 Shades of Noir: The Big Sleep*
> <http://www.imagesjournal.com/issue02/infocus/bigsleep.htm>

4. Mike Figgis' multilinear narrative film *Timecode*, for example, was not only made possible through the advent of high resolution portable digital video cameras, but also took inspiration for its split-screen form from the multiple frames of new media work.

5. Manovich, Lev. *Database as a Symbolic Form*, 1998. < http://www.desk.nl/~nettime/>.

6. 'Multimedia feature: Interactive fiction. But is it story-telling?' *The Economist* 11 Nov. 1995, US edition.

7. Chris Hales' *Jinxed* interactive cinema installation, Oberhausen Short Film Festival Germany, 1997.

8. Barthes, Roland. *Image – Music – Text*. London: Fontana, 1977, p. 95.

9. Rees, Gareth, *Tree Fiction on the World Wide Web*. Web site. <www.tao.ca./~peter/athesis/hypertext/rees94.html>

10. Barthes, Roland. *Image-Music-Text*.

11. Ship of Fools: Terryl Bacon, Jon Dovey, Constance Fleuriot, Liz Milner and Martin Rieser.

12. *Silver to Silicon: Media Myth and Mania* on CD-ROM. London: Artec 1994.

13. In consequence the piece was structured as a binary branching choice 'seven ages of man or woman' interactive biographical narrative, with the player assuming the role of the either male or female 'mogul'. The player could choose between two action options at each level. There were more than 80 interactive tableaux images in the whole game, plus accompanying sound, text and QuickTime movies. A mythic parallel universe of neoclassic futility interweaves the narrative at various key points as a metaphor for the ultimate emptiness of the scramble for media control.

14. Ship of Fools group, *Dreamhouse*, CD-ROM, research project on interactive narrative and new media at the Faculty of Art, Media and Design, University of the West of England, Bristol 1994–6.

15. Barratt is a major home builder and has built housing estates up and down the United Kingdom. As a consequence of the housing boom in Britain in the late 1980s and the subsequent slump, housing

prices fell sharply in the early 1990s, leaving many home owners with mortgages far in excess of the value of their properties. Bradley Stoke in the South West of England experienced the worst negative equity problems in the UK to the point where the town was nicknamed 'Sadly Broke'.

16. *Labyrinth*, CD-ROM and Installation, shown at ISEA 97 in Chicago and exhibited at F-Stop, Bath 1998 and Cheltenham Festival of Literature 2000.

17. Weinbren, Grahame, 'Mastery – ComputerGames, Intuitive Interfaces and Interactive Media, *Leonardo 28*, no.5, 1995, pp. 403–8.

18. Grahame String Weinbren. *Sonata*. London: Institute of Contemporary Arts, September 1994.

19. Dovey, Jon. The Toybox, CD-ROM. Video Positive. Liverpool: Moviola, 1995.

20. Le Grice, Malcolm. 'The Story Telling Machine', public lecture, Watershed Media Centre, Bristol, Spring 1996.

21. Seaman, Bill. CAiiA PhD seminar, Newport College of Art and Design, Spring 1996.

22. Rieser, Martin, *Screening the Virus*, a residency for World Aids Day 1996, commissioned by Artec and Watershed Media Centre as a multimedia pilot for the ArtAids website.

23. Rieser, Martin. *Understanding Echo*. Interactive environment, commissioned by DA2 and SW Arts for the Cheltenham Festival of Literature 2000.

24. Jung, Carl 'Memories, Dreams and Reflections'.

25. Laurel, Brenda. *Computers as Theatre*. Los Angeles: Addison Wesley and Apple Computers, 1991, pp. 188–92; see also Murray, Janet H. *Hamlet on the Holodeck: The Future of Narrative in Cyberspace*. Cambridge: MIT Press, 1997.

26. Davies, Char. *Osmose*, shown at ISEA 95 in Montreal at the Museum of Modern Art and at *Serious Games*, Barbican London, 1997.

27. Bates, J. 1992. 'Virtual Reality, Art, and Entertainment'. *Presence: The Journal of Teleoperators and Virtual Environments* 1(1): pp. 133–8. Details can also be found on the Carnegie Mellon University website: <www.cs.cmu.edu/afs/cs.cmu.edu/project/oz/web/papers.html>.

28. Platt, Charles. Interactive Entertainment *Wired*, vol. no. 1.05, Sept. 1995, p. 63.

29. See Norns<www.creatures3.com>.

30. Neesham, Claire. 'It was the Best of Times …'. *New Scientist* vol. no. 2181. 10 Apr. 1999; see also *Creativity and Cognition*. Conference proceedings. University of Nottingham, 1999.

Interactive Storytelling: The Renaissance of Narration

Eku Wand

A human being sits by the campfire and tells stories – the listeners laugh, cry, ask questions, grumble and shout remarks. A human being writes a novel – the readers can laugh, cry or write letters. A film runs on television – the viewers can laugh, cry, fall asleep or press buttons.[1]

STORYTELLING AND AUDIENCE INTERACTIVITY –
A CONTRADICTION IN TERMS?

Who is not pleased to be told, 'You're such a good listener'? Behind the compliment, all the same, is the question of what an ability to 'listen well' actually means. Is not listening *per se* a *passive* activity and therefore not susceptible either to measurement or evaluation? By what cues do speakers know, or sense, that people are really listening to them? Does it simply come down to attentive glances, mute signs of agreement, invisible oscillations or 'good vibrations'? Depending on the type of performance – a concert, a play, a cabaret act or a reading – 'good listening' certainly also includes more distinct reactions. For the event as a whole, audience participation plays an important role, even if it is something that can merely be reckoned with, but by no means counted upon.

Audience feedback is important in the theatre, in order, above all, to create the right atmosphere, to bring closer to each other the transmitters and receivers or, put differently, tune them to similar wavelengths. Only then can the performers subtly and subliminally exchange information between the memorised lines, concurrent to the rehearsed gestures, and beyond the fixed scenarios. Seasoned performers subconsciously register the timbre of an audience's burst of laughter in reaction to a slip of the tongue, or gauge the degree of sarcasm with which throats are cleared after a pretended ad lib, and respond immediately to the audience mood by shifting the pitch, varying the tempo, or altering the sequence of songs. A number of factors decide how much leeway remains for re-shuffling the numbers in a show, or how much audience interaction is effective or feasible. Due to their largely pre-programmed course, rigidly structured and technically elaborate productions restrict the actors' degree of freedom much more than, say, the deliberately simple performances put on for children, be it with puppets or flesh-and-blood actors.

Seen from this angle, children are especially good listeners. Not only do they quickly identify with the story and its characters, they are also much less inhibited in showing the emotions stimulated by the narration.

THE POWER OF THE AUTHOR AS NARRATOR AND THE BORDERS OF INTERACTION IN REGARD TO AUDIENCE PARTICIPATION

To what degree does the storytelling process, or even the course of the story, change in response to an audience that acts, interacts, interferes? The bards of old were already very much aware of what they wanted to recount. Their manner of interrupting a narrative by asking the listeners questions, by rhetorically deviating from the main plot, by inserting theatrical pauses, were means to the end of building up tension, of involving the listeners, of captivating them. A good narrator so skilfully integrated spontaneous ideas that he could repeatedly return to the planned course of the plot, yet still produce the crucial atmosphere of direct interaction. That was the art of rhetoric.

These interjections must nevertheless be limited in number and length, otherwise the plot becomes unclear and dramatic tension evaporates. That is why parliamentary chairpersons curb the volume of disruptive, but animated heckling, in debates; or, in order to obtain a result, a judge presiding over a court session orchestrates the interaction during the cross-examination. Interaction is a question of timing first, and of dosage second, but above all one of casting. Without a master of ceremonies, no story emerges. Instead, the tale drifts into aimless chattering, and the listeners lose interest.

FROM HUMAN INTERACTION TO MEDIATED INTERACTIVITY

Up to now, 'interaction' has been seen as a direct component of human communication, as an act transacted face-to-face in 'real-time'. The Duden dictionary, a standard authority on the usage and interpretation of the German language, defines 'interaction' as *interrelations between persons and groups*. In the case of analogue media, viewers or listeners initially merely received transmitted broadcasts from the apparatus. Interactive feedback could not be given, particularly in the case of pre-recorded broadcasts, whose reception was deferred. Contemporary users of digital media can directly interact with each other over telephone lines, video-conferencing or live internet chatrooms. (This degree of directness becomes impossible when listening to a message on an answering machine, watching a broadcast recorded on videotape or using a website stored on data servers, since communication is staggered in time and separated, as it were, by the medium.) Interestingly though, early media formats repeatedly experimented with precursors of interaction and interactivity, even if the modern implications of those concepts was not known. Thus, German television in the mid-1970s broadcast a drama that broke down the boundary between pre-recorded and live performance. This 'whodunnit' entitled *Dem Täter auf der Spur* ('On the Culprit's Tracks') did not end with the crime being solved, although there were a number of suspects, but instead cut to a studio where the actors and a live audience were present. The actors – and that was the new angle – remained in character as detective and suspects, while the studio guests were asked to assist the detective by questioning the suspects to conclusively prove guilt. The individual viewing of a broadcast turned into a collective process – the audience had to jointly analyse and evaluate the information furnished by the plot and the easily overseen or deliberately misleading details. It was particularly interesting to observe the behaviour of the actors, who were required to 'improvise to plan'. Unlike the viewers, the cast obviously knew who the murderer was, but were also subordinate to the specifications of the script and the character briefing. However, they were required to deliver spontaneous and flexible reactions to unexpected questions within the scope of the plot.

This television experiment was based on a principle that anticipated a number of issues peculiar to 'interactive storytelling', although, since the audience was involved on-site in a kind of 'real-time metalogue', it was more a case of a live experiment with 'interaction'. For the actors, it was important to receive a thorough briefing on how to behave, react, interact – not just in response to the interrogators – but also in regard to each other, so that ultimately they could spontaneously create 'internal directions'. The actors were practically 'programmed' for their parts without knowing what, and how much, of their internalised repertory would be demanded during the live cross-examination after the broadcast.

FROM THE OPERATION OF MACHINES TO DIALOGUE WITH MEDIA MACHINES

Interactivity, which the Duden calls a 'dialogue between a computer and its user', begins where interaction ends. Only recently, by the way, did the lexicographers accept a word long current in the realm of multimedia; before then, as far as the editors were concerned, 'interactivity' did not exist as a concept at all. By now, most internet users have a precise idea of what to understand by and expect from interactivity. Typical interactivities are the selection of commands from menus, the clicking of buttons or the activation of links, the entry of search words in databases, the adjustment of certain playback parameters such as volume or display forms, as well as responding to questions or messages in contextual dialogue boxes.

However, when comparing the definitions of interaction and interactivity, a glance back over the history of media usage reveals that the 'interactive' must by no means be considered an exclusive domain of the computer. The notorious 'language laboratory' – an experimental method of individually controlled learning, based on analogue technology and magnetic-tape recording – offered a minimal degree of interactivity, but included the content. Pinball machines, by contrast, are low on content, but provide plenty of interactivity. As a general rule, it might therefore suffice to define interactivity as the dialogue between a machine and its user. Whereas, in the context of media that are invariably intended to deliver content, and (among other things), to tell stories and to broadcast messages, the notion of interactivity requires more differentiated consideration. It describes something more than the rules for using an apparatus. In connection with storytelling, therefore, it is of limited usefulness to see interactivity as meaning merely the 'operation' of a machine, in the sense of throwing levers, pressing buttons and pushing pedals. Subsumed into the concept of 'interactivity' is rather a dialogue with people, conducted across the detour of a machine. Firstly, the machine must have something to say to us, to tell us. Something furnished by its makers, something they built-in 'under their breath'. Secondly, the machine must be capable of being a good listener in the abstract sense, namely, a sensitive narrator, who notices input of all kinds and reacts in compliance with a set of pre-defined rules.

INTERACTIVE STORYTELLING: EXTENDED NARRATIVE STRUCTURES AND THE STAGING OF INTERACTIVITY

Thanks to the computer and its rapidly increasing multimedia capabilities, the 1980s and above all the 1990s brought enhanced possibilities for 'programming' a story's backdrops, spaces, locations and events, along with a model for using these constituents and showing how they must change. Over the past 20 years, the possibilities of programming real character attributes, authentic instructions for action and binding behavioural patterns for artificial actors have vastly increased. Likewise, the programming has become more various and elegant, and thus gradually more 'realistic'. In this respect, we can now largely provide the technical options necessary to carry forward a project on the multimedia computer that began on television with *Dem Täter auf der Spur*: namely the nonlinear (or, preferably, interactive) narration of a story.

'Interactive storytelling', as a new discipline of narrative art, faces the task of developing a new species of extended-content script. In other words more plots, more storylines, more occurrences are required. In contrast to a linear novel or film narrative, what initially exists in a writer's mind as a sequence of events (usually composed of many parallel and over-layered strands), must now actually be recorded and made accessible. However, it is important to devise a concept for interactive reception as well as for the fictional content. The many writers – professional and hobby scriptwriters alike – of the science-fiction series *Star Trek* are very familiar with proceedings such as 'manuals' that detail for each figure the *vita*, family tree, character attributes and record of what happened to them in previous episodes. These *vitas*, which are never fully narrated in the individual episodes, are the basis of the so-called 'back story', proper to every scriptwriter's stock-in-trade. Ensuring that narration remains logical and consistent with regard to content, the 'back story' is particularly indispensable for series' writers so that each episode makes sense.

MORE THAN SCREENPLAYS – COMPREHENSIVE RULES FOR MANY DIFFERENT NARRATIVE CASES

Star Trek continues to function primarily as a TV series based on linear narratives and a linear sequence of instalments. This aspect, however, is one which computer-assisted, interactively narrated stories also take into account when stipulating what can be interactively influenced, either consciously or indirectly (the original *Star Trek* games only partially count, since the narrative component is very slight in comparison to the proportion of action and shooting scenes). The way users navigate through scenery and scenes, 'interact' both with locations and, even more importantly, virtual actors, the perspectives from which they view events, the atmospheres and moods encountered and experienced: everything has to be consciously designed and must adhere to fixed rules. This might also be termed the 'staging of inter-activity'.

When it comes to storytelling, then, interactivity initially appeals to the 'good' listener in the user. It appeals to the listener, who shows reactions and communicates something to the speaker (in this case the programme running on the machine), in order to exercise an influence. Compared with the degree of interactivity most contemporary computer games offer (in terms of apparatus and dialogue), this influence may be slight. Yet, it is considerable when compared with traditional media, whose invariably linear sequence (here, any exceptions confirm the rule) is unvaryingly, faithfully and repeatedly reproduced. Admittedly, the way something is (subjectively) perceived can change, just as the effect and meaning of certain songs change over the years. However, if we place intervals, stops and leaps to one side, the course of a story cannot even be influenced, let alone changed, either in its dramatic structure or in its content or message. As Uli Plank puts it, 'all one can do is press buttons, opt in or opt out.'

Compared with the switching on and off of the narrative machines we have so far encountered, interactivity – something perhaps more accurately described as the 'art of designing inter-relationships' – is more concerned with differentiated control knobs, slides and adjusting instruments equipped with a feedback option. 'Interactive storytelling' therefore implies not only the 'good listener' in the user, but also an imaginary 'receptive narrator', who plays for us the part of a system receptive to input. A narrator who, in the figurative sense, glances up from his storyboard, deliberately asks questions, and attentively offers us a virtual ear, tuned to catch quiet murmurs of agreement or dissent. A narrator who involves us in decisions, even delegates the latter, but goes to all this trouble only to rouse the 'good listener' in us all. For a listener curious about the ending is above all one who listens well. That kind of listener is curious, not only to hear the outcome, but also the lead-up, the presentation, the delay tactics – curious, in other words, about the narration.

INTERACTIVE NARRATION OR NARRATIVE INTERACTIVITY?

The relationship between narration and interactivity would appear to be antithetical. Does that make the fusion of 'narration' (the art of captivating the listener with good storytelling) with 'interactivity ' (the art of liberating the user with well-designed man-machine inter-relationships) a contradiction in terms? Is the notion of 'interactive storytelling' a paradox? 'Linear media are becoming part of the content of the world of non-linear entertainment', says Ulrich Weinberg, a professor at the Academy of Film and Television Studies in Potsdam. He continues, 'The entertainment medium of the future is non-linear, virtual and three-dimensional.'[2] He is of the opinion that virtual actors will very soon possess the qualities of real people, in the sense that they exercise a charm that makes one want to observe them. He even speculates that in the future attending a virtual competition involving thousands of players will be potentially more exciting than the television broadcast of the Olympic Games.

Certainly, it is difficult to forecast how in the future people will rate an interactively playable multi-user production. Weinberg's allusion to the sporting character of interactive games separates them from 'narration'. Pure entertainment, including sporting competitions, tells no story – or, at best, the unchanging one of victors and vanquished. If, however, in line with Weinberg's further prediction,

> thousands of actors simultaneously meet up in virtual spaces and enter a parallel world, a plot whose
> framework is predefined, but whose course can be actively determined by every single actor[,]

then it is valid to ask whether it is ultimately permissible to leave the narrative flow to its own devices. Is there not a case for saying that the narrative and interactive strings must be pulled by an author, or mentor, or master of ceremonies?

Who, in this imagined scenario, would be the author, or would there be several authors? If so, how many authors could this kind of story environment tolerate? Will desktop authoring for 'Everyman' naturally follow on from desktop publishing, video and multimedia? Are we all such good storytellers and rules-inventors (not to mention listeners) that a framework is all we need to guarantee ourselves and our co-players a few interesting hours?

Obviously, the experimental artistic handling of interactivity and dramatic structure must be rated differently from scenic narration. If, for instance, we deprive language of its meaning by removing linguistic standards such as sentence structure and semantics, or break down the written word into its raw material of letters and sounds, we can be certain of coming up with experimental onomatopoeia, along the lines of the concrete poetry written by the Austrian poet Ernst Jandl (1925–2000). However, if we subsequently want to tell somebody about this linguistic experience, we must first reassemble the letters in accordance with specific rules, in order to reconvey the content of the story.

THE ART OF STORYTELLING – AND THE INTERACTIVE CHALLENGE IT FACES

Time-tested narrative skills, which have been passed down to us, are the art of omission and the art of good timing. The reporter of an occurrence is neither able to chronologically reflect the events, nor to give a complete account of them. He assumes a subjective viewpoint from which he filters, evaluates and accentuates. The linear sequences he chooses to present as sub-stories are important, as are the 'scenes' he composes with words and gestures, and the emotions he is able to convey or produce. All these descriptions follow a (invisible) storyline. Scriptwriters call this framework the plot – the imagined trajectory of the figures with a role to play (the cast), and the description of a basic conflict.

A specially skilful method of disseminating scraps of information is demonstrated by the thriller genre's usage of pointed or veiled hints, evidence that could incriminate or clear the suspects; surprising statements by new characters who suddenly pop up; or unexpected occurrences showing up everything that came before in a new light. A story's dynamism, tension and entertainment value are ideally the result of the way the narrated reality is selected and apportioned, and of the targeted 'timing' of the turning points.

It is necessary to examine which traditional narrative structure needs to be taken into account, extended or even renewed for the interactive narrative form. Certain specific narrative genres can sometimes be more suitable for interactive adaptation than others. Interactive storytelling is less about re-inventing narration itself, than about exploring specific peculiarities, regularities and rules. At the beginning, the same questions apply: how do I put in place a plot along with locations, characters, and a basic conflict? How, for instance, does the action radius of the viewer (the active player, in this case) relate to the story? Does the narrative perspective need to be limited as a result?

SIGNIFICANCE AND OPTIONS OF THE 'INTERACTIVE VIEWPOINT'

In the early 1990s, a thriller staged from two different viewpoints was broadcast simultaneously on Germany's first and second public TV channels. Running under the title *Umschalten Erlaubt* (*'Switching Permitted'*), the version shown on the first channel was shot from the criminal's viewpoint, while the second channel showed the events through the eyes of the main female character. Both characters went their separate ways, meaning viewers of either version experienced two different stories based on the same plot. Although 'zapping' between these subjective viewpoints was styled 'interactivity', the very filmic chronology of the thriller ultimately provided insufficient impetus to amount to 'interactive storytelling' – in regard both to the making and the viewing.

Nevertheless, this experiment (dubbed, somewhat over-enthusiastically, 'interactive television') at least impressed on a wide audience some awareness of how the narrative perspective could manipulate an audience's perception of a story. It may also have roused in the viewers some sense of the importance of a flexible point of view as an active contributor to a story's reception. A major role is played in interactive applications by the cinematic device of the subjective camera, with players in many computer-game stories assuming the role of the main protagonist and experiencing the plot in the first person. Since the recipient is expected to participate in almost every scene, the suggestion is often conveyed that what happens next is solely dependent on the player's interventions. As regards point of view, a wealth of new, and as yet unexplored, territories have opened up, promising excellent opportunities for integrating and combining these new possibilities with traditional film viewpoints.

With its multimedia story, for instance, the interactive docu-thriller <u>Berlin Connection</u> relies on the players' powers of observation.[3] The protagonist is a British photojournalist dispatched to

Berlin on an assignment. As a professional, he is used to looking at things precisely and seeing them 'in terms of pictures'. Appropriately, *Berlin Connection* conveys its framing story solely by stills, that often, due to minimal motion phases, create a very realistic impression. This is reinforced by a soundtrack blending dialogue with multilayered background noise such as city streets with roaring cars, barking dogs, yelling children or music.

(DVD)

30 *Berlin Connection*, Eku Wand, 1998. The narrative perspective implies formal requirements that exercise an influence on the interface design. Thus, from the perspective of the player and photographer permanent access is possible to important tools such as camera, newspaper, city map and suitcase that expand both the apparatus and the content.

Berlin Connection makes variegated and appropriate use of the starting premise and perspective of the 'photographer-in-a-strange-city' plot. Thus, events repeatedly require the player to grab hold of the virtual camera in order to record scenes that have just been experienced. The displayed image turns into a viewfinder for this purpose, while the humming of a camera motor and the click of the shutter release authentically convey the sense of taking a photo. The user is expected not only to see and 'feel' through the photographer's eyes, but also to be his camera's eye – for only the knowledge subsequently gained by analysing the self-recorded moments makes it possible to advance through the story. The fact that some, but not all, of the self-shot photos prove to be crucial during the course of the story, is an especially good adaptation of a trick used by any good plot-maker. The player is obliged to 'get stuck in', and on one occasion (the love scene hinted at early in the plot), prove his sense of timing. All this clearly illustrates interactive storytelling's potential for directly and effectively drawing the audience into the plot.

THE CHANGE OF VIEWER AS A PRINCIPLE OF THE GAME – AND THE LIMITATIONS OF SINGULAR VIEWPOINTS

The film-based CD-ROM thriller *Psychic Detective* provides another impressive example of how the narrative perspective can be changed.[4] In the role of Eric Fox, a sleuth who has to solve a case of murder, players have the option of assuming the identity of any characters they come into contact with, and from then onward view events from the new perspective until a different identity is chosen. In order to solve the puzzle, which offers 14 different endings, it is necessary to experience all scenes and parallel plots in detail and several times over. The interactive video game nevertheless remains attractive throughout its duration, since the user can assume the role both of victim and murderer. So a host of specific demands are imposed on the script, particularly those concerning continuity.

The creators of the CD-ROM adventure game *Bad Mojo* likewise had an original idea around viewpoint and its resultant visual presentation.[5] Players are treated to a worm's-eye view of the macrocosm inhabited by a cockroach, and thus receive unusually detailed and revealing views of mundane items of furniture in the shabby hotel that constitutes the game and navigation environment. Charming though these images are, the attraction of remaining a helpless roach for the entire game is finite. The narrative interest likewise tends to pale from a certain point on – for instance, when a player is forced to repeatedly explore the same corners in the hope of finding the 'hole' which offers escape to the next scene. At such points, a change of viewpoint (which *Bad Mojo* does offer) can help to make the pictures interesting once more. However, this example shows how important it is to link purely interactive scenarios with autonomous plot sequences that pick up the most recent storyline – if needs be, without regard to the specific situation of the interactively 'acting' main character – and in this way drive forward the story. 'Interactive storytelling', it is becoming clear, demands a functioning interplay of linear narration, active plot motifs, and rules for interactive usage.

THE NECESSITY OF ACTIVE PLOT MOTIFS AND RULES OF PLAY WITHIN INTERACTIVE NARRATIVE CONCEPTS

If chess is used as a metaphor for interactive narration, some basic attributes of the latter become evident: move and countermove. Two possible ends exist: checkmate or draw, but there are a multitude of possible lead-ups to either conclusion. The art of multimedia authoring and direction (interestingly, neither traditional nor new designations have become established for these professions), now consists in deploying an intelligent regulating mechanism to plan and stage linkages that are as varied as possible and adhere to a logical course and appropriate dramatic structure. A multimedia narrative scaffold of set pieces, whose temporal sequence is not necessarily defined and may even be circular, takes the place of the classical linear plot.

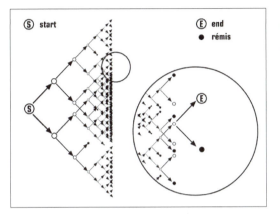

However intricate this temporal sequence may be, and however invisibly it is interwoven with the events, it must remain logical and recognisable so that the viewer/ user/player is able to recognise plot goals he can aim at interactively. The staging of the outcome or, the different endings, must, unlike chess, make do with a manageable number of variations.

Apropos narrative sequences, therefore, it remains necessary to question the legitimacy of demands for 'high-grade', and, if possible, unlimited, interactivity potential, which allows for the random exploration of virtual realities. A staged experience is logically required to move within a demarcated framework or space. Otherwise, the imaginary, but (in my experience) mandatory storyline will ultimately lose significance.

The majority of the so-called 'jump'n'run' computer games could serve as examples demonstrating the opposite. Although based on rough-hewn plots, in reality they unfold the various 'levels' as arenas for the associated games of skill. By the end, the alleged content has long been forgotten and the game is primary. In the 'adventure' computer game genre, by contrast, one often comes across a very successful symbiosis of plot and game. For instance, the share of narration in the *Tomb Raider* series, with its heroine Lara Croft, far surpasses the gaming component.

Nevertheless, on closer inspection the strategic creation and marketing of a virtual (cult) figure deliberately masks the rather modest ratio of story and content to interactivity. Not for nothing, presumably, did the makers allow the heroine to die after the fourth game instalment, only to be resurrected shortly afterwards in a feature film. One should not be surprised to find that in future interactive game-films (or film-games?), the 'flesh-and-blood' pixel heroine Lara Croft, gives priority to narration.

31 Structural diagram of branching narrative, Eku Wand. The possible courses of a game of chess with its multilinear ramifications far exceed anything an interactive narrative scaffold could support – the only clearly defined structural attributes are the beginning and end of the game.

ONCE RULES COME INTO PLAY, IS THERE NO TRULY AUTONOMOUS INTERACTIVITY?

For many, to play interactively means being able to imitate the action radius and sensory experiences of the real environment. Applications and accessory devices attempting to improve the simulation of reality, to enhance the 'sensuality' of the computer machine, have pursued the same direction, be it with control levers and steering wheels for flight and racing-car simulators, or data gloves or virtual-reality helmets fitted with stereo 3D spectacles. Others have approached the reconstruction of real conditions using virtual worlds, populated by virtual representatives in the form of individual avatars, able to be separately controlled by several users. While this successfully generates a genuine realm of possibilities – a cyberspace with an accompanying range of options – the space alone tells no story. Only when plot motifs come into existence within the space does a need to act arise. In ordered circumstances, this need leads to patterns of action, modes of behaviour and even, ultimately, back to rules of play around which the playful handling of a story can develop as virtual role-playing in cyberspace. If this is not the case, anarchic dimensions are fast reached that, because they are uncontrolled, can very quickly become devoid of meaning. This in turn proves that a new story cannot emerge solely due to the complexity or the alleged coexistence of several virtual 'alter egos'. In cyberspace, too, the issues of authorship, agreeing upon rules and the contextual game environment, arise. According to one school of opinion, truly autonomous interactivity ceases to exist once rules come into play. The opposite is actually true. Specifications challenge the players to use their imaginations and strategic intuition in order to get to grips with a role and interact within a fictional game-story environment.

Even a complex simulation-game like *SimCity* is based on a claim demarcated by fixed rules. Only individual human life is surrounded by authentic boundlessness, in which interaction can entail a corresponding degree of unpredictable consequences.

'STRUCTURE IS THE KEY TO UNDERSTANDING THIS NEW MEDIUM'

The above statement is by Greg Roach, one of the first commercial authors, producers and directors of interactive story-games. He adds:

> You have to think in dimensions, in layered text and images, in hologram-type constructions where time can be fluid, where plots can branch, where users are actors groping through and constructing the version of the work they see with the choices they make. Mostly they don't see the whole thing. The whole is apprehended through the exploration.[6]

Thus, renewing traditional, acquired narrative structures is particularly vital in the successful handling of interactive stories. The contribution of a professional author/director – in the sense of the classical film 'auteur' – is indispensable. After all, it is the writer, who not only lays the foundation stones, but also drafts a relatively precise idea. Anybody intending to interactively relate an authored story must be aware of the narrow precipice to be negotiated, in trying to bring

about an intersection between the actual story (as raw material) and the possibilities of the interactive game. This inevitably requires the author to develop well-contrived rules of play that, to
some degree, are artfully inserted turning points, scenes must be devised that hold themselves
accountable to narration and interactivity, pairs of protagonists must be contrasted, and one
must keep the story on course, while at the same time giving the multilayered plot scope for
development.

Impossible though it is to provide instructions for constructing an interactive story or a ready-
made method of networking the components listed above, several attributes have emerged that
help meet the demands for complexity as well as satisfy the resultant requirements. The thriller,
detective story and documentary game genres, for instance, have proved to be especially suitable for game-based plot extensions, just as over the years the increasingly narratised component of adventure games written for computers has resulted in ever more complex storytelling
environments.

In the interactive documentary-thriller *Berlin Connection*, the narrator's juggling of facts and red
herrings is simultaneously composed as a game for the viewer. Having adopted the role of a foreign
photographer suddenly exposed to the underhand practices of an, as yet, anonymous gang, players
must not only find their way about a strange city, but also discover that, if they want to understand
the plot, they must first find out a few things about Berlin's turbulent post-war history. The game provides for this purpose a (fictional) special edition of a daily newspaper celebrating the spectacular fall
of the Berlin Wall. With articles, documentary video clips, radio recordings and photographs for different periods, it recounts key events in the divided city's history after 1945. As well as being generally instructive, this information ultimately assists the course of the plot, which occasionally refers to
the background of the ever more dubious and gripping East-West story into which the viewer stum-
bles as an innocent bystander.

While the author of a classical linear narrative has the task of shaping these plot lines in a way
which is dynamic, entertaining and smooth, the user of an interactive game has to decide where
cuts and leaps take place. Until now, it was left to the author's intuition to sense the effect of his
linear narrative art on his audience, and on this basis provide for the appropriate degree of
dynamism. Whereas, in the case of the interactive recipient's non-linear and, above all, unpredictable 'movement' through the offered spaces of action, it is possible neither to stage nor to guarantee such a fluid dramatic structure.

'Here, the task of writing resembles that of composing a piece of music for a number of different
instruments,' says Janet H. Murray, a US academic and leading authority on interactive storytelling.

> Every element must sound perfect on its own and equally good in unison with the others. The differ-
> ence from music is that in a computer game like *Baldur's Gate 2* it is the player, not the notes, who
> determines which elements are combined, and when this happens.[7]

THE MAIN THING IS TO NOTICEABLY AND EFFECTIVELY ADVANCE THE STORY

At all events, the most important thing is to efficiently and perceptibly drive forward the actual plot. However many details (or 'plot points') of a (sub)story the reader or viewer may have picked up over a period of time, whatever knowledge the 'clicking player' may have already acquired, every plot needs 'nodal points' at various places and times. These points bundle together and analyse the findings gained so far, meaning the players can then act on a new level – faster, more wisely, or perhaps even more confusedly. No matter how linear or how interactive the ultimate form of presentation, a story's central concern remains the resolution of the (main) conflict described at the beginning, be it a crime, unhappy love story, an aspect of society that needs to be changed.

As described above, the first person narrative perspective often makes it necessary for players to experience every plot point directly, and to respond with an intervention. The interactive narrative scaffold must therefore use nodes to link up all the plot points, whether they are associated with locations or persons, and these nodes must initially be invisible to the player.

The scheme runs approximately as follows: plot points deliver important items of information for a story, and simultaneously contain one or more nodes in the form of a question or puzzle. Every node has its equivalent – in the form of an answer – in a different plot point.

Not unlike the popular game 'Memory', questions and answers constitute an invisible carpet that is laid out over the plot points of the game story. Both linear and non-linear links are conceivable. Sometimes merely intersections that speed up the plot exist between individual plot points, sometimes one plot point harbours both question and answer, sometimes different plot points have to be visited several times over in order to investigate certain connections and to make a new plot point accessible or even to allow its manipulation. Finally, by creating a link between two nodes it is possible to close other plot points that have already been 'passed through'. In this regard, the internal narrative structure probably differs most impressively from the linear structures of novels and films.

THE INTERNAL AND EXTERNAL NARRATIVE STRUCTURE

Furthermore, some narrative materials possess an internal structure in regard to the plot, and particularly so in terms of economy. This applies to cases where the active player is able to explore all the plot points, meaning re-usage of the same backdrops is desirable for economic reasons – in order to keep production costs below that of making a film.

One good example is the CD-ROM adventure *The Last Express*, which plays in the Orient Express on the eve of World War I.[8] The action takes place exclusively in the wagons of the famous train travelling between Paris and Istanbul. The player assumes the role of a passenger, has to move through the compartments, eavesdrop on other passengers and build up a picture of the mysterious circumstances. Obviously, a player cannot be in all the wagons at once. This problem is solved by a clock that enables players to leap backwards and forwards on the timescale at will (which is analogous with the route of the train), in order to find out when and how known and unknown passengers boarded and alighted.

Time becomes a supplementary means of adding pressure, since failure to obtain results within a set interval of time causes the player to be thrown out of the game and literally, off the train. The skilfully interwoven parallel storylines result in a gripping and lucid plot motif, whose internal structure is at the same time economically grounded. Such temporal-spatial interdependencies can very much be a further regulating construction for spaces of inter-active action that, on closer inspection, need be neither over-contrived nor too limiting for the plot itself.

THE 'HYPERMEDIA STAGE' – THE GRAPHICAL INTERFACE AS A HYPERMEDIATED NARRATIVE REALM

In the view of the Berlin-based multimedia designer, Andreas Kraft, the monitor must to some degree still tell a story, even if a player does nothing at all. His opinion reflects an important credo that says it is necessary to build up the equivalent of a stage, as opposed to that of a playing field. While in the brainstorming phase the motifs and rules of a plot are still rough, diffuse and modifiable, they continuously assume more concrete shape during the process of development, until the time comes for the visual presentation to be tried out and reviewed. Functional and visual attributes exist for the 'user interface' that are mandatory in implementing the complexity of the inter-active narrative, and, at the same time, represent an external narrative structure. Special attention must be paid to the visually networked identification of sub-plots and useful background information (far exceeding the familiar scope of the boards and cards of conventional games). Here again, the best way of illustrating the vast staging potential of the graphical interface of the computer monitor is to describe specific examples.

The handling of movement and navigation to various plot points in *Bad Mojo* is wholly distinct from the frequently used maps and layout plans. The space is subdivided into grid squares that, as single screens, allow only an objective view of a section of the entire playing area. While this allows unusual insights and views of routine items of furniture – the underside of a table complete with legs, a discarded blob of chewing-gum or similar surprises, for example – it also demands good powers of three-dimensional imagination on the part of the player in order to establish the relationships between the nodes thus identified.

In *Berlin Connection*, it is a matter of acquiring basic historical (background) information on the fall of the Wall by closely studying the special newspaper edition mentioned earlier. Newspaper reports, photos and documentary footage are packaged in a kind of multimedia historical excursion, with a special role being played by the integrated journeys through time. The post-war black market, for instance, is by no means merely an instructive documentary-game, but demands that players (inter)actively take part in the dealings and truly interact with the vendors and customers.

32 *Bad Mojo,* ©1996 Pulse Entertainment/ © 2001 Eku Wand (Montage). The handling of the space in partial views that on the one hand constitute a 2-D game board, but simultaneously merge into a 3-D spatial experience in the mind's eye is an elegant method of doing without the stylistic device of the 'subjective camera'. Each tile represents one monitor page.

33 *Operation Teddybär*,
© 1996 Flammarion/
Index + (original
version)/© 2001
Systhema in der
United Soft Media
Verlag GmbH,
München. The comic-
strip style,
supplemented by
animated sequences
and hyperlinks,
disposes over an
interesting repertory
for adding to the
content and function
of narrative
structures and
simultaneously
delivers a changeable
'stage set', without
seeming forced.

Operation Teddybär imparts historical information through the vehicle of an interactive comic strip depicting the Allied Forces' landing in Normandy in 1944.[9]

At the same time, the hypermedia stage opens up to reveal a documentary section that both leads away from and back to the comic strip. So compelling is the staging that it is difficult to choose between the comic book story and the documentary, meaning the player inevitably ends up visiting the plot points of the comic pages several times over.

A STORY TOLD INTERACTIVELY CAN PRODUCE FEEDBACK – MORE ELEGANTLY AND SUBTLY THAN ANY PREVIOUS GAME FORMS

The failure to register information or make a discovery when following a linear narrative 'merely' makes it more difficult to grasp the connections established by the next node. With some interactive stories, however, viewers may have to obtain specific information, 'experience' certain occurrences, or carry out specific actions before they can even proceed to the next node. Players of *Berlin Connection*, for instance, have to swap certain items on the black market, and, to arrive at the story's solution, must demonstrate powers of deduction and sleuthing akin to those of a detective.

Just as in the children's game 'Blind Man's Buff', where the players assist the blindfolded child by crying 'hot' or 'cold', an interactively-narrated story can produce appropriate feedback – ultimately with far greater elegance and subtlety than any prior form. I mean by this the actual alteration of the mediated background. The background music gets more sinister or soporific; the light fades or brightens; the pace of certain peripheral events noticeably speeds up or slows down. *Berlin Connection* feeds back its reactions by altering the behaviour of people and locations. Thus, a player who gives a wrong answer at some point finds, on returning to the same situation, that informants have suddenly become taciturn or shops have closed. The player might initially react with confusion, but the message is clear.

INTERACTIVE STORYTELLING IS A STYLISTIC DEVICE – AND THEREFORE ALSO A QUESTION OF TASTE

The crucial role played by the graphical-navigational interface in interactive structures is becoming clear. Every image is characterised by the interplay between the user's interactive freedom of choice and the spatio-temporal limitations of his doings. As in a labyrinth (not for nothing is the latter a popular stylistic device in computer games), it is a matter of finding the exits, often within a given period. Players, unable to interactively contribute to the progress of the story, face the threat of the sudden appearance of a new protagonist, a change of scene, an unexpected occurrence or even, at worst, the announcement that the game is over.

Experience shows that frustrations of this nature should not set in too fast or too frequently. The tasks, in other words, should not be too difficult – just as the plot of a thriller should not be over-intricate, otherwise many viewers will be unable to follow and 'turn off' inwardly. If writers of interactive stories want to involve players in their plots, they need to provide them with ways of moving forward, to keep open a 'side-door' for times when all else fails – so that the game remains fun and players can identify with the product.

What is indisputable, is that in order to enjoy interactively narrated stories, people need a certain affinity with the narrative technique. Interactive stories are certainly ideal for people who like thinking about how to resolve a conflict (in thrillers or courtroom films, for instance), or for people who are not just good listeners, but also like posing investigative questions. On the other hand, interactive presentation can also be a good means of presenting material and subjects to audiences tired of traditional media such as books or television.

Seen from this angle, the emergent genre of 'interactive storytelling' is playing its part in bringing about the renaissance of narration in the original sense. Just as the storytellers of old made what, when and how much they told, conditional upon the audience's 'good listening', in order to heighten the tension, entertainment value and level of mental participation; so now interactive stories solicit audience participation in the story and thus help them to more intensively internalise the material.

Translated by Tom Morrison

Notes

1. Plank, Uli. *Digital Storytelling – Tagungsband.* Ulrike Spierling, ed. Fraunhofer IRB Verlag, 2000, p. 195. (Uli Plank is Professor at the Institute of Media Research, Hochschule für Bildende Künste, Braunschweig, Germany.)

2. Ibid., p. 196.

3. *Berlin Connection.* Director: Eku Wand. Publisher: eku interactive, Germany, 1998. CD-ROM (PC and Mac). http://www.berlin-connection.de (11 Jan. 2001).

4. *Psychic Detective.* Director: John Sanborn. Publisher: Electronic Arts, US, 1995. CD-ROM (PC, Playstation and 3DO). http://www.zdnet.com/gamespot/filters/products/0,11114,198363,00.html (11 Jan. 2001).

5. *Bad Mojo.* Directors: Vincent Carrella and Phill Simon. Publisher: Pulse Entertainment, US, 1996. CD-ROM (PC and Mac). http://www.zdnet.com/gamespot/filters/products/0,11114,196680,00.html (11 Jan. 2001).

6. Roach, Greg. '*Greg Roach @ W.R.I.T.E.'94.*' 1994. http://www.cstudies.ubc.ca/write/write94/w_gr.html (11 Jan. 2001).

7. Quoted from: Lischka, Konrad. 'Spiel mir das Lied vom künstlichen Leben'. *Süddeutsche Zeitung,* Munich, 04.01.2001. http://szarchiv.diz-muenchen.de/REGIS_A11640515;internal&action= hili.action&Parameter=computerspiele (11 Jan. 2001).

8. *The Last Express*. Director: Jordan Mechner. Publisher: Brøderbund Software, UK, 1997. CD-ROM (PC and Mac). http://www.lastexpress.com (11 Jan. 2001), http://www.zdnet.com/gamespot/filters/products/0,11114,198971,00.html (11 Jan. 2001).

9. *Operation Teddybär*, Director: Edouard Lussan. Publisher: Flammarion/Index+, France, 1996. CD-ROM (PC and Mac).

Mastery (Sonic C'est Moi)*

Grahame Weinbren

SONIC'S WORLD: PHYSICS AND GEOMETRY

In some recent video games (such as the Sega signature series – *Sonic*, *Sonic 2*, *Sonic 3*, and *Sonic and Knuckles* – and the newer Nintendo 64 games such as *Super Mario 64*, *Donkey Kong* and *Zelda*), both the obstacles that impede the characters, and the devices that assist them are not virtual machines, governed by lighter-than-air laws of cyberspace. They are simulations of springs, ratchets and pulleys, encumbered and regulated by familiar mechanical principles – weight and gravity, force and acceleration, elasticity, leverage. The human player controls animated creatures that need air to breathe, rotors, wings, or gyroscopic platforms to fly, momentum contributed by springs or rocket motors to navigate 'loop-de-loop tracks' and aggressively steep gradients, and trampolines or cannons to propel them to colossal heights.

In this essay I would like to make some observations about a subset of computer games: games that I consider explicitly *cinematic*. The basis of these games is the moving picture, and the player can manipulate a character through a set of environments with registered input a more or less constant possibility. These games are, I believe, the most extreme examples of 'interactivity'. They are the shock troops of new media, always advancing into new territory, at least in their structural characteristics and their unprecedented object-spectator relationship.

The environment of Sonic the Hedgehog and his colleagues, Tails the Fox and Knuckles (an indeterminate species), or that of Mario, the hyperactive toddler-with-a-moustache, is a Newtonian physics demonstration. It is a pool table, a rollercoaster, the world of H. G. Wells and Jules Verne, not that of William Gibson or Neil Stevenson. Unassisted flight, hyperwarp speed, and Roadrunner rates of acceleration (to say nothing of time travel or jacking into databases) are not features of the worlds of most current cartridge games. The milieux these games depict are strangely nineteenth century, un-futuristic, non-science-fictional, though we like to take their international prevalence (not to mention the huge gross earnings of the corporations that produce them) as signs of the encroachment of a future on the present. And, I would say, rightly so.

However, though the physical laws of the depicted environments are within the high school applied mathematics syllabus, the spaces depicted cannot be endorsed by any traditional educational curriculum. Buildings with no visible support structure ascend infinitely, so that characters can keep climbing up and up and up, while abysses descend equally far into the bowels of a virtual

* Earlier versions of some sections of this essay were published in *Leonardo*, vol. 28 no. 5, 1995.

earth. If a character changes direction, going back does not necessarily return him to his initial course. Spatial continuity is either absent (there is no connection between one area and the next), or too present (when, for example, advancing past a certain point brings you back to where you started). To put it another way: the geometry of the space represented in these games is postmodern while their physics remains pre-Einsteinian.

Since the first version of this article was finished in January 1998, 3D games, for Nintendo 64 and PlayStation, have overrun the cartridge game market. In these games a character controlled by the player can move perpendicularly to the plane of the screen, as well as parallel to it – away from the viewer as well as up, down and sideways. These games often include zones from which a character can transmigrate from one place to another (the 'Beam me up, Scotty' principle). Compared with a game like the N64 *Zelda*, *Sonic* feels primitive – almost medieval. But as a general rule the same principles apply. Link, the main character of *Zelda*, is as inhibited as Sonic by the laws of Newtonian physics – until he collects the devices that enable him to breathe underwater, glide across gulleys, and warp to another location. These devices are strictly magical, difficult to obtain, and often need to be mastered themselves. They reinforce the physical limits of the everyday, nonmagical world, the world that Link gradually, item by item, frees himself from. The possibility of movement in three dimensions gives the player a powerful sense of geography and personal placement, as well as an overwhelming feeling of conquest as he liberates the enslaved inhabitants and finally the trapped Princess Zelda – to win the game. The 3D world also encourages the player to move aimlessly, to sightsee, and simply to walk, run, gallop, jump and tumble around. Indeed he is rewarded for non-goal directed meandering: he often finds secret hiding places or insubstantial creatures he can defeat, and wins magic, money, health or useful gear. He also meets off-track characters who challenge him to contests and tests of skill, and in engaging in these minor games, the player hones his own skills with the joystick and buttons, and later finds himself drawing on his practice bouts when he engages a boss or other significant enemy. *Zelda* is a highly intricate environment, with a complicated economics, an awesome cast of creatures, a broad range of landscapes and indoor scenarios, and an elaborated chemistry, biology, geology and ecology so that its world can almost be studied like an alternative version of nature. The game allows its players to feel as if they have acquired genuine skills and knowledge for use in their encounters with tougher and tougher adversaries. It is regrettable that these skills have no application outside the contained world of the game. But over all, my points about the simpler games are confirmed, not negated, by these more recent products.

A first proposal to account for this mismatch between physics and geometry might be that the laws regulating *movement* in the video game need to be immediately comprehensible, while infinite and foundationless architecture and geography do not affect the player's moment-by-moment navigational understanding. The player manoeuvres the keypad with two general aims: *acquisition* – of tools, health, weapons and 'powers'; and *destruction* – of obstacles, enemies, and 'bosses'. The overall goal is to preserve the life of one's character and increase his health whenever it flags so as to reach new levels of play action. It could be said that operating in a world of familiar laws makes the game more 'intuitive.' But this does not seem right. There is a harsh learning curve associated with these games. In a sense, ascending the learning curve is playing the game. A player could equally adapt to a new set of physical laws as he gets in synch with the rhythms of a game and learns how different combinations of buttons make his character jump, hit, kick, shoot, climb, cling and crouch. Indeed in some older games, characters *can* fly without assistance, swim underwater without breathing, and transmigrate from one place to another from anywhere. However, these games are less compelling.

My guess is that the world governed by mechanical laws is designed to create a visceral resistance. The everyday physics of the game world keep the player anchored to his seat, held down by the sense that the laws of the simulation are precisely the laws of the world he is struggling to overcome in daily life: in soccer and basketball in the schoolyard, and on roller-blades or skateboard on the streets and half-pipes. In both the game world and the real world, gravity and friction, if not opponents, are forces to domesticate, while elasticity, momentum, balance and co-ordination are allies. The rhythms of recent games are not based on hand-eye dexterity as much as unexpected accents and changes in tempo. Reaction time, in other words, is no longer the winning ingredient as much as adaptability and familiarity with the ebbs and flows of the game's changing currents. Compare Joan Didion's description of driving on the freeways of Los Angeles in the 1970s:

> Anyone can 'drive' on the freeway, and many people with no vocation for it do, hesitating here and resisting there, losing the rhythm of the lane change, thinking about where they came from and where they are going. Actual participants think only about where they are. Actual participation requires a total surrender, a concentration so intense as to seem a kind of narcosis, a rapture-of-the-freeway. The mind goes clean. The rhythm takes over. A distortion of time occurs, the same distortion that characterises the instant before an accident. It takes only a few seconds to get off the Santa Monica Freeway at National-Overland, which is a difficult exit requiring the driver to cross two new lanes of traffic streamed in from the San Diego Freeway: but those few seconds always seem to me the longest part of the trip. The moment is dangerous. The exhilaration is in doing it.[1]

But the pleasures of surfing the currents, of finding the rhythms of a computer game, can only account for part of its success. The fact is that we cannot beat the computer, and every player knows it. In order to keep us believing the patent falsehood that we might be able to best it at exactly what it does best, the computer depicts a scene of nineteenth century machines, an Adam Smith world of profit and loss, credits and debits, laws we feel we can comprehend and bend to our advantage. But this is a false illusion. The computer eventually will outpace the player. Simulating an opponent, the computer can always win.

The compulsion to play, which is clearly not the same as the compulsion to win, is almost pathological for many players. Time flashes by, obligations are forgotten, while the computer game fills the imagination of the player, despite its minimal rewards and scant storyline. What is it that keeps the player glued to the screen?

In a startling autobiographical memoir published almost 20 years ago, author David Sudnow describes his obsession with a computer game in a style and level of detail that matches the state of mind.

> (…) I serve. I get the first shot right, there's the return, and it'll come right about here, and I'm right about there. Don't miss. Got it. It goes up, hits the correct brick, here comes the return, it's going to be a little further to the right now, so I'm moving to the right. Be careful, don't go too far. So I don't go too far because I'm scared, and instead of bringing the second section under the paddle I bring the middle under it and the ball shoots off to the far right side. Be more careful. So exactly the same thing happens three times in a row, the third shot always hit fearfully in the middle with a full paddle that can't miss the ball but can't hit that brick.[2]

On the screen of *Breakout*, rows of bricks are aligned in front of the back wall of the court (at the top of the screen), and bricks disappear when a puck-like object hits them. The object is to eliminate all the bricks. The puck bounces off a paddle that the player moves along a single axis at the bottom of the screen. The behaviour of the puck is not entirely rational or predictable. Hitting certain bricks changes the speed and direction of the puck's bounce, and at specific points in the game its velocity changes without warning, while different regions of the surface of the paddle also affect the bounce in different ways. *Breakout* was designed in 1976 as an arcade game by then Atari employee Steve Jobs, aided by video game enthusiast Steve Wozniak (!).[3] It was released as a home cartridge game for the Atari 2600 system in 1978, and David Sudnow played this version for several months in 1979. His book is a painfully detailed documentation of his extended attempts to 'beat' the game – hundreds of hours of play are described, move by move, in a writing project that is reminiscent of the early novels of Samuel Beckett.

> I'll pretend it doesn't matter, since I can immediately witness the consequences of caution. Be casual this time and make believe you couldn't really care less one way or the other. Get back that naturalness you had when you woke up. So I go again, and the first two shots are fine, and now comes that third one a little farther to the right, and so I'm casually pretending it doesn't matter that I swing broadly and nonchalantly in that direction, while before the movement to this side was cautious. And now I hit the ball on the very tip of the paddle, which sends it to the left wall.[4]

Sudnow delivers almost 200 pages of this relentless prose, with very little in the way of conclusion or analysis. Though *Breakout* is in some ways quite different from more recent character animation games, Sudnow's description of the game's appropriation of the imagination of the player like an army of occupation certainly applies to Zelda and Sonic; and no one else has undertaken this kind of phenomenological study. The combination of self-consciousness (Sudnow is a psychologist) with his obsessiveness as a player is unique. The very existence of the book demonstrates the authority a computer game can exercise over its player, even when there are no game-characters to identify with, no more narrative than a game of solitaire, and no rewards for winning or even witnesses to a victory. *Breakout* gripped the mind of an adult so firmly that, like a recovering alcoholic, he felt the need to write a book to document his capacity to overcome its power.

What is the source of this power? What is in the compulsion to play and replay the game, missing appointments, losing sleep, sacrificing meals, companionship, and even sex?

Sudnow's battle with *Breakout* is a battle to win consistently. He discounts his occasional 'lucky' strikes in a search for a repeatable victory. In the first part of the book he looks for rules to the game, even going so far as to track down the programmers (he is too late for Jobs and Wozniak, unfortunately, but he finds the software engineers that repurposed the arcade game for home cartridge use). They cannot help him, because the software is constructed not on principles of game theory or a rule book, but on testing and revision: engineers develop a version and then modify it based on observing users' interactions with it. The criterion of a success is that it grips the player precisely as Sudnow was gripped. So he could not expect to find the principles behind the game by interviewing the programmers – their approach was experimental, 'bottom-up'. Since *Breakout* was originally designed as an arcade game, the design objective was that the frenzied player keeps feeding the machine quarters. It is clear what keeps the player playing. His basic desire is for mastery over the apparatus. The point of the game, and I think this can be generalised, is to keep the player between two frontier zones – on the verge of mastery, on the verge of losing control. A little more effort, a little more timing, a little more spring and co-ordination, will reach the next level; and a little less will result in a death. The pleasure is in overcoming what was just a few minutes ago insurmountable. What keeps the boy playing is a promise – the intimation that with enough energy, enough focus, and enough lives, he might master this machine.

Mastery. Even when I write a personal letter now, there are two mental activities involved: the creative act of writing, and word processor expertise, the mastery over the apparatus that I depend on to operate the device with which I write. I've more or less 'learned' the word processor by now, though there are always unexamined features, software upgrades and new output devices. The fact that I can endlessly edit without effort – all you need is … not love, but rather time – enables me to input a text early, perhaps too early, in the writing process. Before the word processor, for me at least, thinking was the first step of a writing project. Now, however, thinking is keying in, a necessary unpleasure. And writing becomes editing.

MASTERY'S DELETION OF THE MASTER

In his essay 'Cyberspace, or the Unbearable Closure of Being', Slavoj Žižek argues that this breakdown of the distinction between writing and editing eliminates the concept of the definitive text. He suggests that a need for a new authority, other than the author of a text, has appeared. This master's (Žižek's term) function would be to adjudicate between competing text versions based on an expertise different from the author's. The computer therefore allows (forces?) the author to abdicate his authority. Žižek calls this the 'decline of the function of the master in contemporary western societies.' He suggests that the illusion of open choice in contemporary media corresponds to the disappearance of acknowledged authority, and in fact results in a decrease of 'freedom'.

> It is when there is no one to tell you what you really want, when all the burden of the choice is on you, that the big Other dominates you completely, and the choice effectively disappears.[5]

However, Žižek is rarely straightforward. He ardently embraces a fundamentally paradoxical approach, where every pivotal concept incorporates its obverse, and it is nearly impossible to extract a coherent position from his jubilant stream of quotations, arguments, jokes and examples drawn from mainstream cinema, literature and politics. He does seem to suggest, however, that interactive technologies (or what he calls 'cyberspace') leave a gap where a symbolic authority formerly existed. The sense of mastery offered by the video game can plug that gap temporarily, allowing the player to regain – for himself – the illusion of authority.

Mastery. Am I arguing that it is a 'drive' like sex, death or survival? Or should we look for a more fundamental psychological principle to account for the game's impoundment of the player's imagination? I wonder if a search for fundamentals is the right approach to the problem. For Sudnow it is the micro-focus of playing the game that keeps him interested – the fact that he is always just short of winning, that a death is always the result of a minor error, an error that should be easy to avoid in the next round. So he always goes on to that next round: he plays it again and again, Sam until he can no longer hold the controller. Sudnow does not expect practice to make perfect. He does not think that reps will increase his skill – and here he contrasts playing *Breakout* to playing the piano – he simply expects not to repeat his previous error. In other words, the game is isomorphic: the structure of each moment of play, in its success and failure, mirrors the structure of the whole game. Winning the game is linking together a series of winning moments, and no more than that. There is no one overall drive governing the player's compulsive behaviour, but rather a series of tiny desires for one small victory after another. Like the structure of a computer programme, the experience of the game and the impulse to keep going are built out of atomic components.

In the character games there is a similar isomorphism between player and character. Mario faces the same task as the player who drives him, though for the player it is a fictional task while for the cartoon creature a (virtually) real one. Exactly as the player is striving for mastery over the apparatus, so the character – whether it is Sonic, Mario, Duke Nukem or Link – is striving for mastery over his environment. This mirroring is one of the factors that leads the player to refer to his character in the first person – 'I just destroyed one of Dr Robotnik's robot machines and liberated his victims' or 'I need more health' or even (spoken with frustration or anger) 'I died'. The fact that the player describes the character's struggles as his own indicates a peculiar and specific kind of identification, and has led recently to the introduction of the term 'avatar' for one's onscreen representative, particularly in networked environments.

IDENTIFICATION: I AM MARIO

Is the relationship of player to avatar different from a reader's or viewer's identification with a character in any work of fiction? Identification has been a major topic in film theory for over 25 years. Recently Žižek has encapsulated and added to this research, writing very elegantly about the contrivances of identification and its connections with 'the gaze' and specific film editing techniques. The essay 'In His Bold Gaze My Ruin is Writ Large' is in Žižek's compilation with the extraordinary title *Everything You Wanted to Know about Lacan (but Were Afraid to Ask Hitchcock)*. Again, it is difficult to summarise the ricochets of Žižek's reasoning; he turns his argument around the concept of gaze, arguing that identification can be directed to a character during the times when the screen portrays that character's point of view. In those moments we can feel as if we are seeing through the character's eyes, and the mechanisms of identification, according to Žižek, are linked with this epistemology.

For my purposes, his most relevant line of argument deals with the shifting of points of view. He sees one of the main functions of montage in the fiction film as enabling the viewer to adopt an ever-changing point of view, shifting from one character to another even within a single scene. Whom I identify with corresponds to my point of view as I find it migrating from one character to another. This thesis is most compelling when Žižek employs it to account for the experience of the horror film. He suggests that in *Psycho* (Alfred Hitchcock, 1963), for example, there are moments, when we find ourselves not only looking through the eyes of the mother of Norman Bates, the embodiment of evil, but also identifying with her to the extent of feeling her unspeakable desires. At the moment Bates stabs Detective Arbogast, we, in identification with Norman's mother, also wish for the death of the prying detective. And this identification with what Žižek calls 'the Thing', i.e. with a creature we regard as morally subhuman whose outlook we find repugnant, is one of the factors that gives rise to the intensity of emotion the horror film generates.

Žižek's subtle analysis of the 'coincidence of our view with the Thing's gaze' culminates in his claim that we do not through this experience gain a greater understanding of Norman's pathology, of the character of the psychopath. At the moment of coincidence of viewpoint, we feel the Thing's wish for the detective's death, without understanding the motives or psychology that bring this desire into being. This is unlike an identification, which carries an understanding (sympathetic or not) of the character whose eyes we see through – a quality that Žižek attributes to our identification with Marion, the secretary who steals the money and is famously killed in the shower. Indeed, Žižek is reluctant to give the name 'identification' to our moment of coincidence with the Thing's point of view, since there are no qualities of character to fill out the experience.

In a video game the 'coincidence of view' is achieved very quickly and by means of a single, elementary device – that the movement of the character is fully determined by the actions of the player. Without my action on the keypad, Sonic is static. My actions bring him to life – and I have to see the world through his eyes to keep him alive. There are few, if any, qualities of character to attribute to Mario, Sonic or Link. Yet the identification is intense. No viewer of *Psycho* would ever refer to Mrs Bates with a first person pronoun, but Mario is me. I am Mario because I am responsible for Mario's

(physical) actions. If Žižek is right, one of the horrors induced by *Psycho* is connected with my experiencing Mrs Bates' despicable desire as my own, while her actions are beyond my control. Thus I feel
her desire without any way to take responsibility: responsibility depends on the ability to act, and, if
necessary, to act against my desires. In a video game, on the other hand, the fact that my actions
determine the actions of the characters endows me with total responsibility. Thus horror is a difficult, if not impossible, emotion to elicit in a computer game: I cannot be induced to desire the unthinkable while I am responsible for the actions of my character – the force driving me is the desire to
keep my character going.

> The idea is that if you consume every Mario artefact you can get your hands on, if you can play the
> Super NES game in a *Mario Brothers* sweatshirt while scarfing down an individually wrapped *Mario
> Brothers* snack, then through some mysterious process of celebrity transubstantiation, you can
> become Mario, or at least take on some of his abilities. It's kind of like Pinocchio in reverse – millions
> of real boys dreaming of some day turning into a digital
> marionette.[6]

So by playing the game I become Sonic, Mario or Link; but not in the sense of feeling their desires
or understanding their motives, since they have neither desires nor motives, not even fictional ones.
As Henry Jenkins points out in an essay I shall discuss in some detail later, '[t]he character is little
more than a cursor that mediates the players' relationship to the story world [...] lack[ing] even the most
minimal interiority.'[7] In contrast, the player does have an interior life, and in manipulating his avatar's
movements, he attributes his own motives and desires, his hopes and fears (at least in relation to
the game) to the character he controls. I need to acquire abilities, better weapons and extended
time, to reach the next level and to win the game; and these attributes are precisely what Mario
needs, in order to stay alive, vanquish his enemies and achieve the next level. Thus in effect my
mental states and Mario's are one and the same: the mindset I read into Mario or Sonic is my own.
It would be surprising if I did *not* refer to him in the first person.

MARIO IS ME. AM I A PSYCHOPATH?

I am Mario. What are the implications of this? In their perceptive collaborative article,
'Nintendo® and New World Travel Writing: A Dialogue', Mary Fuller and Henry Jenkins remark
on the pervasiveness of conquistador and colonialist metaphors in the description (and especially
in the promotional literature) of Virtual Reality.[8] This inspired the authors to make a detailed
comparison of computer games and Renaissance travel narratives by such explorers as
Columbus and Walter Raleigh. Both computer games and Renaissance travel accounts privilege
space traversed over plot and characterisation. This approach yields unsatisfying narratives, since
plot dynamics and character depiction and development are two of the primary conventional
measures of narrative success. In underplaying these qualities, both forms emphasise exploration,
discovery, acquisition and exploitation.

Does it follow that our ten-year-old boys are becoming virtual neo-colonialists as they guide their animated avatars through the environments of data space? How would this state of mind manifest itself? Do they believe that they can master and control their environments more than they used to? Clearly to attempt a general answer to this question would be pointless – but it is remarkable how recent teenage trends seem to emphasise control and empowerment. Skateboarding, roller-blading and snowboarding are skills that depend on developed expertise, and, once mastered, allow the enthusiast to dominate the sidewalks, the schoolyards or the slopes. Body modification, such as piercing and tattooing, suggest that the territory of the body is entirely the domain of its owner. But at the same time, the emphasis on command and control over areas as limited as these might suggest that the commanders feel particularly disenfranchised in other areas of life, areas that are perhaps perceived as more significant. Perhaps part of the interest in video games is in reaction to a sense of powerlessness: with controller in hand one can became master of a world, though this mastery is limited.

The United States government treats the notion of video games causing psychological damage with some gravity. In 1993 and 1994 the House and Senate assembled a joint subcommittee on violence in video games. Of course the members of the committee were not concerned as to whether video games affected the attitudes of their players toward colonialism and conquest: the main issue was the portrayal of violence. The senators and congressmen, as well as the expert witnesses they called, all seemed to accept without question the (untestable) presupposition that violent images provoke violence in those who view them. Dr Robert E. McAfee went so far as to read the following statement into the record, claiming that it represented the official position of the American Medical Association:

> The AMA believes that something must be done to deal with video game violence. We have
> suggested in Congressional testimony earlier this year that perhaps a written message should appear
> on the video game screen at the beginning of each game in which some character is killed, such as:
>
> THIS IS A GAME THAT SHOWS MURDER AND KILLING. IT IS ONLY A VIDEO GAME, BUT IN REAL
> LIFE, MURDER AND KILLING ARE PERMANENT. IT IS VERY WRONG, IT CAUSES A LOT OF PAIN
> AND SADNESS, AND MURDERERS ARE PUNISHED AND CAN GO TO JAIL FOR A VERY LONG TIME.
>
> We also suggest, in the spirit of the video medium, that scenes should be incorporated into games in
> which the consequences of violent acts are depicted in connection with some innocent character
> being injured or killed – scenes such as an ambulance rushing the character to a hospital or cemetery,
> and other characters representing the family and friends of the injured or killed character crying and
> grieving.[9]

I'll leave the ideological underpinnings of this paranoid text to a future grammatologist.

The government's prime example was *Mortal Kombat*, a combat tournament game in which the player selects a character (from a gallery of mugshots) and also selects his character's opponent. The possible contestants form an exotic multicultural assembly, male, female, and of indeterminate gender, from Japanese Ninjas to African warriors. Each character has specific fighting skills, which the player must learn to manage. Some of the deaths are spectacular, including reaching into the opponent's chest and removing his or her heart, or twisting off the enemy's head to harvest a shower of ruby blood. But, finally, *Mortal Kombat* is only an animated costume and make-up exhibition, with little connection to real world violence. The anger and frustration children feel comes from the fact that they invariably play until they lose; until the computer, to which they do indeed attribute qualities of character, wins. Losing to a dumb machine can make anyone mad.

What are the long-term effects of video games on their players? If the characters we control are men without qualities, surely the enemies are also empty shells, bundles of functions not traits, however elaborate their appearance. *Mortal Kombat*'s preferred mode is competition between players rather than against the computer, and the game allows its player to costume his avatar, to select some physical qualities to project his own personality onto.[10] In those games where the primary mode of play is against the machine, the enemies are often two-dimensional cyphers – robots controlled by the dreaded (offscreen) Dr Robotnik in the *Sonic* series, and silly hinged discs with teeth in *Super Mario 64*. In *Taurok* the enemies are a variety of prehistoric beasts and armed foot soldiers, and Link's enemies are a variety of magical and robot-like creatures, from zombies to despots. However, even in most cases these beasts rapidly lose their minimal realism, because even after dying they reappear. Destruction, no matter how bloody, is make-believe: the creature will be reconstituted to attack you later. The economics of software demand repeatable objects. It is unfeasible to build a unique software enemy for each hostile encounter, of which there are hundreds in a game session. Repetition mitigates the bloodiness of the violence. Does it also contribute to a sense of triviality in regard to real world violence? In prison on the day of their arrest, the two Arkansas children who were accused of gunning down their classmates in 1998 reportedly cried for their mothers and tried to exchange their chicken dinners for pizza, obviously misunderstanding the implications of their confinement, if nothing else. Has the culture of video games contributed to their cavalier attitudes? Of course the answer one gives to this question is determined by the presuppositions one makes about a number of fundamental issues, by one's general worldview. To pin the blame on video games in isolation is clearly a case of ostrich thinking.

Is Mario a Christopher Columbus? Does Sonic's world reinforce colonialist values, as Mary Fuller suggests? The point of the video game is mastery – there is never the option of adjusting one's behaviour to fit the environment, e.g. learning and adopting the habits of its natives. (This is not absurd: other games such as *Civilisation II* and *The Sims* can be described in this way.) The only habits the natives have are aggressive behaviours toward the intruder – exactly the qualities the conquistadors attributed to the natives of the New World. Success is based on conquest, not co-operation. As to whether this is the attitude the game communicates, whether the player is left with a desire for mastery over his real world when he puts down his controller – this must be an empirical issue. Many aspects of our contemporary societies reinforce the view that there are winners

and losers in life, and becoming one or the other is largely a matter of outdoing the other participants in whatever game one has chosen as one's own. Like most entertainment, video games reflect
dominant ideologies as much as they originate or communicate them.

MILITARY TRAINING AND REACHING THE NEXT LEVEL

There is one final distinction that I think is important, though I'm not sure I am capable of developing it in sufficient detail. I started this essay with the claim that a player's task in the range of games
I've discussed is mastery over a system of apparatus. I suggested that while Mario's goal was to
master his environment, the player's task was to master his own environment, not Mario's. The
player is looking for an expertise over the system he is playing on, and he achieves this expertise
by guiding Mario through exploration, murder, conquest, pillage and exploitation. Though, as I have
indicated, the player identifies with Mario to the point of referring to him in the first person, there
is a difference between the depicted 'virtual' world that the avatar exists in, and the apparatus that
accomplishes the picturing of the virtual world. The player's task is to master the apparatus by getting Mario to master his world.

> If anything, extreme realism compromises a video game's play-through and hobbles its pacing.
> Lockheed Martin's first draft of *Desert Tank* was a lousy arcade experience, because it was too much
> like a real tank. The vehicle dynamics were great – you could practically feel the terrain rolling under-
> foot. When you fired the cannon, there was a great force feedback effect. But you had to wait for-
> ever to fire again, because real missiles generate so much heat that you have to pause while the
> cannons cool down. This stuff is really key when you're training tank pilots. They have to know all this
> stuff. But it doesn't make for the greatest gaming experience. Taking a minute and a half to reload
> kind of kills the buzz.[11]

This distinction between depicted world and depicting machine collapses when one considers a
type of application that has emerged in the last five or six years. I am referring to military training
simulators, and the games that are based on them. The point of using a flight simulator, for example,
is indeed to learn the apparatus, but, at the same time, the apparatus is a simulation of a fighter
plane, the function of which is, in a word, military. Since the Gulf War, a number of games have
been licensed from, or retooled by, companies like Lockheed Martin that developed training simulators for the military.[12] *BattleTech*, for example, a networked arcade game in which each player
operates his own tank-like vehicle in a battlefield, was developed from a training simulator that was
used by soldiers, who were soon sent to fight in the Gulf War. What the operator experiences
from inside the cabin of the tank is almost exactly what he experiences in the actual field of battle,
since the world outside is brought into the cabin through cameras and other electromechanical
mediation. Being in a real battle is experientially the same as being in a simulator – unless, of course,
a missile hits you. In other words, killing (in contrast to being killed) feels the same whether there
are actual enemy tanks out there or not.

Even the military, however, does not believe that tank simulators in any way prepare the soldiers for the horrors of killing. Other more traditional techniques, centred on drill and basic training, develop those aspects of soldiering. In fact, one of the criticisms of contemporary war (voiced by Lieutenant Col. Dave Grossman in his book *On Killing*) is that the modern soldier is so far removed from the enemy he kills, that he cannot feel the moral compunction that the infantry man, for example, has to overcome when he bayonets his opposite number. Even from a military point of view, this is undesirable. The soldier's effectiveness suffers as does his mental health and his acceptance within the greater society. Grossman suggests that the US military is now deficient in training its soldiers in dealing with the realities of warfare — certainly tank and helicopter simulators do nothing in this direction. This troubling situation results in battle scenes like the so-called 'Highway of Death' at the end of the 1991 Gulf War. US helicopters used their video game-like consoles to guide their missiles into the bodies of teenage Iraqi soldiers as they fled along the road from Kuwait City to Basra after the US recapture of Kuwait. According to Douglas Kellner, the US ground troops who saw the results of this manoeuvre were disgusted and mortified, unprepared for the sight of the actual burned and hideously maimed bodies.[13]

These facts are deeply disturbing. But they are unavoidable facets of the contemporary world. Whether a game is necessarily tainted with militaristic values because it was repurposed from military training devices is a complex issue. Training simulations prepare soldiers for operating weapons and other military apparatus, but fail, according to military experts, precisely in the area of imparting effective soldierly values. For someone who would like to steer children away from the ideologies of war, this is good news. On the other hand, it is possible that *some* military values are passed down — I hope we don't forget too quickly the tragic recent Jonesboro and other high school shootings. Obviously much work remains to be done in these areas, and there is some urgency.

CLOSURE

If the overall force motivating one's play is the desire for mastery, the specific desire that keeps the player in the game is the desire for closure. I want the game to end, and to end with me the winner, a fact that, if achieved, will prove my mastery over its apparatus. As I have suggested, this is a rare treat, and even when tasted, not as satisfying as the craving made one think it would be. According to Lacan, desire is that which is never satisfied. The fact is that most players tire of a game before they beat it, and it is left perpetually open, unfinished, questions unresolved …

NOTES

1. Didion, Joan. 'Bureaucrats', in *The White Album*. New York: Simon & Schuster, 1979, p. 83.

2. Sudnow, David. *Pilgrim in the Microworld*. New York: Warner Books, 1983, p. 130.

3. Information from the Videotopia website at http://www.videotopia.com, retrieved Jan. 1998.

4. *Pilgrim in the Microworld*, p. 131.

5. Žižek, Slavoj. 'Cyberspace, or the Unbearable Closure of Being', Slavoj Žižek, ed. *The Plague of Fantasies*. London: Verso, 1997, p. 153.

6. Herz, J. C. 'Mario über Alles'. *Joystick Nation*. New York: Little, Brown and Company, 1997, p. 136.

7. Fuller, Mary and Jenkins, Henry. 'Nintendo® and New World Travel Writing: A Dialogue'. Steven G. Jones, ed. *Cybersociety: Computer Mediated Communication and Community*. Thousand Oaks: Sage, 1989.

8. Ibid.

9. Robert E. McAfee, MD 30 June 1994, statement of the AMA to the Subcommittee on Telecommunications and Finance, House Committee on Energy and Commerce.

10. William Gibson elaborates the costume fantasy aspect of *Mortal Kombat*-type games in his masterful *Idoru*, in which members of a rock musician's fan club meet in 'virtual space,' each of them presenting herself (or rather her avatar) in costume and character, in fantastic environments they have created as their 'club houses'.

11. Herz, J. C. *Joystick Nation*. New York: Little, Brown and Company, 1997, p. 207.

12. J. C. Herz also makes the fascinating point that all video game technology can be ultimately traced back to US Department of Defense funding. See 'The Military-Entertainment Complex', Chapter 6 of *Joystick Nation*, pp. 197–213.

13. See for detailed discussion of these issues: Grossman, Dave. *On Killing: The Psychological Cost of Learning to Kill in War and Society*. New York: Little Brown and Company, 1996; Kellner, Douglas. *The Persian Gulf TV War*. Boulder: Westview Press, 1992; and De Landa, Manuel. *War in the Age of Intelligent Machines*. New York: Zone Books, 1991.

PART TWO

EXPLORATIONS: A NEW PRACTICE

Crossing and Collapsing Time: Re-constructing (Her)Historical and Ideological Film Narratives on a Transformed Stage

Jill Scott

In this chapter, I would like to address a few components of my current research, which are related to the concept of socially interactive media, and its relationship to the crossing and fusing of time. I will offer to explain my own preferences for non-linear narrative, and how these relate to interactive media generally, and to the creation of new dynamic spaces. My main interest stems from how these investigations further alternative forms of communication and dialogue, and how related memories and associated cognitive processes may be explored through metaphorical objects. The main inquiry is concerned with the combined effects of technology and narrative, and whether the results of this fusion can extend the definitions of space to include a sense of time-lessness. All these investigations have led to a breakdown of the older notions of chronological narrative, observation and characterisation. By presenting history in a new way, as illustrated through my own more recent didactic environmental installations, I hope to show how the results of my research can begin to transform narrative, observation and characterisation into simultaneous metaphors, interactive social-dialogues and new screen-representations. Of prime importance is how these developments can invent refreshing role models for the viewers, who find themselves on a transformed stage.

The main aim for many interactive media artists is to create an experimental multi-user environment, where different levels of transformation of narrative may take place. Embedded within this search for the alteration of narrative, traditional forms of chronological accounts can become very disturbed and segmented. The disruption comes not only from the desire to take in everything and be everywhere at once (as evidenced by the non-linear access of TV channel-switching), but also from the growing need to feature the story of a single character simultaneously with other stories in a broader time-based context. In my environments, computers lend themselves to a thematic set of broken dimensions and related segments, which can be accessed randomly. Over the past 25 years, these have led me to mainly investigate the following three concepts: space and time, historical characters and metaphorical interfaces; including the interdependent relationship between the audience and these concepts.

SMOOTHING SPACE AND COLLAPSING TIME

In my environments, which I currently call 'houses of desire', the focus has been to expand and even transform older concepts of space and time. Firstly, there is the question of whether our old concepts of spatiality and temporality can be redefined through non-linear concepts. This does not necessarily mean that we media artists are uninterested in designing the stage from scratch, in order to enhance the content in our minds, nor in challenging ourselves by the limitations of site specificity. It implies that we are also exploring virtual multi-user concepts by constructing installations, inspired by blurring the lines between solidity and transience.

Secondly, how are shifts in these newer edges or borders of space related to the traditional idea of time or endurance? Is it possible to create some type of new fluid non-dualistic definition of space itself?

Personally, I am concerned with the more emotional and idealistic aspects of these issues, which means I focus on the relationship between the viewer's feelings, and the creation of separate time zones inside the space itself. Therefore, reactive considerations come into play. Do I want the viewers to be able to experience both a private intimate place and a more public social space simultaneously? How do they feedback and identify with these different dualistic levels of space and time, in the very same environment?

According to David Deutsch, the term 'time-travel' can perhaps only be valid when applied to past and present space.[1] He suggests that a rendering of the past can only behave accurately by being faithful to a known image of history. The four environments illustrated here suggest it may be plausible to create a type of interactive and unlimited screen-based space, by encompassing a number of different time zones which allow the viewer to time-travel into the past, the present and the future. The viewers experience this by moving around. The result is closer to what Gilles Deleuze once advocated: the adoption of an entirely new nomadic social system, which should be 'dynamic, spatial and anti-hierarchical.'[2] Although the spatial realm he imagined seems very idealistic, a 'smooth' and 'nomadic' one, which 'liberates the human body's sense of both virtual and real multiple selves inside constructed systems', its goals appeal to new media artists as it is they who are attempting to liberate the passive viewer, allowing them to physically engage in interactive systems (multiple-choice, virtual reality and WWW designs). These systems not only include the novel non-linear potential of computer access, but also connote a *resistance to the older hierarchical systems* and the construction of nomadic environments, where ideas of integration between space and body are played out.

Furthermore, in terms of breaking down borders between the viewer's body and the space that body occupies, Deleuze once considered that a body could be interpreted as devoid of organisation.[3] 'Think of the body without organs, as the body outside any determinate state', he postulated, 'poised for any action in its repertoire; this is the body from the point of view of its potential, or virtuality.' Here, Deleuze urges us to expand the interpretation of body and space, far beyond the meanings attached purely to 'form'. If we interpret his 'body' as the body of the viewer, he also values the viewer's unpredictable actions, and the possibilities of their individual imagination in unlimited space. This sense of unlimited or 'dynamic' space greatly appeals to the media artist, and for me personally, this is enhanced by the crossing of time and by the viewer's desire for immersion. I have discovered that the viewers seem to desire two different types of bodily 'immersion' in screen-space. These are intimacy and expansion. The potential of being enclosed in an intimate screen setting or node seems to appeal for private reasons. Furthermore, they like the feeling of choice between a number of different nodes and the ability to move around them based upon their individual preferences. In this way they enter the realm of the liberated Deleuzian ideal and become wandering nomads. They want to comprehend the overall historical sweep and its related themes, and here a type of collapsed-time is preferable. After they have seen the whole environment, both of the above subjective and objective levels of experience should accumulate, resulting in a type of fused time and smooth space.

This occurs in _Beyond Hierarchy?_ (2000), where intimate experiences into the lives and times of   (DVD) workers, and their respective secrets, are played out. The viewers, by focusing on solo terminals and by moving from one terminal to another, can cross from one time zone into another, in a non-linear fashion. However, the audience can also imagine being inside a huge conglomerate factory (accumulated from many eras of the last century), simply by wandering, observing and interacting with the other viewers.[4] The total experience embodies the interior space of one's own body in relation to the screen (which I would interpret as a protected and enclosed space) and the objective view or the relation to the external and infinite space our bodies occupy (an enlarged and expansive space). The success of the work indicates that the desire for 'immersion' implies both the space of intimacy and that of expansion. This observation is related to the history of performance, conceptual art and experimental cinematic media, when the body was seen as part of the artwork, squeezed between the opposing forces of either supreme objectification or extreme subjectivity.[5] An important contribution from these older art disciplines is the critical development of thematic issues like representation and the human condition, as well as the idea that the personal feelings of the viewers could in some way affect the content.

In _A Figurative History_ (1997), an environment situated in a Japanese style hut, the viewers or   (DVD) participants are asked to react inside intimate nodes of subjective space. However, by engaging with the room in a different way, it is possible to cause a more public scenario to happen. The result is a type of objective meeting, similar to that found in the plays of Bertolt Brecht, who maintained a life-long interest in the collapsing of time, or 'the epic-sweep', as he so aptly called it.[6] However, on Brecht's stage, the viewers cannot physically touch each other or participate to cause the collapsing of time. By comparison, the viewer controls my environments in an attempt to re-construct the atmosphere of a living and sweeping archive or historical laboratory of fused time. Thus chronological time is shattered and scattered by them. The aim is to create a feeling of timelessness by combining an atmosphere of past, present and future in the same space. Therefore my 'houses of desire' is a departure from traditional forms of linear cinema with their beginning, middle, and end, and it continues the evolution of experimental developments in theatre and media.[7]

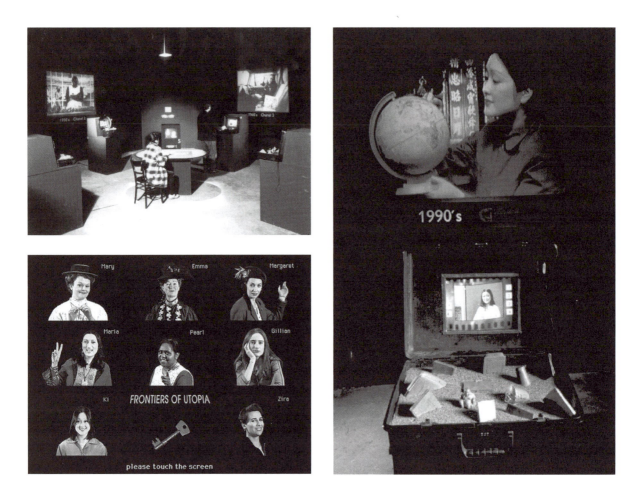

 In _Frontiers of Utopia_ (1995), I extended the traditional rectangular movie house shape, by creating an octagonal ground plan, which housed five small cinematic scenarios. Having already experimented with four and five live-sound environments and related still images in a similar way, I found that when the soundtracks from time zones are played-out simultaneously, by being amplified in the same environment, the viewers enjoy their attempts to mix the soundtracks.[8] _Frontiers of Utopia_ allows the viewers more nomadic visual choice, and at four terminals they can delve into the intimate flavours of idealism or at the central one they can experience the objective thematic viewpoints of a social occasion, which collapses time. These pliant experiences are aided by the familiar social issues of idealism and the relationship between desire and design in a variety of utopias. Working with political, ethical and social issues in the other installations has also helped to formulate the space, and the relation of that space to the viewer's physical participation. While the environments of _A Figurative History_ and _Future Bodies_ explore the fickle house of the history and 'herstory' of the desire to transform the body by technology, _Beyond Hierarchy?_ closely relates to the concept of the industrial 'workhouse' and its idealistic forms of hierarchy. I believe that themes like these help the viewer to integrate, to lose themselves, to become both an intimate subjective and an objective observer, as well as to become a player in the unlimited landscape of crossed and collapsed time. These 'houses of desire', by exploring both the viewer's ideological identification and levels of immersion simultaneously, dissolve the human body and the artwork together.

HISTORICAL AND 'HERSTORICAL' SCREEN CHARACTERS AND US

The computer screens themselves help to blur the lines between the real or constructed space (solidity) and the nomadic viewers (transience), and, on the computer screens, representations of our histories unfold as fabricated screen characters whose main role is to play seductive personifications. Here, I am interested in the creation of transient social metaphors of communication, between the real (viewer) and the re-constructed (screen characters). Not only do successful levels of movement by the viewers in and around the space depend on their intimate dialogue with the screen characters, but also on the amount of ideological identification the viewer can have with them. Primarily, there is the question of what types of characters or digitised identities are best suited to this relationship in the 'houses of desire'. This assumes that presently we are limited by developments in voice-recognition software and therefore, at this point, might look for other metaphorical considerations.[9] A second issue is how to identify with all these characters' ideologies as an 'epic-sweep performance', when only segments of the characters are available for selection. Here we have to take into account the types of collective desire in history, which may best engage the viewer in collapsed, unlimited and dynamic space and time-travel scenarios.

For a number of years, the role models of pioneers and immigrants have been of major interest to me: as seen in the works *Frontiers of Utopia* and *Beyond Hierarchy?*. Here all the screen characters are often full individuals with good and bad moods, trivial pursuits along with deep perceptions, but what they all have in common is that they are the new thinkers of their time. In *Frontiers of Utopia*, extensive research was conducted into the lives of pioneers, an element perhaps left over from my own Australian past. During the relevant inquiry, it became obvious that most of us have been taught that pioneers make history, but most history has been written about famous men by men. What about the stories of pioneer women and their ideals? The dreams of eight ordinary women and their personal concepts of the future became the focus of the environment.

The viewer can meet Emma (anarchist) and Mary (socialist) from 1900, Margaret (capitalist) and Pearl (freedom fighter) from 1930, Gillian (student activist) and Maria (hippy) from 1960, and finally Zira (new ager) and Ki (democrat) from the 1990s. *Beyond Hierarchy?*, on the other hand, represents the major desire to improve one's living and working conditions and focuses on a selected group of six workers. Those chosen to represent this major ideal come from the prominent industries of industrial progress in the twentieth century. These are the ammunitions factories (Sophie 1918); the mining industries (Piotr from 1933 and Lotte from 1952); the expansion of the car industry in the 1970s (Misha); the advent of recycling in the 1980s (Ahmet); and finally, the electronic service industries of the 1990s (Sabine). In both works, I have taken the assumption that histories and 'herstories' are related to ordinary people, and their levels of collective desires and struggles, and not about the progress of capitalistic ideals. The characters are therefore played by

34 (opposite) *Frontiers of Utopia*, Jill Scott, 1995. Collection ZKM and funded by the Australian Film Commission. *Frontiers of Utopia* is a large archive of sounds, images, films, and personal objects drawn from the lives of eight women. The women come from different time zones in the past century and they are all political idealists. An especially designed octagonal environment houses this archive in the form of four outer computer terminals where suitcases and interactive touch screens are located. In the middle of these four terminals, stands a dinner table, where a large photo of all the eight women can be seen. The viewers can either interact with the individual characters and associated sounds and objects, through suitcases, touch-screen terminals or they can select two characters by simple touching them on the photo. Those selected meet across time – a humourous scenario that appears on another screen.

actors with scripts, based on research of real lives and of transient nomads found in oral history archives and books, as well as state and film archives from specific regions.

However in the projects, *A Figurative History* and *Future Bodies,* the screen characters are often exaggerated interpretations of current social desire and debate, and this requires that their very construction be dealt with in different ways. In *A Figurative History*, because the characters represent a set of five radical desires to transform the human body by technological methods, they are constructed using 3D computer graphics and special effects composting techniques. The screen characters artificially match the desires of mythical transformation (Pandora – BC), mechanical simulation (Lady Miso – 1750), biological construction (Frankenstein's monster – 1890), cyborgian incorporation (from the knight – 1550 to the medical cyborg), and finally to the concept of the virtual or downloaded mind (Data body – 1990). They talk about the manipulation of the human body, from the real to the transient, from inanimate to animate and from reconstructed to incorporated, and in so doing, represent an overall historical sweep of these, rather ethically suspect, desires.

Similar interests may even cast the screen characters into virtual rather than solid stage environments, such as those found in the net. For example in *Future Bodies,* the screen characters are entirely nomadic text-based entities, floating in cyberspace. This is because they are based on a dystopic futuristic division of society into the rich (manipulated), the poor (genetically deficient), and the perfect (born genetically perfect). Furthermore, these desires for genetic manipulation are almost impossible to predict in a visual way, and the real-time clashing between the characters and the viewers may affect the screen characters' representations.

In all the above works, technology provides the tool for the audience to meet the screen characters, each one standing in for a particular set of ideologies. These may not only come from the past, but also from the present and future. The viewer is also a character with a set of ideological standards; however, one who uses the computer to traverse continents and compare desires. In so doing, the viewer draws on their own experience to create parallels between periods and locations, technology and nature, class and gender, as well as differing levels of sociality. As Allucquère Rosanne Stone proposes, the main human desire is the need for sociality, and this is the driving force behind the invention of new technologies for communication.[10]

Through technology, a range of screen characters meets the viewer and the viewer meets a diversity of screen characters. This exploration in sociality automatically places the viewer on the mediated-stage, as the main character. This allows for a new level of identification, an extension of what John Fiske calls 'ideological identification';[11] a notion that requires the viewer to take on some performative roles. These can vary from the boss of the character to a type of god or goddess who can cross time, but they always ask the viewer to remain an active participant. Although this is something the audience is normally very shy of undertaking; I have found it best to offer these roles of identity, in relation to a particular theme (for example, our reliance on hierarchies or the ethical implications of re-constructing nature). Consequently, I imagine the audience is interested in performing the unfolding of the theme and offer them some roles to choose from. This is a carry-over from my early performance and installation days in the 1970s, where I would use the audi-

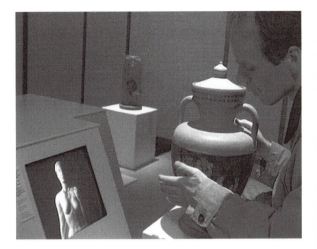

35 *A Figurative History*, Jill Scott, 1997. Funded by ZKM and in the Collection of the ZKM Medienmuseum, Karlsruhe. *A Figurative History* is one installation of a larger work called *Digital Body Automata*, an especially designed hybrid media environment inspired by Japanese architecture. It consists of a small room where five screens and five terminals are semi-embedded into an elevated floor. The five terminals or smart sculptures resemble a Greek vase, a sixteenth-century cog, an IBM transistor, a heart preserved in a glass jar and a knight's helmet. The five corresponding characters to these objects, Pandora, Lady Miso, the Data Body, Frankenstein's monster, and the Cyborg, are all constructed from digital effects and 3D-computer animation. They all wish for various forms of physical transformation. The viewer can either interact with each character separately or select the characters to respond to each other by using these objects. However the objects only function if the viewers touch other viewers as well as touch the objects, as the water in the viewers bodies acts as an electrical conduit.

ence as part of the inspiration for the performance ('Extremities', 1978) or ask them to participate as selected organs of the human body ('Continental Drift', 1992).[12] In order to enhance these roles, it is important to employ a kind of magic, which proves that without the viewer nothing will happen. In most cases the audience is even asked to assume the role of an editor; it is they who unfold the personality of the screen characters' stories; it is they who place the total thematic puzzle together. I simply offer them the fragments, and this means a giving up of linear authorship to varying degrees, in the hope that certain levels of ideological identification will still occur. Therefore, my screen characters are written as relational elements and fragments. I base my method of scriptwriting on the same process as a real-life situation, when one person first meets another person. Chronological narrative cannot adequately simulate the idea of meeting a character, instead it is the association between segments of the screen characters' personality and the personal memories of the viewers themselves, which allows the viewer to have an intimate interactive experience. Associative learning is the way in which the mind works; the links must take place in the viewer's own pace and time. They occur in an unpredictable way, either as connected individual and private references, or as set of related montages tied to the many public and therefore universal desires of sociality.

Naturally, the degree of social success between a screen character and a viewer is helped by

36 *Future Bodies*, Jill Scott, 1999. Constructed in conjunction with ZKM group ('Escape to Beg') for FUSION 99 in Weimar and explored in real-time over the net with ANAT Australia. *Future Bodies* are net-based characters, which only exist in a text format and appear in real-time within the common protocol of a Hotline Chat. They are genetically deficient characters programmed to behave in accordance with a pre-described behavior called Brains. The characters are called Poor, Rich, and Perfect. They can appear as real comments inside the hotline chat and respond to peoples typed in keywords. The program built for them can conjugate and also respond with set parameters of random responses. During the Fusion 1999 event these characters lived in a virtual environment and participants were encouraged to find out more about them as well as edit their moods through keywords.

tricks from traditional film like authentic historical backgrounds and universal reflections of the viewer's own family history or personal experience. However, I have experimented with the idea that the surrounding backgrounds of all the characters should be exaggerated, to see if more universal levels of social identification and perhaps social criticism could be increased. In *Frontiers of Utopia* all the screen characters are set into dreamy artificial backgrounds, a superimposition related to the general conclusion that utopia may be an unachievable frontier, always out of human reach. Alternatively, both the screen characters and their backgrounds in *Beyond Hierarchy?* are manipulated to look like archival photographs, even though they span the history of workers over 100 years. This places them all in an exaggerated historical context, so that the viewers experience the impression of looking back at the twentieth century from a futuristic perspective, an aspect that emphasises the feeling of objectification. By the same token, the screen characters from *A Figurative History*, all appear on a black void, one in which the viewer might assume other artificially-constructed screen characters are hiding.[13] When these talk together, they seem to be representatives from a larger community of other mutants. In other words, the ideology of incorporation between nature and technology lends itself to many fabricated manifestations, of which each screen character is simply a representative.[14] In *Future Bodies,* my current research project, perhaps the characters may roam though the net, to be manipulated by the viewers on a global scale.

As I have suggested above, different environments have been designed to increase the intensity of the viewer's relationship to the characters and the roles they play. They can either choose the order of presentation of many screen characters' personalities, as a series of related segments from separate time zones, or they can cross time on transient pathways and assume metaphorical roles. Their roles are initially determined and directed by the viewer's relation to metaphorical objects (solidity), which trigger the screen characters.

METAPHORS, OBJECTS AND AUDIENCE

The objects, or 'smart sculptures' as I call them, are designed to relate specifically to the time zones of both the overall space and its screen characters. In some of my environments (*A Figurative*

History, *Beyond Hierarchy?* and *Frontiers of Utopia*), the viewer, by using different 'smart sculptures', discovers that she or he can play two separate roles: one private (or local) and one public (or universal). Not only do these roles depend upon the actual metaphors the objects imply, but they also centre on the way the sculptures are used by the viewers. For example the viewer physically touches one of the five objects in *A Figurative History* (a Greek vase – BC; a knight's helmet – 1550; a wooden cog – 1750; an IBM transistor – 1955; and a heart inside a glass lab-jar – 1890). By doing so he or she can privately explore the metaphorical connotations between particular parts of the object, and the associative filmed segment of a screen character. It is through this searching, an intimate experience, that the viewer can assume the role of the history student. However, by touching two 'smart sculptures' and simultaneously linking hands with another viewer, two screen characters can jump linear time. Then they will stop to turn and meet over time. In fact a 'human

37 *Beyond Hierarchy?*, Jill Scott, 2000. Funded by Kultur and Project GmbH; Collection: City of Dortmund. *Beyond Hierarchy?* is a selection of films from the lives of assembly workers from an industrial centre in Germany called the Ruhrgebiet. There are three male and three female workers and they all wish for an end to hierarchical organization. The work was both designed for and inspired by the 'Verwaltungshalle' or administrations centre from a 1910 mine. The space resembles a church in structure, and black and white films of the characters are projected into the arches so that together they look like moving parts of the architecture. The viewer controls the character's sequences from ergonomic chairs located adjacent to the screens on the floor of the space. At one end of the space on the stairwell two viewers must shake hands while simultaneously selecting two of the characters in order to trigger these characters to meet at the other end of the space on a large screen. The ones selected meet on the screen in front of especially selected street demonstrations extracted from archival film footage.

chain' between all the objects and five viewers can cause an ethical public debate to occur cumulatively between all the screen characters.

In both roles (public and private) in *A Figurative History*, the viewer is elevated to a miracle worker, a magical aspect, which is enhanced by the feeling of being connected and therefore an initiator of the conversation. Actually, the 'magic' is derived from the water of the viewer's bodies, which technically runs the interaction.[15]

Alternatively, the more private role of the viewer in *Beyond Hierarchy?*, allows him or her to sit back on luxurious 'media chairs' and intimately control the segments of the workers' lives, as if he/she was the screen character's employer. The public meeting, on the other hand, occurs though an object called '*the secret handshake interface*'. This object places the role of the two viewers metaphorically in the shoes of the screen characters. When two of the viewers shake hands, then instantly two screen characters meet on the street, in front of various famous street demonstrations from 1918 to 1999. Then the respective time zones of the screen characters collapse together, causing humorous generation clashes to occur. The metaphorical role here is of fusion, a merging between the role of the viewer, and that of the filmed workers, together on the same hierarchical plane.

In *Frontiers of Utopia,* the sculptures present the viewer with a local role related to the metaphor of a researcher, combing through endless archives of idealism. Four suitcases with three-dimensional icons, from the time zones of 1900, 1930, 1960 and 1990 are used to comb through the archives. However, the screen characters' historical backgrounds and related sculptures are only accessible when the viewer uses a key to touch and (metaphorically) 'unlock' the objects in the suitcases. A socially public role is taken when the viewers use the very literal interface of a large photograph of all the screen characters eating at a party called 'The Dinner Party'. There they can select two or more screen characters to talk to each other across time. Here again the viewer can perform the imaginary role of a 'time-collapser'.

In all of the above scenarios, the viewer 'acts out' various roles related to the interfaces, but there are surprises. These derive from the potential for electronic interruption between the intimate objects and the expansive interfaces. A favourite surprise of mine is to let the use of the public interface interrupt and affect the private role of the viewer. The viewers in *Beyond Hierarchy?*, who sit in the 'media chairs' playing the bosses, for example, soon lose their editing control of the screen characters, when other viewers use the public interface. In such cases, the screen characters notice themselves talking to another screen character on a second screen. Then they stop to listen, giving the screen characters in the chairs a fright, as well as loss of control.

Currently, I am exploring the potential of such unpredictable circumstances in the net research project *Future Bodies*. Here the surprise may derive from the abilities of a viewer to edit and determine the screen characters' future, by altering their memories in real-time. Erratic reactions are an important part of the process of giving the screen characters a sense of being alive, and of simulating a dialogue.

The above processes of fusion of body with object and unpredictable metaphorical connection extend and redefine our older definitions of the 'interface' itself. As Brenda Laurel has suggested, this term should include the more cognitive and emotional aspects of an actual face-to-face dialogue.[16] By touching a smart sculpture, a symbiotic meeting of two worlds, and therefore two time zones, places the viewer in the role of both mediator and performer, emphasising their physical connection to the interface. Thus, through participation, the viewer becomes a 'modern cyborg', much in the way that Donna Haraway suggests.[17] Furthermore, the joining of these objects together with related gestures allows for the clashing of generations and increases the awareness of related ideologies. In these ways the smart sculptures actually clarify the interrelationship between screen space and the crossing of time, one that can often present us with surprising alternatives. Inside the 'house of desire', the viewer experiences a type of simultaneous interrelationship between a viewing of history/herstory (the private realm) and new social and ethical questions (the public realm). Consequently, the metaphorical objects or 'smart sculptures', as I call them, combine with the viewer's organic body and the screen characters to become accomplices in the same thematic 'house of desires'.

SUMMARY OF RESEARCH

At present, the computer programming required to make these connections between the viewer, the object and the screen character simulates a metaphorical level of sociality. However, this may change in the near future. The machine and we are no longer separate entities and the computer memory is also our memory (i.e. humans construct both memories). For many media artists, the creation of new types of social dialogue between these elements is a major issue in the ongoing research for convivial interactivity. Dialogue has not only been the subject of post-modern research since the beginning of the 1980s;[18] the conceptual simulation and construction of conversations between human character and machine character have been pursued by many scientists in the past (e.g. Andy Lippman).[19] Re-constructing real and virtual connection for a transformed stage is part of an ongoing search for a type of unlimited mediated space. Here creation requires various dynamic metaphors to illustrate and extend the relationship between viewer and content, between viewer and space, and finally between the viewers themselves.

Dramaturgy is no longer a place where the audience sits in the black space absorbed in the flat image of a single screen, watching a story unfold from beginning to end. The new idea is to allow each member of the audience to be a transient nomad and a fully-integrated mediated activator. The viewers unfold the narrative in their own time and space and these pathways are unpredictable. Consequently, this approach simulates the viewers' own desires for a dialogue with each other.

Therefore, the 'house of desires' must be an artistic and educational real-time space, where reconstructed historical associations are an active counterpoint to metaphorical objects and related screen characters. As Liz Grosz, another Deleuzian philosopher, once suggested, the most relevant metaphor for related explorations on the new borders of space-time could be the virtual space of the internet, where 'the post-modern subject may find its correlative and attendant modes of re-spatialisation'.[20] By this, she means that new social relationships may in the future exist between solidity and transience, creating the effect that all moments can become equally important, as scenarios of desire and ideology are played out. Consequently, the viewers, the screen characters, the metaphorical objects and the space itself are beginning to live in corresponding realities and virtualities. It seems computers are currently the medium to present us with the potential to explore timeless re-spatialisation.[21] In the future, I imagine more optimistic and unpredictable transformed stages where the viewers can unfold dynamic new fictions. A stage, which not only crosses time, but also one that presents history in a new non-linear interactive and unlimited landscape: a collapsed and fused socially viable house of ideological representations and metaphors.

NOTES

1. Deutsch, David. *The Fabric of Reality*. Harmondsworth: Penguin, 1997, pp. 294–5.

2. Deleuze, Gilles and Guattari, Felix. *A Thousand Plateaus: Capitalism and Schizophrenia*. Brian Massumi, trans. Minneapolis: University of Minnesota Press, 1987.

3. Ibid., p. 482.

4. Brecht, Bertolt. To find out more about the Berliner Ensemble and the epic theatre see www.gradesaver.com/ClassicNotes/Authors/about_bertolt_brecht.html (Accessed 12 Jan. 2000).

5. For related aspects of objectification and subjectification see the artists Bruce Nauman and Jill Scott in the resource book, Loeffler, Carl and Tong, D. *Performance Anthology. Source Book for a Decade of Performance Art*. San Francisco: Contemporary Arts Press, 1980.

6. Brecht, Bertolt. www.gradesaver.com/ClassicNotes/Authors/about_bertold_brecht.html.

7. See Schwarz, Hans-Peter. *Mediavisions. Media Art History. Are our Eyes our Targets?* Munich: Prestal, 1997.

8. See *Machinedreams 1900*, exhibited at the *8th Biennale of Sydney 1990: Art is Easy*. Curator Rene Block. Published by the Biennial of Sydney and the MCA. Document of *Machinedreams* or *Paradise Tossed* featured in: Hannes Leopoldseder, ed. *Prix Ars Electronica* 1993. Linz: Veritas-Verlag, 1993.

9. To see some of the latest developments in spoken language systems and voice-recognition: www.sls.lci.mit.edu/sls (Accessed 15 Dec. 2000).

10. See Stone's analysis of sociality in relation to the mobile phone and the internet, in: Stone, Allucquère Rosanne. *Desire and War at the Close of the Mechanical Age*. Cambridge: MIT Press, 1995.

11. Fiske, John. *Television Culture*. London: Routledge, 1987–94. Fiske suggests that the process of identification depends on three, non-sequential levels of identification. The first level is characterised by the involuntary merging of the viewer's own identity with that of a given character. Fiske elucidates: 'Central to this is a kind of wish-fulfillment, for the seducing character is claimed to embody many of the unsatisfied desires of the viewer' (e.g. strength, flight, power, immortality). A total identification takes place in the second level, which Fiske called implication-extrication. Here, the subject's identity appears to be lost, wavering between the real and the unreal. The viewer may gossip about the characters as if they were a part of the viewer's world or, alternatively, the viewer may assume the role of the character. This phenomenon is exemplified by the characters of soap operas, whose narratives enter the day-to-day life of the viewer. As an optimistic alternative, Fiske highlighted a third level, labelled ideological identification: 'This emerges from the transcendence of meaning and shifts across to affect the other two problematic stages.'

12. See 'Extremities', 1978. Scott, J. *Characters of Motion*. Straw Man Press, 1982 and 'Continental

Drift', 1992. *Follow Me* magazine, May 1990. 'Artists at Play'. Document of Performance Anne Howel. Sydney Australia.

13. In *A Figurative History* as the title suggests, the word 'figure' is used as metaphor of 'transfiguration' and specifically refers to those mutations and transformations that can be expressed through the medium of computer graphics and digital representation. Each 'trans-figure' represents a distinctive idea, desire and fantasy. Although these 'trans-figures' are only represented by digital and virtual formats, they are nevertheless sympathetically human, scripted on the histories of particular characters with multiple complexities and identities.

14. For example Moravec, Hans. *Mind Children*. Cambridge: MIT Press, 1981.

15. The water of the participant's body actually becomes a conduit closing the gap between positive and negative charges measuring between 10–15 Ohms of resistance. The participant's body is composed of 95 per cent water; thus, it functions as a natural body-conduit connecting the positive and negative metal points on the sides of the objects. When more human bodies are joined together, skin touching skin, the same value of resistance applies, as long as the positive and negative charges are positioned at the correct ends of the chain. In this way the participants' bodies are used to activate the sequences on the video screens, trigger still-frames and turn parts on or off (local mode).

16. Laurel, Brenda. *The Art of the Computer Human Interface Design*. Los Angeles: Addison Wesley and Apple Computers, 1990, p. 19. Empowering a group of users with smart interfaces is, as Laurel agrees, helping to create new visual metaphors for cybernetic and bionic transformation, as well as an understanding that the interface to our environment could be redesigned to suit the needs of many.

17. Haraway, Donna. 'A Manifesto for Cyborgs, Science, Technology and Socialist Feminism in the Late Twentieth Century.' Donna Haraway, ed. *Simians, Cyborgs and Women: The Reinvention of Nature*. New York: Routledge, 1991, pp. 149–81.

18. See Roland Barthes, for whom dialogue meant 'the passing back and forward of poetic and conceptual symbols, associated meanings and themes, not necessarily linear in construction or in sequence which in turn may affect the social, psychological and physiological levels of the participant.' Barthes, Roland. *The Empire of Signs*. R. Howard, trans. New York: Hill and Wang, 1982. See also: Barthes, Roland. *The Rustle of Language*. R. Howard, trans. New York: Hill and Wang, 1986, p. 99.

19. Andy Lippman helped to construct a valuable analysis of dialogue in Artificial Intelligence in the early 1980s, when he proposed that conversations 'should encompass mutual and simultaneous activity on the part of both the participants usually working towards some goal, but not necessarily': as cited in Smith, S. M., Ward, T. B. and Finke, R. A. *The Creative Cognition Approach*. Cambridge: MIT Press, 1995.

20. Grosz, Liz. *Space, Time and Perversion: The Politics of Bodies*. New York: Routledge, 1995, p. 100.

21. This is of course helped by the potential of increasing the number of computers and people working together simultaneously (*Future Bodies*) or the possibility of enlarging the number of people working simultaneously through one computer (i.e. *Beyond Hierarchy?*).

The Space Between: Telepresence, Re-animation and the Re-casting of the Invisible

Toni Dove

> Where does consciousness begin, and where end? Who can draw the line? Is not everything interwoven with everything? Is not machinery linked with animal life in an infinite variety of ways? The shell of a hen's egg is made up of a delicate white ware and is a machine as much as an egg-cup.[1]

In the daily life of industrialised cultures we use a number of technologically-determined interface systems: ATM machines, the internet, video games – even TV remote controls – give us an ordinary or pedestrian experience of telepresence. This experience is of an extended or distributed body. A body that reaches beyond its edges, beyond its skin, and enters into virtual spaces or technical systems where it manifests as action and response. It is a kind of doubling – an uncanny thing – and because it happens frequently in mundane contexts, it is slowly and inexorably re-casting the definition of 'body' through the invisible presences and powers made palpable by technology. At the same time, this ordinary experience of telepresence is helping to re-cast the territories of the invisible previously relegated to the sphere of the paranormal.

Evidence of this shift can be seen across popular culture in a spectrum of projects. The resurfacings of the supernatural and the paranormal have a density and slant that seems to be a new configuration. Human powers are amplified to equal the spectacular techno-developments of virtual spaces and digital special effects. Psychics and witchcraft, second sight and possession, have returned to the arenas of genre fiction with a vengeance. Throughout the narratives of popular culture there is a subtext of boundary anxiety fed by an array of technological advances from genetic engineering and nano-technology to the more ordinary and daily experiences of interface. Where do I stop? What are the limits? Experiences of telepresent agency speak to our mutating constructions of identity and to the limitations of being human. Our edges are blurry.

Familiar genre forms that operate as metaphor and allegory to assist us in assimilating profound changes in our cultural landscape have long been of interest to me in my work. These forms of fiction, combined with the technical evolution of a syntax for the new medium, provide me with a rich window into the fluid constructions of subjectivity at the edges of a culture transformed by emerging technologies. I think of the products of this adventure as philosophical toys. (See also Zoe Beloff's chapter, under The Personalised Interface.)

THE UNCANNY INTERFACE: THE SPLIT BETWEEN THE PHANTASMAGORIC AND THE DISCOVERED UNCONSCIOUS

Part of the resonance for me in the experience of telepresence comes from an interest in the fictional genres of science-fiction and the supernatural, and in the uncanny. The cultural history of these genres is tied to evolving concepts of human consciousness.

The rise of the Enlightenment brought with it a glorification of the rational and the scientific and a marginalisation of the irrational, the gothic and the supernatural. Ghosts lost their credibility. But the repressed does not vanish and the phantasmagoric erupted and resurfaced in new arenas. Commodified, it began a new life in pulp fiction and cheap theatricals – the beginning of a host of popular genres from horror to the supernatural. Internalised, it formed the origins of the unconscious.[2]

The uncanny, the intrusion of an 'other presence' into the familiar and comfortable (a return of the repressed), emerged as a by-product of the anxieties produced by urban crowding and rapidly changing technologies that altered the perceptions of time and space.[3] In the psychological realm the uncanny is frequently represented by the doppelgänger or double – the self-replicated in a form simultaneously familiar and strange that elicits terror. We have all had the chilling experience of a familiar object or person suddenly appearing strange to us – who we thought we knew, we know no longer. The world of appearances splits open and we have a sudden eerie view of a mirror world. The impact of the double is delicately balanced between sameness and difference. The effect can be simultaneously terrifying and poignant or humorous depending on the degree of this difference. The inept human mimicry of the robot R2D2 from the movie *Star Wars* has a different meaning from that of the self-cloned and encountered. The metaphors of the double and of possession seem particularly apt today (the person within a person or the mirror image) as deeply received concepts of holistic identity are challenged and redrawn. The role-playing game is a contemporary illustration of possession. A parallel theme in both the content and construction of my work is the origin and history of popular genre fictions and how they in turn mirror the origin and fluctuations of theories of the unconscious. This tango of theory, ideology, commodification and resistance forms the material through which our concepts of human awareness are threaded. What is required of us as social beings and what are the secrets we keep from ourselves to live socially? A look at what lies beneath and how it comes to the surface.

THE EMBODIED INTERFACE: A DEPARTURE FROM TRADITIONAL CINEMA

I make interactive movies. Cinema is the familiar ground against which I can make strangeness erupt through the responsive powers of interface and interactive structure. The design and actions of interface are a door into an immersive world of storytelling where the nature of cinematic time and space are altered. An embodied responsive interface produces the experience of doubling or extending the body. Characters are inhabited like digital puppets and when a viewer feels their own presence in the screen through the character, it can produce an uncanny experience. The familiar ground of film goes strange and the viewer feels the trace of his or her own actions reflected in the screen. They haunt the movie.

In a traditional film the position of viewer (voyeur) is physically passive – the process of spectatorship is physically still. The film becomes the eyes and point of view of the viewer and the body is left behind or forgotten – we enter the screen. Even in 'action movies', which use the eyes as a visual trigger into the internet of the sensorium to produce physical thrills, the body is largely left behind: inactive – on the shelf, so to speak.

In a responsive interface, the body is active and the experience becomes embodied. A viewer is simultaneously aware of their body – 'in' their body and 'in' the screen. The space between the two is activated. This charged space is a key characteristic of telepresence. It is the space through which the body extends itself into the movie or virtual space. It is the invisible experience of the body's agency beyond its apparent physical edge.

I have been evolving an authoring system for responsive narrative that combines video motion sensing (agency through physical movement) and vocal triggers to allow for a balance between agency and transparency. Agency is the way a viewer feels his or her own presence in the virtual space through the interface. Transparency is the degree to which the interface disappears or falls to the background while the viewer is immersed. The viewer feels the subtle tugs of connection to the movie through its response to their actions. I call this being 'stuck' to the character. It is the magic of this medium and it is this that seems to be disturbing, especially when it is placed in contrast to the familiar ground of film.

THE FUSION OF RECIPES FOR THE SUSPENSION OF DISBELIEF: INTERFACE AND GENRE

An interface has a recipe for the suspension of disbelief embedded in its operations that is similar to the recipes for the suspension of disbelief present in genre fiction. These codes are what we are willing to accept or believe to enter the world of a story. If interface design and genre fiction codes mutually support the vision of a story, an immersive world opens up. The combination of interface and narrative architecture amplifies the voyeurism of film through the sensory apparatus of the body. This amplified voyeurism provides an active exploratory space in which to experience a story. More like an instrument than a game, the combination of motion and/or vocal engagement with an unfolding narrative environment create a heightened awareness that operates almost like trance – a receptive state. It can feel like swimming or flying and engages the body with a virtual environment in a continuous and fluid way. The interface is the osmotic membrane – the means by which we fuse with the virtual space.

The familiar recipes of genre fiction can act in this context like an anchor or a series of signposts to guide you through this unfamiliar terrain. The codes can make us feel at home and act as a door into a world of complex ideas and relationships that are accreting, in a fragmented and slippery fashion, within the physically distracted body of the viewer. It is a potentially hallucinatory form of attention – an attention through inattention, focused by the physical.

In much of the developing area of interactive media, especially in games and multi-user social spaces, the voyeurism of film is transformed by first person action. In this construct, frequently seen in 'first person shooter' games, the viewer enters the virtual space and the viewer's actions have consequences that alter the outcome. In many games narratives are minimal and the rhythm of hand-eye co-ordination actions occur in a virtual space populated by multiple players. Games present challenges that are goal- or reward-oriented and actions have results that move you as an inhabited character or avatar through the space of the game. Speed and motor skill are requisite craft in these environments. The presence of the player as a character in the environment breaks a narrative each time the player acts as it alters the possible outcome of actions and the sequence. Multi-user games, role-playing games, chatrooms, 'MUDs and MOOs' all create a context where narrative is a social and emergent experience. These are significant, evolving, virtual, social spaces rich with possibilities.

But sometimes we want a story told to us as a complete experience – an expression of complex ideas, emotions and metaphors. Are there ways to tell a story that will not be broken through participation? Are there stories in which an amplified voyeurism combines linearity and an emergent narrative through immersion and physical sensation? And why is doing this interesting?

CASE STUDIES: *ARTIFICIAL CHANGELINGS* – A CONVERSATION MACHINE

Artificial Changelings, an immersive, responsive, narrative installation, is the story of Arathusa, a kleptomaniac living in nineteenth-century Paris during the rise of the department store. She is dreaming about Zilith, an encryption hacker with a mission living in the future. Zilith is an 'informal' urban planner redesigning the virtual highways of information data. The character of Arathusa was developed using a conceptual armature based on the social pathologies produced by the social changes that occurred during the Industrial Revolution. This subjective fictional armature – the character and her experience – becomes a glass through which to view the current changes of the technological revolution that are embodied in Zilith, a fractured character with multiple identities and almost no interior life. Urbanisation, merchandising, the mechanisation of travel and industry, and the birth of film are viewed against the evolution of information technology as part of the conversation between viewer and characters. These references form an unstable ground against which the physical experience of a virtual conversation with two characters in different centuries unfolds. *Artificial Changelings* is more like a conversation with a schizophrenic video android with a history, than it is like a traditional plot-driven film. Things float to the surface and form accretions.

PROJECT DESCRIPTION

A large curved rear projection screen with its curve bowing towards the audience hangs in a dark room like a large lantern. The choice of the curved screen was designed to pull the experience a step further away from film and to make the screen into a presence, an entity. In front of the screen on the floor are three flat black rubber floor pads approximately 3 by 2.5 inches each, in a line moving away from the screen. Embedded in the front end of each pad is an electro-luminescent

38 *Artificial Changelings*, Toni Dove, 1993–8. An installation shot from the exhibition 'Wired' at The Arts Center for the Capitol Region, Troy, NY, 2000.

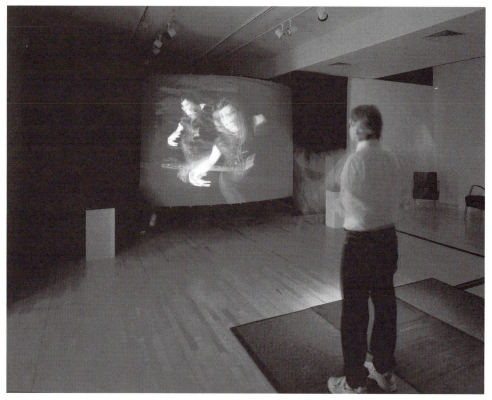

label that lights when a viewer steps on the pad. A fourth smaller pad is behind the three. The pad closest to the screen is labelled 'Close-up', next is 'Direct Address', then 'Trance/Dream' and finally the smaller pad, 'Time Tunnel'. Over the pads are two hanging lights and a small surveillance camera.

A non-interactive credit sequence with a brief introduction to Arathusa, the nineteenth-century character, opens the piece in a dark room. Following this, the overhead lights come up creating a dim pool of light over the pads. The piece – a voice – invites the viewer to enter the story space. The viewer steps back and forth on the pads to trigger video and uses body movements to move a character's body, generate speech, and create sound environments. When a viewer steps on a pad, the label lights to indicate that zone of video is active. Movement from pad to pad dissolves and changes video images. In Close-up a viewer is inside a character's head, hearing interior monologue or seeing from her POV. Stepping back to Direct Address puts the viewer in conversation with a character or in physical interaction – speaking, dancing, or sometimes hearing a third person narrator tell a fragment of story like a memory. In the third zone, Trance/Dream, the viewer enters an altered state and the imagery is dream-like and fantastic. The fourth smaller pad is the Time Tunnel. This pad triggers a video clip that switches to the other century of the story and the Trance/Dream pad lights up. The viewer then enters the other century of the story through the dream space. Once a zone is triggered the viewer's body move-

ment causes a re-animation of the video frames as they are played. This is not based on the linear 30 frames per second-video standard, but frame by frame, backwards, forwards, and at different speeds and in different non-linear configurations. Sound is triggered as layered, sequential and random fragments of speech or dynamic, sampled environments responsive to the viewer's moving body.

39 *Artificial Changelings*, Toni Dove, 1993–8. Three stills from the installation: 'Arathusa Dreaming', 'Multiple Ziliths', 'Zilith in the Time Tunnel'.

As a viewer physically navigates the story space through movement on the pads and movement picked up by the surveillance camera that feeds data to the video motion sensing system, an accretion of information builds knowledge of the character. The structure is based loosely on the model of conversation: you push on the character and gradually something is revealed, some of what happens is in your control and some is not.

Viewers seem to start out learning the system by trying to control the character. This manipulation is difficult to manage as the nature of the motion-sensing connects you to the character, slips away, and returns. The system parses motion below our level of comprehension. We tend to see gestures as discrete 'objects' — a fast gesture or a slow one. The motion sensing system sees a gesture as a complex arc of escalation, plateau and de-escalation. A movement repeated will not necessarily repeat a result. What the viewer is left with is a broken sense of connection that continually returns. This contributes to the uncanny sensation of the film gone strange. The characters in the movie are connected to you — attached to you in a palpable way that is not quite comprehensible. Movement through time and space, in and out of POV, contributes to a sense of the familiar gone awry. Viewers often end by mirroring the character. This is a phenomenon we see in human conversation. Two people feel empathy and express it through body language during conversation by mirroring each other's movements. In *Artificial Changelings* the viewer mirrors the character to enhance the feeling of connection.

When *Artificial Changelings* was completed and I started to watch viewers engage in the experience, I was surprised by the unnerving quality of the interface. This is due in part to its juxtaposition against the familiar, cinematic character of the imagery. I had not expected it to be disturbing or to engender what some refer to as out-of-body-experiences, what I think of as 'in body' experience. The sensation of connection – what someone referred to as 'that "thuuk" like a Vulcan mind meld' – led me to think much more specifically about the suspension of disbelief recipe of the interface and how it could be used to support and intensify a story.

SPECTROPIA: AN IMMERSIVE DATE MOVIE FOR TWO

A tale of supernatural possession became a logical place to explore the combination of genre fiction tropes and the uncanny interface which was evolving in the authoring system developed for *Artificial Changelings*. *Spectropia,* a project currently under development, is an interactive feature length narrative designed to be responsive to two viewers or performers at a time – an immersive date movie. Its length – almost that of a feature film (70 to 90 minutes) – suggested to me both serial form and a stronger narrative through line.

The story opens in a time reminiscent of the late eighteenth century, but strangely inverted, as if seen through a looking-glass of dimly-remembered and mutated images, the future in England, 2099, a world of artificial surfaces where knowledge spans only a person's experience and recorded history is forbidden. This culture of consumption floats on islands of garbage; saving anything is punishable by law. Spectropia, a girl in her teens, lives in the salvage sector of an urban centre known as the Informal Sector. The sector's function is compacting trash to lift the island above sea level as the water is slowly rising. Spectropia's companion, a duck android (part animation and part wireless robot), runs a black market business in retro objects. The duck is a baby-sitter bot, *in loco parentis*, programmed by Spectropia's father who disappeared while searching back in time for a lost inheritance. Driven by a feeling of abandonment, Spectropia searches for clues with a scanning machine of her own invention. The machine reads garbage and generates life-like historical simulations that she can enter and that respond to her voice and movement. This illegal research into the past takes her to 1930s New York after the stock market crash. Obsessive scanning short circuits her machine and traps William, a handsome ghost, in her workshop. Her machine then transports her to William's time and place, New York city 1931, where she finds herself in the body of a sophisticated older woman and amateur sleuth – Verna DeMott. A strange romantic triangle, time travel, and a mystery involving possession take the couple on a journey – clues appear written in invisible ink, hidden in locked boxes, broken lockets, at the end of dark tunnels and winding stairs, in towers. Spectropia uncovers the mystery of time travel on her machine: clothes are the passageway between the centuries. A garment slips off her shoulder as erotic attraction builds and 1931 trembles, dissolves and fades to the future. She is yanked forward in time only

40 *Spectropia*, Toni Dove , 2001. (top) Spectropia scans a piece of garbage and a simulation appears. (below) The Duck. Spectropia is played by Paz de la Huerta. (*Spectropia* is being developed with support from the Institute for Studies in the Arts at Arizona State University and ThunderGulch/LMC, NYC and is funded in part by the Greenwall Foundation, The Rockefeller Foundation, The National Endowment for the Arts and the New York State Council on the Arts.)

to scan herself back again to finish the puzzle. The tension between repression and release drives the narrative forward to its climax, in which economic disaster is only partially averted, romance is both thwarted and rewarded, and Spectropia returns to the future with a new understanding of her own past.

The narrative structure of the piece echoes the economic and emotional structures it depicts. The infinite deferrals of desire present in consumer culture and advertising are viewed through economic events that emerged in the 1920s – the instalment plan and buying on margin. The narrative (an uncanny ghost story) is haunted by the phantom of credit, the thing that isn't there, and by the desire created by commodity culture that is never satiated. This is paired with a voyage into the mysteries of adolescent sex – of approach and retreat, desire and repression, as each step towards physical intimacy pulls our heroine back to the future. The object of desire is unstable, fuzzy – it keeps changing or morphing in an endless chain. The thing keeps slipping away. It is the desire itself that ultimately creates pleasure, the experience of eternally delayed conclusion as a thing in itself – anticipation, frisson, and the adrenaline of seduction never quite consummated.

PROJECT DESCRIPTION

Spectropia is designed as a serial in three parts to create a greater flexibility of presentation. It can be seen as a theatre piece performed by two players for an audience or performed by the audience itself with guides, or as an installation in serial parts. Eventually I would like to see it as a living room experience networked so that two people can view it from the same or different sites. The initial 'movie instrument' has an interface that builds on the basic design developed for *Artificial Changelings*. Several physical floor buttons allow two viewers to share the navigation through three zones of video material. Motion-sensing uses viewers' body movements as a trigger for conversation, soundtrack alteration, and re-animation of video action. Wireless head microphones allow for vocal commands to navigate video space, for pitch and amplitude tracking to allow viewers to sing to the movie escalating the soundtrack, and for speech recognition and synthesis so that viewers can talk to smart characters that will talk back. The two viewers in the piece each become a main character in each century of the story and they must co-operate to allow conversation to unfold between characters, to make their way through suspense-drenched physical space and to negotiate physical interactions with each other (karaoke flirting). Navigating between zones can shift point of view, allow a viewer to look around the video space, or enter a character's private thoughts. Intermittently the action splits and viewers must follow one character or choose to try and see both lines of action simultaneously. It is as if the viewers put on the characters like smart costumes. I think of *Spectropia* as a techno-variation on Japanese Bunraku Puppet Theatre, in which black-clad puppet masters perform on stage, articulating nearly life-sized puppets. In *Spectropia* viewers are shadows in the story and manifest a relationship with each other through the characters on the screen.

When Spectropia time-travels and finds herself in the body of Verna, the dislocations she feels in another time and in another person, and the questions both she and Verna have about this circumstance, are underlined and supported by the viewers' own experience in the interface. Is this possession and time travel or a sophisticated simulation – a form of role-playing? Where does she go when I am in her body? Can two people occupy the same body at the same time? Do we ever really know the people we love? A metaphor of haunting runs through the story. Alternating states of awareness and amnesia organise the multiple identities that seem possible within characters in the story. The definitions of multiple personality disorder and their relationship to memory aided me in creating the 'cubist personality machine' that became the interactive narrative structure and a kaleidoscopic fractured mirror for the story itself. A multiplicity of POVs are experienced physically, through the spatialised construction of the virtual space. This is echoed in the design of the characters and cemented by the continuous physical engagement that forms a distraction, a trance-like form of inattention, into which the story seeps.

41 *Spectropia*, Toni Dove , 2001. Sally is played by Helen Pickett.

Sally Rand Close Up – viewers converse with Sally using speech recognition and synthesis through a head mounted wireless microphone. (Photo: Zoe Beloff.)

Sally dressing room – viewers can name objects (balloon, radio) or say Sally's name using a head-mounted microphone and a close-up image appears that responds using speech synthesis. (Photo: Sam Levy.)

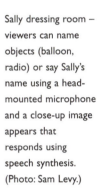

Sally Rand Bubble Dance – viewers sing or speak to Sally through a microphone and she dances; the video and soundtrack responds to the viewer's voice. (Photo: Sam Levy.)

AN ARCHITECTURE OF PERCEPTION – DESIGNING INTERFACE AND NARRATIVE STRUCTURE

In *Artificial Changelings* content unfolds through an accretion that imitates the unfolding of a conversation. It is a double portrait and in narrative terms, primarily exposition. I think of it as an engine. Its continually cycling random selections of alternating behaviours mix with the navigational choices of the viewer to create an approximately 30-minute experience that varies widely from viewer to viewer. It is never completely the same.

In developing *Spectropia*, I have attempted to push further into narrative and immersive territory. I wanted a piece of longer duration and a story with a narrative arc. The addition of vocal elements to the interface will now be designed more specifically to enhance and move forward story elements. For instance, the simulations created from Spectropia's garbage 'holodeck' include characters the viewers can speak to that will speak back and relay historical information necessary to the story. In another example, a segment of intense suspense is spatialised – suspense becomes a place to hang out where time is like rubber and the viewer navigates the video space using verbal commands. The responsive environments are designed to echo body perception and with this in mind, they are also redesigning cinematic vocabulary. I wanted to make a movie that would take itself apart as you were watching it and reassemble, wrapping itself around you.

In some ways *Spectropia* will be both more linear and more responsive than *Artificial Changelings*. In developing it I am thinking about the way that perception is constituted as sensory input in the body and I'm designing a responsive system that will assemble a perceptual space. This will locate the body in relationship to the virtual architectural space of the narrative, to the interior space of characters (through unstated thoughts, feelings and perceptions), and to the space of characters' relationships – and by implication the viewers' – through both conversation and intimate physical action. *Spectropia* feels to me more like a building than an engine. Perhaps this is because it is anchored by narrative and attempts, in the design of the three navigable zones, to create a palpable sensation of environment in the way that our body perceives itself to 'be' somewhere. 'Being' somewhere is a complex set of inputs and relationships and not only about the proximity of walls or ceilings.

This design for me is always filtered through the language of cinema – looking at its rules, taking it apart, attempting to understand how it works in order to rebuild it. It is as if I were making up my own film language, so that when we shoot it's not about shot/reverse shot, but a shot structure that will later assemble around the user to create an immersive world. This charges the space between the body and the screen, creating ecstatic 'in body' connections, while it escalates the voyeurism of cinema. I think that the intensity and repetition characteristic of trance play a part in the viewers' experience, both in the pacing and intensity levels of the story, and in the way it plays out through the movements of the body in concert with the images and sound. It forms the potential for what I would call a material ecstatic experience. This returns to my idea of the ordinary or pedestrian experience of the body's invisible agency, and the re-casting of the paranormal in material terms: a new invisible.

THE AUDIENCE AS PERFORMER/REBUILDING THE CONCERT HALL

One of the mutating or dissolving boundaries that interests me in the process of inventing an authoring system for responsive storytelling is the breakdown of the barrier between the audience and the performer. Telepresent interfaces have contributed to this – interactivity in all its forms creates an active viewer that departs from our conventional nineteenth-century view of the passive audience and starts to migrate into the territory of the performer. When we pull this relationship out of the home – out of the private sphere of one computer/one person – it becomes more apparent that this is a potentially radical change. In what spaces will this be presented? By what tools will it be made? By what sources shall it be funded and for what audiences? A new medium generates an entire spectrum of recipes for financing, production, distribution, presentation and publicity. It also generates its own architecture – think of the movie theatre or the museum. In the beginning everything is a *kluge* (or 'quick fix') – a retrofit, a misuse of existing tools and spaces to imagine a thing that might exist.

I imagine a space with a projection system that creates large-scale dimensional images not bound by a perceivable screen. I imagine moveable seats, the possibility of scheduled shows with human guides, and a great deal of flexibility. I imagine living room systems enabled by broadband that allow for the distribution to niche audiences of what is by nature infinitely reproducible work. I imagine game/entertainment consoles of the future with compelling interfaces that use speech and sophisticated sensors and have the possibility for networking users to a complex mix of cinematic and animated imagery and sound.

In the meantime, if I want to write a song I have to build the piano and the concert hall – using existing tools designed for something else – and this, I think, is part of the adventure. Making interactive movies is working in a medium that doesn't exist yet, like a Zoetrope inventor in the nineteenth century, working before film became a medium. Only the initial flickerings exist. It is working between things – between disciplines, between something that was/is and something that will be.

GENRE AS ALLEGORY

A final word on the concept of genre fiction, on the pleasure of recognisable forms and the way they seduce an audience to come along with you on a strange journey. I am increasingly interested in the idea of allegory in genre, in using the familiar recipes of genre fiction to express complex and sometimes difficult concepts in an accessible way. To slip things in, using a coded familiar form, that presented straight on would be difficult or perhaps unacceptable – in an entertaining way. I should mention the importance of pleasure here – the gift of pleasure, of fun. I think of *Alice's Adventures in Wonderland* (Lewis Carroll), a story that has captured the imaginations of generations – it was a critique of the monarchy. *The Wind in the Willows* (Kenneth Grahame) was an essay on class, *The War of the Worlds* (H. G. Wells), a close look at colonialism. Stories help to form the values of a culture and also provide a language to subvert them. They help acclimatise people to change, help to allow the absorption of new ideas and to enrich the imaginary of culture, that mysterious generative pool that seems to have such a profound effect on the atmosphere, and on the quality of our lives.

NOTES

1. Butler, Samuel. *Erehwon*. Penguin Classics, 1985, as quoted in: Ansell-Pearson, Keith. 'Viroid Life: On Machines, Technics and Evolution'. Ansell-Pearson, ed. *Deleuze and Philosophy: The Difference Engineer*. New York: Routledge. 1997, p. 197. Also quoted in Sobieszek, Robert A. *The Ghost in the Shell: Photography and the Human Soul 1850–2000*, Cambridge: MIT Press, 2000, p. 12.

2. These thoughts on the history of the uncanny are indebted to: Castle, Terry. *The Female Thermometer: 18th Century Culture and the Invention of the Uncanny*. Oxford: Oxford University Press, 1995; and: Clery, E. J. *The Rise of Supernatural Fiction 1762–1800*. Cambride: Cambridge University Press, 1995.

3. Vidler, Anthony. *The Architectural Uncanny*. Cambridge: MIT Press, 1992, pp. 3–66.

Intersecting the Virtual and the Real: Space in Interactive Media Installations

George Legrady

> The production of space is a search for a reconciliation between mental space (the space of philosophers) and real space (the physical and social spheres in which we all live).[1]

To experience space is to engage with it through one's presence, to possess it by being immersed in it, in the way one possesses space when inside a room, in a park or on the streets. Computer-generated virtual, immersive environments create the illusion of space by simulating visual clues such as boundary delineations, which allow us to perceive directionally and to circulate. Internet space is a metaphoric space accessed through a technological window, linking individuals in real-time across geographical territories. In the process of interacting with the digital world, we can consider 'real space' to be the site where our bodies can come into contact with the technological devices by which we experience virtual space. Social space then, becomes the site where we gather to watch each other coming into contact with the technological devices used to engage with virtual spaces.

Real-time data streams of digital images, texts and sounds make it currently possible to trespass across geographical and cultural boundaries, exponentially exacerbating aspects of Walter Benjamin's famous analysis on the nature of art production and its reception within a technologically-driven society. My sense of perspective requires an initial readjustment when I am confronted with a culture-specific experience that I know belongs to a specific geographical, cultural space, but becomes accessible anywhere where I can log into the internet. For instance, listening to NPR (National Public Radio) played through a 'RealAudio' internet plug-in on my laptop computer in Budapest, broadcast from New York, and received through an Ethernet connection while working simultaneously on the same computer in some other application.

Artists who create in digital media can produce works that do not require embodiment in any physical object. These works are free from the constraints of materiality, since they exist as numeric data on highly transportable storage devices such as hard drives, disks and CD-ROMs that can always be 'materialised' when needed. Digital works can be experienced in any given time and any given (institutional) space, or simultaneously in different geographical spaces through the web environment, making it possible for real-time interaction between multiple users or producers.

These forms of distribution seem to imply experiences freed from the constraints of the material world, but in fact, these experiences are highly shaped by the reception devices through which users come into contact with the transmitted information. For artists and communicators who want to create a specific experience, conceptualising the interface environments, within which the digital-based interactive artworks are to be experienced, becomes as much an integral component in the design process as the design of the interaction and the visualisation of its information data.

When digital-based artworks enter 'real' institutional spaces such as libraries or museums, a number of issues come to the foreground. If the work exists as a CD-ROM or on the internet, does it shift function from being an artwork to being a reference when presented in the library section of a museum? What are reasonable contractual obligations when a work published as a CD-ROM, but intended as an installation in a public context, is presented within the museum exhibition space? What kinds of experiential differences can be generated through a work designed for both the public viewing of the exhibition and more private home reception on the internet or CD-ROM?

INFORMATION AS PRODUCTION MATERIAL

Digital media works are by nature information-based. The two forms of artistic production which seem prevalent are the parallel art world strategies of either authorship or appropriation. Artists either invent perceptual or experiential simulations through computer programming, code production, or produce by processing existing digitised data, sorting and storing them in data-structures. The creative activity is a two-fold process: one begins by collecting and organising data which is then followed by the process of interface design — a form of narrative construction resulting in indexes, links, sequences and interfaces, which can generate the information flow and give meaning to the content. These approaches are to some extent a consequence of the nature of the medium, in as much as digital data consist of discrete units of information stored as digital numbers, which can be transformed and regrouped easily according to algorithms designed by the authors.

In the second half of the nineteenth century, the growth in the visualisation of information was enhanced by two discoveries: the photographic process, followed by the half-tone printing technique. Scientific visualisation, such as Marey's and Muybridge's documentations of movement in time recorded photographically, began to circulate first as both information and later as art. Many artists such as Duchamp, Léger, Picabia, who were working in the age of mechanical production, incorporated expressions of scientific data into their work. In the late 1960s, the conceptual art movement and systems or process-based artists such as Hans Haacke considered social information data as the material element for their projects. Digital media art practice has followed in the steps of these approaches, but it can be argued that information management in itself does not necessarily result in art. There is the expectation that the artwork transcends its materiality to some extent, that it generates a synthesis on a higher level. Recontextualising data may be thought of as a strategy of aesthetic practice, for instance: relocating news information into the gallery space can add a second level reading to the presented material. This sort of a shift of non-art information into the gallery space signifies an aesthetic gesture, as it is an action denoting intentionality. Recontextualisation and presentation generate meaning by themselves, resulting in an alteration in the way the information is perceived.

In the mid-1980s I began to write software that would transform digitised video stills in various ways. A few years later, I completed my first work that was purely software based, designed to be accessed interactively through a computer.[2] Enthused by discussions generated between linguists and computer science professionals about the potentials of computer programming software production as an arena for metaphoric expressions, I explored digital information processing and computer programming as forms of creative practice. My aim was to create programmes that would address logical propositions and inconsistencies in philosophical discourses emanating out of Claude Shannon's Information Theory. I was interested in the relation between noise to signal as a way of defining meaning in communication, and in what this approach would mean to the way we interfaced with technological hardware. My approach aimed to address the technological functioning and the design of interfaces, rather than to generate a techno-phenomenal event, or its aesthetic by-product. After having absorbed computer programming's logic, my work moved towards the production of databases, archives, methods of classification, information structures that dealt with historical inscription or reflected a cultural perspective whose data were accessed according to an organising principle expressed through an interface metaphor.

Many of these software works were given expression on the computer monitor, generating data in visualised form. I was both concerned and satisfied that these time-based, visualised events could exist without the necessity of producing a physical variant. My background in photographic practice was an important reference in the realisation that the meaning of these works would be marked by the mode of their access and presentation. For data that exists in the virtual, technological hardware, interaction becomes the mode of retrieval and the means of experience.

IMMATERIALITY AND PRESENCE

Digital media software products, sent into the world for distribution and consumption, have none of the physical properties normally associated with commodity objects, for instance: weight, volume displacement or material presence. Their immateriality makes handling, storage and distribution relatively easy, as they are brought to life within the virtual space of the computer, a hardware that can be thought of as the access interface into the virtual environment. Software by itself stored on a CD-ROM or other media is not usable until activated within the computer. This technological information storage and retrieval procedure does have analogue, pre-digital era corresponding precedents: film being the primary medium that comes to mind. The cinematic experience occurs when the film's content, encoded in image and sound data stored on a cellular media, is brought to life and made visible through activation by a piece of hardware, the projector.

The cinematic experience normally requires a public and social space in which it is to take place and therefore embodies a social experience. Viewers come together at a preset time to experience the event. They are physically present, orchestrated within a designated space in a determined format consisting of the arrangement of seats directing the audience's gaze towards a screen, a historical extension of the theatrical stage. The audience's communal presence within this institutionalised space becomes the occasion for the experiencing of the cinematic work. Radio, television and even telephone reception can also be understood as defined and ritualised reception spaces, most often private rather than public, but nonetheless situated within a social context. Interactions via telecommunication involve the body's physical presence and participation in some socially-defined manner, and even though these transmissions are ubiquitous, a kind of continual virtual presence, ritualised spaces with their own regulated conventions have evolved for their reception. Examples might include the radio industry's redirected focus from the home to the mobile automobile environment, after being superseded by television viewing in the social spaces of the living room, or local communal meeting places.

We can briefly refer back to Walter Benjamin's discussion on the historical conditions of production in his 'Works of Art in the Age of Mechanical Reproduction' to reflect on the digital artwork's value within the current situation of technological production.[3] Digital media works possess many of the attributes that release them from the conditions that Benjamin identified as giving rise to the phenomena of acquiring mythic, or cult value, which he defines as the 'aura' surrounding the unique artwork object. Digital-based works are immaterial, they can be everywhere, they have no originals. Authenticity is not a determining issue as all copies can potentially be seen to have equivalent value. This translates into greater handling flexibility for public institutions as acquisition, storage, transport, insurance and installation costs are drastically reduced. It is only when digital interactive artworks are presented within the public institutional space of the museum that they are brought into dialogue with history and its ideological discourse.

In comparison to the unique artwork, which has acquired 'aura' and value as a result of provenance and other factors, embedding it into the process of commodification; digital immaterial works also acquire value through representation within the framework of the museum's institutional space. Works that exist in the virtual domain of the internet, storage media or CD-ROM are given physical material expression through installations that are often based on curatorial and technical decisions determined by budgetary and other administrative factors. For instance, availability of technological media hardware, the viewing space that they occupy, and visitors' physical presence in relation to the scale of the work (within the allotted architectural space) become highly pertinent constituting properties that shape the reception and meaning of these immaterial media works. It is conventionally suitable to present internet and CD-ROM projects on a computer monitor on a table, but, given the spectacular aspect of museum spaces, can such a presentation formula, normally associated with information access, sustain the work's value as artistic experience, or does such a presentation format invariably diminish it to the level of reference material?

INTERSECTING PUBLIC SPACES WITH THE VIRTUAL

In the introduction to her article on immersive technologies, Katherine Hayles comments that the promises of VR (virtual reality) leading to an 'out of body' experience have not fully taken into

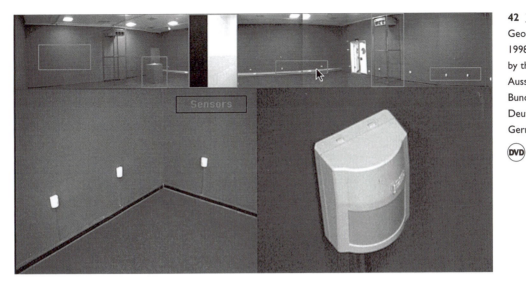

42 *Tracing*,
George Legrady,
1998. Commissioned
by the Kunst-und
Ausstellungshalle der
Bundesrepublik
Deutschland, Bonn,
Germany.

(DVD)

account the interface requirements of such interactions.[4] She identifies the interface mechanisms as highly grounded in physical, bodily experiences. One has to connect and access data through keyboards, trackballs, gloves, monitors, visors, microphones and headphones, etc., all of which make us highly aware of our bodies' physical contact with the devices. In fact, these can produce unintended bodily experiences, such as various forms of injury, if their usage is sustained over long periods. Once these devices enter circulation, they become part of the general common knowledge, conventionalised through familiarity. Over time they lose their strangeness, we forget the metaphorical discrepancies as we adapt our own bodies to accept their particular functional limitations.

These delivery devices have entered the museum environment as the dominant means by which digital works are presented. The most common device used at this time is the desktop, electronic publishing computer with monitor and mouse: a standard, multi-purpose, information-processing device that can be easily recycled from the exhibition floor to the library or curatorial offices. During the past decade, these computers have become steadily conventionalised to mean office work, information retrieval or game-playing. For some situations, these references may not pose a problem, but for others, this approach does not allow for a full experience of the digital work.

Audiences enter the museum environment in search of a public, artistic experience, rather than library-style research/information reception, unless that is a contextualising component determined by the artist. Participating in an interactive work within the context of a museum space implies engaging with spectacle and a form of audience performance. The experience is performative, in the sense that the audience is engaged as both performer and spectator: performing through the interaction with the work, functioning as spectator through the observation of what occurs when the other audience members are in performance mode. Needless to say, the audience's engagement is a necessary component of the interactive work, since it positions the viewer into creating presence: and it is only through the audience's actions that the work can reveal its complex layering of choices and multiple events.

The interactive installation takes place in a spatially delineated, architectural space. It and the surrounding area is a localised, socialised space, a site of discourse, and therefore an intrinsic, constituting element, pertaining to the full meaning of the work. This surrounding space situating the work and its reception can either be left to chance, or carefully planned. In either case, it functions as a key component of the work. My approach has been to extend the work's meaning into its surrounding space, describing its architectural presence and boundaries through various aesthetic devices such as image projection, wall partitions, wall coloration, text quotes, printed images, sounds and sound isolation zones. In the recent installations, the technology has been extended to carefully record the audience's presence and movements and to meaningfully use that information as a way by which to direct the content flow in the work.

In the public context of the museum environment, the audience trades space in exchange for time. Public spaces do not offer the kinds of comfort of private spaces. Private space, such as the home or office, implies self-determined time-management to research, to examine in detail, to go into greater depth. Digital media works that can be accessed in such environments, for instance CD-ROMs, or web works, are experienced through the various standard computer hardware that viewers have at hand. An additional factor, that recontextualises any information passing through it, involves the particular framing that a data provider might impose, continuously reminding us of its existence. It may be a moot point, but in such situations, the artist cannot influence the physical and contextual frame through which the artwork is received. The focus shifts towards immediacy and issues of mass audience accessibility, or accessibility across geographical space and time. One has to recognise that within the framework of the digital information communication environment, an interactive artwork's intrinsic value as art experience lies in a synthesis of two components. The first consists of the content and information flow of the work, all aspects of which are normally determined by the artist, and the second consists of the conditions of its delivery, exhibition and reception: aspects of which are beyond the control of the work's author.

NOTES

1. Lefebvre, Henri. *The Production of Space*. Donald Nicholson-Smith, trans. London: Blackwell, 1998, back cover.

2. *Equivalents II* was first presented in *Iterations: The New Digital Image* curated by Tim Druckrey for the International Center of Photography, New York. It later travelled extensively in *Photography after Photography*, an exhibition curated by Hubertus von Amelunxen and the Siemens Kultur Programm, Munich.

3. Benjamin, Walter. 'Works of Art in the Age of Mechanical Reproduction'. Hannah Arendt, ed. *Illuminations*. New York: Schocken Books, 1985.

4. Hayles, Katherine. 'Embodied Virtuality: On How to Put Bodies Back into the Picture', Moser and Douglas, eds. *Immersed in Technology: Art and Virtual Environments*. Cambridge: Banff Centre for the Arts/MIT Press, 1996, p. 1.

Virtual Reality – Tautological Oxymoron

Malcolm Le Grice

For a short while one of my forms of relaxation was flying a light single-engine, high wing mono-plane. I particularly enjoyed taking a flight around the bay area of San Francisco – around Berkeley along the Bay Bridge over Treasure Island, then I would fly as low as I could get away with over the pyramid in the centre of the city and out over the Golden Gate into Marin County, then make the circuit back over the water to Oakland. I particularly liked to do this in the late evening as the sun was going down and the lights of the city were coming on. One night I had started a little later than usual and instead of turning north over Marin I went south down the coast. After almost an hour I realised I had flown further than I intended and on impulse decided I would carry on down the coast aiming for Los Angeles. It was already past eleven, LA would still be some 300 miles away, my early Cesna could not make much more then 120 miles in the hour, and I calculated I should need to refuel on the way. I reckoned I would not get there until two in the morning or even later but made up my mind to go for it. I planned to find one of the smaller airfields, which seem to be all over the west coast, where I could land and take on fuel. I picked one out just before Santa Barbara. As there was a light wind coming in from the east I radioed in and flew into the runway from the west. There was no beacon so I prepared for a visual landing, always a bit tricky in the dark, but the lights showed the runway clearly and I approached at about 60 miles per hour cutting the throttle and lowering the flaps watching the altimeter carefully. I still hit the ground with a bit of a bump and a bit further up the runway than I should have been but otherwise it was a good landing.

I refuelled quickly, taxied to the end of the strip and took off again into the sea breeze, banked steeply left and set off again with the sea on my right and the foothills of the Sierras on my left. By one-thirty and still some way to go, I must have become drowsy. Though I was alone in the cock-pit, I thought I heard Emily call out 'Are you coming to bed?' Then after what seemed some time, her voice again, only closer. Distracted I suddenly noticed that the altimeter reading was low. Now you may know but I did not, just before you get to LA there is a ridge of hills, which seem to come down all the way to the sea. Having lost concentration I had drifted inland and lost height. In desperation I pulled back quickly on the stick without enough throttle. I went into a stall and ploughed into the side of a hill. The plane ended up nose down and tail in the air with Emily standing behind me in her dressing gown – 'What on earth are you up to – it's two o'clock – I just woke up and wondered where you were.'

Sheepishly and rather irritated I said, 'I was flying down to Los Angeles – I wanted to see if it was there.'

'What do you mean – you wanted to see if it was there?'

'Well I knew all the Bay Area was there and found that it seemed to continue down the coast – I wanted to see if LA was there as well.'

'But at two in the morning.' She paused, 'And is it?'

'Is it what?' I said.

'Is it there – Los Angeles – is it there?'

'I still don't know – you disturbed me and made me crash', which was not strictly true. It was my fault not hers. 'I shall need to go back to Oakland and start all over again and it takes nearly four hours in the Cessna – and I can't go more than ten minutes in the Lear-jet without crashing.'

'Well you do what you like – I'm going back to bed.'

OK – unharmed after my crash – I was determined to find out – so I reset to Oakland – set the time to daylight and started again. Four hours later I found LA – it was there – but not in so much detail as San Francisco. And, what is more I made a good landing amidst the 747s at LA International airport.

Here my soliloquy was interrupted for my cigar was smoked out and a new one had to be lit. So I smoked again, and then suddenly this thought flashed through my mind: 'You must do something, but inasmuch as with your limited capacities it will be impossible to make anything easier than it has become, you must, with the same humanitarian enthusiasm as the others, undertake to make something harder.' This notion pleased me immensely … moved by a genuine interest in those who make everything easy, I conceived it as my task to create difficulties everywhere.[1]

WHAT ARE THE CONTINUITIES AND DISCONTINUITIES OF VR WITH OTHER FORMS OF REPRESENTATION?

Wherever we try to put the historical origin, maybe the cave paintings, or early carving of figures, it does not matter too much, humankind seems always to have had a fascination with the representational facsimile. We like to construct and experience images, which not only symbolise or call up the recollection of objects but also actually look like the objects they represent – stand in for them as if they were really present. Certain cultures and religions have resisted the power of the image, Puritan or Islamic for example, but even here this has needed to be an active resistance constantly reinforced against a very strong psychological or cultural driver.

Without falling into the trap of presenting a progressive change as improvement, we can see a broad historical development of the form of facsimile representation. We could characterise the earliest known instances as having an increasing command of the representation of the object. In the main, these were the human face, body, animals, and other common domestic objects. These representations, whether images on flat surfaces or three dimensional models in wood or stone, show a developing facility for the representation of shape, texture, colour and three-dimensionality – the curve of a cheek, the folds of fabric – for example. As is well known, a major development in representation took place progressively during the fourteenth century. Gradually the rules of visual perspective were codified so that not only was there a facility in the painted representation of objects; there was also an increasing command of the way in which these objects were represented as having a rational and consistent relationship to each other in space. Objects in the foreground consistently obscured objects deeper in the represented space and their reduction in relative size was consistent in relationship to their represented depth. Subsequent psychological understanding and relativistic forms of representation from Cézanne to the Cubists and Futurists have brought into question whether the visual (subjective) experience of objects in space conform to their measurable or mathematical, optical physics. However, the conventions of perspective provided an objectification of spatial relationships, which counteracted ideological hierarchies, even if they did not displace them, by those of the physical and by implication, scientific, world – the world of measurement and mathematical models.

The idea that this mathematical concept of spatial representation paved the way for a mechanical form of reproduction passing through the simple optics of the camera obscura to the development of photography, however commonplace, is sound. Again though, the security of the technological description of such developments masks the psycho-cultural function of such developments – the fascination with the facsimile – the desire for and pleasure taken in the encounter with an illusion, giving to the senses an experience which can stand-in for the real. We might define at least two aspects to this desire and pleasure. One is the passive desire for magic – the pleasure we take in being fooled, and maybe in a more sophisticated way, to savour the interchange between knowing and not knowing the truth behind the illusion. The other we might name as a 'syndrome' – Pygmalion, Petrusca or maybe Frankenstein – the desire to create, from our own power, the body which is ultimately alive and real as we are – 'a walkin' talkin' livin' doll'.

Resuming the historical sweep, defining the means rather than the motives: the attempt to produce ever more adequate illusions of more objects and objects in space led, in its mechanical aspect to the attempt to add more and more sensory features to the illusion. The addition of colour, stereoscopy and the most spectacular: the addition of movement through the invention of cinematography and together with this the later addition of sound. Within this cinematic history, the sensory enhancement has included the immersiveness of wide-screen, SurroundSound and (though short-lived in part because of the clumsiness of the technology) stereoscopy in cinema and even the odd attempt to add touch and smell. All these developments might be seen as evidence of a desire to create a greater and greater similarity between the sensory experience of the representation and experience of the 'real' world.

There is a trap here. By habit, we assume the creation of a facsimile representation is a matter of matching sensory experience between the representation and the real world. Also, by a deep tradition we assume to test if we are encountering reality or illusion by exploring it with sensory functions beyond those incorporated in the representation – 'I shall believe it when I can touch it' says Thomas. However, the process of adding sensory parameters either to the representation, or to the test for its reality, is not the whole story.

Other features (and I shall try to define three) not strictly sensory, are entered into the equation of the visual representation. The first of these is narrativity. Thus far, my analysis has concentrated on the visual and auditory illusion. With the addition of movement through cinematography, or more precisely, with the development of a visual representation incorporating temporality, it soon became evident that the representation of movement itself was insufficient to satisfy the facsimile desire as it became extended in this new medium. The rate at which the novelty of seeing the illusion of the world in motion wore off is testament to this. The desire rapidly transfers to a wish to see a representation that conforms to our experience of the real world in the sense of behaviour, as well as of perception. Of course, the representation of human behaviour was not new – it is as ancient as storytelling, Greek drama and more recently (in this broadbrush history) the novel. What was new in the twentieth century was the fusion of the representation of behaviour with a visual and auditory representation simultaneously predicated on the maximum possible suppression of the distinction between the illusion and the real: an immersive illusion where the encounter with the representation stood in for, and was, in many of its sensory and other aspects, indistinguishable from an encounter with the real. In theatre, the conflict of the hard, undeniable presence of actors together with the conventional artifice of scenery and stage required a suspension of disbelief. On the other hand, narrative cinema, with its flow of action, naturalistic acting, and photographic realism, increasingly involved not so much a suspension as a suppression of disbelief. The act of collusion by the spectator in cinema – desire for its magic transport – resists recognition of the artifice in favour of immersion in the illusion. This desire not to 'wake' is similar, as Freud made us aware, to the way the dream itself helps us resist waking. That we may draw a parallel between the 'dream-work' and a 'film-work' is tempting except that in the dream it is our unconscious which makes the construction while the film's construction is made for us. Do we dream it or does it dream us?

The second new condition, instantaneity, is of a different order and, unlike narrative (though there is a further complexity to be discussed), it is fundamentally new within our field of representation. Instantaneity in representation is a condition made technically possible by remote communication systems, initially telephone, then radio and television. Instantaneity evinces an apparent presence manifested through sensory facsimile experienced at a distance from the originating event, but, crucially, experienced at the same moment as the event is taking place. It brings to representation an entirely new feature, which is both illusion and reality simultaneously. The illusory factor remains the sense of presence constructed from the sensory facsimile and the reality factor derives from the belief (or knowledge) that the representation is taking place at that same moment as the event in the real world. There is a significant difference if we watch, on TV, Brazil play Italy in the final of the World Cup exactly as it is taking place than if we watch it recorded even a few hours after the game. This difference is evident despite having resisted finding out the final score before watching the recording. When we watch it 'live' we are sure, or at least believe we are sure, because evidence available from other aspects of the context is overwhelming, that not only do we not know how the match will end but that no one else in the world knows this either. They do not know because it is unknowable – the event is continuing in the uncertainty of the present moment. When we watch the recording, we may not know the outcome, but we know it is already known, the event will have happened already. In the 'live' broadcast, we are able to share in the continuous uncertainty, which is fundamental to the lived moment. In a way, this sense of presence remains illusory: we are clearly not present at the game when we watch from our living room; we are still unable to see beyond the frame and sensory parameters which are determined by the camera operator and the limits of the technology, and more crucially we are unable to; we cannot run onto the pitch and take the ball nor incite our fellow spectators to do so. Just as the sensory features of representation are always limited and do not reach a perfect correspondence with the real so the condition of instantaneous presence has its limits. However, in the passive sense, as spectators, we remain able to share that edge of uncertainty as real events unfold. Though of a different kind to the sensory parameters of the representation, this condition of instantaneity is an abstractable quality of the representation, like its colour or frame and it is equally subject to manipulation or falsification.

Until the technological achievement of instantaneity in representation, the image was always retrospective. The picture, whether painted or mechanically produced, recorded a moment in the past and brought it to us in our present. Our passivity not only resided in the act of spectatorship (a fundamental difference between the condition of maker and spectator, storyteller and listener) but also in the awareness that the image belonged to a moment, which had passed. That moment was no longer a matter of uncertainty or intervention. Of course, there was a different kind of uncertainty if that image had a bearing on the present – if it was a document in evidence. This concept of evidence is most dramatic when determining culpability in law, but still applies less spectacularly in every holiday snap shot – Is this really how we look? – Did we really do that? – We were there! For the image in evidence – the image as a document – the question of truth displaces that of illusion in the relationship with reality but the same issues of the limit of sensory parameters apply in both cases. For the image used in evidence, as well as the possibility of falsification – Was this image retouched? Was the filmstrip or audiotape edited? – There is also uncertainty based on the limits of the medium – What is going on in that blur or the point where the grain reaches the edge of its resolution? – Whose is that face half cut off by the edge of the frame?

The image used in evidence encounters the instantaneous in two ways. The first by standing in for what was a past instantaneity – a moment that had its cruciality – which seems to be made more or less reliably available to us because it was made contemporaneously. This is a condition we most associate with mechanical recording, photography, film and sound recording but it does also exist in the drawn and painted image, and even in the written word. The second way in which the image in evidence encounters instantaneity is in its bearing on unfolding events. By carrying forward its documentation from one moment to another, it may become a time bomb affecting the unfolding present.

If we review the cinematic (and this is the complexity I suggested) from the perspective of instantaneity we see one major aspect of cinema's illusion as the feeling that as we watch its narrative it is taking place in the present and we are present as it is taking place. This pre-dominant present tense mode of cinema can be equally true whether the story is set in a historical or contemporary period or even if it is set in the future. Even within the codes of cinema, the flashback begins instantly to involve us as if the action were present. Again, we must be cautious, as the word in the form of the story is also capable of evoking a kind of instantaneity, an illusion that we are present at the events unfolding. However, it is only through the achievement of an instantaneity in representation, which is actual – as with Brazil versus Italy – that we can measure the special condition of the illusion of presence as it has emerged in cinema. Perhaps it would be helpful to make a subtle distinction between a con-dition of illusion where the representation makes the apparent object present for us, and a condition where we seem to be brought into the space and time of the event. This later case is where we have become inscribed into the scene, in the first instance by perspective and in the second, into the temporality or action by the narrative. Here the crucial power of its illusion is our sense of presence at and in the event. The adequacy of the sensory illu-sion, where the object is brought into our presence, when added to the effect of our inscribed presence in the scene through the narrative, is a heady cocktail and is distinct in the cinematic from the written or theatrical story. It is also distinct in its being constructed from building blocks of photomechanical evidence. These are, as we 'know', falsified with lights, contrived actions and actors. They are constructions not records of the unfolding, uncertain world, but we collude in effacing the construction in order to experience the nar-rative as if it were present for us and we were present with it. This presence and illusion of instantaneity is based on our apparent implication in the plot. We seem to care what hap-pens as if it were happening to us. We identify with one or other of the characters – and here, 'identify' means a transfer of our psychological self to that character as if it were our-selves – and curiously we seem able to identify with more than one and shift our identifi-cation between them.

Whatever the psycho-social or psycho-cultural cause, it is evident that the dominant form for the cinematic, as we find it in the cinema and on television, has become an ultra-naturalistic rep-resentation at every level from the *mise-en-scène* through to the behavioural stereotypes and codes of acting, linked to a form of montage and camera placement or movement which heightens the illusion of instantaneity. This form reaches a kind of peak in the episodic soap opera where the illu-sion of instantaneity is raised by the continuity of apparent daily development. We are drawn into watching the daily episode as if it were happening on that very day, and like the 'live' football game, were subject to the same uncertainty. The experience we have derived from the truly instanta-neous seems to be transferable as another quality of the illusion even though a retrospective rep-resentation. Curiously, the highly extended duration of the narrative over months and years enhances rather than breaks the integration of the events of these illusory lives into our own. Again, at the centre of our collusion seems to be a desire for representations where the distance between the representation and the experience (not just the look) of real life should be as small as possible and may be treated as non-existent. Sociologically this is evident by the way in which soap opera characters, more so than the mediocre stars that play them, become 'real-life' people in the news. Indeed, their emergence as stars with a persona different from their soap opera role might inhibit the extended illusion of instantaneity.

So where is the distinction between reality and illusion? If the main test of the distinction is based on sensory factors in deciding the presence or apparent presence of the object then there are a number of serious difficulties. However much we attempt to extend the sensory parameters, frame, or 'neutrality' of the mechanics of the representation, these will always be limited by the medium and the represented object will always have sensory extension beyond these limits. In any case, our senses are severely limited; they reside within a very narrow portion of the electromagnetic spectrum whether we are using them in an encounter with the real or a representation. In addition to the sensory limits of our encounter with either the real or the representation, both are psycho-culturally coded in interpretation, and psychological evidence suggests this cultural coding extends to perception as well. Furthermore, the medium used for a representation, at the point at which we encounter it, has itself the condition of an object in its own terms. The modernist enterprise in all the arts stressed the reality of the representing object, either reducing its illusory elements or countering their representational function. For example, Picasso's incorporation of a piece of the 'Journal' onto the surface of the painting acts as an illusionist (pictorial) representation of the newspaper, but simultaneously it acts as the actual object: the piece of newspaper retaining its identity as itself as an actual physical presence, and asserts itself as a material form on the surface of the canvas. Instances like these not only exploit the contradictions in coded interpretation but also question whether a binary distinction between illusion and reality can be maintained. Each of these difficulties arises from the way in which a representational facsimile brings to our senses a pattern which is sufficiently close to an encounter with the real object as to be confusable with it — if only for a moment, or — if only with a colluding desire for the eye or ear to be fooled. What potentially breaks this problematic more than any other factor is the dynamic flux of reality and particularly the crucial edge of presence when actual events in which we are implicated are unfolding. We see from the traditions of narrative and particularly the cinematic that this flux itself can be represented in another order of illusion where the behaviour of people and objects become the material of the representation. We also see how the condition of instantaneity in presence can also have its place in the representational form. So difficulties in maintaining a valid test of a visual illusion on the basis of its sensory similarity to the object, equally apply as difficulties when transferred to the 'behavioural' similarity between an enactment and the experience of human relationships as they unfold in the real world. The crucial distinction seems to be 'cruciality' itself (thank you, Lenny Henry).

It would seem that the only viable basis for retaining a concept of the real is this 'cruciality' of our encounter. We might then define the real as being the arena of irreversible consequence. And for each of us individually, this is the arena in which the actual consequence of our developing life is determined, not always a matter of choice, but always a matter of our implication in the dynamic unfolding of events. At its most dramatic it is evident in mortality and loss and in the echo of this in the impossibility of owning – holding on to – any moment. More positively it is evident in potentiality and transformation and in the exercise of choice, power or creativity. A concept of the real, which is based on our encounter in the dynamic world of uncertainty and irreversible consequence promises to displace the dichotomy between the real and the illusory, and certainly between the real and the representational by incorporating the representation as a particular case of the encounter with the real. Here the distinction is not one of opposition but of status – what part does the representation play within the real?

But we are jumping ahead. I offered to define three factors, which needed to be considered in the relationship between the facsimile representation and the real. The first was narrativity, the second was instantaneity, and the third is interactivity.

If the early traditions of (pictorial) representation can be characterised by the representation of the object to us – confirming our power over objects – and if the more recent state of our representational (cinematic) technologies have placed us as spectators within the representation of unfolding events, then interactivity seems to offer a representation of our intervention in those events. Where the cinematic implicates us as spectators through the processes of identification supported on a layer of photographic, sensory simulation, and an illusion of instantaneous presence, interactivity promises us implication as protagonists. I and others have rehearsed many of the arguments surrounding the narrativity of interactive forms (for example articles by Cameron, Le Grice, Weinbren and Wright in *Millennium Film Journal* no. 28, Spring 1995) – the changed position and role of authorship, the branching or parallel narrative against fundamental synthesis of imaginary worlds and the changed condition of identification as the spectator becomes protagonist. Here the subject is Virtual Reality and, in my argument, its continuity with a psycho-cultural enterprise from pictorial representation using perspective to the dynamic 'narrative' of represented events. Though VR can be differently defined, and another history proposed, its most prominent device is the incorporation of an Euclidean concept of space, interpreted through vanishing point perspective where the viewpoint is capable of movement rather than having a fixed station. In addition, the virtual space is capable of investigation through the interactive intervention of the 'spectator' or protagonist. My aim is not to predict the future path for VR or interactivity within this broad field. Some of that future is already with us from: simulation – my flight to LA; computer adventures, violent or sophisticated; computer art by Jeffrey Shaw and many others; attempts at interactive cinema with the audience pressing buttons; or interactive digital TV where the viewer may select viewpoints in sports coverage. My aim is to try to understand certain of the fundamental issues, as this new capability within media becomes language and convention, more or less continuously with the social or cultural functions of existing media and particularly where it seeks to develop as art.

If we return to my attempted definition of the real as the arena of irreversible consequence, one overwhelming feature is that we become implicated in the consequence by our actions and choices. Our identities in this way become the trace of our imprint in the world as it moves from potentiality through the uncertainty of the present into history. Our history of choices in their turn deter-

sent. We should not forget though that this exercise of choice and
...mited by our social environment – those things beyond our con-
...stances – the poor Kosovan seeing family, tortured, killed, home
...ness may be virtually (that word) non-existent. Interactivity, as we
...ral and particularly in the constructions of VR, seems to model the
...action and its effect on the development of a facsimile represen-
...nges, and maybe radically changes certain conditions in art and
...y alter the issue of our relationship to illusion, representation and
...ed a fiction in cinema by passive identification with one or other of
...ter the action as a protagonist does not radically alter the role the
...vation to engage in it. This is particularly the case as the structure of
...o outcomes must be just as predetermined by the work – through
the (computer) programme – as is the linear outcome of a classic film. In the interactive VR the outcomes may be multiple or we may fail in our objectives, quest, and not satisfy our desire. However,
these changed (extended) parameters of the representation only continue the process of illusion by
incorporating another set of features we find in the real world. As such the form of the engagement
does not extend beyond the programmed parameters of the work.

I have attempted to describe a developing historical process in the field of facsimile representation – a broad sweep: object-representation enhanced by the addition of increased sensory parameters; the command of coherent spatial representation added through perspective; subsequent
mechanisation through photography; the addition of motion and temporality through cinematography; the fusion with sound recording; and with the conventions of narrative. All this produces an
art where the adequacy of the representation – its power as facsimile – is extended to the representation of behaviour and action providing an immersive sensory experience sufficient to stand
in for, stand instead of, an experience of the real world. It provides for us an experience where,
while engaged in it we must suppress the contradiction between the representation, the represented and the material reality of the artifice. I have also added into this sweep the effect of actual
instantaneity, the capacity for live broadcast, its prefiguring device in the illusion of present (tense)
in the experience of cinema narrative and its subsequent influence on the extended, episodic naturalistic soap which has such a dominant place in contemporary culture.

The most recent phase in the expression of the Pygmalion syndrome, VR, provides an interactive immersive environment, which simulates not only the look (potentially the feel and other sensory parameters) but also incorporates, through interactivity, an extended illusion of presence.
'Objects' are present for us and we are apparently present for them. This is confirmed by our ability
to traverse the space at will and further confirmed by our ability to interact with the objects and
change the outcome of depicted (narrative) events. But the contradiction remains, however convincing the illusion – and the illusion of behaviour is more fundamental than any visual illusion of
objects – the incorporation of our effectiveness into the representation is not the same as our
action in the arena of real consequence. The modernist enterprise in art, as with Kierkegaard's

determination to 'create difficulties everywhere', drew attention to this contradiction largely by the juxtaposition of illusion and the affirmation of the presence of the work as 'object'. Except for the experimental film, which remains a separate form, this modernist enterprise has had no influence on the developing conventions of cinema or its incorporation into the conventions of television. Representation there remains without contradiction and devoted to illusionist immersion. VR, in its popular manifestation, appears to seek continuity with the traditions set by the cinematic – sensorily convincing facsimile and engaging narrative – but with the added illusion of effective involvement in the action. However, VR as the basis of an art form continues to need a way in which the contradictions between engagement in the arena of irreversible consequence and incorporation of interactivity as a parameter within a representation can be integral to the experience of the work.

If, as I maintained, the only viable definition of the real is engagement in the arena of irreversible consequence, and that the distinction between reality and illusion is not one of opposition but of status, then the incorporation of contradictions in the VR artwork is a necessary aspect of providing our 'cultural language' for evaluating this status.

NOTES

1. Kierkegaard, Søren. *Kierkegaard's Concluding Unscientific Postscript*. Lowrie, W. and Swenson, D. F.,
    trans. Princeton: Princeton University Press, p. 164 ff.

Recombinant Poetics: Emergent Explorations of Digital Video in Virtual Space

Bill Seaman

The authorship and inter-authorship of virtual space opens out a new set of potentials for the exploration of digital video. In this chapter I will focus on the use of digital video in relation to other media elements in _The World Generator/The Engine of Desire_, authored by Bill Seaman with Gideon May as programmer.[1] _The World Generator_ is an artwork that has been shown in galleries, museums, the UCLA Visualisation Portal, and in the context of IT conferences. The work is shown as a large-scale data projection and is interfaced from a table with built-in navigation and selection tools. Central to the contemporary exploration of digital video is the ability to operate on and spatially position video within virtual environments. We must remember also that video can be a container for entirely synthetic computer-graphic material, recorded images of differing physical environments and/or any combination of the two.

I have been investigating what I call Recombinant Poetics.[2] Works that explore Recombinant Poetics enable the examination of operative media-elements within specific, construction-oriented virtual environments. Inter-authorship is achieved through use of such systems. Recombinant Poetics is concerned with the combination and recombination of media-elements in the service of generating emergent meaning through interactivity. Context, decontextualisation and recontextualisation are explored in a dynamic authored environment by a vuser (viewer/user) operating within the constraints of the authored system.[3] Such environments are characterised by Rhizomatic space,[4] and differ from the earlier combinatorial exploration of interactive video, as generated via interactive laserdisc (although one can address earlier interactive video through the conceptual lens of Recombinant Poetics).[5] In terms of video functioning as a media-element, a series of potentials are opened up within virtual space. The ramifications of these potentials are relevant to questions of both form and content. It must also be noted that many different artists can be seen to be exploring Recombinant Poetic processes at this time.

I am exploring a contemporary application of the word 'poetics'. The definition needs to be seen in terms of an art practice in which 'imaginative' and evocative relationships are explored through the interactive experience of media-elements of language, image and music/sound within a computer-based, digital environment.

Eric Vos, in the journal _Visible Language_, edited by Eduardo Kac, in a text entitled 'New Media

Poetry – Theories and Strategies', describes a poetics of 'new communication and information technologies' that he suggests 'could not have been created and cannot be experienced in other environments.' He describes 'a poetry based on the integration of characteristic features of these technologies in the strategies that underly the writing and reading of poetic texts.' He states:

> … We are dealing with a virtual, dynamic, interactive, immaterial poetry … We call this basis theoretical rather than poetical because it expands the habitual domain of poetics to include considerations of communication and information theory, semiotics and interart relationships.[6]

This definition is to a large extent exemplary in terms of my own objectives, although I do not value written and/or spoken text above other media-elements in a hierarchical manner within Recombinant Poetic works. Recombinant Poetics is not primarily a logocentric poetics. My work enables the exploration of a conflation of logocentric and non-logocentric language-vehicles. It is by all means an 'interart' poetic to which I refer.

In Recombinant Poetics, like in new media poetry, the work is 'not already there; it is not a package for but a parameter of the poetic communication process.'[7]

Emergent meaning is also experienced through a 'virtual existence'. Digital video becomes one of many media-elements to potentially be addressed through authored computer-based processes.

A VIRTUAL VIDEO ENVIRONMENT

The World Generator/The Engine of Desire is a generative virtual environment. The virtual interface is comprised of a series of spinning container-wheels and is physically interfaced through a table, track-ball, positioning-ball and two selection buttons. This interface enables the participant to generate and navigate virtual worlds in real-time. One spins the container-wheels and selects from a vast collection of media-elements and digital processes. The media-elements that can be positioned and repositioned in this mutable world include 3D objects, sound objects, digital video stills, digital video loops and an elaborate poetic text.

VIDEO AS TIME-BASED OBJECT IN A VIRTUAL WORLD

Video is explored in the environment in a number of ways. On the rotating container wheels are miniature video-based icons. The participant rotates the wheel and activates the video to play in a thumbnail version. This small video appears as a video still until it is activated. When the user chooses a video it is entered into the space as a 2D digital projection in space. This is like a small screen that one can navigate around and/or through, within the virtual space. This video screen is surrounded by an 'aura'. This 'aura' is a sphere that designates that the video is the selected object in the space and can be operated upon. Thus the video functions as a time-based object in the virtual space. When the video-object is selected a number of different functions can be accessed via the container-wheel menu system. These functionalities can be applied to the selected video object potentially altering: the level of transparency, the scale, and the aspect ratio. Behaviours can also be applied.

BEHAVIOURS

Media-behaviours can be described as predefined behavioural attributes authored into the functionality of the generative virtual environment. These behaviours become activated or are encountered by the 'vuser' (viewer/user) during interaction. A specific behaviour can be attributed to a particular media-object. The selected element subsequently behaves in a particular manner, i.e. the element spins, rotates, levitates, moves in a spiral, etc. A behaviour can be selected by the participant through a specific menu choice of a particular 'glyph' presented on the menu system. When a selected media-element is highlighted by the 'aura' (the selection device that enables functional choice of media-elements within the system), then a behaviour can become attached to the video-object. Behaviours are pre-authored as one set of menu choices and can potentially be attributed to any of the media-elements. Potentially, behaviours could also be triggered in relation to particular actions or human behaviours that the vuser of the system undertakes. There is great potential in the implementation of higher levels of authored behavioural attributes. This might include the authoring of intelligent behaviours that could reconfigure media material in a 'meaningful' manner through voice- or gesture-recognition programming.

VIDEO APPROACHED IN DIFFERING STATES WITHIN THE VIRTUAL ENVIRONMENT

If a participant uses the container-wheels to place a 3D object into the environment, a moving video texture map can be applied to the object. This becomes a dynamic use of video in the virtual space. Hybrid media-objects are generated by this technique, which abstract the video based on the shape of the 3D media. An emergent aesthetic is here achieved through combinatorics. Claude Berge was one of the founding members of OULIPO (Ouvroir de Littérature Potentielle) – a group that explored both analogue and digital combinatoric poetic methodologies early on. In the book *Principles of Combinatorics*, Berge provides this definition:

> What is Combinatorics: We wish to offer here a definition of combinatorics, which depends on a very precise concept of 'configuration'. A configuration arises every time objects are distributed according to certain predetermined constraints. Cramming miscellaneous packets into a drawer is an example of a configuration … The concept of configuration can be made mathematically precise by defining it as a mapping of a set of objects into a finite abstract set with a given structure; for example, a permutation of n objects is a 'bisection of the set of n objects into the ordered set 1, 2, .. ., n'. Nevertheless, one is only interested in mappings satisfying certain constraints.[8]

One cannot help but see the relevance of OULIPO as a precursor to the 'configurations' and reconfigurations of Recombinant Poetics. As we trace the development of OULIPO we see an expansion of Oulipian explorations including the employment of computer-based systems as well as extensions of OULIPO into many other fields. OU-x-PO (where x = the field in question) was articulated by François Le Lionnais and functions as a generative means to enable infinite expansion into new fields, e.g. painting, mathematics, history, etc.[9]

In *The World Generator* the spatial juxtaposition of multiple objects to multiple movies enables a vast number of possible aesthetic reconfigurations. An object can be selected via the 'aura' and differing functionalities can be applied as described above. Thus the same initial video material can take on very different states during the exploration of inter-authorship of the virtual environment. The proliferation of video-objects in a virtual environment is computationally intense. The environment has been optimised to play only one video-object at a time. This object is turned on and off based on the virtual proximity of the participant within the environment. All of the still images included in the system are also derived from digital-video and can also be applied as texture maps and/or viewed as flat virtual stills within the environment.

The very nature of exploring the contextually controlled dynamic of a work of art is extended through this computer-based mechanism. The potential for generating complex abstract images arises as the vuser moves through a series of meaning states. They can witness how meaning becomes emergent through personal interaction within a generated context. The work strikes a balance between order and chaos, enabling the vuser to take an active role through experiential examination. This environment is always constrained by the media-collection that is made available to the vuser during use. Having a specific collection of media-elements is central to focusing the probability of generative meaning production.

As media-elements are combined, both in real-time and through temporal arrangement, a depth of subtle experience is generated, enfolding many different meaning-states through interaction. A specific loading of the fields provides a set of potentials, which is experienced as the vuser conceptually positions and negotiates the collection of media-elements. Each media-element provides a field of potentiality, leading to an ongoing perceptual summing. The engaged activity of the vuser drives, in part, the potential conveyance of media-elements. There is an intermingling of the intention of the artist/author with that of the vuser. This is brought about through the use of a specifically authored media-collection, as examined through the alternate intentions of the vuser as they manipulate and explore that collection through environmental interaction. The mutable architecture of this variable media-collection is carefully considered to heighten the potential for combinatorial media resonance.

VIDEO ABSTRACTION FACILITATED VIA TEXTURE MAPS

It is interesting to observe the levels of abstraction that one can generate through the exploration of variables inherent to the system. One can begin with a recognisable moving video image or video still. From this initial state a heightened level of abstraction can be achieved via interactivity. Abstraction is here achieved through texture mapping, spatial positioning, multiple behaviours and transparency. The dynamic use of video enables one to add a differing quality of aesthetic 'warmth' to the environment lending a unique feel to the generated virtual world.

VIDEO AS A POTENTIAL MEDIA-ELEMENT IN A NON-LOGOCENTRIC MIXED-SEMIOTIC SPACE

Form and content are always inextricably linked in a circle-like manner – a work that focuses on content must always take some form, and a work which explores form always carries content. They cannot be separated. *The World Generator/The Engine of Desire* enables the poetic construction of spatial configurations of differing signs. Peirce's definition of the sign is extremely elegant in that it is sufficiently open to help elucidate the complexity of sign usage in a generative virtual environment. All of the media-elements that are contained by my generative virtual environment can be considered as signs in terms of this definition, including digital video and video stills:

> A sign [or representation] stands for something to the idea, which it produces, or modifies. Or, it is a vehicle conveying into the mind something from without. That for which it stands is called its object; that which it conveys, its meaning; and the idea to which it gives rise, its interpretant.[10]

My artwork is a conveyor mechanism that enables the spatial configuration and reconfiguration of signs, as well as the inter-penetration of signs. These signs can potentially function by 'conveying into the mind something from without'. Each individual media-element 'stands for something to the idea, which it produces, or modifies'. I use the term recombinant sign (used by many authors) to refer to the operative nature of signs within the work. Signs function to qualify or 'modify' other signs in alternate generated media-contexts. The conveyance of digital video shifts in relation to constructed contexts that are generated through the operative use of the work. Here, digital video and video stills function as poetic language-vehicles.

FIELDS OF MEANING – AN EMERGENT APPROACH TO THE PERCEPTION OF VIRTUAL CONTEXT

One approach to meaning is through the concept of 'fields of meaning'. Jacques Derrida suggests that meaning can only arise through qualities of difference (différence).[11] The term 'différence' is a pun in French, simultaneously pointing to difference and to deference or to put off until later. *The World Generator* is a contemporary 'difference' (différence) engine, that enables a non-logocentric spatial approach to emergent meaning through computation.[12] In *Writing and Difference* Derrida speaks about force and 'a certain pure and infinite equivocality'.[13] It is this particular quality of meaning production that I am exploring through my techno-poetic engine. In this form of spatial environment, or authored virtual 'volume', there is a play of forces, each contributing in a subtle manner to the nature of how meaning arises in the mind of the vuser. Derrida points to the complexity of these forces, which extend far beyond simple binary relations.[14] *The World Generator* enables a specific play of forces, visualising, making literal and rendering operative Derrida's notion of meaning 'force'. The evocative nature of video is just one of these meaning forces.

The World Generator is an engine of location, dislocation and re-location of media-elements – an engine of spatio-temporal simultaneity. It is the operational nature of this device, a 'fissuring' and fusing engine that enables one to explore emergent meaning. Meaning arises at the demise of any singular fixed meaning. Saint-Martin, in *Semiotics of Visual Language*, posits this notion of 'difference' from another perspective – *'a spatial continuum is not a given datum but a construction of perception itself.'*[15] Navigational exploration, as well as differing generative qualities of interactivity, present an exciting aesthetic experience of emergent meaning production. The concept of the field, as borrowed from physics, becomes central to an emergent approach to the complexity of media within my generative virtual environment. Umberto Eco in *The Open Work* speaks about the field suggesting *'now a complex interplay of motive forces is envisaged, a configuration of possible events, a complete dynamism of structure.'*[16] The dynamic play of multiple planes of forces of difference (différance) contribute to the perception of a perceived or evoked sum. Meaning is always in a state of becoming in such a work. A finite set of media-elements is entertained through a vast set of potential combinatorial abstractions.

In terms of the visual field, Saint-Martin speaks about relations between coloremes, where a coloreme exhibits a visual field of force.[17] Thus, we shift from the force of the word to alternate visual forces. Saint-Martin attributes this notion of forces to Gurvistch from his *Théorie Du Champ de la Conscience*, where the 'percept' arises out of a 'field of forces'.[18] *The World Generator* enables the dynamic arising of juxtapositions or neighbourings of coloremes. It also enables the inter-penetration of alternate coloremes to form the perception of emergent coloremes. Saint-Martin further examines relations between this approach as it relates to the 'phonetic unit of verbal language':

> This definition of the element of visual language as a continuous and spatialised topological entity, endowed with somewhat fuzzy boundaries, would appear incompatible with the accepted view of the phonetic unit of verbal language, only if one neglected to consider the actual elasticity of this latter notion. In effect, the phoneme is constituted of a cluster of auditory variables within extended limits and it can also, according to the individual case, play the role of a morpheme or even of an entire phrase.[19]

Virtual exploration makes palpable the 'elastic' nature of both visual and textual language. Saint-Martin goes on to specifically elucidate the field-like quality of visual perception and the notion of meaning force. The notion of the summing of meaning forces becomes central to the production of meaning and moves away from examining language from the perspective of individual signifying units towards a perception of dynamic perceptual energy processes. Saint-Martin states:

> Considering the agglomerates of matter which constitute the semiotic carrier of visual language, visual semiotics has every reason to abandon previous paths and to adopt an epistemology which is more in agreement with the dynamism of observed phenomena. It will recognise that matter is not inertness, but energy.[20]

As Bachelard expresses it:

> It is energy, which becomes the fundamental ontological notion of any modern doctrine of matter, even the principle of individualisation of material substances. Any atomistic philosophy must, because

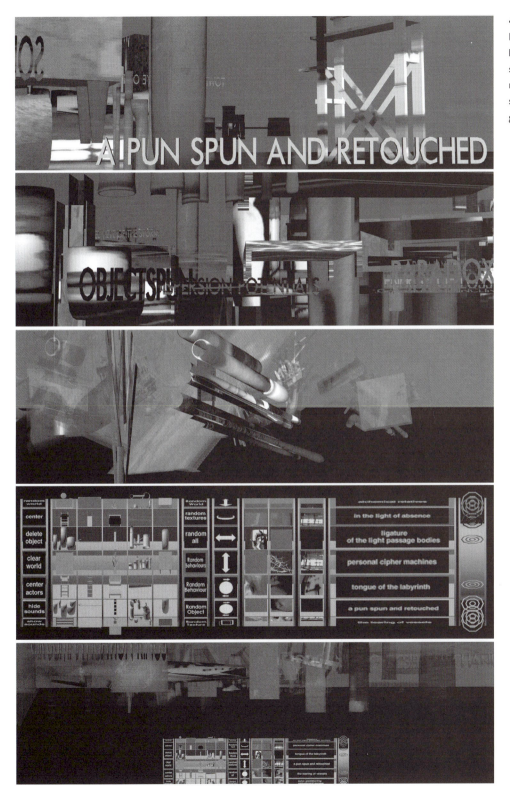

43 *World Generator*, Bill Seaman, 1998. The bottom two images show the control reels, the top three show audience generated landscapes.

of this fact, be reformed. One must decide whether the real has a structure in relation to its qualities or whether it produces dynamic phenomena as a result of its structure.[21]

… In a certain sense, the basic element of visual language can only be a psychophysical entity defined by both the subjective and objective aspects of a percept.[22]

My work seeks to approach a virtual/literal world of energy processes, exploring both the 'subjective and objective aspects of the percept'. Along these lines, in a paper entitled 'Toward a Field Theory of Post-Modernist Art', Roy Ascott has outlined an approach to meaning in the arts. In it he discusses the potentials of a specific behavioural mode of psychic interplay as a particular generative methodology:

I would like to look at the attributes for a new paradigm for art, a field theory that would replace the formalist modernist aesthetic. It takes as a focus not form but behaviour; not an information model for sending/receiving of messages in a one-way linearity but the interrogation of probabilities by the viewer; it looks at a system in which the art work is a matrix between two sets of behaviours (the artist and the observer) providing for a field of psychic interplay which can be generative of multiple meanings, where the final responsibility for meaning lies with the viewer.[23]

The notion that meaning is contingent on context and that context can be generated through viewer interaction is pivotal. This device can act as a conduit of exchange between the author of a generative media-world and a vuser, further co-authoring an emergent space. Interaction promotes an engagement with an environment populated with media-elements: recombinant music/sound, spatial text, juxtapositions of computer-graphic objects, images, digital movies, as well as attached behaviours, all functioning as relative fields of meaning force. These fields act upon one another and form this recombinant cyber-polysemic field of fields. Digital video cannot be isolated in terms of the work, but must be seen in relation to the meaning force of other media elements. Each media-element potentially functions as a 'field of meaning' and exhibits a form of force that influences the perception of other chosen media-elements during interaction.

VIDEO AS QUALIFIED BY VIRTUALLY ADJACENT TEXT, IMAGE AND SOUND

The reading or understanding of a recombinant poetic environment will be perceived by a vuser as the sum of the evocative 'forces' exerted by the various media-elements brought into relative proximity. It must be noted that this environment is time-based and is not fixed; the sum of these 'forces' is cumulative and transitory in nature. Brian Massumi in *A User's Guide to Capitalism and Schizophrenia* states that 'meaning is force':

This gives us a second approximation of what meaning is: more a meeting between forces than simply the forces behind the signs. Force against force, action upon action, and the development of an envelopment: meaning is an encounter of lines of force, each of which is actually a complex of other forces. The processes taking place actually or potentially on all sides could be analysed indefinitely in any direction.[24]

Media-elements have been authored with an intentional polyvalent nature in *The World Generator*. An individual media-element may exhibit a set of divergent forces enfolded within one 'modular media variable', arising in relation to alternate contexts of juxtaposition that are brought about through interaction, i.e., a pun has more than one evocation, contributing to an environment of 'forces' moving simultaneously in differing directions. Polyvalence can manifest an experience that is potentially greater than the sum of its parts, depending on the media-collection employed. Media-elements become nodal and define a set of relations over the distance of virtual space and time; later becoming related to a series of alternate authored media-elements, which add to the connective nature of the environment. Multiple conceptual relations are brought about through recontextualisation.

Writing about emergent examples of virtual architecture in *An Evolutionary Architecture*, Frazer describes another perspective on the employment of the notion of the 'field'. He states: 'The history of the form is the history of the field.'[25] As digital video is employed and variously juxtaposed, it also takes on an accretive meaning. It is this dimensional holistic quality of a virtual environment that separates it from many past poetic forms. Even a fragment of a media-element can contribute to the summing of a set of conveyances, as evoked within the configuration of conjoined fields. This environment is 'always whole', and each 'fragment' is both whole within itself, as well as part of a larger whole.[26]

Hayles has chosen to elucidate a notion of fields of meaning in her book *The Cosmic Web: Scientific Field Models and Literary Strategies in the Twentieth Century*:

> The field concept, as I use the term, is not identical with any single field formulation in science ... In marked contrast to the atomised Newtonian idea of reality, in which physical objects are discrete and events capable of occurring independently of one another and the observer, a field view of reality pictures objects, events and the observer as belonging inextricably to the same field; the disposition of each, in this view, is influenced – sometimes dramatically, sometimes subtly, but in every instance – by the disposition of the others.[27]

The World Generator experientially enables the examination of the inter-penetration of media-elements. These elements are always 'interconnected'. They are paradoxically simultaneously modular and are available for processes of aesthetic alteration, abstraction, inter-penetration and interchangeability. In a computer-based context there is always a conflation of matter and energy processes that enable interaction. It was the analogy of the paradoxical characteristics of light – being alternately a wave and a particle – that led me to the exploration of poetic elements that could take on different meanings based on their substitution in alternate contexts. It also led me to acknowledge how different meanings can arise depending on how the vuser is conceptually approaching the media.

Media interrelations are brought about through the operative nature of *The World Generator*. Time-based exploration of mutable context and emergent conceptual material are generated through poetic construction and navigation of intermingled fields. I have explored notions concerning the field in poetic works and artistic statements beginning in 1980.[28] Hayles further develops her thoughts on the concept of the field:

> The Twentieth Century has seen a profound transformation in the ground of its thought, a change catalysed and validated by relativity theory, quantum mechanics and particle physics. But the shift in perspective is by no means confined to physics; analogous developments have occurred in a number of disciplines, among them philosophy, linguistics, mathematics and literature … The essence of this change is implicit in the heuristic models adopted to explain it … A dance, a network, a field – the phrases imply a reality that has no detachable parts, indeed no enduring, unchanging parts at all. Composed not in particles but of 'event' in constant motion, rendered dynamic by interactions that are simultaneously affecting each other.[29]

I seek to metaphorically invoke the paradox of complementarity where the environment can either be seen in the light of waves (an intermingling of fields) or particles (modular-media elements) depending on how it is observed. One can look at individual media-elements as presented in a menu system within my techno-poetic mechanism, or one can view a constructed world of interrelations generated from those individual elements. The mechanism does represent a 'network of events' as well as a changing 'energy field'. In terms of energy fields, the layers of authorship in my techno-poetic mechanism enable a focused procedural set of artefacts to be generated. The economy of means – condensations, puns, polyvalent imagery, etc. – act as vehicles of this compression and when unpacked reveal various spokes or alternate layers of meaning.

One can begin to address the idea of environmental context in terms of 'flows', and approach the notion of a 'reciprocal precondition between expression and content', one can observe my techno-poetic environment in terms of an enfolded set of energies functioning on different levels of abstraction and codification.[30] The entire process functions through a series of translations and interminglings of enfolded energy flows.

PATAPHYSICS AND E-PHANY PHYSICS

In the light of the emerging experiential media domain that is made operative within *The World Generator*, 'Pataphysics' can be seen as a relevant 'authored' precursor. Pataphysics was coined in 1911 by Alfred Jarry in his book *Exploits and Opinions of Dr. Faustrol, Pataphysician*. Jarry developed a fascinating set of ideas concerning a new science within this self-proclaimed 'neo-scientific' novel. In this fiction Jarry presents the following definition of Pataphysics:

An Epiphenomenon is that which is superinduced upon phenomenon (…) Pataphysics (…) is the science of that which is superinduced upon metaphysics, whether within or beyond the latter's limitations, extending far beyond metaphysics as the latter extends beyond physics. Ex: an
epiphenomenon being often accidental, pataphysics will be, above all, the science of the particular,
despite the common opinion that the only science is that of the general. Pataphysics will examine the
laws governing exceptions, and will explain the universe supplementary to this one; or less ambigu-
ously, will describe a universe which can be – and perhaps should be – envisaged in the place of the
traditional one, since the laws that are supposed to have been discovered in the traditional universe
are also correlations of exceptions, albeit more frequent ones, but in any case accidental data which,
reduced to the status of unexceptional exceptions, possess no longer even the virtue of originality.

Definition. Pataphysics is the science of imaginary solutions, which symbolically attributes the properties of objects, described by their virtuality, to their lineaments.[31]

It is interesting that Jarry was discussing virtuality in 1911. There is a larger contemporary context
that this definition can be seen to inform. I am here concerned with the authorship of a poetic
physics in virtual space. One important relation that figures into new approaches to digital video with
virtual environments comes from what I have coined E-phany Physics. E-phany Physics is defined by
an author/programmer, encoded to become relevant within a constructed computer-based environment and need not adhere to the laws of actual physics. E-phany Physics is the art/science of a
physics that is authored with a computer-based system, conjoining an actual space with a virtual or
illusion-based space – this may also be a psycho-acoustic space. A computer-mediated environment
may be actuated through differing constructed interfaces that enable a set of relational media-arte-
facts to be made to appear in a consistent manner. The sensual stimulus generated through interaction with such environments can be more or less palpable. E-phany Physics can define the relative
'appearance' of the behaviours of virtual objects, video-objects and/or characters, as they are inter-
acted with in a virtual space. Although such an artificial physics is authored, the illusion of such an
environment can be articulated back into physical space through various forms of haptic stimulus –
imagine Alice in Wonderland rendered physical…. Thus an odd co-mingling or superimposition of
virtual artificial physics and actual physics can be explored. There is always an actual physics, which
becomes involved in the production and transmission of the artificial physics to the participant. This
points back to Jarry's 'science of that which is superinduced upon metaphysics.'

THE SLIPPERY NATURE OF THE FIELD
Barthes' notion of 'anchorage' – in the age of the hyperlink and virtual space, the morph – is no
longer adequate to address the unfixity of the recombinant sign. Navigation in cyberspace is about
mobility, passage, linkage, processes of association, 'lines of flight'[32] and Barthes' 'relay'. I am not suggesting that I want to destroy the precision of language-image relations; on the contrary, I seek to
observe their actual complexity in relation to the mutability of this techno-poetic environment. No

single media-element is potentially more important than another in terms of signification within environments that are mutable or reconfigurable. In fact, various hyperlinks, virtual proximities and/or trajectories through media, as chosen by an interactor, can potentially (if not wilfully) shift a particular 'anchorage'. Specific forms of drift (non-anchorage), as well as shifting and temporary 'anchorage', as Barthes describes it, have long been explored in poetic works. In the techno-poetic mechanism, the removal of anchorage enables the experiential observation of mutable context. In this case *The World Generator* enables an experiential understanding of how meaning can shift in relation to contextual change.

It is understandable that one would seek to be entirely articulate with text. Alternately, I am very much interested in the nature of ambiguity as a poetic vehicle and in how meaning is emergent over time within particular contexts. By intentionally loading a system with a resonant selection of specifically ambiguous media-elements, each carrying multiple potential conveyances, one can experientially observe how meaning is emergent in relation to context through the process of inter-authorship.

In terms of pictorial elements, I have intentionally loaded the system with computer-graphic objects that may suggest alternate readings when juxtaposed with one of the other members of the collection of media-elements housed in the techno-poetic mechanism. An emergent, time-based context of meaning is generated. Snippets of information are constantly encountered in hypertexts. We do not begin with the assumption that they are meaningless, we observe the construction of the context and how it articulates the meaning.

All language depends on context for understanding. The subtlety of context cannot be underestimated nor the environmental relations which inform it. In the use of language-vehicles, we continually revise our understanding and augment, or layer with previous understandings, that which we have derived from alternate contexts. In other words, thought draws upon the patterns of use that are made available to us through memory. Thought is weighed against current circumstance. This ongoing process of perceptual awareness always impacts on the understanding of context.

This notion of a persistence of conceptual 'presence' takes on a pivotal role in the volatile electronic environment that characterises *The World Generator*'s 'virtual' space. Peirce's process of 'modification' is always in an ongoing mode of application.[33]

I am suggesting the need for the formulation of a contemporary theory of environmental meaning as it is generated and explored within computer-based environments. The concept of fields of meaning presents a rich set of constructs to build upon.

EISENSTEIN'S RELEVANCE

In *How I Became a Director*, Eisenstein suggests the following about the birth of montage:

> From the process of production, a technical term has passed into linguistic currency, designating a mechanical assembly, a set of water conduits, or machine tools. The beautiful word for such a construction is – 'montage'.[34]

Eisenstein also spoke about 'montage' in relation to the notion of a machine-like juxtaposition of fragments: 'Montage is a beautiful word: it describes the process of constructing with prepared fragments.'[35]

The World Generator, made operative through computer-science, literalises the operational nature of a juxtaposition of 'prepared fragments'. I am seeking to construct a bridge between science and art exploring a concept analogous to the employment of media 'fragments' as a poetic construction strategy. The 'fragments' spoken of above suggesting that this system could be 'like a machine', elucidated in terms of film technology, is central to my discourse. In the historical sense, this again restates the notion of a hardware/software paradigm: film (software), working in tandem with a machine (hardware) – the projector, whereas computers enable random access to data, as well as abstraction and manipulation processes, film is a linear, time-based medium. It is the computer that facilitates ease in the ordering, re-ordering, and complex virtual spatial positioning of time-based digital video. In film, montage is facilitated by the cut, where film passes in front of an illuminating source, bringing about the viewing of an alternate image. In virtual reality, the image is constantly being generated through light emissions. Although the space appears continuous, it is generated through on/off alterations of pixels, comparable to the filmic cut but functioning on a minute, computer-based scale. The appearance of designated media-objects is generated by the virtual proximity code, which activates changes in pixel states. These changes are made in groups and thus generate the illusion of the particular spatial media-relation. The filmic cut occurs in the time/space of the film pull-down, between individual frames; virtual change occurs in the time/space of a grouping of pixel changes and is equal to the refresh rate of a given computer.

The mechanism created for my project makes potential filmic (digital video) 'fragments' and other media-elements operative to the user of the system, dimensional in a different way to that of film. These fragments can potentially be organised in a virtual space – positioned and repositioned across a media landscape.

Like Eisenstein's montage, media-elements, when juxtaposed, generate a 'creation', which is greater than the sum of its parts:

> The basic fact was true and remains true to this day, that the juxtaposition of two separate shots by splicing them together resembles not so much a simple sum of one shot plus another shot – as it does a creation. It resembles a creation – rather than the sum of its parts – from the circumstances that in every such juxtaposition the result is qualitatively distinguishable from each component element viewed separately.[36]

It is this aspect of 'creation' that is central to the generation of emergent meaning. Eisenstein further articulates his concept of creation:

> The strength of montage resides in this, that it includes in the creative process the emotions and the mind of the spectator. The spectator is compelled to proceed along that self-same creative road that

the author travelled in creating the image. The spectator not only sees the represented elements of the finished work, but also experiences the dynamic process of the emergence and assembly of the image just as it was experienced by the author.[37]

Unlike Eisenstein, there is not a pre-edited entity that the participant experiences, but there is, however, an operative realm of probability, in which the menu system functions as a constant. The participant becomes actively involved with inter-authorship – a heightened engagement, in which the participant 'experiences the dynamic process of the emergence'.

Eisenstein was influenced to some degree by Japanese poetics, in particular the compressed form of the 'Tanka'. He was well informed about the use of hieroglyphs: 'Hieroglyphs developed from conventionalised features of objects, put together, express concepts ie. the picture of a concept – an ideogram'.[38] He went so far as to suggest that a 'Tanka' could be seen as a kind of shot list. He wrote:

> From our point of view, these are montage phrases. Shot lists. The simple combination of two or three details of a material kind yields a perfectly finished representation of another kind – psychological.[39]

It is this psychological space, generated through the perception of the spatial juxtaposition of media-elements that contributes to an exploration of emergent meaning. Eisenstein pointed towards the conjunction of the denotative (text) and the depictive (picture) in Japanese arts, stating:

> Not only did the denotative line continue into literature, in the Tanka, as we have shown, but exactly the same method (in its depictive aspect) operates also in the most perfect examples of Japanese pictorial art.[40]

The functionality of *The World Generator/The Engine of Desire* presents a new technological form of spatial montage. Where Eisenstein explored fixed splices of filmic time, I am exploring a splice of volumetric space, or virtual graft. Visually, this is manifested in two ways in the generative world – the vuser sees menu items and when one is selected, observes this media-element entering the space through a spatial dissolve and/or digital cut. The vuser, through their choice, brings about dynamic cut-like changes in the dimensional space. These decisions enable instantaneous, evocative collisions or inter-penetrations of media-elements.

Eisenstein, in speaking about montage, suggests that it was a form of 'collision': 'A view that from the collision of two given factors arises a concept'.[41] He continues, relating such an idea to metaphors from physics:

> Recall that an infinite number of combinations are known in physics to be capable of arising from the impact (collision) of spheres. Depending on whether the spheres be resilient, non-resilient or mingled.[42]

This quote falls neatly into my discussion of fields of meaning, E-phany Physics and meaning force as described earlier. Eisenstein explores this notion of force from the perspective of 'conflict'. He goes on to say:

> So, montage is conflict: as the basis of every art is conflict (an 'imagist' transformation of the dialecti-cal principle). The shot appears as the cell of montage. Therefore it also must be considered from the viewpoint of conflict.[43]

Although virtual reality is spatial, it is constructed through the presentation of a sequence of spatial two-dimensional views of a three-dimensional space. Immersive virtual space is generated simul-taneously by presenting two slightly different perspectives of the three-dimensional space. I have chosen to show only a singular high-resolution data-projection in displaying *The World Generator*. Although the technology has changed from film to the computer, we are still experiencing an expanse of vision – individual frames that are merged through engagement with the persistence of vision facil-itated within this time-based technology. Conflict, or meaning forces (as I have referred to them above) are juxtaposed within this virtual terrain, both through spatial location (at any given moment arising from the perspective of the vuser), and time-based relative proximity (derived through vuser interaction with the system). Media-elements can be juxtaposed presenting digital cut-like transitions within the environment through slow spatial revealing (as derived during navigation), radical juxta-position brought about through media-behaviours, and selected engagement with computer-based processes presented on the menu and by vuser selection and placement within the environment.

Eisenstein outlines a series of relevant 'cinematographic' conflicts, which I believe directly relate to the operational nature of the techno-poetic mechanism:

> Conflict of graphic directions (lines – either static or dynamic);
>
> Conflict of scales;
>
> Conflict of volumes;
>
> Conflict of depths;
>
> And the following conflicts, requiring only one further impulse of intensification before flying into antagonistic pairs of pieces:
>
> Close shots and long shots;
>
> Pieces of graphically varied directions;
>
> Pieces resolved in volume, with pieces resolved in area;
>
> Pieces of darkness and pieces of lightness;
>
> Conflicts between an object and its dimension – and conflicts between an event and its duration;
>
> The compression of all cinematographic factors and properties within a single dialectical formula of conflict is no empty rhetorical diversion;
>
> We are seeking a unified system for methods of cinematographic expressiveness that shall hold good for all its elements. The assembly of these into series of common indication will solve the task as a whole;
>
> Experience in the separate elements of the cinema cannot be absolutely measured.[44]

I would suggest that the word 'conflict' specifically embodies Eisenstein's interest in certain height-ened forms of meaning force. I have outlined earlier the dynamic functionality of my device. We can see the parallels to Eisenstein's list of 'conflicts' to operations that are made interactive within the generative virtual environment (although meaning force can be seen to be functioning on a more subtle 'force' level). I have spoken of the time-based summing of meaning forces and my interest in loading fields of meaning with particular subject matter to achieve an outcome, which is greater than the sum of its parts, although I am pushing beyond the confines of film. Eisenstein posits this description, which also sheds light on experience in my generative virtual environment:

These stimuli are heterogeneous with regard to their 'external natures', but their reflex-phys-iological essence binds them together in iron unity, physiological in so far as they are 'psychic' in perception, this is merely the psychological process of a higher nervous activity.

In this way, behind the general indication of the shot, the physiological summary of its vibrations as a whole, as a complex unity of the manifestations of all stimuli, is present. This is the peculiar 'feel-ing' of the shot, produced by the shot as a whole.

The basic indication of the shot can be taken as the final summary of its effect on the cortex of the brain as a whole, irrespective of the paths by which the accumulated stimuli have been brought together. Thus the quality of totals can be placed side by side in any conflicting combination, thereby revealing entirely new possibilities of montage solutions.[45]

Eisenstein foresaw the neural collage that makes up experience – a registering of experience that happens 'irrespective of the paths by which the accumulated stimuli have been brought together.' He was keenly aware of the emergent conceptual realm brought about through the exploration of media. He even foresaw the genetic relations that are also inherent to my approach:

As we have seen, in the power of the very genetics of these methods, they must be attended by an extraordinary physiological quality.[46]

It is the operational characteristics of my device that take my practice to a different communicative space than filmic montage. My virtual environment is constructed of a multiplicity of visual media-elements and can be seen as singular computer-based shots, which nest these varying components.

The nature of spatial 'patterning', brought about through interactive techno-poetic construction, enables one to explore 'neighbouring' relations in a dynamic manner.[47] *The World Generator* functions as a discourse mechanism that seeks, as a subtext, to help us understand a set of dynamic meaning-relations and to potentially apply that knowledge to situations, which may arise outside of the device.

CONCLUSION
The exploration of digital video within a generative virtual environment presents a series of exciting new potentials for computer-based media. The non-logocentric approach to media-elements

through various forms of generative abstraction presents a new emergent form of evocative media exploration. The concept of fields of meaning and meaning force suggests the beginning of a new approach to understanding interactive media in a dynamic manner where meaning is emergent based on individual interactivity within particular authored and inter-authored environments. The re-understanding of montage in terms of virtual space helps to illuminate such a non-fixed media space. Virtual space presents an exciting new environment for engaged exploration of video imaging.

NOTES

1. *The World Generator/The Engine of Desire* – see my PhD dissertation entitled 'Recombinant Poetics: Emergent Meaning as Examined and Explored within a Specific Generative Virtual Environment' (Seaman, 1999).

2. Recombinant Poetics: The term 'recombinant poetics' was created by the author in 1995. It was introduced to Roy Ascott as a potential area of investigation at CAiiA during ISEA (Sept. 1995) and registered within the application title in Dec. 1995. Work delineating the concept was first published on the World Wide Web in April, 1996 on the CAiiA website: <http://caiiamind.nsad.gwent.ac.uk>. Subsequent research has shown a related metaphorical use of the word 'recombinant' by Mitchell in his discussion of 'recombinant architecture' (Mitchell, William J. *City of Bits. Place, Space and the Infobahn.* Cambridge: MIT Press, 1995, p. 47). Other artists and researchers have used the term 'recombinant' in a metaphorical manner, including Arthur Kroker (Kroker, 1994) and Diana Gromala. Gromala is currently working on a book called *Recombinant Devices: Ideologies of Virtual Design.* Doug Kahn, in *Wireless Imagination* (Kahn and Whitehead, 1994, p. 13) also suggests poetic relations to DNA in the work of William Burroughs and Brion Gysin. Sergei Eisenstein, in *Film Form* (New York: Harcourt, Brace & Co., 1949, p. 67), speaks of the 'genetics' of montage methods. The Critical Art Ensemble have also written about the 'recombinational sign' (Critical Art Ensemble, 1994). The exploration of modular, recombinational systems can be witnessed in my artwork as early as 1981.

3. The term 'vuser' was coined by Seaman May 1998.

4. Rhizomatic space – Deleuze, Giles and Guattari, Felix. *A Thousand Plateaus: Capitalism and Schizophrenia. Vol. 2.* Brian Massumi, trans. Minneapolis: University of Minnesota Press, 1987, p. 21.

5. See such artists as Lynn Hershman-Leeson (then Lynn Hershman), Luc Courchesne, Grahame Weinbren, Peter D'Agostino, Michael Naimark, Ken Feingold and myself (among others) working with interactive video.

6. Vos, Eric. 'New Media Poetry – Theories and Strategies.' *Visible Language.* 30.2, 1996, pp. 216–17.

7. Ibid., p. 219.

8. Berge, C. *Principles of Combinatorics.* John Sheenan, trans. New York/San Francisco/London: Academic Press, 1971, pp. 1–3.

9. Mathews, H. and Brotchie. A. *OULIPO Compendium.* London: Atlas Press, 1998, p. 320.

10. Peirce, C. *Collected Papers. Volume I–VIII.* Cambridge: Harvard University Press, 1931, p. 171.

11. Derrida, Jacques. *Writing and Difference*. A. Bass, trans. Chicago: University of Chicago Press, 1976, p. 23.

12. Babbage, *Charles. Charles Babbage and his Calculating Engines: Selected Writings by Charles Babbage and Others*. New York: Dover Publications Inc., 1961.

13. Derrida, Jacques. *Writing and Difference*, p. 25.

14. Ibid., p. 20.

15. Saint-Martin, F. *Semiotics of Visual Language*. Bloomington/London: Indiana University Press, 1990, p. 71.

16. Eco, Umberto. *The Open Work*. A Cancogni, trans. Cambridge: Harvard University Press, 1989, p. 14.

17. The coloreme defined: 'A zone of the visual linguistic field correlated to a centration of the eyes. It is constituted by a mass of energetic matter presenting a given set of variables. This primary element of visual language is made up, from a semiotic point of view, of a cluster of visual variables …' (Saint-Martin, 1990, p. 5) He goes on to say: 'The coloreme is immediately structured as a topological region. Visual perception is realised through a positioning of the eye in the direction of the visual field, called an ocular centration or fixation … Given the richer visual potentialities of the two central sources of vision, we have defined as a coloreme the area of the visual field which is the product of two interrelated zones:

    (1) a central area more precise, dense and compact, corresponding to foveal vision; and

    (2) some peripheral layers, less dense, but still rich in colours, corresponding to macular vision.

    On the objective plane of representation, the coloreme corresponds to any coloured quality located at the termination point of an ocular fixation and contributing to the formation of a visual percept. The very definition of the percept as an entity structured as a field of forces (Gurvitsch, 1957, p. 114) requires that the minimal unit by semiotics to a visual language be a material zone sufficiently large for perceptual mechanisms to be realized.' Saint-Martin, p. 6).

18. Gurvistch, A. *Théorie Du Champ de la Conscience*. Paris: Desclé de Brouwer, 1957.

19. Saint-Martin, 1990, p. 7.

20. Ibid., p. 9.

21. Bachelard, G. *L'Activité Rationaliste de la Physique Contemporaine*. Paris: Presses Universitaires de France, 1951, p. 135 as found in Saint-Martin, 1990, p. 4.

22. Saint-Martin, 1990, p. 4.

23. Ascott, Roy. 'Toward A Field Theory of Post-Modernist Art'. *Leonardo Vol. 13*. Cambridge: MIT Press, 1980, pp. 51–2.

24. Massumi, Brian. *A User's Guide to Capitalism and Schizophrenia. Deviations from Deleuze and Guattari*. Cambridge: MIT Press, 1992, p. 11.

25. Frazer, J. *An Evolutionary Architecture*. London: Architectural Association, 1995, p. 112.

26. Ibid.

27. Hayles, N. Katherine. *The Cosmic Web: Scientific Field Models and Literary Strategies in the Twentieth Century*. Ithaca: Cornell University Press, 1984, Preface II.

28. The exploration of notions related to the field concept began in 1980 with my work *One Around Which/A Substitution Trajectory in Relation to Subatomic Particle Observation* – Congruent Circular Architecture, 1980; I have also used the concept of fields of meaning to describe my work for many years ie. see the artist statement 'Foci/Resonance', Seaman 1986.

29. Hayles, 1984, p. 15.

30. Deleuze, Gilles and Guattari, Felix. *Anti-Oedipus: Capitalism and Schizophrenia*. R. Hurley, M. Seem, and H. R. Lane, trans. Minneapolis/London: University of Minnesota Press, 1983, pp. 241–2.

31. Jarry, A. *Selected Works of Alfred Jarry*. Roger Shattuck and Simon Watson Taylor, eds. New York: Random House, 1965, p. 192.

32. Deleuze and Guattari. *A Thousand Plateaus: Capitalism and Schizophrenia*. p. 21.

33. Peirce, C. *Collected Papers. Volume I–VIII*, p. 171.

34. Eisenstein, Sergei. *Film Form*, New York: Harcourt, Brace and Co., 1949, p. 245.

35. Aumont, Jacques. *Montage Eisenstein*. L. Hildreth, C. Penley, trans. London: BFI, 1987, p. 150.

36. Eisenstein, Sergei. *The Film Sense*. J. Leyda, trans. New York: Harcourt, Brace, Jovanovich Inc., 1974, p. 8.

37. Ibid., p. 32.

38. Eisenstein, *Film Form*, p. 25.

39. Ibid., p. 32.

40. Ibid.

41. Ibid., p. 37.

42. Ibid.

43. Ibid.

44. Ibid., pp. 38–9.

45. Ibid., p. 67.

46. Ibid.

47. Saint-Martin, 1990, p. 69.

The Construction of Experience: Turning Spectators into Visitors

Luc Courchesne

The world surrounds us, and how we experience it depends both on what is going on in it and what we are up to. For many artists and experimenters the challenge arises when, looking around for inspiration, we attempt to materialise our vision with the means available to us.

This is hardly new. To some nineteenth-century painters and photographers who had, as Oettermann suggests, 'discovered' the horizon, it must have seemed natural to abandon the frame and its imposed point of view (familiar in painting) for a wider, horizontally unedited form of visual representation.[1] Introduced by Aston Barker in Glasgow in 1783, the panorama and its off-shoots were at the forefront of imaging development throughout the next century, and remained a popular attraction until cinema was introduced. The theatrical presentation of moving images suddenly drew the crowds away from the rotundas displaying the still panoramas.

By the turn of the twentieth century, the new generations of entrepreneurial image-makers had abandoned, out of sheer technical difficulty and for economic reasons, the project of developing a cinematic panorama, and made do with the frame's imposed point of view. They were to spend the next hundred years crafting the language of the cinematic experience and expanding its narrative form.[2]

Cinema evolved its unique way of telling stories, yet it never really questioned the basic architecture it inherited from the theatre, with the audience facing the stage. Nevertheless, it appears to have kept alive the plan of growing more immersive. This is exemplified, for example, by Abel Gance's multiple-screen feature film *Napoléon* in 1926, or by Waller's *Cinerama* in the 1950s and today's IMAX and OMNIMAX technologies.

In parallel, computing technology has brought about new ways of creating, manipulating and displaying images and sounds. Its capacity to input, process and output data has given birth to the notion of real-time interactivity and of viewer/audience participation. The birth and rapid growth of the computer game industry is certainly one bold outcome; so is the work of a broad base of artists and experimenters stemming from visual arts, music, performance or cinema who have concurrently (since the late 1970s) explored and questioned the potential of interactivity and measured its implication for a spectator turned user or visitor.

The computer is also fostering new expressions of the nineteenth-century quest for the ultimate panoramic experience – through QuickTime VR and other flavours of manipulable immersive still- or moving-imaging techniques. There is a host of devices: going from the head-mounted displays or moving windows (for the generation in real-time of a view of a computer model or of a portion of an immersive picture), to a rapidly growing number of micro-environments, that immerse visitors in the video or data content.

In light of all of this, and of our fast-changing cultural landscape, I would say that the media artists who are currently doing installation work are in the forefront of those inventing a medium, a medium whose impact in the future will be comparable to that of cinema in the not so distant past. This medium will be built around three basic features: interactivity and the connectivity coming from late twentieth-century computer and networking technologies; the moving image, inherited from cinema and television; and the immersivity created by the panorama artists of the early nineteenth century.

My work has been leading in that direction since the mid-1980s. In this chapter I will look at the structures of content and interaction that have evolved from it, and will illustrate the challenges of using the computer creatively and of working toward an aesthetic of interactivity and immersivity. I will also explain why, in my opinion, it is not appropriate to speak of narrativity in relation to an interactive work.

CASE STUDY

When looking for a voice of my own in the early 1980s, my models were visual artists and experimental film-makers such as Michael Snow, Stan Brakhage, Hollis Frampton and Robert Frank. They showed me the level of freedom that could be exercised over a seemingly contrived and coded medium such as film, but it would have been impossible for me to follow in their footsteps; as of the mid-1970s, affordable video had displaced film as the medium of choice for experimental work. My initial intention in using video was to work at crafting linear transformations and to see how I could alter the experience of space in my installations. But the medium became truly useful to me when I discovered it could be manipulated and reconfigured in real-time.

At first editing was what attracted me the most: One side of me wanted to be handcuffed, curious to find out what happens to the initial concept when all the time-based decisions are made prior to shooting. This strategy led to single-sequence videos such as *Bob Rosinsky's Sister* (1982), *Paula* (1983) or *Past and Future Wheel* (1983); the other side leaned toward the opposite extreme: a movie of broken bits offering endless editing possibilities. Originally, when I asked my colleagues at the MIT Film/Video Section to tell the story of Goldilocks to the camera for *Twelve of Us* (1982), I simply wanted to gather material, a collection of reconfigurable bits of video, in order to compose a poetico-surrealist story of my own. The idea proved impractical but the process pointed to the concept of an automatic storytelling machine, a movie structured as a deck of cards being reshuffled for every viewer.

This happened shortly after I saw a demo of the laserdisc-based *Aspen Movie Map*.[3] Several months later, in early 1984, some of us at MIT embarked on a group project titled *Elastic Movies* where we were to experiment with computer-controlled laserdiscs and explore storytelling in an interactive authoring/viewing environment. The work was completed in the fall of 1984 and premiered in 1985 for the opening of the Media Lab. What we then called 'polylinear storytelling' or 'reconfigurable video' was renamed shortly after 'interactive video'; which has been the realm of my experimentation, expression, and art ever since. With computer control of video sources in real-time, I could reconcile both sides of my early videographic taste for carefully defined concepts and endless editing.

THE FORM OF INFORMATION

(DVD) Breaking the material into bits and pieces is worth little to me unless there is some sort of underlying structure and mechanism. My first solo project, _Encyclopedia Chiaroscuro_ (1987), was an experiment in hypervideo. The content was divided into four parts, which represented my own cosmogony: people, places, ideas and light. These parts were then organised into a virtual object made of nodes and links, which was designed to be manipulated in real-time.

My intention was to use and interpret the visitors' movement, using an infrared sensor placed in front of the screen, to navigate within this structure and to form a videostream in real-time from a substantial bank of video sequences, related to each of the four poles. As a result, each visitor conducted her/his own personal exploration of this cosmogony. For example, stillness was interpreted as interest and produced a continuity in the 'storyline'. Movement, on the contrary, broke this continuity, as if the programme were trying to regain the visitor's attention.

The authoring shell developed for this work – programmed in C – allowed me to define video sequences, and their order in as many screen sets as needed. I could thus determine what the programme would do after playing the sequences of a particular set: loop or go to a new screen set; I could also define what would occur within a particular sequence if an event was detected: go to the beginning of the screen set or jump to another set. This allowed me to create situations where, for example, a character lost in reverie on screen reacted to someone entering the room.

In practice, visitors, noticing that their movements impacted on the succession of images, generally engaged in a sort of dance with the installation. To relieve the frustration felt by a good number of them who wished for more control I added a push button that instructed the programme in the way the infrared sensor did. From being reactive, the installation became participatory. As a result, the work began to be understood as a kind of scratch-video apparatus meant to be brutalised.

In all interactive work with input and output devices addressing the spectator turned visitor, a more or less immersive space is defined. Minimally, it may consist of a bare computer, but in most cases an attempt is made at integrating equipment, content and visitor into a coherent environment. In _Elastic Movies_, the environment is that of a corridor where a passer-by is invited to respond via a keypad to voiced orders being cast from a piece of furniture. In _Encyclopedia Chiaroscuro_, the screen is enlarged with the result that the visitor is somewhat dwarfed. From an object to be manipulated in _Elastic Movies_, the installation is redefined in _Encyclopedia Chiaroscuro_ as a space in which the visitor is invited to enter.

44 *Encyclopaedia Chiaroscuro,* Luc Courchesne, 1987.

This project taught me the importance of building familiarity into the interactive piece so users feel comfortable with how to think and behave in relation to it. As I was embarking on a new project, one question kept surfacing: What metaphor could help integrate technology and content so that visitors would be drawn to engage immediately with the work? *Portrait One* (1990) was an attempt to answer it.

PAYING RESPECT TO OLD HABITS

I had read somewhere that the human face is the image most easily recognised and the one for which we have, in any culture, the widest and most subtle range of interpretations. Equally familiar to us is conversation, an essential survival skill and something we learn and practice from a very early age. So it seemed obvious to me that (given the limits of interactive techniques and the attraction computers and related technologies have for people) a computer-based work that strove to graduate from a mere machine display towards an experience rooted in aesthetics, and perhaps even in art, needed to carry bold content. I thus undertook to craft a virtual persona with whom one could have a conversation and possibly build a relationship. By deciding to revisit a perennial art form, the portrait, I hoped to also demonstrate that computer-based art could be considered art *tout court*. After sculpted, painted and photographic portraits, there could well be a new form of portraiture, based on interactive video, in which fragments of behaviour recorded from a real human being are used to create the impression of an encounter.

The interaction between the character played by actress Paule Ducharme and her imagined conversation partner was written prior to the recording as a series of linear developments: 'Hello!'; 'Do

you have a minute?'; 'What is your name?'; 'What are you doing here?' etc. I used HyperCard as an authoring tool.[4] Questions addressed to the character are grouped on 'cards' by sets of two to four; each question is a 'button' linking to another 'card' that defines and plays a video sequence related to the question; this video 'card' is in turn linked to another 'card' showing a new set of questions. After ending a particular development, I could step back a few 'cards' and imagine alternative questions (attitudes) with their own development. For instance, in formulating the second or third question on a card, I imagined the visitor in a different mood or another visitor altogether.

The editing process lasted well after the work was premiered in February 1990. Exhibiting the installation to different audiences systematically inspired changes and additions to fine-tune the interaction between the character and visitors. The final version of the installation includes six languages that were added as the work travelled. The work was later adapted for CD-ROM (1995) and the web (1999).

This process of building complexity through addition makes it almost impossible to visualise the structure of the work other than in a very schematic way. In *Portrait One*, every interaction starts and finishes with the character looking away, apparently absorbed in its thoughts. Any line of interaction will take the visitor through some of the content, explore some of the topics and define some kind of relationship; and no matter what, it will always end with the character returning to contemplation. One ironic measure of success felt by visitors with the character in *Portrait One* has been how long can one carry on the conversation before being 'dumped'. In fact, not unlike in real life, showing sensitivity for the character usually creates more room for conversation, which translates into better developed topics, and longer conversations.

Overall, the installation has been successful in shifting the debate from the technology used, to the aesthetics of interactivity. Because the metaphor of conversation is so strong, once a visitor suspends disbelief, the work's imperfect mechanics and crude interactive mode are forgotten and the experience remains consistent and coherent no matter what happens. You could always blame the woman portrayed or yourself for any oddity, and the limit of her scope could be attributed to an attitude. The character's attitude is in fact technology-based. With such a structure and the limits of laserdisc or computer memory, it was not possible to keep adding on, and some lines of development simply had to be closed. This translates into the character's tendency to shut itself off to certain topics and visitor's advances.

The positive response to *Portrait One* encouraged me to further develop the concept of conversation-based human-computer interaction. In *Family Portrait* (1993), in order to strengthen the

illusion of a growing relationship between a character and a visitor, I added 'levels of intimacy' to the conversational structure. At first, the questions are general and quite banal (level 1); then, after proper introductions (transition 1/2), the discussion develops to cover what the character does, how it does it and perhaps what its motivations and beliefs are (level 2). As the conversation edges into personal considerations, the character will test

46 *Family Portrait*, Luc Courchesne, 1993.

the visitor to decide whether or not the conversation should go any further (transition 2/3) and, if so, affirmative, the character will probably agree to discuss very personal issues and show its feelings (level 3); at that point, if its mood (generated at random) is properly dealt with by the visitor (transition 3/4), the character may end up confessing something he or she 'never told anyone' (level 4) and this ends the encounter. I used this canvas to conduct interviews with my subjects in documentary portraits.

Grouping characters to create virtual societies also helped strengthen the illusion of presence in my installation work. Some of these societies were constructed as documentaries from interviews with real people such as in *Family Portrait*, and others were written as fictions such as *Hall of Shadows* (1996).

The eight characters in *Family Portrait* can be addressed individually, but to get a sense of who they are in relation to one another, you have to meet with several of them. In the process, the struc-

47 *Hall of Shadows*,
Luc Courchesne,
1996.

ture of the group becomes apparent and produces an account of what it was like to live in Marseille in the summer of 1992.

In *Family Portrait*, I achieved limited interaction between the characters when left to themselves or when, in the course of the conversation with a visitor, a topic of particular mutual interest surfaced. This gave me the idea to create a fictional work, constructed more like a theatrical play. This time, with a fully-developed technique for orchestrating interactions between the different stations, the four characters are given a life of their own and made to appear quite content to be among themselves until visitors, approaching them tactfully, point to the limits of their existence. From this moment on, the four characters seek to escape and ask the visitors to help them to this end. If in all my interactive work, the visitor's experience typically ends with their decision to leave, there is this time a definite end that can be attained when the installation shuts down for a moment … before it resets and the characters return to their initial life. To get to this point, visitors have to understand the idea, implicit in the title *Hall of Shadows*, that the characters are actually their own shadows.

In *Hall of Shadows*, I accumulated data on a particular conversation between a visitor and a character to construct a context for the encounter; the character is made to remember this data for use later as the dramatic line develops. This feature made it possible, for example, for a character to 'know' the name, sex, age, origin and occupation of a visitor and to use this data when introducing this visitor to other members of the virtual group.

PORTRAITS AND LANDSCAPES

Besides developments of the conversational structure, the technique I used to display video images further helped enrich the experience of an encounter between visitors and virtual characters. In *Portrait One*, instead of placing a monitor in front of the viewer, I used glass to reflect the video image in space. This was originally designed in order to superimpose the computer and video screens and to create a single visual object for the viewer. It turned out that watching the video reflection instead of the source image lessened the reference to video and television and enhanced the impression of the character's presence. It thus helped transform the installation into a conversational space.

From the single character in *Portrait One*, I built *Family Portrait* around four stations defining a space that was intended as a forum where the society of visitors met with a society of virtual beings. When the dynamics and connections between the virtual characters became apparent, visitors were often forced into a similar interaction among themselves. I expanded on this idea in *Hall of Shadows* by making this interaction among visitors a condition for the development of the plot. I also used video projectors to enlarge the representation of characters and show more of their bodies. As in the previous portrait installations, I reflected images on large glass plates to give the impression that both visitors and virtual characters inhabited the same museum gallery. This approach to installation, sometimes referred to as augmented reality, is interesting in that it achieves a good degree of immersivity without the expense of covering the whole space with images.

In *Passages* (1998), visitors can convince the characters, four New Zealanders, to take them to one of their secret and favourite places in and around Wellington. This piece, which I started to develop in 1996, was my first attempt to take the action outside of the confines of a gallery. For this work, which featured both people and landscapes, I used reflection on glass plates and favoured the ghostly presence of the characters to the continuity of the landscape, with the result that the two sections of the panorama are significantly split apart.

Passages, a two-channel 180° panorama, is a transition work that leads right into <u>*Landscape One*</u> **(DVD)** (1997), a four-channel 360° panorama. This time, the space is the main subject, and exploring it is the goal. The encounter with virtual characters remains though: to walk around and explore, visitors have to be invited by characters turned guides. In *Landscape One*, each character represents a strategy about exploring the garden in which the action takes place, and its journey is coloured by the type of relationship it has with visitors. The space is thus more metaphorical than real and the language used to navigate mostly points to relationships and attitudes in life.

The work is constructed as a loop of about 12 minutes representing a 24-hour cycle. In this artificial day, the same things always happen at exactly the same time: Right after sunrise, a partying couple walks through the scene, set in a public park right in the centre of Montreal; later in the morning, a jogger with his dog passes by; around noon, a family comes for a picnic until a mid-afternoon thunderstorm chases them away; when the sun finally shines again in early evening, a woman returns to pick up the bag she had left and disappears before sunset; at night one can hear that there is a lot of action around, without really seeing anything of course. Any of these characters can be hailed and talked into taking visitors somewhere. When that happens, the whole installation space moves the visitor along the path defined by their guide. All the scenes were recorded using four simultaneously running cameras, edited into four video streams and played in synchronisation to appear as a single and coherent 360° image.

As in the previous interactive four-channel work, *Landscape One* allows up to about 12 people in at the same time, with interaction shared between the four stations. This time, I used four rear-projection screens, instead of the usual glass reflectors, to make a quasi-closed space and create a better sense of immersion. The experience highlighted the challenges and rewards of panoramic imaging and, for the next project, I was ready to embark on a blind date with anything that could

48 *Landscape One,* Luc Courchesne, 1997.

make the production of interactive video panoramas simpler and more affordable, both to produce and to exhibit.

In my earlier work, I always tried to give visitors a sense that they were in an environment, rather than in front of a screen. But there is a threshold when augmented reality becomes really augmented and redefines the experience of space. This threshold is determined, for a visually-driven species such as ours, on how much is offered to the eye. The use of darkness, which draws on a visitor's imagination to fill the space, is a wonderful device to this end, we have come to expect the wealth that immersive visual information provides.

Since *Portrait One* I have been using ceiling-mounted screens with reflectors underneath for the presentation of characters. Starting with *Family Portrait*, I've arranged these screens and reflectors to suggest a sort of interior space, which visitors have to inhabit to come to experience the work. In *Passages*, I tried to use the same technique without succeeding in reducing the gap between the two reflected images to an acceptable point. This is why I used rear projection in *Landscape One*.

As I started on a new installation project in the Summer of 1999 and started looking for a way to produce a seamless single-channel panoramic viewer, I had the idea, after testing several other options, of merging the four screens and reflectors used in previous work and of morphing their boxy shapes into cones. A donut-shaped anamorphic video image of a panorama like the one pro-

duced by commercially-available lenses, could thus be projected directly onto this slightly conic screen placed above the head of the viewer and the perspective restored by reflection to make the image visible from inside.[5]

49 *Panoscope 360°,* Luc Courchesne, 2000.

The initial tests in October 1999 showed the concept to be workable, and I spent the next couple of months refining it and building a prototype introduced at Siggraph in July 2000 as the Panoscope 360°.[6] The simplicity and affordability of such a technique for authoring and presenting immersive and interactive content now allows for single-user or small-group types of installations. This is clearly an advantage in any interactive environment where it is essential to understand the genesis of visitor-triggered events.

As new input modes such as voice-recognition become practical and affordable, a personal interactive and immersive device is becoming a viable authoring and delivery option that could grow into a widely-used platform. The concept for the Panoscope 360° includes a recipe for recording, authoring and presenting interactive panoramic content. If widely adopted, a repertoire of 'panoscopic' works could start to develop.

The first project I had for the Panoscope 360° was a sort of 'movie map' titled *Space by Number* (2000). The piece uses voice for input: once inside the device, a visitor navigates a space by calling numbers appearing at decision-points. The current 'panoscopic' project is inspired in part by Pasolini's film *Theorema*: Visitors enter a territory to be explored; their wanderings may lead them to a house occupied by a group of people whose life appears quiet, neither exciting nor boring. The leading role in *Theorema* is now played by the visitor, who has the opportunity to influence the course of these people's lives one way or another, before leaving them to their fate. This is unless an unexpected event creates a new situation.

THE BIG PICTURE?

Interactivity and immersion have been important keywords for a good ten years in the circles of media artists working with installation. It is also widely accepted that the current computer interface is not the information display we need to reach the full potential of interactive media. Cinema and television are good storytelling devices, but will always fall short of providing a believable interactive experience. In my opinion, cinema couldn't become immersive without a deep transformation of its content's structure and development, and if it did it would have to be called something else. By definition, and as demonstrated by early nineteenth-century panorama work, in expanding the field of view, immersive imaging frees the viewer's body and multiplies the possible points of view; choosing what to look at amounts to picking a subject and making something of it. Any immersive medium is thus by nature interactive and transforms spectators into visitors.

As I suggested earlier, it is thus not appropriate to speak of narrativity in relation to the construction and experience of an interactive work. The way I see it, the only narrative, if it materialises, will originate from the visitor after she or he experiences the work and not from the work itself, which is constructed as a context for experience.

Panorama artists of the nineteenth century introduced immersive imaging and artists/engineers of the late twentieth century developed data manipulation and interactive techniques. Cinema was born out of a practical technique for creating moving images and proved that the right form/content formula can find its audience and grow into an industry. The combination of the three things (immersion, movement and interactivity) should be the basis of the next mass medium and the cultural expression of a society moving into the twenty-first century and looking for it's own identity. The importance and scope this medium could take would be further augmented by the possibilities that networks offer to break the isolation of single computers and their users. Machine intelligence, always falling short of visitors' expectations, is advantageously replaced by human intelligence, sensitivity and unpredictability.

Like all installation artists involved with computers and networks, the challenge faced at the turn of the twenty-first century is similar to that of the Lumière brothers and Edison a hundred years ago, and of Barker a hundred years before that: a formula that perfectly integrates medium, content and participants has still to be invented and developed. Once it is found we will have the basis of an industry of new media turning the spectator into a visitor and the storyteller into an author of worlds in which the visitor is invited to behave and bears the consequences of his or her actions.

Is this a recipe for games? Life is life, and games, like art, more often than otherwise find their inspiration in life. With today's technologies, interactivity and connectivity are very visible and often awkward. In time, as humans/machines, and humans/humans systems of exchange develop in richness and fluidity, the notion of levels of interactivity, or of distance, will disappear and be replaced, it is to be hoped, by discussions on pleasure, beauty and the aesthetics of experience.

On one point as regards interactive artworks, artists/authors will make the difference between games and art. Asking the question simply demonstrates that we haven't yet seen the D. W. Griffith, Orson Welles, Buñuel or Pasolini of the constructed experience.

NOTES

1. Oettermann, Stephan. *The Panorama: History of a Mass Medium*. New York: Urzone, 1997, p. 408.

2. There have been a few examples of cinematic panoramas, most of which turned out to be technical and economic failures. The balloon ride presented at the Paris World's Fair in 1900 took an audience of about 100 people up and around Paris. The story goes that the show was definitely cancelled after three showings when a projector operator died from the explosion of the power plant specially built for the installation. Before that, so-called 'moving panoramas' representing, for

example, a journey down the Mississippi River had been successfully developed and toured in the United States and Europe. The authoring and display technology was nevertheless too difficult and costly to maintain and operate.

3. The *Aspen Movie Map* is an interactive video installation recreating the experience of driving through the city of Aspen, Colorado. It was created between 1979 and 1982 by a collective from MIT's Architecture Machine Group and the Film/Video Section.

4. HyperCard is an authoring tool, the first one of its kind, introduced by Apple in July 1987. It allows people with limited programming skills to design applications. HyperTalk, its programming language, can be embedded into objects in HyperCard to perform almost any operation. I've used it as a primary authoring and presentation shell in all my interactive video work since 1989. It incorporates for example video controllers for the laserdisc-based projects or the current QuickTime DV and HD (High Definition) projects. From the beginning, I used it to display the questions allowing visitors to 'communicate' with the characters and to play the characters' responses. Later on, I used it to remember a few things about the conversations and build a context where characters can be made to seem more sensitive to visitors and where a particular relationship can 'grow'. I also used it as a network management tool to have any number of virtual characters behaving as a group.

5. The Remote Reality panoramic lens is designed for making single shot QuickTime VR still images (www.remotereality.com). I have used the same lens on video cameras.

6. Information on the Panoscope 360° can be found at http://panoscope360.com.

Movies after Film – The Digitally Expanded Cinema

Jeffrey Shaw

The history of the cinema is a history of technological experiment, of spectator/spectacle relations, of production, distribution and presentation mechanisms that yoke the cinema to economic, political and ideological conditions, and above all it is a history of creative exploration of the uniquely variegated expressive capabilities of this remarkable contemporary medium. Despite cinema's heritage of technological and creative diversity, it is Hollywood that has come to define its dominant forms of production and distribution, its technological apparatus and its narrative forms. But the current hegemony of the Hollywood model of movie-making, despite its frenetic recourse to special effects, is about to be relegated by the radically new potentialities of digital media technologies, and that's why the rise of the video game and location-based entertainment industries are such significant phenomena. These new contexts seem to be setting an appropriate platform for the further evolution of the traditions of experimental and expanded cinema.

Though it is still early in the process, one can identify focal features of this emergent domain of the digitally expanded cinema. The technologies of virtual environments point to a cinema that is an immersive narrative space, wherein the interactive viewer assumes the role of both cameraperson and editor. And the technologies of video games and the internet point to a cinema of distributed virtual environments that are also social spaces, so that the persons present become protagonists in a set of narrative dis-locations. Our net condition is a circumstance, a contingency and a predicament. It has made our screens into lattices that hide and expose the territories of newly-formed intelligent information spaces. The often trivial technological convergences that are being heralded here are just the tip of a much more interesting iceberg – the synaesthetic convergence of all our modalities of perception in a conjoined space-time of real, surrogate and virtual formations. These shared environments of any and every level of embodiment are also social spaces in which the artwork is no longer a mere accoutrement, but may define the very structure and cosmology of those spaces and their activities.

CONTAINED FICTIONS AND AUGMENTED REALITY

One can talk about two underlying currents in media art. The first configures the audiovisual experience within a bounding border, setting up a detached relationship between the viewer and the fiction, which is constructed inside that frame. Such an enclosure, be it the frame of a painting, the proscenium arch of a theatre, the casing of a TV set or the black border of a cinema screen, delineates and separates the fictional space from the real space – it sets up a magic window which spectators gaze through into aesthetically contrived spaces. The opposing tendency wants to get rid of the frame so that there is no magic window, so that the created space is released as an immersive experience, which is somehow embedded in the real world. Prefigured by the baroque, the current term for this is 'augmented reality' (as distinct from 'virtual reality'); a strategy whereby one builds fictional constructs that augment the real world and that are conjoined with the real world and its inhabitants.

In the history of the cinema the correspondence between framed and frameless narrative spaces has been especially characteristic. The development from a theatrical proscenium arch format to CinemaScope, IMAX and OMNIMAX enlarged the cinematic frame until it virtually disappeared from the viewers' field of view, while eccentric experiments with 3D, Sensorama and Smellorama also demonstrate the cinema's native immersive yearnings. Yet it seems to me that despite these expansive and sensational forms, such cinema remains what it was, a framed and contained space of removed experiences. Films like H. C. Potter's *Hellzappopin* (1941, US) admit and exploit this discrepancy as the provenance of extravagant humour.

A more radical effort to deconstruct the framework of this illusory space and transgress the normal boundaries of the viewing experience can be found in the 'expanded cinema' works made by experimental film-makers and artists in the 1960s and early 1970s. Anticipating the contemporary domain of digital interactivities, a distinguishing characteristic of this work is its attempts to establish audience participation in one form or another, so that the actuality of the viewing environment is thereby interpolated with the virtuality of the cinematic environment. One such example was the *Movie Movie* (1969), an Expanded Cinema performance specially created for the (DVD) Experimental Film Festival in Knokke-le-Zoute, Belgium.[1] It took place in the foyer of the festival building, with the audience sitting on the stairs and balcony. The authors – Jeffrey Shaw, Theo Botschuijver and Sean Wellesley-Miller, dressed in white overalls, first brought in a large inflatable structure and unrolled it on the floor. Then it was gradually inflated while film, slides and liquid-light show effects were projected onto its surface. The architectural form of this inflatable structure was conical with an outer transparent membrane and an inner white surface. The projected imagery first impinged lightly on the tightly inflated outer envelope and then appeared on the semi-inflated inner surface. In the intermediate space between the transparent and white membranes, various material actions were performed to materialise the projected images. This included the inflation of white balloons and tubes, and the injection of smoke.

This work set out to transform the conventional flat cinema projection screen into a three-dimensional kinetic and architectonic space of visualisation. The multiple projection surfaces allowed the images to materialise in many layers, and the bodies of the performers and then of the audience (many of whom spontaneously threw off their clothes) became part of the cinematic spectacle. In this way the immersive space of cinematic fiction included the literal and interactive immersion of

50 *Movie Movie*, an
Expanded Cinema
performance,
Jeffrey Shaw,
Theo Botschuyver,
and Sean Wellesley-
Miller, 1969.
(Image: Jud Yaklut.)

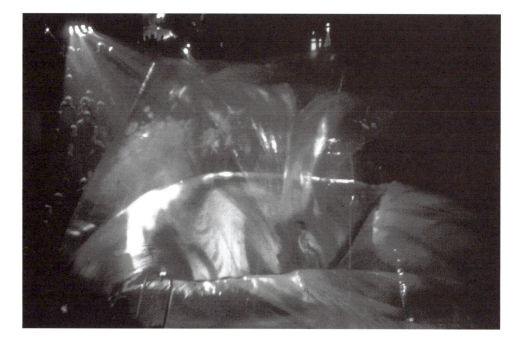

the viewers, who modulated the changing shapes of the pneumatic architecture, which in turn modulated the shifting deformations of the projected imagery. A sensual conjugation of actuality and fiction was achieved through a mediated dematerialisation of their respective boundaries. Such a convergence of architectonic and cinematic space clearly prefigures the modalities of mediated architecture that today are being built in cyberspace, such as *Asymptotes'* virtual Guggenheim Museum (www.guggenheim.com).

The *Movie Movie* also incorporated an innovative and interactive approach to the design of its acoustic space. The *Musica Electronica Viva* (Rome) were closely involved in the scenography, creating an intense and loud density of electronic sounds, that were interactively modulated by the musicians via a spatially-distributed sound amplification system, placed both outside and inside the inflatable structure. From within, the performers and members of the public could manipulate the shape of the inflatable structure, dragging its membranes in one direction and another, and in so doing change the shape of its acoustic spaces. Thus, this soft interactive, light-weight architecture allowed the public to dynamically modulate the live performance of the music and add another level of immersive conjugation of the body, architecture and mediated manifestation to the cinematic experience.

INTERACTION MODALITIES AND IMMERSIVE SPACE
The digital domain is above all distinguished by its variegated range of new interaction modalities. Needless to say all traditional forms of expression are also interactive to the extent that they are must be interpreted and reconstructed in the process of apprehension. However, digital interactivity offers a new direct dimension of user control and involvement in the creative proceedings.

The traditional cinema's compulsive spectacle/spectacle relationships will be transformed as the growing spectrum of input/output technologies and algorithmic production techniques are applied to the digitally-expanded cinema.

Cinema builds hyperrealities, space-time constructs that are conjoined to the presence of the spectator in the darkened magical space of the movie theatre. From Cinerama, to 3D to spherical Omnimax, the cinema has yearned to construe its fictions in a space of equivalence to the real. The holy grail, as in all forms of art, is presence, the experience of *being in that place* that induces a totality of engagement in the aesthetic conceptual construct of the work. The goal is not the totalitarian spectacle that overwhelms and belittles the viewer, rather it is the sublime demonstration that affirms each viewer's unique position and critical relationship to the representation. Furthermore, the new networking technologies allow these cultural experiences to extend themselves into virtual social spaces that can constitute a further level of immersion.

conFiguring the Cave is a computer-based video installation that undertakes a set of technical, pictorial and interactive strategies to identify various paradigmatic conjunctions of body and space where the human figure is used as a psycho-geographical locus for multiform spatial representations.[2] *conFiguring the Cave* was one of the earliest art works to be created using the CAVE™, a unique form of a virtual reality environment developed at the University of Illinois. The work was commissioned for the permanent collection of the NTT InterCommunicationCenter in Tokyo where it was first installed in 1997. In the original environment, high-resolution, real-time, computer-generated stereoscopic images are projected onto the three walls and floor of a specially-constructed room, creating a totally immersive virtual reality experience for the viewers.

The user interface in this interactive installation is a near life-size wooden puppet that was shaped like the stereotypical artist's wooden mannequin. Specially-engineered with electronic measurement devices hidden within each of its moveable joints, this puppet is situated in the centre of the projection area and can be manipulated by the viewers to control the transformations of the computer-generated imagery.

conFiguring the Cave constitutes seven differentiated pictorial domains. Together they offer a consonant exploration of the manifold relationships between body, space and language. The imagery has been created using a unique set of algorithmic software tools developed by Bernd Lintermann at ZKM, that is able to generate an emergent complexity of mutable forms and organic abstractions, which are conjoined with representative and symbolic images. Movement of the puppet's body and limbs dynamically affect changing parameters in the real-time image-generating software, and particular postures of the puppet cause specific visual events to occur. Most significantly it is the action of moving the puppet's hands to cover and then uncover its eyes, which causes the transition from one pictorial domain to the next.

The American composer Les Stuck has created seven sound compositions for the seven pictorial domains in this work, which is presented via an eight-channel spatialised sound system that augments the three-dimensional qualities of the stereoscopic visual environment. The sound compositions, like the imagery, are interactively affected by the viewer's handling of the interface

51 *conFiguring the Cave*, Jeffrey Shaw, permanent collection of the NTT InterCommunication Center in Tokyo, where it was first installed in 1997.

puppet's body and limbs, and thus contribute to a synchronous unity of both visual and audio transformations in this work and its overall synaesthetic singularity.

conFiguring the Cave embodies a meta-language of functional relationships between bodily and spatial co-ordinates. These relationships are both physical and conceptual, creating an anthropomorphic world that connects to the long history (in all cultures) of conjecturing the body as the locus and measure of the universe. At the same time this work is located in a post-modern exigency, which has flung the body into a vertiginous space of deconstructed co-ordinates and equivocal complexity. The old harmonies are brought into question in the fragile co-variance of the representative surrogate body (the puppet) located in a measureless space of reticular forms (the seven domains). Yet there is a new balance this work seeks to formulate through a meta-language of images that are able to construe a stage of meaning that is an interactive extension and coherent sanction of our contemporary human condition, both separated from and connected to historical configurations.

PERIPHERAL VISION AND DISTRIBUTED NARRATIVES

The accomplished Chilean film-maker Raul Ruiz, has in his writings condemned the compulsive attributes of the central narrative in the Hollywood cinema, and calls for strategies, whereby the autocracy of the director and his subjugating optical apparatus, can be shifted towards the notion of a cinema that is located in the personally discoverable periphery.[3] How exactly to achieve this seems to me to be a very pertinent challenge, and I see solutions being offered by new methods of visualisation and utilisation.

The biggest challenge for the digitally-extended cinema is the conception and design of new narrative techniques that allow the interactive and emergent features of that medium to be fulfillingly embodied. Going beyond the triteness of branching plot options and video game mazes, one approach is to develop modular structures of narrative content that permit an indeterminate, yet meaningful number of permutations. Another approach involves the algorithmic design of content characterisations that would permit the automatic generation of narrative sequences that could be modulated by the user (for instance by using a genetic model of selection). And perhaps the consummate challenge is the notion of a digitally-extended cinema that is actually inhabited by its audience, who then become agents of and protagonists in its narrative development.

Place-Ruhr extends the traditions of panorama painting, theatre and cinematography into the vectors of simulation and virtual reality.[4] *Place-Ruhr* is a personal portrait of the Ruhr valley, and in the virtual landscape that is its stage, performers present to the exploring viewer the past, present and future transmutations of its geographical and geological patrimony into a profound arena of human exigency.

The *Place-Ruhr* installation itself is a rotating platform, which allows the viewer to interactively rotate a projected image within a large circular projection screen and explore a three-dimensional virtual environment, constituting an emblematic constellation of panoramic locations and events. By inviting the viewer to step onto a rotating platform, *Place-Ruhr* forces them to abandon their bodily relation to the surrounding real space and enter the fictional space that the work offers. This happens quite unconsciously – only after the viewers step off this rotating platform do they realise they have to relocate themselves in the real space again. Such kinesthetic experiences are the reason why motion-platform technology is so compelling for simulation purposes and for the ever more popular location-based entertainment ride films. Using these technologies the artwork can address and engage not just the audiovisual senses but the whole body of the participant.

Place-Ruhr presents a virtual landscape containing 11 photographic cylinders that actualise particular sites in the Ruhr area. The viewer can navigate this three-dimensional space, and enter these panoramic cylinders. Once inside, the represented imagery becomes a completely surrounding cinematic sequence which fills the projection screen and presents the recorded circumstance as an immersive event. The identity of each of the 11 sites is defined by its environmental scenography (both real and artificial) conjoined with a time-based occurrence that has been staged there. These events are approximately one minute in duration, and repeat themselves continuously in a seamless loop. Similarly, the landscaped architecture of 11 cylinders repeats itself infinitely in all directions. The overall ground surface of this landscape is inscribed with a diagram of the Sephirothic 'Tree of Life' in figurative relation to which the 11 Ruhr site cylinders are situated. This diagram is coupled to a map of the underground mining tunnels in the Dortmund area.

On the platform there is a column with an underwater video camera. This device is the inter-

52 *Place-Ruhr*,
Jeffrey Shaw, 2000.

active user interface, its buttons and handling allow the viewer to control his movement through the virtual scene as well as cause the rotation of the platform and of the projected image around the circular screen. A small monitor within this housing also shows the ground plan of the virtual environment with reference to the user's location there.

A microphone on top of this interface camera picks up any sound that the viewer makes, and this causes the release of continuously moving three-dimensional words and sentences within the projected scene. Originating in the centre of the screen, the physical arrangement of these texts in the virtual environment is determined by the path of the viewer movements while they are being generated. These texts have a temporal five-minute life span; becoming more and more transparent until they disappear. They constitute a trace and transitory memory of the viewer's presence there.

Place-Ruhr's stage is a virtual landscape populated by its 11 cylinders of moving visual formations – a constellation of theatrical cinematic events that the viewer can visit and examine in whatever order he or she chooses. In other words it is a modular interactive theatre where two kinds of spaces are conjoined – the cinematically-represented spaces, and the spaces of the virtual environment in which these cinematic events are geographically located.

Such a spatial conjunction evokes the new conditions of interactive narrative and its possible modalities of operation. On the one hand there is the set of autonomous narratives embodied in each of the panoramic video recordings. On the other hand there is the hyper-narrative of interactive relations and experiences that is effected by the viewer's explorative journey within the virtual environment. Because this journey is in effect a process of viewer control over both the camera and editing of the pre-recorded cinematic data, it enters the domain of a technologically augmented theatre where each performance becomes a unique retelling of its embedded scenographies.

NOTES

1. *Movie Movie* – Theo Botschuijver, Jeffrey Shaw, Sean Wellesley-Miller, 4th Experimental Film Festival, Knokke-le-Zout, Belgium, 1969 – Production Sigma Projects Amsterdam.

2. *conFiguring the Cave* – Agnes Hegedues, Bernd Linterman, Jeffrey Shaw, Leslie Stuck, NTT InterCommunicationCenter, Tokyo, 1997 – Production ZKM Karlsruhe.

3. Ruiz, Raul. *Poetics of Cinema*. Paris: Editions Dis Voir, 1995.

4. *Place-Ruhr* – Jeffrey Shaw, Vision Ruhr, Dortmund 2000 – Production ZKM Karlsruhe.

'Emotions Encoded'*

Merel Mirage

> Formerly, I dreamed I was a butterfly flying around and
> enjoying itself. I did not know that I was Chuangtse.
> Suddenly I awoke and was Chuangtse again. I did not know whether it was
> Chuangtse dreaming that he was a butterfly,
> or a butterfly now dreaming it was Chuangtse.
> Thereafter Chuangtse, the Taoist philosopher from ancient China, asked himself:
> 'Am I a man who dreamed of being a butterfly, or am
> I a butterfly dreaming myself to be a man?'

The world on the other side of the screen. A place where one can dream. For more than three years I have been sitting behind the computer screen, acting and reacting in parallel worlds, all running at the same time. Worlds in windows, piled up on my desktop. Windows for Netscape browsers, for downloading software, for graphical applications, for private and business correspondence, for the programming of my website, for discussion groups, for talk sessions with friends, and for real-time connections to virtual communities, such as 'beachside' at MIT's MediaMOO, or 'Stonehenge fields' at LambdaMOO. A busy digital life. The more windows I decided to open, the more I got involved in the life on the screen, and the stronger impulses I needed from reality to make me aware of its existence; the sound of sirens, the smell of food, or my name being called.

CASUAL ENCOUNTER

One day, for a project I was working on, I wanted to know what happens with the silkworms in the process of making silk.[1] I made a search on the net. After passing by several sites that only talked about the beauty of silk and not about its production, I landed in a China discussion group where I met a person who could explain the process in detail, and who voluntarily added a personal opinion:

> Since I consider a silkworm to be an unimportant animal, I don't find it a problem to know that for
> the silk socks I buy, millions of silkworms were dropped in ovens and gasified alive, in the middle of
> their process to become butterflies.

* This article first appeared in an earlier form in *Leonardo*. vol. 30, no. 5, 1997, pp. 377–83.

I could not agree to this, and we ended up having a provoking discussion ranging from butterflies to Wittgenstein. Then, casually, we started to e-mail back and forth, and, from an anonymous source of information, this person became a regular visitor on my screen, a presence I got used to and even started to appreciate. It was an experience just like real life, in which you come across many people but like some more than others.

> Did you also have that vivid feeling all night after our connection? It was as if you were sitting right next to me. I feel comfortable understanding you more and more. Thanks for being so open. We exchange so much about everything, I could be connected with you the *whole day*.

Since I found it rather curious to have a cyber-acquaintance, I saved all our textual exchanges from the start – not knowing that from this ordinary beginning would come more than 1,500 pages of communication.

We were just two out of millions of people who had spontaneously connected themselves to the ever-flowing stream of digital data. Uncountable cross-linked locations between human minds inhabiting computer networks. Little islands of consciousness, all alone, scanning, sensing and tracing not only information, but also other forms of life in cyberspace. Anonymous human beings from all over the world, digitally connected:

> Are you there?

CONVINCING EACH OTHER

No smell, no gender, no age, no beauty, no reality. Instead, real-time interactivity and unlimited possibilities for the imagination. I was dating a virtual stranger. Fear of fantasy and cyber-lies:

> Today is the day of the rose, you
> give a rose to the person who signifies
> most to you, so I give this one to you
> —<-<-{@

> Please don't blow me up in your
> fantasy, don't imagine me as a lover,
> see me as a friend.

Is any sort of human emotional exchange possible through the wires? Or is sharing in cyberspace an illusion, and are we just triggered by textual anonymity and misled by the sensation of our own thoughts bounced back to us? Do words hurt in cyberspace? There is no frame of reference like there is in our material world. (Francis Picabia says somewhere, 'Our heads are made round so our minds can change direction.') Each time you log on, you can have a new presence and identity, but you can't define it, and you don't know what effect it has, nor what origin it has, nor what time it has. Who am 'I' in here? And what is the fate of our virtual selves in this world without fixed models for space and character recognition?

> I've never considered you a dream behind the wires.
> If not a dream, then what am I for you?

The fact that my friend pretended to be a male student of my age made me somehow believe 'him', knowing that the net is still mainly populated by white males between 18 and 40 years of age. Nevertheless, we spent considerable energy in convincing each other about our sincere intentions and true identity:

> The medium is not the exciting thing.
> You are.

The relationships that are being formed in this undefined space are based purely on each other's willingness to believe in a variable truth. Everything could be simulated, or even programmed. Paranoia in virtual reality is not a disease any more, but a realistic attitude.

Once I asked him, 'How can you prove that you are what you say you are?' He said, 'Why are you so paranoid?' I said, 'Because in the net you never know.' He answered, 'Sure, but if you spend all your time doubting about the truth, you will never have pleasure.' That was a convincing argument, and I gave up seeking for solid soil.

Being confronted with those experiences and questions, I understood that sooner or later you can no longer deny the fact that you are not only an anonymous hunter for information, using the internet as a tool, but first and foremost a form of self in cyberspace. But what would happen to you if you accepted this delusive reality of the computer world? Fear of drifting away from humanity and private identity. Is this decision to act and react upon unproven facts perhaps the first step for your virtual self on its evolving way towards its life in virtual reality?

Parallel to my virtual discoveries, in real life, through the search for silkworms, I had come across a beautiful butterfly book full of amazing creatures. Out of them all, the one that intrigued me the most was a genus called Morpho, meaning 'form' and evoking 'transformation', 'metamorphosis'. I liked the Morpho because of its suggestive colours. The upper sides of its wings, visible in flight, are blue and remind one of the sky, of an empty and free space. The undersides of its wings, visible while resting, are dark brown and remind one of the earth, of a defined and solid space. It is like seeing a transformation from earth to heaven, body to soul, life to death, in each flap of the Morpho's wings.

The search for new forms of identity in the internet has created numerous social environments such as MOOs, MUDs, and IRC.[2] These are online, text-based virtual worlds, populated and created by users who communicate with each other in real time. During my journeys through these worlds, I encountered a continuous flow of bare confessions from strangers, shamelessly exchanging in intimate language their worst fears and highest hopes. In an environment that seems so anonymous and safe, hidden emotions are unlocked and stare back at us. The insecure and curious self comes out, freed from the constraints of reality, and it has nothing to lose. It exposes itself to anyone who wants to use or abuse it; it discovers a borderless virtual playground.

One of these MOOs became the setting where my friend and I met, where our initial casual exchanges changed into regular encounters. Uncertainties, fears and joys were experienced in a new context:

We do exist, don't we?

Coming back from buying the butterfly book, I did a net search on Morpho and found someone's diary notes on a journey through the rain forest:

It's as if the ever-shifting mists are in an ecstatic dance with the vine-laden trees, and the giant blue luminescent butterflies, Morpho peleides, are playing joyfully between these planetary-level lovers. The electric blue flash of the incredible Morpho seems to illuminate the shade of the forest, which is intensified by the luxuriant tangle of lianas.[3]

For a moment it was difficult to realise that I was sitting in a closed room with 20 buzzing computers around me. I wanted to see the Morpho.

LONGING

It felt strange if my cyber-friend and I had no contact for a day. And when I had to work through the night, he kept a window open for me so I would not feel alone. What is going on here? I began to ask myself. I had a very busy social and professional life to look after, and I didn't want to wait around for a shadow in a computer that took so much time and energy.

Actually I'd prefer that we could look at the same screen. I feel so stupid, sitting here alone. It gives no satisfaction back. Doesn't it feel platonically plastic?

On the other hand, what exactly was wrong with it? Was it so bad that there was a level of reality missing? At least this was a relationship that wasn't influenced by gender, age, features, class and nationality, and it seemed to satisfy me on a spiritual level. Emotion has its own reasons about which reason knows nothing at all, as Pascal said somewhere. I could not just stop here in the middle. I wanted to go further and explore the boundaries of this virtual jungle.

One day I realised that even seeing his name in my e-mail box made a shot of adrenaline flow through my blood. Emotions, real or not, were influencing my brain and penetrating my reality. I fought against this growing digitised affection:

You are my cyber-friend. Don't get real please!

Why did I need to feel the blood flow through my veins again to realise how far my mind had travelled on its own? It must have been the absence of these (bio)logical reactions in virtual space that
made me physically numb and made me fly so far.

The needs of the body were forgotten, and cyberspace became an endless playground for the
soul to wander freely, like a butterfly. But when the body tried to join the life of the soul and
expected physical stimuli, the endless playground shrank rapidly to a space full of limitations:

We are living in a dream, until the dream can't go further.

Around this time, I discovered the existence of the Garden of Butterflies at the castle in Bendorf-
Sayn, Germany, and went there to see the Morphos in reality. These butterflies, which are native
to the tropical rain forest, are obviously not made to live in white-netted butterfly gardens in
Germany. They are used to sticking their tongues in fermented fruits and to flying higher and higher
while attracting others with their radiant blue. Here in the garden, they still instinctively tried to fly
higher and higher, but much too soon they reached the white nylon net, the frontier of their territory. Once they realised that they were not free, they frantically fluttered and fluttered against the
bright white net, trying to get out, to the other side, the free space. The desperate sound of their
wings flapping against the nylon, or even against the glass behind the net, hurt me inside.

SPLITTING POINT

Erosion of reality by digital virtuality. Real energy is spent to keep the virtual self alive. What makes us
sacrifice hours of reality for being wired?

I can't see you as an insignificant net-thing any more. You are part of me now.

Time goes fast behind a computer. Users are eager to give much of themselves and to forget the
needs of the flesh. Under the surface of the net is a big stream of human voluntary input. There is
a lot going on, on another level, flowing faster and faster. Being logged on, and living virtually – it
starts to physically hurt after a limited amount of time. Computers are not so friendly to the
material part of us:

My eyes hurt, and my fingers are
getting weaker. I feel tired by the idea
of typing more.

Our story, which had been going on for almost a year now, became unsatisfying:

In the end it's only the blank screen
that stares back at me.

The inevitable longing of the mind provoked the body to react. But for the needs of the body there was no solution (yet). It just sat there, day after day. In the Garden of Butterflies there had been a cupboard full of fresh cocoons. The butterfly attendant allowed me to take two of those with me to film the birth of a Morpho. At home, I carefully attached them to a tree branch, sat next to them, and waited the whole night through. With the first morning light, the life inside the little green cocoons began to move with short shocks that made them swing on the branch. The chrysalis was preparing for the final step towards its transformation.

Then, all of a sudden, I heard a sound like cracking plastic. It was the sound of the first tropical butterfly breaking out of its solid cover at six a.m. In half a second, the round thick body tumbled out of its cocoon and pumped its blood through the veins of its folded, wrinkled wings until they could not grow any bigger. The rest of the butterfly blood, which smelled like perfume, dripped on my floor, and created a pink splashy pattern on some white papers. Once hatched, the Morphos hung upside down, still connected to their cocoon, to dry, to test their tongues by rolling them in and out, and to wait until they were ready for take-off. This motionless drying period took just long enough for me to bring them back to the Garden of Butterflies and set them free. In their very first flight, they hit the glass. Five weeks later they were dead. I found their worn-out bodies in some bushes and took them home with me. It is surprising how much of a connection you can feel for a butterfly after attending its metamorphosis.

Being logged on, feeding my virtual life, I felt more and more as if my body was a cocoon, left passively on a chair while my soul, transformed into a butterfly, was having impossible adventures deep down in the endless and timeless constructions of the net. This gap between body and mind was the first boundary I hit in cyberspace. It caused a splitting point between reality and virtuality. (With every new machine, a new form of accident happens.)

Psyche, in ancient Greek, means 'soul' and also 'butterfly'. In the story of Psyche and Eros, the two lovers were initially forced to experience their love in total darkness, like two strangers meeting on the net. One night, Psyche was overcome by curiosity, lit a lamp, and discovered that her unseen lover was Eros. They were severely punished for this revelation of reality and had to suffer a period of pain and separation before they could come together in the real world.

We got trapped in a different reality. I feel the distance. It's made of expectations.

We couldn't go on like this. We had to choose. If we chose our virtual friendship, we would have to ignore our emotions and the desires of the body to be satisfied. If we chose reality, we would risk being disappointed and losing all we had shared over the net. In the end, we felt too human, too much flesh and blood, to be able to ignore the body, and we chose to test reality and meet:

If we don't like each other, it's not the end of the world. I can't wait to see you.

TIME STOPS HERE

Virtual time stopped. We met in reality. In front of the cafe I saw a man waiting who could be him. While I was walking towards him, I thought, 'What am I doing? I can still get out of here, turn around, and pretend not to be me.'

I was expecting to wake up any moment. It was as if my dream dissolved into reality. The closer I came, the more reality forced me to transform the image I had seen in mind into the man standing there. The two worlds were not comparable, were un-dissolvable. I felt that we had to start from zero: nothing but a stranger was standing in front of me. But how surreal – a stranger who asks you about your dinner with Andrea last night and who brings you your favourite fruits. How could this develop, this feeling of being so distant, and so close at the same time?

One thing was clear to both of us: cyberspace gave taste to reality. After having met in real life, no matter with what result, the virtual exchange seemed lifeless, and so that part of our story got lost in the internet.

TRANSFORMATION OF FANTASY INTO REALITY

In my mind, an artwork about this one-year experience in cyberspace was already made. It naturally sprang out of the situation and developed itself. So often I had imagined the butterfly, wandering in different moods through the textual worlds of the net while leaving its cocoon motionless behind. I had seen it flying around and enjoying itself, and I had seen it hitting the screen in its attempts to escape. Eventually this vision triggered me to turn my idea into a reality perceivable by others: an artwork in which I would try to portray the emotional involvement of a virtual self and its dichotomy between reality and virtuality.

But where to start? I now had to bring together two contrasting elements: the existing large body of text consisting of our 1,500 pages of net exchanges, and the delicate appearance and disappearance of the butterfly, which still had to be created from scratch. I started by reading all 1,500 pages again. It was an interesting experience to reread so many moments of my own daily exchange with another person, in so many spontaneous and unconscious moments, over a period of one year. It was as if a year of my life was frozen and came alive again. A figure took shape. It gave me a vivid experience of observing myself from another angle and from an objective distance. I realised once more how much the making of art is connected to life.

Initially the whole text seemed relevant, but using all the details for the work wouldn't bring me anything new. Moreover, to try to uncover the essence of the story by leaving out all extra data was a challenge that could add something to my own understanding of the story. So I started an exhausting process of reduction. In one month, 1,500 pages were cut down to nine. It was like doing surgery on my own past. To these nine pages, I added three pages of fiction and cut another five. Now I had seven pages of text in which I had examined every single phrase for its functionality and meaning in the artwork to come.

The final text follows a dramatic curve that shows the development from the casual first encounter, to the realisation of mutual liking, to the fear of cyber-lies, to the belief in each other's words, to real longing, and finally to a splitting point between reality and virtuality.

I wanted the text to be like a model, a timeless and placeless abstraction of actual locations, people and emotions; a docudrama that could happen any time to anyone. Therefore, I left out any reference to definite elements like gender, people's names, geographical places, and even a clear indication of the number of participants. The text should express a universal experience through an individual approach.

The text, an essential part of the total work, is seen in the work as a digital stream of exchange that is being typed on the foreground of a computer screen. Reading the exchange on the monitor, the spectator gets the feeling of being an observer looking into an ongoing dialogue between two (or more) strangers in cyberspace. Emotions are expressed by words, words translated into digital data, digital data reinterpreted as words, and words perceived as emotions. It's a constant flow of human feelings: emotions encoded.

Later I called the completed work: _Subject: emotions encoded_.[4]

(DVD)

VIRTUAL MORPHO

Simultaneously to the work on the text, I visited the Garden of Butterflies again, this time to film the behaviour of the Morphos and to record the sound of their wings hitting the glass. (Just try to follow a butterfly with a video camera sometime!) The surprising and colourful appearance and disappearance of a butterfly can make you wonder: Is this real? Its natural freedom, and its seemingly casual attitude towards direction, make you forget about the constraints of reality.

I realised that the real Morpho would not be a good actor in the work, and I certainly didn't want to force it to hit the glass over and over again until we got the right shot. Besides that, after doing some tests mixing the video images of the Morpho and the dialogue, it was clear to me that the real butterfly's overwhelming beauty and natural behaviour outshone anything else on the screen. This butterfly, no matter how much I digitally processed it, could never give the feeling of having been born in cyberspace, like my relationship.

I decided to look for a computer animator to create a photo-realistic three-dimensional animation of the Morpho. From the four hours of video footage of the real Morpho, I selected ten minutes of favourite images that would fit the dramatic structure of the text. This selection of real-life footage became the reference and inspiration for the animator to capture the elusive realism of the butterfly. Polygon by polygon, he recreated the motion and energy of the Morpho on his screen, striving for more and more realism. The wire-frame skeleton of the butterfly was already convincing, but when he added its surface texture – made from photos of the dead Morphos that had been born in my room – I saw the virtual Morpho that I had been waiting for.

In the context of the work, this virtual butterfly represents that part of you that was born in cyberspace and that wants to feel real. It moves in between the text and the background, and it behaves in accordance with the dramatic progress of the text. Initially it is just flying around and

53 *Subject: emotions encoded*, Merel Mirage, 1996.

enjoying itself, but the more emotional the exchange becomes, the more its awareness of reality increases, and the more the butterfly realises the limits of cyberspace and feels trapped. It starts to move frantically and bumps into the screen in its attempts to reach the other side. The glass of the screen, at first almost unnoticeable, becomes an uncrossable barrier between the butterfly and reality. The sound of the butterfly bumping into the screen reinforces our awareness of this barrier.

If only the butterfly would turn its back to the screen and fly away, it would be free (can you ever be free in an endless space?), but it would have to forget about its body. It would have to separate its material and immaterial presence.

After mixing the Morpho and the text in the editing, the result was a ten-minute choreography made for a butterfly with a textual docudrama set in cyberspace, performed on a computer screen.

MOCK-UP

The heart of the work – the screen in which the docudrama takes place – now had to be placed in an environment in which a visitor would be able to physically experience it. I built a life-size mock-up of a typical work space that could exist anywhere: a floor, a wall, a table, a monitor and a chair.

Next to the table, close to the monitor, stands a natural plant. It is on this side of the screen, the side that the butterfly wishes to reach. The plant represents its expectation of reality.

Seen from a distance, a visitor sitting in front of the screen becomes part of the set-up itself, somewhat isolated from the real world. And sitting in front of the screen yourself, you become less aware of the environment and more submerged in the exchange that is happening on the screen. When no one sits in front of the screen, it displays a background of moving patterns. And as soon as a visitor sits down, the text and the butterfly appear, and the life of the screen becomes perceivable. This interactive element of the work reflects on the basic fact that the net is a parallel but invisible space as long as no one decides to connect to it. Walking around the set-up, you see the back of the wall, with the back of the monitor and cables coming out. You realise that perceivable space stops here.

OTHER WORLDS

Two days before the premiere of the work in a gallery in Berlin, the plant, a Monstera, was still missing.[5] Through the snow, we drove around to all the tropical garden centres in town to find this last missing piece.

The worlds you land in while making art are always surprising: becoming a regular guest in the insectarium of a zoo (where a female praying mantis devours the head of a cricket right in front of you); visiting all the garden centres in Berlin (where you find jasmine and orange trees blooming in the middle of winter); witnessing two tropical butterflies popping out of their cocoons in your room (leaving behind the sweet smell of butterfly blood); and seeing a virtual Morpho being created out of exactly 3,666 polygons.

The day of the opening my ex-virtual friend came to see the show. For both of us, it was a surreal experience. To the other visitors we were just two more anonymous spectators. We stood outside and watched people interact with our story. For us the story had ended, but for the public it had only started.

Chrysalis

I surrender the day
in a chrysalis of dreams
my shadow unfolds
its wings and takes
flight, leaving me
to face the silken
secrets inside
the cocoon alone,
the silver fossils
of life
discarded
in the press
of the day
crawl forth from
white shells,
burst with sudden
growth on the
walls of the
night
chanting
kaleidoscopes

Anonymous[6]

NOTES

1. This was my Poem*Navigator piece, which is on the web at http://art.cwi.nl/stedelijk/capricorn/ mirage/start.html. My most recent work dealing with the internet and public space, _Holy.nl_, can be found at http://www.holy.nl

2. MUD stands for multi-user dimension or multi-user dungeon, the latter name stemming from MUD's origins as an online version of the role-playing game Dungeons & Dragons. MOO stands for MUD object-oriented as MOOs are object-oriented programming environments. Both MUDs and MOOs are virtual worlds, but MUDs are usually set up as highly structured role-playing games, while MOOs are more open role-playing environments. IRC stands for Internet Relay Chat and is a simpler form of a virtual meeting place than either MUD or MOO.

3. Rain forest quote found on the web at http://gate.cruzio.com/~hawk/arc1.1/allan.html.

4. This piece was produced at the Academy of Media Arts, Cologne, Germany, with computer animations by Jordi Moragues and sound by Moore/Kiefer/Schipke.

5. The show was at the Neue Gesellschaft für Bildende Kunst, Germany, Dec. 1996. This work has also been shown at the Venice Biennale Club Media Exhibition, 1997, the World Wide Video Festival, Stedelijk Museum, Amsterdam, 1997 and the exhibition Interact! at the Wilhelm Lehmbruck Museum in Duisburg, Germany, 1997.

6. Poem found on the net at http://sdcl-www.colorado.edu/public_html/Ken/poetry/chrysalis.txt.

An Ersatz of Life: The Dream Life of Technology

Zoe Beloff

I work with moving images: film, stereoscopic projection performance, and interactive cinema on CD-ROM and websites. My ongoing project is an exploration of what could be described as 'the dream life of technology' (not what technology is or was, but what people believed or desired it to be).

In the last century, there existed a multiplicity of cinematic apparatus. My dream is to open up the moving image once again to new languages of vision. The cinemas I imagine are marginal, fragile, sometimes coalescing only momentarily in the act of projection. They create parallel universes, calling into question corporate visions of progress with their digital utopias. I wish to reawaken the psychic charge that was unleashed by the birth of photography, film and audio recording. At the same time I have no desire to turn back the clock, rather, I wish to explore critically the deep assumptions built into the machines through which we understand our world.

CINEMA INCOGNITO
I am inspired by the writings of a great cinematic alchemist, Raul Ruiz, specifically this short passage from his book *Poetics of Cinema*,

> I will recount the life of cinema past, present and future, as though it had never existed, or had never been anything more than sheer conjecture. I will try to lay out some of the philosophical problems that this vanished art proposed, and I will seek to explain its journey incognito through the grammatical city known for the moment as virtual reality.[1]

What sets fire to my imagination is just this conjecture, the possibility of a reinvention of cinema that moves us imaginatively from the past into the future.

A CHANCE ENCOUNTER BETWEEN A QUICK CAM AND A FILM FOUND AT THE FLEA MARKET
In the summer of 1995, with no money to shoot film and no place to show my work, I began my first digital project in the form of QuickTime movies. The computer was simply something I had around the house. Challenging myself to make a movie a week, I opened my own cinema on the web. It was the beginning of *Beyond* in serial form. Early motion picture serials and toy projection devices inspired me. The computer is today's home movie projector. I liked the idea of cinema trickling down the phone lines into people's homes.

My QuickTime movies in *Beyond* were made 'live' without digital manipulation, by re-photographing film and text with a Quick Cam ($99 black and white video conferencing camera), using effects that would not have been out of place in Méliès' studio. Just as the earliest film-makers struggled to find a new visual language through the newly-developed technology of cinema, so I aimed to invent, in a personal way, a new articulation of space and time, that both grew out of cinema, yet went beyond it.

I think of the computer as a way to 'jot down' ideas in the form of images and sounds. Unlike most digital work, my CDs were really spontaneous and created over time, so that they became actually a record or sketchbook of my investigation and thought process as it happened. There was no predetermined 'master plan', just some rough ideas in my head: nothing was written down. Rather, one line of research led to another, one text to another. Movies were improvised with what I found at the flea market on Sunday mornings. In fact, my projects would have been impossible to plan in advance. Chance played a tremendously important part. Besides, I didn't always know what I was going to do in a QuickTime movie until I actually set it up and performed in front of the camera. Frequently I was projecting film, playing music and performing all at the same time, so I couldn't see what I was doing until after it had happened. I have always secretly felt that making these QuickTime movies was more like 'casting a spell' than conventionally shooting a film.

PHILOSOPHICAL TOYS

What I make could be described quite simply as 'philosophical toys', heirs to nineteenth-century devices such as magic lanterns, Zoetropes and hand-cranked projectors. I often describe this apparatus as forming the secret history of QuickTime movies, producing images that are tiny, unstable and, most importantly, interactive. They remind us that interactivity, far from being a new phenomenon, was integral to the production of the nineteenth-century moving image.

I've deliberately stuck with the word 'toy' to describe my CD-ROMs because to my mind, the cinematic toy is not simply a machine in miniature; it has an extra expenditure of energy invested in play, in the pleasure of the moment. 'Machine' suggests something altogether too functional, too goal-oriented. In the conventional cinematic apparatus, a film is put on the projector and the machine is switched on for a certain duration until the film runs out. However, most philosophical toys are constructed around loops, which remove us from linear time into an altogether more hypnotic state. Classical cinema knows only 'next', the philosophical toy, only 'now' and 'again'.[2]

INTIMACY

In its classical form, cinema signifies the creation of an illusionistic world that exists apart from us; governed by its own temporal laws, its own spatial laws and above all oblivious to us, a great machine that effaces all traces of its production. And if we are to enter into it, we must leave our corporeal selves behind. Capturing us in its glare, it holds us still and obliterates us in the dark. In contrast, my CD-ROMs are designed specifically for an audience of one. An intimate dialogue is created.

AN INTERFACE

The CDs are constructed by linking QuickTime movies and QuickTime VR panoramas to create the illusion of a world that invites the viewer to explore a new kind of mental geography. They find themselves travelling through time and space, encountering my virtual alter ego, which, as a medium that interfaces between the living and the dead, leads the viewer on a journey that is as mysterious, as it is unpredictable. Very simply, QuickTime VR panoramas are virtual 360° spaces that one can explore by dragging the mouse around the space. They are constructed by 'stitching' together in the computer 12 still photographs taken in rotation. The viewer can zoom in and out and, by clicking on 'hotspots', access the short movies. *Beyond* contains 20 panoramas and 80 QuickTime movies.

The location is an actual abandoned asylum, dating back to the nineteenth century. It stands in for many places, both real and fictional (from Charcot's clinic at the Salpêtrière, to Roussel's fictional world of *Locus Solus*, to the destroyed buildings of the two World Wars, to the Paris Arcades of the Second Empire, to the ruins of the great world expositions).

A PHANTASMAGORIA OF PROGRESS

In practice, digital technologies are the most fleeting of media, as hardware and software mutations bring in their wake ever-faster obsolescence: a faster way of forgetting. Walter Benjamin wrote about the beginnings of this phenomenon in his Arcades Project, seeing nineteenth-century capitalism as a hellish time in its endless promotion of the new:

> The dreaming collective knows no history. Events pass before it as always identical and always new.
> The sensation of the newest and most modern is, in fact, just as much a dream formation of events
> as the eternal return of the same.[3]

As I began working on *Beyond*, I felt that these issues should urgently be addressed. Benjamin wished, through examining the past, to make the mechanisms of our own delusion, or own dream state, clear to us. He aimed to do this, not through examining the big events of history, but through examining its scraps and remains: images, objects, buildings, the landscape of the

54 'L'Eve Future' panorama from *Beyond*, Zoe Beloff.

everyday that has been discarded. He spoke of, not life-remembered, but of life-forgotten; illu-minated at the very moment of its disappearance. It is just this debris, washed up at the flea market, that I hope in my own way to make speak again, but differently – to illuminate the pres-ent through the past.

I was not interested in being literal or illustrative, but instead in letting the past breath through small discarded objects. For example in *Beyond* the 'dead' are represented by fragments of home movies from the 1920s to 1940 found at flea markets, as well as early film footage from the Library of Congress Paper Print collection. Long outdated forms resurfacing anew in the digital realm fas-cinated me. Such are panoramas. Actual panoramas painted around specially-constructed circular rooms were a popular form of entertainment in the nineteenth century. Long since forgotten, they now reappear on the computer as QuickTime VR.

MENTAL GEOGRAPHY

The possibilities opened up by interactivity allowed me to realise ideas of mental geography that previously could only be described rather than actually experienced in art. A geography described in the words of Baudelaire as: '*A city full of dreams where ghosts accost the passers-by in broad day-light.*'[4]

Unlike film or video, my CDs are designed to be experienced more than once. Each time the viewer enters *Beyond*, they can choose a different route. There are no maps, because, to me it is a city of the mind, a city of metaphor, it is a virtual city, in which the ordinary laws of geography do not apply.

Ideas, in the form of movies, cluster around particular rooms or space. There are two methods of travel: literally, on foot, a filmed simulation of walking from place to place. Panoramas are also linked by narrative movies, thus trains of thought connect the viewer from one place to another. Baudelaire became a key figure in *Beyond*, perhaps because he was the first great writer of the modern city, the first modernist. It was he who first defined this idea of 'mental geography' as a state of mind: the city shot-through by allegory. My QuickTime movie based on his prose poem, *Symptoms of Ruin*, could serve very well as an introduction. Here, by describing his dream of a fan-tastic endless and impossible building, which only he knows is on the verge of collapse, he is per-haps actually describing his mental state and his own body. A body slowly dying, exteriorised in the form of a '*building attacked by some hidden disease*'.[5] He was the archetypal flâneur, while my work might also be considered as an exercise in digital flânerie.

(DVD) In my next CD-ROM, <u>Where Where There There Where</u>, based on Gertrude Stein's play *Doctor Faustus Lights the Lights*, 'stage sets' have become QuickTime VR panoramas within which the actors, as embedded video loops, perform. By clicking on a character, a QuickTime movie appears, which tells us their story and leads the viewer on their journey. Each time it is played, the viewer can choose a different route and discover new ways to interpret the characters.

The logic of the interface is that immediately upon entering a panorama, if you click on a char-acter, you will see a movie that follows the train of thought, inspired by the previous one, but if you turn 180°, the character will now lead you off on a tangent, a new idea.

And yet I am I reminded of the words of Dziga Vertov: 'Kino-Eye uses every possible means in montage, comparing and linking all points of the universe in any temporal order.'[6]

Are interactive technologies simply a banal literalisation of these ideas that he realised so forcefully in his films? Does 'click and point' spell the end of metaphor? I wonder.

SPECTACULAR SYMPTOMS

What fascinates me is that the birth of mechanical reproduction opened up almost limitless possibilities in the mind of the nineteenth-century viewer. Was it simply that people were just more gullible and that now hard science has dispelled their fantasies? I don't know. One could argue equally the converse: that because something was conceivable, then it became, perhaps, possible. My thesis is that if something (which we now take for granted) like photography, was experienced as an uncanny phenomena (which seems to undermine the unique identity of objects), creating a parallel world of phantasmal doubles; then the possibility of the production of, for example, Spirit Photographs was not nearly as implausible as it might be today. In *Beyond*, I felt these were important issues to address, that with the onrush of today's technology, our capacity for wonder, to dream through our machines, was closing down.

VIRTUAL MACHINES

All technologies are also mental constructs, we think through them, but at the same time they define the boundaries of our thoughts. My CDs are very much about these mental constructions, cinemas of the mind. I see them as twins. As philosophical toys. *Beyond* is a dualist machine. *Where Where There There Where* is a logical and materialist machine. The key figure for me here was Raymond Roussel, the first great constructor of fantastic machines in the twentieth century. It is Roussel's madness, in the form of his novel *Locus Solus*, that is at the heart of *Beyond*. Here we are confronted with a symptomatic work, symptoms of fact, symptoms of fiction, symptoms of an age, each I believe illuminating the other. Written in 1914, *Locus Solus* simply recounts a tour of the estate of a famous inventor, Martial Canterel (who was modelled on Edison). One by one, bizarre mechanical inventions are described in a style, at once dry and fantastic.

What I began to discover was that a work of fiction, written by a so-called madman, or at least

55 'The Furnace Room' panorama from *Where Where There There Where,* Zoe Beloff.

56 'Locus Solus'
panorama from
Beyond, Zoe Beloff.

in the words of his doctor Pierre Janet, 'a singular neuropath', was not nearly as bizarre as it appeared on first reading. Instead, this book might better be regarded as a strange mirror reflecting back symptomatically and with almost uncanny clarity the crossroads of media technology and psychology, at this time. Roussel's explanatory mania always goes beyond the fantastically detailed mechanical descriptions of moving parts, cogs and wheels, to become, as it were, case histories. The resulting machines can be seen as the outcome of some kind of psychological disturbance on the part of his characters. These machines are the externalisation of the mind at work.

RE-ANIMATION

Most resonant for me was Roussel's description of the *Ice House*. It reveals a series of dioramas that are open to public viewing behind glass. Within each little stage, an actor performs the same melodramatic set piece over and over again with uncanny exactitude. These scenes become truly strange when we discover that all the so-called 'actors' are dead. Through electricity, Martial Canterel has mechanically re-animated these dead people. They are not conscious, but instead, once revived, repeat unconsciously (with unvarying motions) the most traumatic moments of their lives, in a suitably chilled environment: hence the *Ice House*.

> **Vitalium**
>
> At last, after a great deal of trial and error with corpses submitted to the required degree of cold, Professor Canterel prepared on the one hand Vitalium and on the other Ressurrectine. The latter was injected as a liquid into the skull of some defunct person from a laterally pierced opening, solidifying of its own accord around the brain. It is then only necessary to put some point of the internal envelope into contact with Vitalium, for the two new substances, each of them inactive without the other, to release a powerful current of electricity, which penetrating the brain and overcoming its cadaveric rigidity, thus endows the corpse with an impressive artificial life.[7]

What are we to make of this grotesque scene? In my view a little research reveals that it was at the time, perhaps, much less strange than it appears to be now. Here it is very interesting to note, as has been pointed out in an essay by Vanessa Schwartz, that up until the turn of the century, the Paris Morgue was an extremely popular place of public entertainment.[8] Schwartz connects this spectacle along with panoramas and the wax museum as pre-cinematic entertainment that this new technology more or less killed off. And in a sense it is this turning point that we discover in Roussel's writing. For the dead in his 'Ice House' are not unlike those frozen figures that would mechanically be brought to life in the earliest movies.

Remember that the first films were shown initially with a still-frame up on the screen that would then suddenly come to life as the projectionist cranked the projector. At the same time these films, less than a minute long, were often shown as loops so that the same gestures were repeated with uncanny precision over and over again.

AN ERSATZ OF LIFE

In his book, *Life to those Shadows*, Noël Burch wrote that:

> Edison's wish to link his phonograph to an apparatus capable of reproducing pictures is not just the ambition of an astute captain of industry; it is also the pursuit of the fantasy of a class become the fantasy of a culture: to extend 'the conquest of nature' by triumphing over death through an ersatz of life itself.[9]

Central to my work is this theme of death and artificial resurrection. The machine mediating between these two states. I believe that this legacy, so often forgotten, of the suppression of death, continues to haunt the creation of virtual reality.

AN ELECTRIC BRAIN

Again in my next CD-ROM *Where Where There There Where* I came back to the Ice House as a kind of guiding metaphor. To just stop and explain for a moment, in 1996, I was approached by the Wooster Group Theatre Company and asked to do something, in relation to a new work that they were rehearsing. The work is called *House/Lights* and is related in a very idiosyncratic way to Gertrude Stein's play *Doctor Faustus Lights the Lights*. In no sense was my work to be a document of the play itself. Rather one might describe it as a satellite work. It exists purely in the virtual realm. Here, Roussel's description of the dead body as electrical automata insensibly acting out the most traumatic moment of its life became in my mind the Steinian figure caught in a loop of language. Her Doctor Faustus sold his soul to the devil for the secret of electric light, only to discover he had no soul to sell. Only then, in anguish, he discovers that he cannot die, for without a soul he is in essence already dead or like any machine neither alive nor dead.

WITTGENSTEIN'S DREAM

The year 1938, the date that Stein wrote *Doctor Faustus*, was a time of transition between the old analogue world and the birth of the digital realm, and it is this transition that I wanted to be reflected in the work itself. In the sense of both finding a contemporary formal equivalent in digi-tal media for the radical restructuring of language performed by Stein's text, as well as a playful philosophical investigation of the relationship between electricity, logic and language games, that her work inspires.

We enter this world through a true story, that of Wittgenstein's escape into the cinema:

> Wittgenstein insisted on sitting in the very first row of seats, so that the screen would occupy his entire field of vision, and his mind would be turned away from the thoughts of the lecture and his feelings of revulsion. His observation of the film was not relaxed or detached. He leaned tensely for-ward in this seat and rarely took his eyes off the screen. Once he whispered to me, 'This is like a shower bath!' He wished to become totally absorbed in the film no matter how trivial or artificial it was, in order to free his mind temporarily from the philosophical thoughts that tortured and exhausted him.[10]

But as in all dreams, the repressed returns. It is these hidden conflicts, the ones that are repressed below the surface of the play, that I wished to bring to light. Indeed the whole project brings to life cinematically the conflicts between the virtual machines built by Stein, Pavlov, Turing and Wittgenstein on the eve of World War II.

HIS MASTER'S VOICE

My first question was of course: who is Doctor Faustus? All we know is he discovers the secret of electric light and he has a dog that says only, 'Thank you'. Perhaps he was really Doctor I. P. Pavlov who had conditioned this reflex in his dog? But then I asked what could the relationship between electricity and conditioned reflexes possibly be? I discovered how conditioning revolves around very simple binary opposition. A stimulus is either 'on' or 'off' just like the circuits of a computer.

A whole new way of thinking about thought was coming into being based around 'Truth Tables' or 'Boolean Algebra'. It was these ideas, in the work of the mathematician Alan Turing, which were to lead not only to the very existence of 'Universal Turing Machines', or as we now call them, com-puters, but also to the concept of Artificial Intelligence. Turing believed that the binary configura-tion of electrical circuits could lead to thinking machines or 'electric brains'. He believed that the mind could be encoded mathematically, that an electric brain was theoretically quite possible. Wittgenstein thought just the opposite: that it was a logical impossibility, a linguistic absurdity.

Though Stein was clearly fascinated by language and logic, I'm not suggesting that she was aware of these discussions that were going on in Cambridge. Rather, I was interested in layering these ideas over each other, in the hope that they might illuminate each other in productive ways. Thus my desire became to work with Stein's text not as a story but as a set of logical operations or 'application', within which I can 'input' my own 'data'. So in my version, Doctor Faustus can be sub-stituted by Pavlov or Turing, and Mephisto can become Wittgenstein in his role as devil's advocate.

The Wooster Group actors can become Turing Machines, who 'output' the text in the form of printed paper tapes that issue from their mouths.

57 'The Devil and the Electric Dog' panorama from *Where Where There There Where*, Zoe Beloff.

A WINDOW OR A DOOR

Ultimately the computer is simply one apparatus of many that I use in my work. My QuickTime movies allowed me to sketch out ideas that I am currently fleshing out through resurrecting lost or forgotten technologies, particularly 3D projection, to explore the histories of (what we think of as) virtual reality. In my CDs I attempted to evoke an imaginary landscape beyond or behind the screen of the computer. More and more, I am fascinated by conjuring up phantoms that come out to greet us, that invade our own three-dimensional space. My recent stereoscopic film *Shadow Land or Light from the Other Side* (tbc) is based on the 1897 autobiography of Elizabeth d'Espérance, a material-ising medium, who could produce full-body apparitions. It suggests how one might think of a medium as a kind of 'mental projector' and the phantoms as representations of her psychic reality. Visually the film explores the origins of what we think of as the virtual. While twentieth-century cinema can be described as a 'window into another world'; the nineteenth century conceived of spectres that could cross over into our own world. Currently I am working on an installation, *The Influencing Machine of Miss Natalija A.,* that uses stereoscopic diagrams and interactive video to con-jure up the hallucinations of a schizophrenic.

TIME MACHINES

As I have tried to demonstrate, all media technologies could be said to be shot-through with this idea of artificial resurrection, with time and death. They are time machines. Cinema is a time machine of movement. Stereo photography brings about the artificial reconstitution of space, con-gealed now like waxworks or the dead frozen behind glass in the morgue. Is it then so strange that people believed in the literal possibility of travel in time? I end *Beyond* with a quote from Pierre Janet, who actually believed in the possibility of time travel: 'The past exists and endures in a place we do not know and cannot go.'[11]

But one might add, that in its own way the past does endure in film, in photography and now in the digital realm. It is up to us to imagine the rest.

NOTES

1. Ruiz, Raul. *Poetics of Cinema*. Paris: Editions Dis Voir, 1995, p. 107.

2. My website *Illusions*, an exploration of the relationship between digital medial and cinematic toys, can be found at http://turbulence.org/Works/illusions/index.html.

3. Benjamin, Walter. *The Arcades Project*. Cambridge/London: The Belknap Press, 1999, p. 546.

4. Baudelaire, Charles. 'Les Sept Vieillards'. *Les Fleurs du Mal*. Francis Scarfe, trans. London: Anvil Press Poetry, 1986, p. 177.

5. Baudelaire, Charles. 'Symptômes de Ruine'. *The Poems in Prose*. Francis Scarfe, trans. London: Anvil Press Poetry, 1989, p. 206.

6. Vertov, Dziga. *Kino-Eye*. Kevin O'Brien, trans. Berkeley: University of California Press, 1984, p. 16.

7. Roussel, Raymond. *Locus Solus*. R. C. Cunningham, trans. London: John Calder, 1983, p. 118.

8. Schwartz, Vanessa R. 'Cinematic Spectatorship before the Apparatus: The Public Taste for Reality. Fin-de-Siècle Paris'. Linda Williams, ed. *Viewing Positions*. New Jersey: Rutgers University, 1994.

9. Burch, Noël. *Life to those Shadows*. Ben Brewster, trans. Berkeley: University of California Press, 1990, p. 7.

10. Malcolm, Norman. *Ludwig Wittgenstein: A Memoir*. London: Oxford University Press, 1958, p. 27.

11. Quoted in Ellenberger, Henri F. *The Discovery of the Unconscious: The History and Evolution of Dynamic Psychiatry*. New York: Basic Books, 1970, p. 354.

The Good Cook: A Vertical Axis versus a Horizontal Axis in Interactive Narrative Construction

Michael Buckley

The notion of games with the viewer as a player (or detective) is well-documented and frequently used in the making of interactive multimedia works. It is my contention that the dramatic potential of the medium has yet to be fully exploited. My CD-ROM *The Good Cook* explores the new role of the viewer/participant in interactive media.[1] It investigates how interactivity affects the nature of storytelling, the issue of form and content, and the structure of a dramatic work in interactive form. The work further explores the 'deep syntax' of conceptual meaning that can be developed in this media.

Like most of my work, *The Good Cook* is based (in part) on real events. A series of conversations I recorded in the kitchen of a restaurant between a cook and his assistant form the backbone of this piece. Other sources include remembered personal childhood stories, snatches of song and some fictional material. The construction of *The Good Cook* is a new way for a viewer to 'interrogate' a subject. The content is not as fixed as in a 'filmic essay' by a film director. Interactivity provides exciting new ways for a viewer to read and interpret a subject. *The Good Cook* is almost like a candid, face to face dialogue with the subject. A certain 'intimacy' is engendered. Unlike time-based linear forms, interactive media offer the possibility of presenting a subject in a way that allows the user a richer plurality of viewpoints. It removes the time constraints of the standard one hour format of TV/video programme.

THE GOOD COOK IS A NARRATIVE STEW TO DIP INTO ...

The work attempts to replicate the state of insomnia using an interactive medium. It explores the psychological make-up of a character (a cook), as he tries to come to grips with his sense of identity during a tormented night of 'no sleep'. Randomness plays an important role in this interactive. *The Good Cook* is based on the premise that memory is inherently unreliable. Memories and reveries are not always accurate. Reflecting this idea, a viewer of the work gets alternative and sometimes conflicting thoughts from the cook within various sections of the narrative. A new version of the cook's life may be presented each time the interactive is viewed. This is primarily achieved

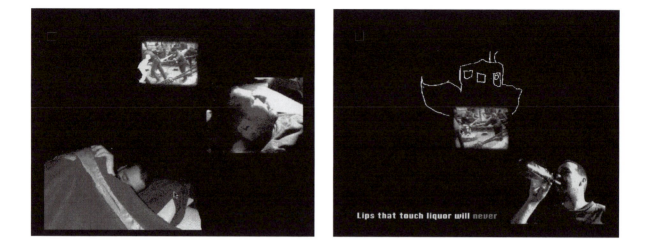

58 *The Good Cook*,
Michael Buckley,
1999.

through the use of random sound loops that carry over into new sequences as the work is explored. As the cook hears voices, songs and stories from the past, he tries to remember the people of his forgotten reveries. Throughout the interactive, phantoms appear as silhouettes and sound loops that continue to repeat and haunt him.

A stream of consciousness of his internal ramblings unfolds … His mind continually wanders over the workings of the day. He remembers the abuse that was thrown back and forth between the dishwasher and himself. He battles the forces of darkness within himself. He is consumed by those rejected, unrealised and repressed energies that return to haunt and torment him. Memories are interspersed with incidents from his childhood that he tries hard to remember – the spiders, his father, being locked up in the toilet all night as a five-year-old, and his mother crying. He remembers the tattoos on his father's arm: the clipper ship, the hanged monkey and the naked girl. Until he resolves these tormented memories, he cannot rest. Called by the 'herald' of insomnia, the cook embarks on a journey of discovery into the nether regions of his own soul, or perhaps his cooking pot (the aroma of memory).

WRITING FOR MULTIMEDIA

As an artist, I am not interested in trying to ape literature (the novel) in the manner of Hollywood cinema. Interactive media fails at this level. Interactives seem more akin to a poetic discourse where the content can be viewed and replayed, and is 'read' as you would a poem. The viewer needs to work at the construction of meaning. It is a looser, more playful experience, where repetition brings new insights. There are plenty of psychological studies that show the pleasure of repetition. We feel more comfortable when we know something, become familiar with something or someone. Viewing *The Good Cook* over a few sessions is similarly like getting to know someone over a period of time. An important aspect of writing for multimedia is creating the right landscape or environment and 'tight conceptual framework' for the work. The writer must consider how the viewer enters into the landscape and how this frames their experience of the work. Too often in multimedia, a viewer has to leap around in a work that is designed like the glossy pages of a magazine. This experience tends to lack engagement and to be ephemeral and shallow.

In *The Good Cook*, I try not to mimic the style of cinematic language, where the set and action changes are constant and detailed. Like the staging of a play, interactives need only a few set designs (landscapes) with minimal costume changes. *The Good Cook* is limited to one main actor (the cook) and three or four minor players; the waitress, the kitchen hand, the cruel father and the cook himself as a child. All the drama is located in his bed or in his kitchen. Interactives can also be compared with radio plays where the viewer fills in the gaps suggested by audio cues and where themes/ideas are more open-ended or open to interpretation. Humour plays a major role in *The Good Cook*. It aids audience identification with and understanding of the subject. Does the Cook wallow in his own unhappiness or self-pity? Does his cynicism carry him through?

I'll let all these thoughts dribble out of my throat, out into the void ...[2]

CONCEPTUAL FRAMEWORK

A chief characteristic of the mind is that it is constantly describing itself. I use the 'restlessness of the mind' as a conceptual model for *The Good Cook*. This work is influenced by the clinical psychiatric state of 'Echolalia'. It is a form of stuttering where an involuntary repetition occurs. It can manifest itself in people trying to manage anxiety. *The Good Cook* explores this phenomenological landscape of uncertainty and anxiety and repetition.

In a state of ceaseless flux, the mind goes about weaving and 'un-weaving' itself ... Likewise, human consciousness struggles in perpetual pursuit of meaning, a persona, or a form. Even at levels far below the zone of the conscious, definition and clarity, unconscious forms and relationships exist. Sometimes within the struggle for meaning, the admission of fugitive impressions or idle thoughts can produce floods of emotion that may overturn the checkerboard of logic we have created. Our reveries, memories and thoughts become a confused, turbulent activity in contrast with an outer world of coherent, concrete complexity. Insomnia can enforce this conscious struggle for meaning. We continually attempt to redefine ourselves, and reappraise past events. In our minds, we act out new interpretations and variations continually reworking our memory for new scraps of useful information. We use conjecture and probability to do this. Our minds accumulate an immense collection of memories. The deeper or further back our memories of the past, the sharper our doubt in the present or future. A phenomenon of uncertainty accumulates.

OBJECTS AND PICTURES

Objects can be seductive. If you organise objects into a context, they become seductive by implication – the swinging monkey, the objects in the cook's kitchen, the shadows, the sailing ships. The work creates a desire to know more about these objects. They become metaphors for ideas. When you move into a picture, you consciously discover details you can name. The picture sets things into motion and creates further pictures that merge from scraps of information, ideas, and ways of providing meaning. They can be used as a form of language, without necessarily using written or spoken text. Similarly, music and sound effects can influence the viewer.

The Good Cook is a discontinuous narrative. It apes the way people talk and have conversations. A conversation is going on between the viewer and the cook, as the viewer explores the interactive and finds out more about what the cook has to say. The character leaps from scene to scene, without the story construction of conflict and resolution, often required in a conventional narrative. The work is a kind of 'split' monologue where the past and present continually entwine. The cook's thoughts do not run in a linear narrative sequence but are interspersed throughout the CD-ROM. Gradually all the bits of dialogue come together, although this does not happen until the work has been viewed several times.

In the use of overlaying audio material through looping, language itself becomes fluid. Words mean different things in different contexts, contradictions are constant, old words and phrases give new words new meanings when overlapped. *The Good Cook* can be viewed as a social interactive. This style could easily be transposed as an oral history project. It explores the personality of the speaker rather than just reading a subject's memoirs and looking at their photographs (the written or verbal memoirs). In *The Good Cook* the viewer is directed down into the 'nitty gritty' of the character. The viewer quickly discovers the character's voice and the selectivity of his memories. Through this process, the viewer builds up a psychological framework of the character. It's like trying to find an explanation as to why a character behaves the way he or she does.

INTERFACE FUNCTIONALITY

It is important for interactive works to leave room for the viewer to bring some of their own creativity to a work. *The Good Cook* has a few essential signposts so that a viewer can easily move around in this work that has more than 30 sections. The opening offers the choice of an introduction (rather like a trailer to a movie) or the menu page. The introduction sets the tone and style for the work. The menu has a cast button which works like programme notes for a play. Each character is briefly introduced with a phrase that hints at their personality. The menu (or the base) is made up of hours of the night, 1.00 am, 2.00 am and so on. These can be clicked onto to go into those hours of the night. There are roughly seven sections within each hour of the night. Each section begins with a Bible quote. This aids the viewer in knowing they are entering into a new sequence. In the top of each section is a small square that the viewer can click to get to the end of that section. This can aid a viewer if they feel they are 'lost'.

At the end of each section there are three choices: a clock, which will take the viewer back to the main menu; a still photo which will take the viewer back to the start of that section; and a QuickTime movie, which will take the viewer to the next section. This is a random work so there is no real need to follow it sequentially. However, there is an ending at 5.00 am.

The end of the night is a little forest of upturned chairs.[3]

A HORIZONTAL AXIS VERSUS A VERTICAL AXIS

Interactive works can prepare a space for an encounter between viewer and object. They can follow two different axes — the horizontal axis of ego consciousness and rationality, which tries to figure things out, and the vertical axis of psychic depth, which plumbs dream and myth to present figures and images. Instead of the centre stage literalism of most film and television pieces, a vertical axis in multimedia introduces new possibilities and powers of interpretation. The viewer becomes more involved in the artistic process of the work and becomes aware of things seen and unseen, words heard and echoed into the moments of confusion, sensing the dark as a place of shadow, of the other.

The viewer in turn organises their perception into habituated patterns of response, making the strange familiar through strategies of identifying and naming, through replaying and hearing repetitive turns of phrase. A 'sensing' process evolves from the attentive viewer's willingness to explore aspects of the work. We become familiar, we begin to comprehend and predict certain patterns in characters and scenes from everyday life. Interactivity gives us this ability to become familiar with, to repeat, to re-acquaint ourselves with a work. The vertical axis does not need to mimic the cause-and-effect patterns of rational behaviour. Interactives need not rely on form and content through their story structure as might be the case in cinema. But it is possible to borrow certain principles from this form to act as guides and signposts in building an interactive.

The base of *The Good Cook* is built like sections/scenes from a play, but should not be viewed as a direct equivalent. Interactive media in part destroys the holistic integrity of the storyteller and listener, singer/song, author/reader, director/viewer. There is no original first ground, no homeland …

'INTERACTIVES ARE NOT CINEMATIC!'

During a stay in Ireland (1997) I read a critical work *Beckett and Myth* by Mary A. Doll, a noted Beckett academic. Her writing resonated with my approach to interactive multimedia.[4] Mary Doll's writing suggests that Beckett's mythic pattern is an inversion of the traditional heroic quest (departure, encounter and return). Beckett's quest is thoroughly non-heroic, involving three mythic moments, regressing, encountering and sensing, somewhat like being in a middle of a journey. Similarly, the cook is a character in search of his soul, as he remembers and searches out characters from his past and present. He does not complete his quest. He is continually in a state of search.

Mary Doll suggests that:

There is an undersurface of all things, a voyage into the unconscious, an evocation of the unsaid by the said. The relation between the earth and the underworld, alive mythically but hidden to logical thought processes.

For the cook his insomnia is a night of hell with nothing and everything going on forever. However, beneath the cracks in his consciousness, myths and psychic energy seep through. Shadows hide layers, voices echo, repeat and loop. Objects contain depth. Bodies, torsos, limbs and faces fuse, evolve and haunt his memory. Characters appear out of the black and are highly disturbed or disturbing. Stories rarely come to an end. Like myths they build upon basic patterns, and give the viewer the possibility to create endings and recreate beginnings. In *The Good Cook*, the logic of games or of the heroic quest pattern simply will not do. Like dreams or nightmares the CD-ROM requires us to live in them. Deepest feelings get touched, truths get contradicted, uncertainty prevails, the pot of the unconscious is stirred. In the cook, problems aren't raised in the beginning and resolved at the end. Rather, the cook engages in a continuous stirring of the self in which time becomes the present tense, the senses become alive; common sense is replaced as an immersive quality that covers the viewer. An analytical approach is logically, sequentially and hierarchically overturned in the process.

Deconstruction theory suggests that a text constructed by an author, whose life contains a definite history and clear bias, is reconstructed by a reader whose life differs from that of the author and whose perspective is framed differently. The text in fact becomes different to that which the author intended through the action of the viewer. This notion can be placed within the context of

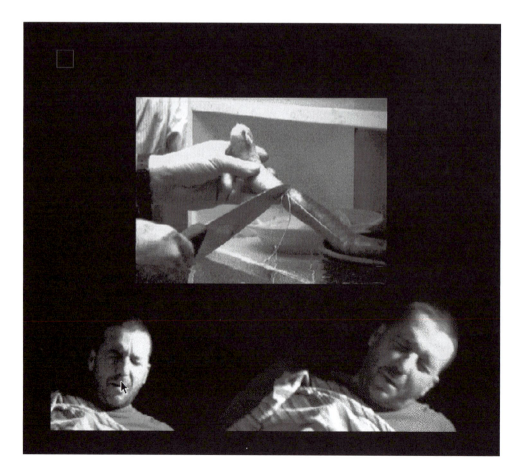

59 *The Good Cook*,
Michael Buckley,
1999.

interactive multimedia where it can further undermine a clean Cartesian split between author and reader, subject and object, text and context. In this new space an observant viewer is definitely expected to engage in making meaning. In giving up the old pact of reality, where art mimes the surface and films fulfil expected roles and promises, mythopoetic work must reorganise otherness. Objects, images, mirages, dreams, hallucinations, ghosts, voices, disembodied characters come from the unconscious. The viewer needs to let go of habituated patterns of perceiving.

Mary Doll suggests:

> By shutting out reality the viewer is enticed to wander in the fragments and archaic remnants of the unconscious, the emotionally charged picture language of dreams, myths, primitive rites.[5]

The shift down into the vertical axis takes us into the roots of poetic discourse … the psyche releases us into rivers of time … one is at sea. *'I'm on a sea of fat!'*

The artistic process is one of unveiling. To rend veils of things hidden from things perceived. One is cast into a different way of experience where one can encounter with amazement, enchantment and terror: figures, animals, images and ghosts, floating in a sea of uncertainty. Interactive media can offer us moments of enchantment, when images and objects can come forth from darkness, space and language. The viewer no longer needs to operate inside the sealed jar of literalism, dictated by the director's gaze in time-based media, but rather, enter into a mythical quest of discovery. Objects and pictures speak wordlessly to deeper recesses of being. The viewer engages with objects on the screen, as if they were stones to overturn and reveal what's underneath.

NOTES

1. Buckley, Michael, *The Good Cook* (CD-ROM), the Australian Film Commission, 1999.
2. Ibid.
3. Ibid.
4. Doll, Mary A. *Beckett and Myth: An Archetypal Approach*. New York: Syracuse University Press, 1988.
5. Ibid.

Mongrel's *National Heritage*: Reporting the Experience

Graham Harwood

WHAT IS MONGREL?

Mongrel is a mixed bunch of people working to celebrate the methods of London street culture. It was set up with the people who helped make *Rehearsal of Memory*, which is a CD-ROM made with patients/prisoners of Ashworth, a top security mental hospital. Mongrel is centred on Matsuko Yokokoji, Richard Pierre-Davis, Mervin Jarman and Harwood. We set up projects and invite others to join in on specific ones.

NATIONAL HERITAGE

The Mongrel project <u>National Heritage</u> grew out of a specific need, location and time. It attempted to address the wide-spread practice of using new communications technology for the dissemination and organisation of various forms of eugenics, nationalism and racism. The project deployed cultural strategies and uses of digital technology that undermine and strategically play with the expectations of radicalisation in a manner which usurps them. In addition the project drew attention to, and created dialogues about, the implicit racism in the construction of hardware, software and surrounding discourses in the use of new technology in arts and culture.

60 *National Heritage: Heritage Gold,* Mongrel.

Richard Pierre-Davis:

National Heritage was conceived as a response to all the hype surrounding the internet and in particular far right activity on the net. It snowballed into its own identity with input from various artists collaborating on the project with Mongrel steering the ship into a one-finger salute to the PC clones and all them fronting fakers worldwide.

National Heritage had three main project centres: *Natural Selection* is an internet search engine working in exactly the same way as any other one of these vast pieces of software that find data on the web, but adds a twist of its own.[1]

Harwood:

Well basically, it's the same as any other search engine. The user types in a series of characters that they wish to have searched for. The engine goes off and does this and then returns the results. If you're looking for sites on monocycles, that's what you get. If you're looking for sites on elephants, that's what you get. As soon as you start typing in words like 'nigger' or 'paki' or 'white' you start getting dropped into a network of content that we have produced in collaboration with a vast network of demented maniacs strung out at the end of telephone wires all over the place. The idea is to pull the rug from underneath racist material on the net, and also to start eroding the perceived neutrality of information science type systems. If people can start to imagine that a good proportion of the net is faked then we might start getting somewhere. And as a search engine, from Europe it runs faster than most US-based search engines. Enlightenment and a cheaper phone bill – you can't lose.

Colour Separation was a large print poster constructed from photos of over one hundred people who in some day-to-day way are related with the core Mongrel group. These images were transformed into eight unglamorous stereotypes of black/yellow/brown/white men and women.

Matsuko Yokokoji:

Colour Separation is an element of the *National Heritage* 'campaign'. It functions as a poster and also as a free distribution paper. We made eight stereotypes and four masks. That's the system. It makes a chart of the nonsense of racial categorisation. We could see the myth of racial classifications. In Japan when I was growing up in the 60s and 70s, we knew about it through the media. We knew that black people look like Stevie Wonder, we knew that white people look like Marilyn Monroe. So we actually tried to build these stereotypes out of the photographs of faces of real people. And what we found, in trying to make these stereotypes of the four colours, but mixing in the ideas of the stereotypes from other people in Mongrel too – a real mix – was that these stereotypes were completely unattainable. What we ended up with then were completely untypical stereotypes. Antistereotypes. No glamour at all! The kind of people you'd see walking the streets in London. The masks perform operations on the faces. They stitch them up. They are roles that move across the entire spectrum of classification that we represent, across all the untypical stereotypes. You have white masks on black skin, but you also have black masks on black skin, yellow, brown, whatever ... It produces a more complex tangle of interrelationships and conflicts.

National Heritage, the installation, allowed users to abuse one or more of the unglamorous stereo-types constructed for *Colour Separation*.

WHERE DID THE PROJECT START?

It started in the reductive transition from analogue to digital. Once this change has been made, computer technologies allow for the infinite reproduction of a digital image without further loss of quality. The question for us was: whose image or images are being reproduced infinitely without loss of quality – and to whose benefit? To examine this question we initially needed to look into specific social relations and plausible possibilities for a diverse new media.

Constructions of race in the form of mental images are much more than simple pointers to bio-logical or cultural sameness. They are constructs of the social imagination, mapped onto geo-graphical regions and technological sites, and they can raise some pretty specific questions; such as 'when was the last time you saw someone black, yellow or brown in the Apple developer maga-zine?' or 'Why was the Nippon operating system so expensive in Japan?'

Fabrications of race have traceable links to historically-specific relations such as those informing the experience of slavery, migrant labour, colonisation, or of friends and family. Clearly, racial images are pregnant with the political processes from which they emerge and to which, in turn, they contribute, and images of different races articulate the political and economic relations between races in societies.

IMAGES IN CYBERLAND

What insights can we gain by looking more specifically at the images in 'Cyberland'? Although some magazines favour images of Japanese women fondling their modems, 'CyberEurope' and 'Cyber-USA' offer us an almost complete absence of 'mongrelised', black or Asian material and for that matter a lack of any impure or 'filthy' social relations. This lack, or convenient forgetting, of certain kinds of images in the techno-cultural sphere goes far beyond simply reflecting the self-interested, distinguishing experiences and aspirations of the authoring Digerati™ and their 'suck-up' class of consumers.

At the turn of the nineteenth century, the construction of the Chicago skyscrapers marked a similar, albeit less ambitious, attempt at forgetting. The Chicago elite merely tried to rid itself of the butchers' stench from America's biggest slaughterhouses with the watchwords 'Let's not deal with the rotting carcass. Let's build a palace in the sky.'

Digital cloning has helped call into question accepted notions of originality and genius, allowing a re-evaluation of the codes of cultural production – just as long as this does not include the filth of uncomfortable social relations. Given even the racialisation and elitism of cultural objects such this book, you might still think that underneath you're all still loveable. The multicultural 'let's-get-on-with-each-other-and-get-happy' number has for a long time been one of the main tactics for hiding hard, difficult debate behind a 1960s-style 'love-in'. Mongrel cultures have come too long a way acquiring intellectual rigour to be fobbed off with a flower pushed up the barrel of their gun.

BOMBARDED IMAGES BY DIMELA YEKWAI (AN EXCERPT)[2]

Black bastard, Nigger, Coon, Savage

Cannibal — did you eat your mother?

I hear she is gone missing.

Hi (son) sun-shine

Fuck your mother last night?

Monkey, Nappy head, Nigger brown, Ethnic, Exotic, Uncivilised, Scroungers, Lazy bums, BOY,

Coloureds, Muggers, Negroes

Not tax evaders — they don't work

Thick lip baboon

You (were) are lucky, we civilised you, had to tame you first

Ungrateful, not even a thanks for us enslaving you

GIVING YOU A CULTURE

What about that, green monkey?

See we had to try and

Stop you fucking it!

Spreading AIDS all over the place

I am only telling you this for your own good

While I castrate you

No dick no fucking and the green monkey is safe

That leaves me to service your woman

After all these nigger woman like it plenty

Don't want her to go mad and drown our lily-white babies.

Will give her some half-breeds to keep her quiet while she forget YOU

NATURAL SELECTION

This part of the campaign attempted to creatively address the widespread use of the internet in the dissemination and organisation of various configurations of nationalist and racist strategies, in concert with what is termed the 'new eugenics'; a collection of techniques that put biological engineering in the service of market forces. The project comprised the building of an internet search engine and directory for the purpose of spotlighting these activities, in an attempt to undermine their aesthetic and technical frameworks. This was accomplished through the process of various contributing artists making links between material that already existed online, and strong narratives that the artists created which were based on their research into local real world contexts for the subject.

The directory was structured in order to draw attention to, and to create dialogue about, racism implicit in the construction of hardware, software and in discourses around the uses of new technology in arts and culture. A search engine is a piece of software that looks for keywords such as titles, subject areas, author names and so on, on the internet-based World Wide Web – much in the same way that a library database does. A directory is an internet resource based on the use of a search engine which provides additional referencing and commentary to a list of specific links within general or specific subject areas.

As a way of imposing order on the fruitful chaos that the super-abundance of supply over demand has created on the web, search engines and directories are some of the most important and most visited sites on the internet. The production of software in this context is dedicated to knowledge organisation and information retrieval: a field largely seen as the domain of linguists and computer scientists. This immediately brings with it a range of problems that are at once both cultural and technical. The technology underlying search engines and databases – set theory – is based on creating classifications of information according to arbitrarily or contingently meaningful schemes. It is in the application and development of those schemes, with all their inevitable biases and quirks, that the aesthetics of classification lies.

Natural Selection attempted to create such a piece of software based on artistic principles. Through the search engine component of the project, the artists deconstructed and made obvious these biases and quirks, not only by searching online, but also by investigating the local actuality in which they operate.

Matthew Fuller:

Natural Selection's use of other search engines' material is an example of an ongoing technical conflict, which is obviously a very live one since it messes so heavily with control of proprietary culture masquerading as social resource. (Something extended in the cracked software projects in *Natural Selection* such as *Heritage Gold*.) Echoing this, like most of Mongrel's work, *Natural Selection* doesn't shrink away from difficulty. If people are going to check it out, they need to be looking for more than a punchline, or a nice neat 'anti-racist' or 'multicultural' solution. The nineties have seen a near complete homogenisation of language around race. A *fait accompli*, which trivialises the deep texture of language, culture and racialisation. We seem to have entered an era of a miserablised 'politics of semantics' represented by arguments over phrases such as Bill Clinton's, 'It depends on what the meaning of "is" is' and London's Metropolitan Police Commissioner Paul Condon's nervous wordplay in trying to avoid the acknowledgement of institutionalised racism in the police. At the same time, *Natural Selection* delves into this politics of semantics as it is constructed through software conventions and the protocols built into the World Wide Web.

Natural Selection was produced by Matthew Fuller and Harwood for Mongrel. Many strategies were employed on the search engine and these are a few:

• *Islam and Eugenics*[3] by Hakim Bey: an anarcho-Sufi from the United States and author of many books including the classic of the 1990s underground *TAZ* (Temporary Autonomous Zone), looked at the history of eugenics from a series of heretical Islamic points of view.

- *BlackLash*,[4] a cracked free downloadable, is the game of the streets. It allows you to choose between four black stereotype, fighting characters, then slay your way to freedom through swarms of insectoid cops and Nazis.
- *Aryan Nations*[5] is a journey through the English language in pictures. The history of words shows us that the language of the 'pure English' had already been overrun by the language of the colonised.
- *The Critical Art Ensemble* produced a site featuring an internal document from genetic engineering consortium BioCom.[6] In it we see how genetic engineering of children along racialised lines may be being prepared for release onto the consumer market.
- *Heritage Gold*,[7] a cracked version of Photoshop 1.0, is another classic from the MongrelSoft Empire. This piece of software is the standard heritage editor for all diversity professionals. Download it (for free) now and give your family tree a pruning.
- *Yardie's Immigration Advisor*,[8] Mervin Jarman's work, shows, among other things, the fastest way for a Yardie to get past British immigration – a hilarious collision of officialese, Tel Aviv realism and pure criminal mindedness!
- *Save the Internet* or *National Spiritual Internet Awakening*.[9] Some people think the internet is a global mind. It is, but one that's gone nuts. This site is dedicated to saving the internet's mental health and we thought it was so crazy we copied it.
- *Skrewed*[10] is a celebration of nationalism in music. You thought it was just military marching bands? Check how stupid it can get … This site is by author Stewart Home and musician Daniel Waugh.
- *Bombarded Images*[11] is Dimela Yekwai's powerful poem and story. She considers herself to be in the tradition of village 'Warner women'; bringing words from beyond into the digital age for a celebration of the individual and collective self.

It was clear to Mongrel and its collaborators that search engines have acquired immense positional importance in the network, acting as a gateway (both in the sense of allowing and blocking access) to material on the web. As a technical and media context, it is one that is riven with the most inexplicable density of political and cultural machinations. We felt while this investigation was important, that we should also deal with the 'street' and produce images that could offer no sense of progression or could be read as delivering the message that 'racism is over'.

Mongrel, from its own cultural complexity, and through dealing with *Natural Selection*, developed, during this time, a particular take on progressive anti-racism as experienced in London. Our view is one that admits that racism is multi-faceted and not the preserve of any one social group or another. Addressing the current manifestations of racism is certainly not about shaming, blaming or being guilty. These particular tools generally belong to a time in which an aspirational group of black people was yet to be established and were primarily used in the United Kingdom of the 1980s to establish a new black social elite (that would act as a reliable buffer zone between the haves and have-nots). It became a matter of urgency to have an acceptable black face sitting on

municipal authorities after the economically costly riots in London, Manchester and Liverpool in
the early 1980s. The standard view of social racism is that it manifests itself formally within the
structural leftovers of European colonialism and can be statistically proven to exist within economic and cultural power centres. This structural inheritance, because of its formal nature (both
within legislation and in its inability to control the reproduction of minorities' own self-image) can
be addressed 'easily' by rewriting the rule books and helping a few 'intelligent' blacks to get into
business.

Mongrels on the other hand, see racism through a bruising experience of the world, see it
essentially as migratory and multifaceted, and offering no promise of ending. We witness racism in
individual indifference, masquerading as tolerance; masquerading as the other's disinterest, and in
individual geographical and economic limitations. This complexity requires an individual to search
for specific lines of cultural and personal misinformation and to decode how these data form into
images of the 'other's' intelligence. Then they must accordingly determine how this image acts on
the social, economic structures of society locally and at large. The individual uses this understanding personally – to escape from their social, geographic, economic isolation, inherited from a col-
onial past. This is seen as useful for the self-interest of all people, white as well as black. Out of this
particular viewpoint grew *Colour Separation*.

BRITISH AIRPORT AUTHORITY (BAA)[12]

Mervin Jarman:

You see growing up in Jamaica it is endemic that you learn to improvise, in other words 'tun yuh
hand an mek fashion' seen. Now the BAA thing goes out to a primary group of yardies mentionable
those who are thinking that the grass is greener on the other side, and the overall analogy of that is
not necessarily. The language thing is or has become a form of cultural identity so no longer am I just
a English speaking person but to express one self in this kind of broken English dubbed patois (patwa)
contemporary it adds flava and undermine bureaucracy. I believe though that it is important for you
to understand the fundamentals of my implications and method of construction; to answer the question on the style and chaotic method that seem to be the underlying composition. You have to
imagine things from behind my mask where unstructured and chaotic deranged behaviour is the most
intelligent and effective means of communication without being detected specially when dealing with
various authority and institutional organisations. This is how the lie becomes the truth vice versa. BAA
is consequently absolved from the fact that this policy of abuse and brutality has been perpetrated
against me and others, whose only crime is to want to travel the world like Columbus, Marco Polo
and the great Admiral Penn and General Venables, with the only difference being there is no 'design'
to it as there was with the Lord Protector, Oliver Cromwell. And the opposite is true if you were to
visit Jamaica.

COLOUR SEPARATION

Constructed from photos of over one hundred people who are related in some day-to-day way with the core Mongrel group. Each artist, with their friends and family, is represented in their genetic 'heritage', one or more of the following geographical regions – Africa, East Asia, North Europe and South Asia – indicated respectively by skin pigmentation ('black', 'brown', 'yellow', 'white'). The head images were then digitally merged, made anonymous and separated again to arrive at four distinct racial types, both male and female. The eight composite and anonymous portraits were

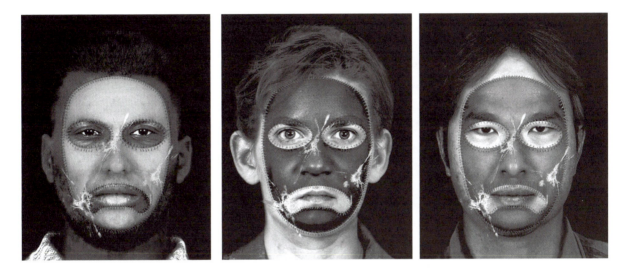

then masked. (Masking appears in the project in a manner similar to this example: Masking the face of an anonymous portrait encourages the viewer of a poster to be caught up in a racial dichotomy. The viewer is unsure why the base face has the skin of another face sewn onto it.) Then we added images of spit so the viewer could detect signs of racial abuse but not identify who is the abuser or who the abused.

61 *Colour Separation,*
Mongrel.

Harwood:

These are people that never existed. These images wear the masks of the other stereotypes. The masks are spat on. On the cover we have a white man wearing a black mask covered in spit. We have no idea who has done the spitting. Is it a white man fed up of his friend pretending to be black? Has he been spat on because he is a black-masked man who is white underneath? In this work as in the rest of society we perceive the demonic phantoms of other 'races'. But these characters never existed just like the nigger bogeyman never existed. But sometimes …
reluctantly we have to depict the invisible in order to make it disappear.

Ten thousand copies of *Colour Separation* were distributed through various outlets in London, the rest of the United Kingdom and abroad. This project eventually produced a series of 40 images featuring the head and skin from the project's contributing artists, also the artists' friends and family, and from groups local to the communities where we worked. We found that in the United Kingdom, where the work was largely ignored, that art's central positioning on ideas of race, racism and national identity had been overlooked for a long time. While many black artists have been active in this field, the work produced rarely positioned itself against the aesthetic and administrative *modus operandi* that housed it. One consequence was that a self-image emerged in an art-going public for whom it was usual to assume that those attending 'intellectual pursuits' and 'culturally prestigious events' etc. were above the mundanity of racial conflict and, indeed, positively cultivated a view of themselves as 'anti-' or 'post-' racist.

We felt that giving a few black British artists the odd bit of gallery space was being used as a pretext for the careful shunting of these problems to the outside of the 'purified' high-cultural sphere. Racism thereafter can be located only in the vast majority of people not attending culturally prestigious events. In other words, those people who live in subordinate English street cultures. Exclusion from this elevated world can thus be seen as a self-inflicted condition. It is 'common sense' then that such English street cultures are racist get-togethers of 'ignorance and filth' and conversely that to produce a work of art, in a culturally prestigious location, about race, racism and national identity would be to unnecessarily preach to the converted.

But the politics of race and culture have changed. The idea of a narrow self-righteous art-loving post-racism is, frankly, laughable. The self-confidence of subordinate English street cultures in dealing with issues around race is demonstrable in their endemic philosophy of 'mixing it up' and in their mongrel anthems. This is not a suggestion that racism has declined in any measurable form, but that the ground on which it built its foundations is shifting. Art-loving post-racism is made even more laughable by the self-righteous moralism of the evangelical art-cadres who espouse it. In considering alternative technological arts practice and its relationship to cultural privilege, it is important that we think again about the principles that underlly artistic judgement. The idea of universality in art forms the basis of aesthetic judgement. It is the root onto which are grafted the principals of taste. Cultural domination is achieved by 'taste' acting as a measure of distance between those of us who are tasteful and those others who are not.

Universality is a convention that was itself constructed out of debates in which racial difference was a central issue. Long before scientific racism had gained the upper hand, Hegel was arguing that the central difference between Blacks and Whites was a cultural and perceptual one. Hegel wrote that blacks 'do not have the ability to appreciate the necessary mystery involved in the creation of truly symbolic art, thus placing them outside the realm of authentic aesthetic sensibility.'[13]

The critical dialogue in the English art scene between its professionals – curators and artists – and its audience clearly relies on a set of historical principles produced during Hegel's era, a period when slavery, bond servitude and forced child labour were still a large part of western civilisation. Aesthetic judgement remains a fundamentally politicised concept. We need to destroy the boundaries put into place by specific arts disciplines, professionalisation and the hierarchy of taste. We can start by inviting in the mongrel forms of culture with their diverse and inclusive 'filthy' social relations. We can deal with the rotting carcass of Hegel's 'truly symbolic art' by burying it.

BEYOND *NATIONAL HERITAGE* – A VIEW TO THE FUTURE

National Heritage culminated in an installation at the 'Next Five Minutes' in the Waag Amsterdam, a former sixteenth-century anatomical theatre situated at the geographic centre of Amsterdam's canal zone. In the past, criminals and deviants were dissected in order to be studied by the merchant classes. We worked with the peoples of the Bijlmer, a housing estate on the outskirts of the city and home to a large immigrant community to reveal the racialisation within that city. The dialogues were fed directly into the installation, which used the faces from *Colour Separation* and had the audience symbolically spitting on them. This action in turn rewarded the user by revealing the bruised hurt of this particular racialisation. Through this installation it became clear to Mongrel that there was a need for other voices to be heard, and we began to think about tools and techniques that would allow more open structures to be populated.

Intelligence has long been associated with ruling elites, but in recent years it has become more and more associated with Intellectual Capital. This Intellectual Capital can be defined as knowledge that can be converted into profit, encompassing inventions, ideas, general know-how, design approaches, computer programmes, processes, and publications. One off-shoot of this association is a hardening of attitudes, tolerances, and the finer grading of what constitutes intelligence. Notions like 'Intellectual Property', 'Intellectual Assets' and 'Human Resources' have stained the older, looser meanings of 'capacity for understanding' or the 'ability to perceive and comprehend meaning.'

Those intelligences that confirm the ascent of Intellectual Capital, make wealth, because that's what you do if you're 'intelligent'. Wealth ensures high standards of formal education for use in the attainment of more wealth, thus the 'intelligent' create a self-fulfilling prophecy that allows the social elite to imagine that they are truly more intelligent than the rest of us. The problem with this drift in meaning is that it interferes with our ability to forget past notions of what constituted intelligence in the person you just spoke to and move on to what constitutes intelligence in the person with whom you are now talking. This is an essential strategy for Mongrel, operating in charged social atmospheres.

Understanding the nature of another's intelligence and remaining agile enough to spot it, in whatever form it may be manifested, is essential to Mongrel's understanding of collaboration. Having established the key criteria of respecting other intelligences, we can now think about moving on from *National Heritage* to an openness, which within this context means something that is inherently amenable to change in terms of form and function, to accommodate the cultural and social variety of local groups (family groups, older people, youth groups, ethnically diverse groups).

To this end, Mongrel created the *Linker* software, which produces dialogues with other mongrels' fast artefacts of digital culture.[14] A crucial thing about these dialogues is that we found people wanting to produce something that looked good, and meant something, but didn't want to have to invest months in teaching themselves something like Adobe Photoshop or Macromedia Director (which are configured to be most useful to experts). Technology, as we have discovered, whatever the media hype, is not inherently open to all contexts. The social structure and the architectural spaces that house new media projects must actively be made available to people. At the same time, having specific social and technological skills on hand to inform the new initiate, or maintain equipment, or constantly rethink what constitutes openness in the project space is hard, gruelling and expensive work.

Openness in a technological project has no possibility of taking hold unless the most marginalised individual in the group, whatever their ability or assumed ability, is brought into the centre of the workshop. We have had such incidents while working with people with disabilities, who had no physical or emotional way to tell us of their needs. This is an extreme situation, but one in which the workshop leader has to make difficult decisions, how to include someone who cannot signal either their desire, or aversion, to be included. I would take the decision to include them based on what I believe is the essentially social nature of being human.

The point to be made again and again is that the group has a social dynamic that requires that the most marginal (either physically located in the room or emotionally positioned within the group or culturally determined) needs to be constantly folded back into the centre of workshop activity. Mongrel will usually attempt to accomplish this by drawing on aspects of the intelligence of the individual when dealing with their lived experience. There can be no doubt that we all display such intelligence all the time – usually unacknowledged. To respect this intelligence and draw it into the centre of social activity is a first step to an open project.

METHOD AND APPEARANCE

When Mongrel operates we often appear to the uninitiated to be chaotic, arrogant, disorganised, lazy and having far too much fun to be working intelligently. It is often forgotten that Mongrel has a large cultural and experiential reservoir to draw on. Over the last five years we have dealt with our own social and cultural complexities, as well as those of other 'mongrels' met along the way. Because of this misunderstanding of our working practices, we feel that it is necessary to explain some of the principles we employ.

When Mongrel makes a decision to become involved in a workshop/project, we do so at both the formal organisational and the subjective level. We enter into a state of total curiosity: curiosity towards others and ourselves. We use our total curiosity to think about history – both our own and theirs; the material world as well as the realm of the imaginary. It is our job in the workshop to unravel motivations: ours for wanting to do the workshop and theirs for wanting to participate. The workshop, if it is going well, should contain numerous contradictory motivations for the group to represent itself using *Linker*. We have to keep ourselves open and let these representations contend with each other. After all, in an unequal world, the struggles around the question of who is able to make themselves visible, and who is not, and for what purpose, is central to any worthwhile reflection on how we see the world and what representations of the world we are fed.

The workshop group usually pre-defines its identity long before entering into a workshop with us. The group usually imposes this on the mongrels working with them. Mongrel usually retaliates with sets of lived experience. This sets up a charged atmosphere in which the power structures of the event become transparent. We use both the contradictions and similarities in the client group to wind up the situation. The contradictions both annoy and encourage the client group into action. Anger and intolerance at your own belittlement is a useful energy for dealing with the boredom of constant social embattlement, but can only be entered into in a safe space, after the transparency of power structures have been revealed.

NOTES

1. Mongrelx.org/Project/Natural/index.html/
2. Mongrelx.org/Project/Natural/Venus/index.html/
3. Mongrelx.org/Project/Natural/Hakim/index.html/
4. Mongrelx.org/Project/Natural/BlackLash/index.html/
5. Mongrelx.org/Project/Natural/Byju/index.html/
6. Mongrelx.org/Project/Natural/Biocom/index.html/
7. Mongrelx.org/Project/Natural/Heritage/index.html/
8. Mongrelx.org/Project/Natural/BAA/index.html/
9. Mongrelx.org/Project/Natural/NSA/index.html/
10. Mongrelx.org/Project/Natural/Skrewed/index.html/
11. Mongrelx.org/Project/Natural/Venus/index.html/
12. Mongrelx.org/Project/Natural/BAA/index.html/
13. Cited in: Gilroy, Paul. *The Black Atlantic. Modernity and Double Consciousness.* London: Verso, 1993.
14. Mongrelx.org/Project/Linker/index.html/

Glossary

Acrobat

Adobe Acrobat is a software package that converts various document formats into a form that can be reliably displayed by any end user who has Acrobat Reader software installed on their machine. Text and graphics are all embedded into the document. Increasingly the format is being used in the printing industry for the safe transfer and interpretation of designs and in other situations where layout of mixed media is important. Acrobat files have the file extension PDF (portable document format).

Antialias

Antialiasing usually refers to graphics, though applies to other media such as sound and text. It refers to the apparent smoothing of media, which is achieved by the slight blurring of otherwise hard edges to improve the viewing or listening experience of digital media.

Avatar

An avatar is the icon that is the digital representation of an individual.

Bit

A 'bit' (from 'Binary digIT') is the smallest unit of information a computer can use. Eight bits make one Byte. A single digit number in base-2, in other words, either a 1 or a zero. Bandwidth is usually measured in bits-per-second.

Bitmap

A bitmap is an image file in which every pixel displayed on screen has a value which is held in memory. There are many bitmap file formats including BMP, TIF, GIF, JPEG, PSD. Vector images, on the other hand, store only descriptive information about an image.

Browser (web browser)

A browser is a type of software application or program that allows the user to view web pages. There are different types of browsers; some only allow the user to view text, but browsers such *Netscape Navigator* and *Internet Explorer* for instance allow the user to view images and other media that may be integrated into a web page design.

CD-ROM

A CD-ROM (Compact Disk – Read Only Memory) is a storage device than can hold up to 650Mb of data. It has become a convenient way for publishers of multimedia materials to distribute their products. Increasingly people are using this medium as a way to store or make back-up copies of their work. This has become possible with the introduction of affordable CD-ROM writers and the fall in price of CD blanks.

Cross platform

If an application is cross platform it means it will run on computers irrespective of the operating system. Usually cross platform refers to the two main operating systems for PCs: Windows and Mac OS.

Cursor

The cursor is the mark displayed on the screen controlled by the movement of your mouse or according to the point at which you are typing. It takes different forms: an arrow shape is its default state. Over text it changes to an 'I-beam' and over a hot link it will change to a hand shape indicating that you can click the mouse button to perform a task.

Digitisation

The process of converting analogue (wave-based information) to the digital information (ones and zeros) that can be used by computers. Also known as encoding.

Domain name

The unique name of the server and a suffix that identifies the location of the server or the type of organisation that maintains the server. Domain names are often used in URLs. For example, the domain name, 'microsoft.com' is part of the URL 'http://www.microsoft.com/'.

Download

Downloading describes the process of retrieving and saving files from the internet. Web pages, for instance, are downloaded from internet servers (storage and delivery computers) to be displayed on the user's computer through a browser. Often downloading is used to describe the process of permanently transferring files. All sorts of files can be downloaded including whole software programmes.

DVD

Digital Video Disk or Digital Versatile Disk is a recent standard for high capacity Compact Disks, holding a minimum of four Gigabytes.

E-mail

E-mail is electronic mail used for sending messages and attachments (documents or files included with a message) across the internet. A word-processed essay as well as images and other documents can be refined and sent either as an e-mail attachment.

Floppy disk

A floppy disk is one of many kinds of computer file storage device. Like the hard disk on your computer, a floppy disk will allow you to save a copy of a file to it. Floppy disks have the advantage of being portable. This allows files to be opened on different computers. Compared to other storage devices they are quite 'small'. This means their capacity to store files is limited (to 1.4 Mb). They are still more than adequate for most people's needs, such as storing word-processed documents.

FTP

File Transfer Protocol is an internet protocol that enables file sharing between file servers and client machines.

GUI

Graphical User Interface, the graphical representation of the computer operating system, such as Windows, Mac OS or X11 on the screen.

HCI

'Human-Computer-Interaction is a discipline concerned with the design, evaluation and implementation of interactive computing systems for human use and with the study of major phenomena surrounding them.' (after ACM SIGCHI)

Home page

A home page is the page that first opens up when you start your browser. A home page is also the name given to the entry page of a website.

HTML

Hypertext mark-up language, a language used for creating documents for the World Wide Web. HTML uses special code that tells web browsers how to display elements such as text and images in a document.

HTTP

Hypertext Transfer Protocol, a protocol used for exchanging HTML documents and other files on the World Wide Web.

Intelligent Agents

Intelligent Agents are pieces of software that have a request for information put to them and then travel over the network seeking out that information.

IRC

Internet Relay Chat.

ISP

Internet service provider, a company that provides connections to the internet.

Java

Java is an object-orientated, platform-independent programming language that is commonly used to create Java Applets, which are small applications, typically developed for the web.

Modem

Modems are found either inside or attached to your computer and often use telephone lines to pass information between computers on the internet. When you go online, your modem will call another modem at the offices of your ISP – and the two modems will communicate (i.e. move information between them).

MOO

A multiple user environment on the internet, based on object-oriented technology. The original was created by Pavel Curtis at Xerox Parc (Lambada MOO). The interactive structure and communication between participants/users is based on domain-specific languages, software architectures and object-oriented frameworks. See also MUDs.

MUD

Multi-User-Dungeon, -Dimension or -Domain. Text-based virtual reality environments on the internet, in which users are represented by avatars (fictitious personae). They represent real-time chat forums with a narrative structure, often a fantasy and adventure game, in which users are able to add more internal structures onto the database that mirrors the existing world.

Newsgroup

A newsgroup is an internet-based discussion area that has an agreed topic. Newsgroups are accessed using news reader software from Usenet (the internet system reserved for newsgroup discussion). Newsgroups exist to discuss most areas of interest.

Pixel

Pixels are the units that describe how a computer screen displays information. Monitors typically have a resolution from about 72 dpi (dots per inch) to 96 dpi.

QuickTime

Video compression and display system produced for Apple Mac computers but can also be viewed by Windows machines.

QuickTime VR

Derived from QuickTime, QTVR allows 360° interactive panoramas to be developed and viewed.

RAM

Random Access Memory. A computer can hold information in memory without having to write it to disk. This makes computers operate much faster when dealing with short-term information.

Rollover

A rollover is an interactive screen device (such as a button) that has a changed state when the user's mouse cursor moves over it. To rollover is the act of moving the mouse cursor over a screen object.

ROM

Read Only Memory as in 'Compact Disk – Read Only Memory' (CD-ROM).

Search engine

Many search engines exist that scan the World Wide Web in order to locate web pages (and other internet resources) to satisfy a user's query. Some websites, such as university websites, have their own search engine which will search just their site. These search engines make the World Wide Web very powerful and it is worthwhile for all users to spend some time getting to know how to use the search engines properly.

Server

A server is often thought of as a computer on the internet that contains files like web pages that other people can access. Actually it is software installed on a computer that operates like a telephone exchange. That is, it receives calls or requests for information and delivers the requested information.

Software

Software is what a computer (hardware) uses. It takes many shapes and forms. Without software a computer would be little more than a collection of metal and plastic. Software is the general term that describes all kinds of computer programmes and files.

Streaming

Streaming allows audio and video to be played across the internet in real-time. With most audio and video on the internet you must wait until the whole media file has been downloaded to your computer before it can start to play – streaming media will start running immediately.

TCP/IP

Transmission Control Protocol/Internet Protocol. The basic protocols controlling applications that use the internet.

URL

Uniform Resource Locator, a unique name or number that specifies the location of a file on the internet. A URL consists of a protocol, such as 'http://' that specifies a web page, followed by a server or path name. For example, the URL for the Microsoft website is 'http://www.microsoft.com/'.

Vector

Vector graphics files record image information by the mathematical description of curves, rather than recording pixel values as is the case with bitmap images. This makes vector graphics files smaller in file size and highly scaleable.

Video

Digital video is useful in multimedia applications for showing real life – such as people talking or real life illustrations of concepts. Its main drawback is its very large file size. To make them usable video files need to be compressed.

Virus

A virus is a malicious programme. They are transmitted from computer to computer by infected files, such as word-processed files, and run when the file is opened. Some viruses are designed to run only on a particular date, and some can do considerable damage to the contents of a computer's hard drive.

VRML

Virtual Reality Modelling Language, the standard for displaying 3D data in web browsers. VRML is the navigation specification behind 3D objects and environments on the web. HTML creates 2D environments. 3D VRML worlds are used to host things like chatting and gaming, where users represent themselves using avatars.

Web page

An HTML document that can include text, images, sounds and movies, as well as links to other web pages and files.

Web server

A computer that can deliver a web page when requested to do so by a web browser. Each web server on the World Wide Web has a unique address.

Website

A collection of web pages (also known as HTML documents) on the same web server. The pages on a website typically cover related topics and are usually interconnected by links. Most websites have a home page.

Window

Window describes the viewing area for an application. Some applications support the use of several concurrently opened windows, though only one will have the 'focus' – this means it is the current live window with which the user is interacting.

World Wide Web

The graphical, multimedia portion of the internet. The most common files on the World Wide Web (WWW) are HTML documents, which are also known as web pages.

Bibliography

Aarseth, Espen. *Cybertext – Experiments in Ergodic Literature*. Baltimore: Johns Hopkins University Press, 1997

Acconci, Vito. *Avalanche Magazine*. New York, Fall 1972

Adorno, Theodor W. *Negative Dialectics*. E. B. Ashton, trans. London: Routledge, 1973

—— *Minima Moralia*. London: New Left Books, 1974

—— Horkheimer, Max. *Dialektik der Aufklärung. Philosophische Fragmente*. Frankfurt am Main: S. Fischer, 1978

—— *Aesthetic Theory*. Gretel Adorno and Rolf Tiedemann, eds. Robert Hullot-Kentor, trans. London: Athlone Press, 1997

Alpers, Svetlana. *The Art of Describing: Dutch Art in the Seventeenth Century*. Chicago: University of Chicago Press, 1983

Arrighi, Giovanni. *A Persuasive Account of the History of Capitalism. The Long Twentieth Century*. London: Verso, 1994

Ascott, Roy. 'Toward A Field Theory of Post-Modernist Art'. *Leonardo Vol. 13*. Cambridge: MIT Press, 1980

Aumont, Jacques. *The Image*. Claire Pajackowska, trans. London: BFI, 1997

—— *Montage Eisenstein*. L. Hildreth, C. Penley, trans. London: BFI, 1987

Babbage, Charles. *Charles Babbage and his Calculating Engines: Selected Writings by Charles Babbage and Others*. New York: Dover Publications Inc., 1961

Bachelard, G. *L'Activité Rationaliste de la Physique Contemporaine*. Paris: Presses Universitaires de France, 1951

Balász, Béla. *Der Geist des Films*. Halle, 1930

Barthes, Roland. *Image – Music – Text*. London: Fontana, 1977

—— *The Empire of Signs*. R. Howard, trans. New York: Hill and Wang, 1982

—— *The Rustle of Language*. R. Howard, trans. New York: Hill and Wang, 1986

Baudelaire, Charles. 'Les Sept Vieillards'. *Les Fleurs du Mal*. Francis Scarfe, trans. London: Anvil Press Poetry, 1986

—— 'Symptômes de Ruine'. *The Poems in Prose*. Francis Scarfe, trans. London: Anvil Press Poetry, 1989

Baudrillard, Jean. *The Perfect Crime*. Chris Turner, trans. London: Verso, 1996

Benjamin, Walter. *The Arcades Project*. Cambridge/London: The Belknap Press, 1999

Benjamin, Walter. *Illuminations*. Hannah Arendt, ed., Harry Zohn, trans. New York: Schocken Books, 1986.

Berge, C. *Principles of Combinatorics*. John Sheenan, trans. New York/San Francisco/London: Academic Press, 1971

Bloch, Ernst. *The Principle of Hope. Vol 1*. Neville Plaice, Stephen Plaice and Paul Knight, trans. Cambridge: MIT Press, 1995

Bolter, Jay David and Grusin, Richard. *Remediation. Understanding New Media*. Cambridge: MIT Press, 1999

Bordwell, David and Carroll, Noel, eds. *Post-Theory: Reconstructing Film Studies*. Madison: University of Wisconsin Press, 1996

Blumenberg, Hans, ed. *Poetik und Hermeneutik IV. Terror und Spiel*. Munich, 1971

Buddemeier, Heinz. *Panorama, Diorama, Photographie. Entstehung und Wirkung neuer Medien im 19. Jahrhundert*. Munich, 1970

Busche, Jürgen, ed. *Quantentheorie und Philosopie. Vorlesungen und Aufsätze*. Stuttgart, 1983

Burch, Noël. *Life to those Shadows*. Ben Brewster, trans. Berkeley: University of California Press, 1990

Bush, Vannevar. 'As We May Think'. P. Mayer, ed. *Computer Mediated Communications*. Oxford: Oxford University Press, 1999

Butler, Samuel. *Erehwon*. Harmondsworth: Penguin Classics, 1985

Castle, Terry. *The Female Thermometer: 18th Century Culture and the Invention of the Uncanny*. Oxford: Oxford University Press, 1995

Chion, Michel. *Les Musiques Electro-Acoustiques*. Aix-en-Provence: INA-GRM, 1976

—— 'Le Son au Cinéma'. Paris: Cahiers du Cinéma, 1985

—— *L'Audiovision*. Paris: Nathan, 1990

—— *La Musique au Cinéma*. Paris: Fayard, 1995

Christie, Ian and Taylor, Richard. *Reconsidering Eisenstein*. London: Routledge, 1993

Clark, Hilary. 'Networking in Finnegans Wake'. *James Joyce Quarterly*, vol. 27, no. 4, Summer 1990

Clery, E. J. *The Rise of Supernatural Fiction 1762–1800*. Cambridge: Cambridge University Press, 1995

Cornwell, Regina. 'Touching the Body in the Mind'. *Discourse* 14.2, Spring 1992

Crichton, Michael. *Jasper Johns*. New York: Harry N. Abrams/Whitney Museum, 1977

Currie, Mark. *Postmodern Narrative Theory*. London: Macmillan, 1998

Davis, Douglas. *Vom Experiment zur Idee. Die Kunst des 20. Jahrhunderts im Zeichen von Wissenschaft und Technologie. Analysen, Dokumente, Zukunftsperspektiven*. Cologne, 1975

Deane, Paul. 'Motion Picture Techniques in James Joyce's "The Dead"', *James Joyce Quarterly*, vol. 6, Spring 1969

De Landa, Manuel. *War in the Age of Intelligent Machines*. New York: Zone Books, 1991

Deleuze, Gilles and Guattari, Felix. *A Thousand Plateaus: Capitalism and Schizophrenia*. Brian Massumi, trans. Minneapolis: University of Minnesota Press, 1987

—— *Anti-Oedipus: Capitalism and Schizophrenia*. R. Hurley, M. Seem and H. R. Lane, trans. Minneapolis: University of Minnesota Press, 1983

—— *Rhizom*. Berlin: Merve, 1977

Derrida, Jacques. *Of Grammatology*. G. C. Spivak, trans. Baltimore: Johns Hopkins University Press, 1977

—— *Writing and Difference*. A. Bass, trans. Chicago: University of Chicago Press, 1978

Deutsch, David. *The Fabric of Reality*. Harmondsworth: Penguin, 1997

Didion, Joan. 'Bureaucrats'. *The White Album*. New York: Simon & Schuster, 1979

Dinkla, Söke. *Pioniere Interaktiver Kunst. Von 1970 bis heute*. Ostfildern: Cantz Verlag, 1997

Doll, Mary A. *Beckett and Myth: An Archetypal Approach*. New York: Syracuse University Press, 1988

Druckrey, Timothy. *Iterations: The New Digital Image*. Cambridge: MIT Press, 1994

Duchamp, Marcel. *The Creative Act*. Text of a talk given April 1957, at the American Federation of the Arts, Houston. Published as a phonograph recording. New York: Aspen Magazine, 1967

Eco, Umberto. *The Open Work*. A. Cancogni, trans. Cambridge: MIT Press, 1989

Eisenstein, Sergei. *Film Form*. New York: Harcourt, Brace and Company, 1949

—— *Notes of a Film Director*. New York: Dover Publications Inc., 1970

—— *The Film Sense*. J. Leyda, trans. New York: Harcourt, Brace, Jovanovich Inc., 1974

Ellenberger, Henri F. *The Discovery of the Unconscious: The History and Evolution of Dynamic Psychiatry*. New York: Basic Books, 1970

Erlich, Victor. *Russian Formalism. 3rd Edition*. Yale: Yale University Press, 1981

Fabo, Sabine. *Joyce und Beuys. Ein intermedialer Dialog*. Heidelberg: Universitätsverlag C. Winter, 1997

Fassler, Manfred. 'Stile der Anwesenheit'. Brigitte Felderer ed. *Wunschmaschine Welterfindung*. Vienna: Springer Verlag, 1996

Field, Syd. *The Scriptwriter's Workbook*. New York: Dell, 1987

Fiske, John. *Television Culture*. London: Routledge, 1987–94

Foucault, Michel. *Dits et ecrits. Sélections, Vol. 1*. New York: New Press, 1993

Frazer, J. *An Evolutionary Architecture*. London: Architectural Association, 1995

Freud, Sigmund. *Drei Abhandlungen zur Sexualtheorie*. Vienna 1905. *Three Contributions to a Theory of Sex*. A. A. Brill, trans. New York: Modern Library, 1938

Friedman, Ted. 'Making Sense of Software'. Steven G. Jones, ed. *Cybersociety*. London: Sage, 1995

Fueloep-Mueller, René. *Phantasiemaschine*. Leipzig, 1931

Fuller, Matthew. 'The Mouths of the Thames'. *Next 5 Minutes 3. Workbook*. Amsterdam, 1999

Fullerton, John and Söderbergh Widding, Astrid, eds. *Moving Images: From Edison to the Webcam. Stockholm Studies in Cinema*. Luton: John Libbey, 2000

Gauntlett, David, ed. *web studies: Rewiring Media Studies for the Digital Age*. London: Arnold, 2000

Gilroy, Paul. *The Black Atlantic. Modernity and Double Consciousness*. London: Verso, 1993

Greenaway, Peter. *The Stairs*. Geneva/London: Merrell Holberton, 1994

Grond, Walter. *Der Erzähler und der Cyberspace*. Innsbruck: Haymon, 1999

Grossman, Dave. *On Killing: The Psychological Cost of Learning to Kill in War and Society*. New York: Little Brown and Company, 1996

Grosz, Liz. *Space, Time and Perversion: The Politics of Bodies*. New York: Routledge, 1995

Gurvistch, A. *Théorie Du Champ de la Conscience*. Paris: Desclé de Brouwer, 1957

Hales, Chris. 'The Interactive Filmmaker's Challenge'. Fullerton and Söderbergh Widding, eds. *Moving Images: From Edison to the Webcam. Stockholm Studies in Cinema*. Luton: John Libbey, 2000

Haraway, Donna, ed. *Simians, Cyborgs and Women: The Reinvention of Nature*. New York: Routledge, 1991

Harvey, David. *The Condition of Postmodernity: An Enquiry into the Origins of Cultural Change*. Oxford: Blackwell, 1989

Hayles, N. Katherine. *The Cosmic Web: Scientific Field Models and Literary Strategies in the Twentieth Century*. Ithaca: Cornell University Press, 1984

—— 'Embodied Virtuality: On How to Put Bodies Back into the Picture'. Mary Anne Moser and Douglas MacLoed, eds. *Immersed in Technology: Art and Virtual Environments*. Cambridge: MIT Press, 1996

Hayman, David. 'Nodality and Infra-Structure in Finnegans Wake', *James Joyce Quarterly*, vol. 16, no. 1/2, Fall 1978

Heidegger, Martin. *Being and Time*. John Macquarrie and Edward Robinson, trans. Oxford: Blackwell, 1962

Hein, Birgit. *Film im Untergrund. Von seinen Anfängen bis zum unabhängigen Kino*. Frankfurt am Main/Berlin/Vienna, 1971

Herz, J. C. 'Mario über Alles'. *Joystick Nation*. New York: Little, Brown and Company, 1997

Hickethier, Knut. *Film-und Fernsehanalyse*. Stuttgart/Weimar: Verlag J. B. Metzler, 1996

Hoberman, Perry. 'Free Choice or Control'. Hannes Leopoldseder and Christine Schöpf, eds. *Prix Ars Electronica 96*. Vienna/New York: Springer Verlag, 1996

Hollander, Anne. *Moving Pictures*. Cambridge: Harvard University Press, 1991

Hughes, Bob. *Dust or Magic?* Boston: Addison Wesley, 1999

Huyssen, Andreas, Scherpe, Klaus. *Postmoderne. Zeichen eines kulturellem Wandels*. Reinbek: Rowohlt Verlag, 1986

Iser, Wolfgang. Der Akt des Lesens. *Theorie ästhetischer Wirkung*. Munich, 1990

Jabès, Edmund. *The Book of Questions*. Paris: Editions Gallimard, 1963

Jarry, A. *Selected Works of Alfred Jarry*. Roger Shattuck and Simon Taylor Watson, eds. New York: Random House, 1965

Jones, Steven G. ed. *Cybersociety: Computer Mediated Communication and Community*. Thousand Oaks: Sage Publications, 1989

Kaprow, Allan. *Some Recent Happenings*. New York, 1966

Kellner, Douglas. *The Persian Gulf TV War*. Boulder: Westview Press, 1992

Kelly, Kevin. *Out of Control: The New Biology of Machines*. London: 4th Estate, 1994

Kemp, Wolfgang, *Der Anteil des Betrachters. Rezeptionsästhetische Studien zur Malerei des 19. Jahrhunderts*. Munich, 1983

Kierkegaard, Søren. *Concluding Unscientific Postscript*. W. Lowrie and D. F. Swenson, trans. Princeton: Princeton University Press, 1968

Kluszczynski, Ryszard W. *Film-Wideo-Multimedia*. Warsaw: Instytut Kultury Warszawa, 1999

Kreimeier, Klaus. 'Das Kino als Ideologiefabrik'. Berlin: *Die Kinemathek* no. 45, Nov. 1971

Kress, G. and van Leeuwen, T. *Reading Images: The Grammar of Visual Design*. London/New York: Routledge, 1996

La Biennale di Venezia. *XLII Esposizione internationale d'arte*. Arte e Alchemia. Venice, 1986

Laurel, Brenda. *The Art of the Computer Human Interface Design*. Los Angeles: Addison Wesley and Apple Computers, 1990

—— *Computers as Theatre*. Los Angeles: Addison Wesley, 1991

Lefebvre, Henri. *La Vie Quotidienne dans le Monde Moderne*. Paris: Gallimard, 1968

—— *La Production de l'Espace*. Paris: Anthropos, 1974

—— *The Production of Space*. Donald Nicholson-Smith, trans. London: Blackwell, 1998

Leopoldseder, Hannes, ed. *Prix Ars Electronica 1993*. Linz: Veritas-Verlag, 1993

Leopoldseder, Hannes and Schöpf, Christine, eds. *Prix Ars Electronica 96*. Vienna/New York: Springer, 1996

Levinas, Emmanuel. *Totality and Infinity: An Essay on Exteriority*. Alphonso Lingis, trans. Pittsburgh: Duquesne University Press, 1969

Lévi-Strauss, Claude. *Structural Anthropology*. Claire Jacobson and Brooke Grundfest Schoepf, trans. Harmondsworth: Penguin, 1972

Levy, Pierre. 'The Aesthetics of Cyberspace'. Timothy Druckrey, ed. *Electronic Culture*. New York: Aperture, 1997

Leyda, Jay, ed. *Eisenstein on Disney*. Calcutta: Seagull Books, 1986

Lippman, Andy. *Moviemaps: An Application of the Optical Videodisc to Computer Graphics*. Siggraph proceedings, 1980

Loeffler, C. and Tong, D. *Performance Anthology. Source Book for a Decade of Performance Art*. San Francisco: Contemporary Arts Press, 1980

Lyotard, Jean-François. *The Postmodern Condition: A Report on Knowledge*. Geoff Bennington and Brian Massumi, trans. Manchester: Manchester University Press, 1984

Lyotard, Jean-François. *Lessons on the Analytic of the Sublime*. Elizabeth Rottenberg, trans. Stanford: Stanford University Press, 1994

Malcolm, Norman. *Ludwig Wittgenstein: A Memoir*. London: Oxford University Press, 1958

Marx, Karl. *Das Kapital: A Critique of Political Economy. Vol 3*. Friedrich Engels, ed. Moscow: Progress Publishers, 1962

Massumi, Brian. *A User's Guide to Capitalism and Schizophrenia. Deviations from Deleuze and Guattari*. Cambridge: MIT Press, 1992

Mathews, H. and Brotchie, A. *OULIPO Compendium*. London: Atlas Press, 1998

Mitchell, William J. *City of Bits. Place, Space and the Infobahn*. Cambridge: MIT Press

Moravec, Hans. *Mind Children*. Cambridge: MIT Press, 1981

Murray, Janet H. *Hamlet on the Holodeck. The Future of Narrative in Cyberspace*. Cambridge: MIT Press, 1997

Museum für moderne Kunst, Stiftung Ludwig Wien, ed. *Split Reality: Valie Export*. New York/Vienna, 1998

Neale, Steven. *Cinema and Technology*. Bloomington: Indiana University Press, 1985

Nelson, Ted. 'A New Home For the Mind'. P. Mayer, ed. *Computer Mediated Communications*. Oxford: Oxford University Press, 1999

—— 'Getting it out of Our System', *Information Retrieval. A Critical View*. George Schecter, ed. Philadelphia, 1966/Washington DC, 1967

—— *Literary Machines*. South Bend, Edition 87.1, 1987

Neuhaus, Wolfgang. *Die Vernetzung der Fiktionen*. Telepolis 2000, http://www.heise.de/tp/deutsch/inhalt/sa/4245/1.html

Oettermann, Stephan. *The Panorama: History of a Mass Medium*. New York: Urzone, 1997

Parker, Phil. 'Reconstructing Narrative'. *Journal of Media Practice*. vol 1, no 2. Intellect 2000

Peirce, C. *Collected Papers. Volume I–VIII*. Cambridge: Harvard University Press, 1931

Perec, Georges. *Life: A User's Manual*. Harvill Press, 1988

Peters, Susanne. *Wahrnehmung als Gestaltungsprinzip im Werk von James Joyce*. Trier: WVT, 1995

Pissarro, Camille. *Letters to his Son Lucien*. John Rewald, ed. Lionel Abel, trans. 4th edn. London: Routledge, 1980

Rhode, Eric. *A History of World Cinema*. London: Allen Lane, 1976

Rieser, Martin. 'Interactive Narratives: A Form of Fiction?' *Convergence* 3.1. Luton: John Libbey, Spring 1997

Riley, Terence. *The Un-private House*. New York: Museum of Modern Art, 1999

Roussel, Raymond. *Locus Solus*. R. C. Cunningham, trans. London: John Calder, 1983

Ruiz, Raul. *Poetics of Cinema*. Paris: Editions Dis Voir, 1995

Saint-Martin, F. *Semiotics of Visual Language*.
Bloomington/London: Indiana University Press,
1990

Salt, Barry. *Film Style and Technology: History and
Analysis*. London: Starword, 1983

Schwartz, Vanessa R. 'Cinematic Spectatorship before
the Apparatus: The Public Taste for Reality in Fin-
de-Siècle Paris'. Linda Williams, ed. *Viewing
Positions*. New Jersey: Rutgers University, 1994

Schwarz, Hans-Peter. *Mediavisions. Media Art History.
Are our Eyes our Targets* Munich: Prestal, 1997

Scott, J. *Characters of Motion*. Straw Man Press, 1982

Silverman, Kaja. *The Accoustic Mirror. The Female Voice
in Psychoanalysis and Cinema*. Bloomington:
Indiana University Press, 1988

Smith, S. M., Ward, T. B., and Finke, R. A. *The
Creative Cognition Approach*. Cambridge: MIT
Press, 1995

Sobieszek, Robert A. *The Ghost in the Shell:
Photography and the Human Soul 1850-2000*,
Cambridge: MIT Press, 2000

Spiegel, Alan. *Fiction and the Camera Eye. Visual
Consciousness in Film and the Modern Novel*.
Charlotteville, 1976

Spierling, Ulrike, ed. *Digital Storytelling – Tagungsband*.
Fraunhofer IRB Verlag, 2000

Stone, Allucquère Rosanne. *Desire and War at the
Close of the Mechanical Age*. Cambridge: MIT
Press, 1995

Sudnow, David. *Pilgrim in the Microworld*. New York:
Warner Books, 1983

Vattimo, Gianni. *The Adventure of Difference:
Philosophy after Nietzsche and Heidegger*. Cyprian
Blamires, trans. Baltimore: Johns Hopkins
University Press, 1993

Vaughan, Dai. *For Documentary. Twelve Essays*.
Berkeley: University of California Press, 1999

Vertov, Dziga. *Kino-Eye*. Kevin O'Brien, trans.
Berkeley: University of California Press, 1984

Vidler, Anthony. *The Architectural Uncanny*.
Cambridge: MIT Press, 1992

Virilio, Paul. *Polar Inertia*. Patrick Camiller, trans.
London: Sage, 2000

—— *A Landscape of Events*. Julie Rose, trans.
Cambridge: MIT Press, 2000

—— *Strategy of Deception*. Chris Turner, trans.
London: Verso, 2000

Vogler, Christopher. *The Writer's Journey*. London:
Michael Wiese, 1992

Vos, E. *New Media Poetry – Theories and Strategies*.
Visible Language, 1996

Weibel, Peter. 'The Post-Gutenberg Book'. Center
for Art and Media ZKM, ed. *Artintact 3*. Artist's
interactive CD-ROMagazine. Karlsruhe, 1997

Willett, John, ed. *Journals 1934-1955. Bertolt Brecht*.
Hugh Rorrison, trans. London: Methuen, 1993

Williams, Raymond. *Television: Technology and Cultural
Form*. London: Fontana, 1974

Wilhelm Lehmbruck Museum Duisburg, ed. *InterAct!
Schlüsselwerke interaktivet Kunst*. Ostfildern:
Cantz Verlag, 1997

Wright, Will. *Six Guns and Society: A Structural Study
of the Western*. Berkeley: University of California
Press, 1975

Youngblood, Gene. *Expanded Cinema*. New York:
Dutton, 1970

Žižek, Slavoj, ed. *Everything You Wanted to Know
about Lacan (but Were Afraid to Ask Hitchcock)*.
London: Verso, 1992

—— ed. *The Plague of Fantasies*. London: Verso,
1997

Index

Page numbers in *italics* indicate illustrations; n = footnote (only where there is separate information of interest)

New Screen Media – Operating the DVD-ROM

The DVD-ROM is designed to run on computers with the following minimum specification:
- 64 MB free RAM
- QuickTime: Version 3.0 or later (version 5.0 installers are supplied on the disk). It is desirable to allocate 40Mb RAM to the QuickTime Player for optimum performance.
- Macintosh: Mac OS 8.5 or later
- PC: Windows OS 95/98/NT/2000

Instructions for use:
1. Open the disk
2. Launch the appropriate version of the disk software by double clicking on the icon: RUNME(Mac) or Runme.exe(PC)
3. Clicking on the main, darker menu bar options near the top of the screen ('Contents/Orientations/ Explorations/Glossary') activates submenus below. The small green arrows to the left of the screen scroll the options presented – alternatively you can click directly on any of the words within the submenu. Current selections move to the far left of the screen. Text is presented in paged form, and these pages are turned using the small green arrows at the foot of the page.

- The *Orientations* section is contextual and theoretical. The *Explorations* section illustrates examples and issues. If a series of small images appear to the left of screen you can activate titles and the media type description on a rollover. Clicking will open them in the main window . With video, a further click enlarges to full screen. Clicking again reduces to the window size.
- Interactive works are selected in the same way as video or still images – however, a double click on the main window image is required to launch the application. You can exit an interactive piece by either pressing the escape key (esc) or in the case of Zoe Beloff's interactive work (Mac only) by Applekey+full-stop [.].
- Navigation of QuickTime VR movies:
  Macintosh and PC: to zoom in – hold down Shift key, to zoom out – hold down Control Key.
- An A-Z of Quicklinks at the bottom left of screen allows automatic access to the artists listed in the scrolling window.
- Any web address in blue will launch your internet browser and connect directly to the appropriate website. If you do not have a permanent connection to the internet you will have to connect to your ISP before the links will work.
- Users of some older computers may experience slow response when playing some of the interactive pieces directly from the DVD. You may wish to copy the relevant folder(s) to your hard drive and launch the pieces from there. Allocating more memory to your chosen Director player may also improve performance.